European Security beyond the Cold War

Four Scenarios for the Year 2010

European Security beyond the Cold War

Four Scenarios for the Year 2010

Adrian G.V. Hyde-Price

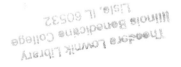

The Royal Institute of International Affairs · London

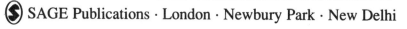

SAGE Publications · London · Newbury Park · New Delhi

First published 1991

SAGE Publications Ltd
6 Bonhill Street
London EC2A 4PU

SAGE Publications Inc
2455 Teller Road
Newbury Park, California 91320

SAGE Publications India Pvt Ltd
32, M-Block Market
Greater Kailash – 1
New Delhi 110 048

British Library Cataloguing in Publication data
Hyde-Price, Adrian
  European security beyond the Cold War: Four
  scenarios for the year 2010. - (Royal Institute
  of International Affairs)
  I. Title   II. Series
  327.094
  ISBN 0-8039-8557-6
  ISBN 0-8039-8558-4 pbk

Library of Congress catalog card number 91-052897

Printed in Great Britain by Billing and Sons Ltd, Worcester

Contents

This book is dedicated to my Mother and Father, for all their love and support over the years

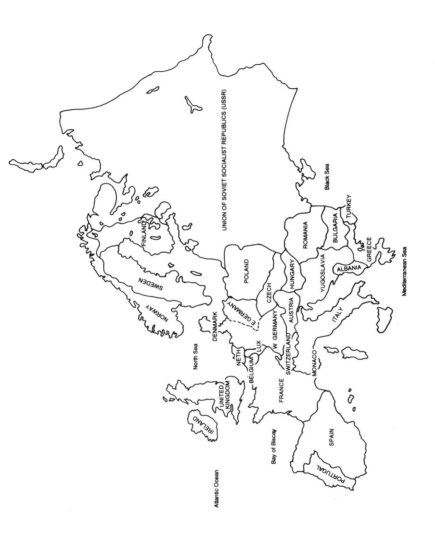

Preface

Writing this book has not been easy. I began work on it in January 1989, and by the autumn had completed chapters on – amongst other topics – the two Germanies, Eastern Europe and the Soviet Union. Shortly afterwards, communism in Eastern Europe collapsed, and it soon became apparent that German unification was not far off. Writing a book on European security at a time when Europe itself was experiencing its greatest period of political and strategic flux since 1946–47 has been a demanding task. It would have been impossible had it not been for the help, advice and encouragement from my friends and colleagues at Chatham House and in the wider international security community.

I hope this book will prove of use to all those interested in the problems of European security after the cold war. It considers the implications of the momentous events of 1989 – the year the cold war ended – and 1990, against the background of the fundamental transformations that have been reshaping Europe over recent years. The manuscript was completed at the end of December 1990, and I am aware that, at the time of writing, the outcome of a series of important developments is still unclear: the European Community's two inter-governmental conferences on economic and monetary union and political union are about to begin in earnest; NATO is conducting a major Strategic Review; the CSCE has acquired a more institutionalised structure, but its precise role and responsibility in the new Europe is still being discussed; the Congress of Peoples' Deputies is meeting in Moscow at a time of growing crisis in the country; the break-up of Yugoslavia seems ever more likely; and above all, events in the Gulf seem to be moving inextricably towards war. In attempting to consider what sort of security-structure Europe might have in 2010, I am reminded of Hegel's words of caution at the end of his Preface to a *Philosophy of Right*:

> One word more about giving instruction as to what the world ought to be. Philosophy in any case always comes on the scene too late to give it. As the thought of the world, it appears only when actuality is already there cut and dried after its process of formation has been completed .... When philosophy paints its grey on grey, then has a shape of life grown old. By philosophy's grey in grey it cannot be rejuvenated but only understood. The owl of Minerva spreads its wings only with the falling of the dusk.

So far I have spoken only of the difficulties I faced in writing this book. I should also say that writing it has been one of the most intellectually rewarding and pleasantly absorbing experiences of my life. Working on these issues at a time of such extraordinary change in Europe was both stimulating and enjoyable. It has also brought me into contact with a wide range of intelligent and interesting people, many of whom I now count amongst my closest friends. Finally, I hope above all that in writing this study of European security beyond the cold war, I have been able to communicate to the reader some of the excitement I have felt when thinking about the issues involved in Europe's uncertain future.

Adrian Hyde-Price
London, 31 December 1990

Acknowledgements

This book is the product of my three years spent as a Research Fellow on the International Security Programme at Chatham House. I am deeply indebted to those at Chatham House who have helped, encouraged and advised me during the writing of this study, and to all at the institute who helped make my sojourn there one of the happiest and most rewarding periods of my life.

I owe a special debt to John Roper, who encouraged me to undertake this ambitious study of European security, and who has provided invaluable help and advice at all stages since. Working with John was not always easy, but it never ceased to be stimulating! I am also deeply indebted to Professor Fred Halliday, who found time to read and comment on the completed manuscript at a time when he was busy with events in the Gulf. I am most grateful to him for his incisive and encouraging comments.

During John's year as Acting Director of Studies, Phil Williams became the International Security Programme's Director. I am grateful to Phil for his advice on the opening chapters of this book, and for chairing the series of study group meetings at which my first drafts were discussed. William Wallace, as Director of Studies, provided guidance and encouragement throughout my three years at Chatham House, as did the Institute's Director, Admiral Sir James Eberle.

There are many others at Chatham House who I would like to thank for their constant support and kindness: Alex Pravda, Neil Malcolm, Peter Duncan and Lenny Geron; Helen Wallace, Louis Turner, Jonathan Stern, Trevor Taylor and Peter Ferdinand; Phedon Nicolaides, Philip Robins, Mark Curtis and Michael Grubb; Lesley Perry and Katie Williams; Jo Statler and Phillippa Venn; Lucy Seton-Watson, Chris Cviic and Manda Gifford; Jenny Foreman and Liz Parcell; and Susan Boyde, Mary Bone and Mary Wood. Pauline Wickham deserves a special mention for her advice on style and on how to prepare the manuscript for publication. I would also like to thank the ISP's Programme Assistants over the years, who have given me invaluable administrative support: Tracy Jarvis, Sue Swasey, Hannah Doe, Britta Martini-Miles and Elaine Eddison. Finally, let me thank Marie Lathia for initiating me into the mysterious world of PCs and WP.5, and Edgardo Fippi and his colleagues, who helped make Chatham House such a friendly place to work in.

Whilst at Chatham House, I had the privilege to be given a desk in the elegant surroundings of the Duke of York room. I soon realised that I was a fortunate interloper in what was clearly the intellectual hub of the institute! I would like to extend a special thanks to my room-mates over the years, who provided day-to-day friendship and intellectual sustenance; in particular, Gerry Segal, Alyson Bailes, Michael Clarke, Satoshi Okumura, Norbert Ropers and Hans-Hendrik Kasper.

The first drafts of this book have all been discussed at study group meetings held between January 1989 and February 1990. Without the constructive criticisms made by my friends and colleagues at these meetings, this book would be much worse than it is now. I would therefore like to thank all those who took the time to participate in one or more of my study-groups, including: Chris Bluth, Olivia Bosch, Nigel Brind, Andrew Butfoy, Barry Buzan, Stuart Croft, John Cross, David Dunn, Geoffrey Edwards, Thomas Enders, Jonathan Eyal, Ian Gambles, Mike Gapes, Eric Herring, Gerard Holden, Ieuan John, Keith Kyle, Mary Kaldor, Margie Lindsay, Donald MacLaren, Edwina Moreton, Renee De Nevers, Hella Pick, Jonathan Powell, Gwyn Prins, Michael Pugh, Holger Ruthe, Philip Sabin, Peter Siebenmorgen, Michael Smith, Barbara Wells, David Wedgwood-Benn, and Nick Wheeler.

I am also grateful for the written or oral comments I received from Hannes Adomeit, Walter Andrusyzyn, Vladimir Baranovsky, Gerd Basler, John Baylis, Frank Blackaby, Ken Booth, Yves Boyers, Frédéric Bozo, Andre Brie, Robert Brinkley, Katherina von Bülow, Anne-Marie Burley, David Calleo, Michael Cox, Ian Cuthbertson, Richard Day, Jürg Döring, Judit Gömöri, Dan Hamilton, Peter Hardi, Sergei Karaganov, Gennady Kolosov, Egbert Jahn, Zdzislaw Lachowski, Robbin Laird, Ekkehard Lieberam, Bernd Löwe, Lars-Erik Lundin, Bernd Löwe, Lubomir Molnar, Harald Müller, Nick Rengger, Uwe Nerlich, Barbara von Ow, Alexei Pankin, Jérome Paolini, Ingo Peters, Adam Daniel Rotfeld, Paikiasothy Saravanamuttu, Gebhard Schweigler, Hans-Joachim Spanger, Jane Sharp, Witold Pawlowski, and Ole Waever. Their criticisms have helped greatly improve the quality of both my arguments and presentation: I am of course responsible for the book's remaining shortcomings and weaknesses.

A book such as this would not have been possible had it not been for the intellectual stimulation provided by a series of international conferences and seminars I attended between 1987 and 1990. These conferences were a vital source of new ideas and different approaches, and helped me understand how different the problems of European security looked when approached from different national or political perspectives. In the first place, I would like to thank the Aspen Institute of Berlin (especially the Institute's then Assistant Director, Margarita Mathiopoulos), who invited me to participate in a series of four study group conferences on the theme of 'Perspectives for a "European House" within the Framework of the CSCE-Process'. These meetings brought together a group of young Americans and Europeans from all the main CSCE participating countries, and were held in Berlin, Paris, Budapest and Bonn/Berlin between April 1988 and June 1989. Furthermore, I would like to thank the Atlantic Council of the United States, who invited me to the 14th Young Leaders Seminar in Hamburg and Berlin (November 1989); to Martha Dassu and her colleagues at the Centre for the Study of International Affairs for joint CeSPI-Friedrich Ebert Foundation workshop on 'The New European Security Order' in Rome (July 1990); to Mary Kaldor, and the other participants at the East–West Seminar on Global Security and Arms Control at the Moscow State Institute of International Affairs (MGIMO), in July 1989; Ludgar Eling and the Konrad Adenauer Foundation, for their conferences on European security in Wilton Park and Paris; Lars Wallin and the Stockholm Swedish Defence Research Establishment (FOA), for their symposium on 'NATO and the WTO in the 1990s' (June 1990); to all the staff at the Wilton Park conference centre, particularly Nicholas Hopkinson and Richard Latter; and to the Osaka Chamber of Commerce, who invited me to address the plenary session of the G-BOC Conference in Japan in September 1990.

Finally, I would like to thank the MacArthur Foundation, whose generous financial support greatly assisted the work of the International Security Programme over recent years.

List of Abbreviations

ABM	Anti-ballistic missile (Treaty)
ACE	Allied Command Europe
ADE	Armoured division equivalent
AFV	Armoured fighting vehicle
ALCM	Air-launched cruise missile
APC	Armoured personnel carrier
ATACM	Army tactical missile
ATTU	Atlantic-to-the-Urals
BAOR	British Army of the Rhine
C^3I	Command, control, communications and intelligence
CBM	Confidence-building measure
CBW	Chemical and biological warfare/weapons
CDE	Conference on Disarmament on Europe
CDU	Christian Democratic Union (FRG)
CFE	Conventional Forces in Europe
CIA	Central Intelligence Agency
CMEA	Council for Mutual Economic Assistance
CoCom	Coordinating Committee for Exports
Cominform	Communist Information Bureau
Comintern	Communist International
CPSU	Communist Party of the Soviet Union
CSBM	Confidence- and security-building measure
CSCE	Conference on Security and Cooperation in Europe
CSU	Christian Social Union (FRG)
EC	European Community
ECE	(United Nations) Economic Commission for Europe
ECU	European Currency Unit
EDC	European Defence Community
EFA	European Fighter Aircraft
EMU	Economic and Monetary Union
EPC	European Political Cooperation
ERW	Enhanced radiation warhead
ET	Emerging Technologies
EUREKA	European Scientific Co-operation Project
FAR	Force Action Rapid
FDP	Free Democratic Party (FRG)
FOFA	Follow-on Forces Attack
FRG	Federal Republic of Germany
GATT	General Agreement on Tariffs and Trade

GDR	German Democratic Republic
GLCM	Ground-launched cruise missile
GNP	Gross National Product
GSFG	Group of Soviet Forces in Germany
ICBM	Intercontinental ballistic missile
IEWSS	Institute for East–West Security Studies (New York)
IISS	International Institute for Strategic Studies (London)
IMEMO	Institute for World Economy and International Relations (Moscow)
IMF	International Monetary Fund
INF	Intermediate-range nuclear forces
IPW	Institute for International Politics and Economics (East Berlin)
LRTNW	Long-range theatre nuclear weapons
MAD	Mutual assured destruction
MBFR	Mutual and Balanced Force Reduction (talks)
MBT	Main battle tank
MIRV	Multiple Independently Targeted Re-entry Vehicle
MLRS	Multiple launch rocket system
MUD	i) minimum unacceptable damage, or ii) mutual unilateral disarmament
NATO	North Atlantic Treaty Organization
NPG	Nuclear Planning Group (NATO)
NPT	Non-proliferation treaty
NVA	National Peoples' Army (GDR)
OECD	Organization for Economic Cooperation and Development
OMG	Operational Maneuver Group
PCF	Communist Party of France
PCI	Communist Party of Italy
PGM	Precision guided munitions
POMCUS	Pre-positioned overseas material configured in unit sets
PRC	People's Republic of China
RAF	Royal Air Force
RIIA	Royal Institute of International Affairs ('Chatham House', London)
RUM	Related unilateral measures
RUSI	Royal United Services Institute (London)
SAC	Strategic Air Command
SACEUR	Supreme Allied Commander Europe
SALT	Strategic Arms Limitation Talks
SDI	Strategic Defense Initiative
SED	Socialist Unity Party of Germany (GDR)
SHAPE	Supreme Headquarters Allied Powers Europe
SIPRI	Stockholm International Peace Research Institute
SLBM	Submarine-launched ballistic missile
SLCM	Sea-launched cruise missile
SNF	Short-range nuclear forces
SPD	Social Democratic Party of Germany (FRG)
SSBM	Ballistic missile submarine
START	Strategic Arms Reduction Talks
UN	United Nations
USAF	United States Air Force
WEU	Western European Union
WTO	Warsaw Treaty Organization

1
Introduction

For the third time this century, the old order in Europe is crumbling. Post-war Europe – the Europe of Yalta and Potsdam – proved a remarkably stable and predictable place for nearly four decades. Now, however, it has entered a period of flux, in which old verities and past assumptions no longer hold. Since the mid-1980s, the pace of change in East–West relations has accelerated beyond what anyone thought possible. Thanks to the profound changes in the Soviet Union in recent years, the strategic map of Europe has been redrawn. After nearly four decades of East–West confrontation and cold war bipolarity, the dramatic events of late 1989 have produced a watershed in post-war Europe. The developments in this *annus mirabilis* were unique in that never before had such profound change in a crucial region in the international system taken place without war or bloody revolution. In 1789, 1815, 1870, 1914 and 1939 – at all these moments of far-reaching political and strategic change in modern Europe – violence constituted the indomitable 'midwife of history'.

The contours of the emerging political and strategic landscape in Europe are only dimly perceivable – if at all – and much remains clouded by uncertainty and ambiguity. In the early 1990s, the overriding concern of Europe's decision-makers will be to contain the disruptive effects of the strategic earthquake of 1989: looking beyond this, however, the task is to develop a fundamentally new security system for Europe. A security system which incorporates the political, economic and military changes of recent years, and one able to provide a flexible but secure framework for a durable peace in Europe.

The purpose of this book is threefold. First, to define what is meant by the term 'European security system', and to analyse its historical evolution, motive forces and structural dynamics. Second, to identify the key factors affecting the future development of the European security system over the next 10–20 years, and to consider the implications of the changing security agenda in Europe and the global system. And, third, to outline some alternative scenarios of the European security system in two decades' time, in order to explore some of the long-term implications of current trends and policy-options in the European security area.

The structure of the book follows from these three aims. In the remaining pages of this introduction, I shall briefly consider the specific dynamics of the European interstate system and the nature of the post-war East–West conflict. I will then define the key terms employed in the book. Finally, I will argue that the study of European security is itself about to undergo a conceptual change, comparable to that which occurred in the 1950s in the light of the impact of nuclear weapons on the international system.

The main body of the book is divided into three parts. The first begins with a brief survey of the historical development of the European security system, and then moves on to consider the secular trends which have been gradually eroding its underlying foundations. The second part provides a more detailed analysis of the key determinants of change in Europe, including Soviet perestroika, post-communism in Eastern Europe, the process of integration in Western Europe, German unification, changing transatlantic relations, regional differentiation in Europe, and the evolving structure and balance of military power on the continent. Together, these constitute the decisive variables in the changing security order in Europe. In the third part, four scenarios of Europe in 2010 are outlined and analysed. The aim of these scenarios is not to try and predict the future, but to explore some of the possible outcomes of current trends and policy-options, and to assess what impact these alternative security frameworks might have on the stability of the European interstate system. In the concluding chapter, we will consider the implications of the broader changes in the international system for the nature of security, stability and change in Europe in the 1990s and beyond.

The European Experience of War, Conflict and Social Change

Europe's security problems derive from the specific dynamics of its inter-state system.[1] After the collapse of the fragile *pax Romana* in the fourth and fifth centuries AD, Europe developed as a fragmented and polycentric entity. The political and cultural diversity of the European continent was in part a function of its variegated geography, with a landscape fractured by mountain ranges, large forests, broad rivers and climatic variations. This political fragmentation had the fortunate effect of allowing a variety of different forms of economic and social organisation to develop, including the market – which was to prove decisive in the continent's rise to global prominence. The combination of competing economic systems, and a plurality of centres of political and military power, gave Europe its distinctive socio-economic dynamic, which distinguished it from other world civilisations.

By the early Medieval period, the fragmented and polycentric nature of European political and economic life had given rise to a relentless struggle for power amongst a shifting coalition of states. This struggle for power took place within a 'Europe' which was defined primarily in religious terms, ie by the conflict between 'Christendom' and Islam. With the coming of the Reformation, however, a religious divide within Christianity added to Europe's internal conflicts. Nevertheless, the competitive interaction of the European states stimulated new innovations in economics, science and technology. It was this which gave Europe its peculiarly vital and dynamic societies. With the development of the world market – spurred on by European trade and commerce – Europe was able to establish a dominant place for itself in the international system by the sixteenth century.

At the same time, the decentralised European balance of power produced an endless search for military superiority by individual states, which resulted in a costly arms race and a series of ever more bloody and vicious wars. In contradistinction to many other world civilisations, however, no single state or group of states was able to achieve political dominance by virtue of a monopoly on the decisive military technologies of the age. This meant that no 'gunpowder empire' – equivalent to those which existed between 1450 and 1600 in Muscovy, Tokugawa Japan or Mogul India – emerged in Europe.

The specific nature of the European security problem in its historical dimension, therefore, stems from this inescapable paradox of European development: the continent's pluralist and fragmented political structures stimulated a constant process of economic and scientific innovation, but they also produced a succession of ever more destructive wars between these rival states, empires and alliances.

The European state system which emerged at the end of the Middle Ages was thus characterised by ceaseless diplomatic activity and frequent wars amongst its member states, within a genuinely multipolar structure. In the sixteenth century, Spain, France, Austria and England were the leading powers of Europe. In the early seventeenth century, they were briefly joined by Holland and Sweden, although these were later eclipsed by Russia and Prussia (Spain too was to lose its leading position in the mid-seventeenth century). By the end of the seventeenth century, the European interstate system had finally matured into a genuine multipolar balance of power structure, in which there were five great powers (France, Britain, the Habsburg Empire, Russia and Brandenburg-Prussia) and a myriad of lesser powers.

One distinctive feature of this state system was the continued existence of almost all of the states of Europe (with the notable exception of Poland). This was by no means the case with other state systems (as the rise and fall of a plethora of mighty empires in the ancient world makes abundantly clear), and was the outcome of a constantly shifting but generally maintained balance between the principle European states. For nearly four centuries, the pluralist and multipolar interstate system in Europe which emerged at the end of the Middle Ages was able to contain the successive bids for hegemony by the Spanish, Austrians and French.

However, the internal equilibrium of the European state system was fatally undermined by the rise of German power at the end of the nineteenth century. The formation – by 'blood and iron' – of a centralised German state possessing substantial industrial, financial and human resources, and with enormous political and military potential, was to lead to the disintegration of the balance of power in Europe.[2] Without American intervention in 1917, it is possible that Germany might have won the First World War, and it was only the involvement of the Americans and the Soviets – Europe's two great flanking powers – which prevented German domination of the continent in 1939–45. The years from 1870 to 1945, therefore, are the years of the disintegration and collapse of the multipolar European interstate system which had existed for over four centuries. The security system which developed in Europe after 1945 was fundamentally different from that which had previously existed, and was constructed in a radically transformed political, military and economic context.

With the crushing of Nazi Germany and the construction of a new security system, Europe has enjoyed one of the longest periods of uninterrupted peace in its turbulent history. Paradoxically, however, it has become the site of the greatest concentration of military force the world has ever seen. Furthermore, the relative peace – or, more correctly, the absence of war – in Europe, and the stability of the post-war system, have been based until recently on an artificial division of the continent, with all its deleterious consequences for Europeans, from both the East and the West. This ambiguous and contradictory military-political arrangement is the child of the controversial post-war settlement, which is frequently traced back to the conferences of Yalta and Potsdam. Dissatisfaction with it over the years has led to repeated and periodic demands for what President Mitterrand called *sortir de Yalta*, but until relatively recently it seemed that the post-war structure was too stable and dependable to be dismantled in favour of an untested alternative.[3]

The structures and dynamics of the security order which emerged in post-war Europe can only be understood in the context of the East–West conflict in Europe, a conflict which has dominated the politics and strategic concerns of the European continent for the last four decades. It is this conflict, above all others, which has provided the motor force of the post-war security order, and which has decisively shaped the character and the key institutions of the European security system.

The East–West Conflict in Europe

The East–West conflict in Europe developed as a consequence of the specific conjuncture of political, military and economic forces at the end of the Second World War. It is closely associated with the cold war, with which it is sometimes equated, although the term 'cold war' itself refers more accurately only to those periods of intensified confrontation since 1945 (1947–53, 1958–61, 1979–85).

When discussing the nature of the East–West conflict, there are a number of points to be borne in mind. First, the 'East–West conflict' is not a simple conflict involving one specific dispute, but is a complex configuration, involving a series of overlapping and criss-crossing patterns of conflict and cooperation. It is the result of a series of processes, which have developed on a number of different levels (global, regional and national), with a number of different elements (economic, political, ideological and military), through a series of different phases (heightened confrontation, partial detente).[4]

Second, the East–West conflict can be seen as one of the five different 'conflict formations' identified by Dieter Senghaas.[5] Senghaas argues that these conflict formations are *Handlungszusammenhänge* ('action sets') which structure the international system along a series of broad political, military and economic axes, each with its own form and identity. The other four conflict formations are conflicts within the West, conflicts within what was once known as the 'world socialist system', the North–South conflict and regional conflicts in the Third World. These different conflict formations, according to Senghaas, interact and impinge upon each other in a variety of ways, but each has its own internal logic and dynamic.

Third, to speak of the East–West **conflict** is in some senses misleading, in that East–West relations have exhibited tendencies towards both conflict **and** cooperation. From the time of Stalin's death onwards, there were a series of attempts to regulate and manage the East–West conflict, and to develop codes of behaviour for the 'adversarial partnership' or 'competitive coexistence' into which the East–West relationship was soon to evolve. This was particularly evident after the twin crises of 1961–62 (over Berlin and Cuba), and again in the 1970s. The relationship between the two military-political alliances thus involved a complex dialectic between cooperation and conflict, as the protagonists sought to develop a security structure for Europe which was capable of adapting to a process of peaceful and stable change.[6] Some powers were more orientated towards the status quo than others, but all sought a stable and predictable security order in Europe. At no stage, therefore, did the East–West conflict ever become a struggle to the death between irreconcilable enemies.

Finally, the East–West conflict is the result of a process of multiple causation, or 'complex overdetermination' to use Louis Althusser's term.[7] This process involves the interaction of five basic elements, which together provide the motive forces of the post-war European security system. These five elements are:

1. **Superpower rivalry** – this can be seen as a structural imperative inherent within the bipolar world system which emerged in the wake of the Second World War.[8] The struggle for global hegemony between the two dominant powers had a decisive impact on the rest of the international system, and served to legitimise the dominant role of the USA and the USSR within their respective power-blocs. At the same time, this bipolar structure, with a managed – albeit abrasive – superpower conflict, provided a stable framework for managing conflicts in an otherwise anarchic and turbulent global system.

2. **Ideological antagonism** – this was the result of the clash of two rival socio-economic and political systems, with different values, organisational principles and political practices.[9] Its origins can be traced back to the period of instability after the First World War, with the Bolshevik revolution, the rise of the Comintern, and the clash of Marxist and liberal *Weltanschauungen* (encapsulated in the rival platforms of V.I. Lenin and Woodrow Wilson in 1918). However, it was only in the wake of the Second World War that it became a decisive factor in global politics, given the spread of communist power and influence in parts of Europe and Asia. Indeed, R.J. Vincent has argued,

> The history of East–West relations in the modern sense of that expression, as the contact between socialist countries and western liberal democracies, is in an important sense the history of a dispute about human rights .... In the Cold War, the ideologies of human rights held by the Soviet Union and the United States met head on, and the contest was the fiercer for the strength of conviction on both sides. The ideas of the protagonists about human rights were not mere preferences which outsiders could take or leave, but commitments the spread of which measured progress in the contest between the superpowers and, in turn, strengthened or weakened the domestic legitimacy of their governments.[10]

At the same time, however, this was not simply a conflict **between** different social systems, but one **within** societies in both East and West. It was the international expression of a tension at the heart of modern societies, between the pursuit of liberty on the one hand, and that of equality on the other; between individual versus collective rights; and between the market and social justice. In this sense, it was a 'schism within a single civilization, a secular version of the earlier religious divide ...'.[11] The ideological dimension of the cold war thus has its roots in the strains of modernisation and industrialisation, and was in part a reflection of the socio-political divisions that these processes generated (and which became a particularly sensitive political issue in the immediate post-war years in Europe).

3. **Traditional Great Power rivalries** – this constituted an important element of the East–West conflict, as traditional Great Power conflicts over the balance of power were incorporated into the broader East–West antagonism. This can be seen from the British concern about 'Soviet expansionism', which in many respects was simply a continuation of the earlier rivalry between the British Empire and Tsarist Russia. However, at the heart of the traditional power-political concerns of the Europeans was the German question. The division of Germany in 1948–49 seemed to provide a working solution to the problem of German power in Europe, but at the same time, this division created an inseparable connection between traditional Great Power rivalries in Europe and the broader East–West conflict.

4. **National-ethnic conflicts in Europe** – although the East–West conflict provided a regulatory framework for managing and containing some of the ethnic and national tensions in Europe within the two alliances (ie, the Hungarian–Romanian and Graeco-Turkish disputes), it nevertheless overlapped with and reinforced some of the other tensions latent in Europe: ie, between the Germans and the Slavs (which provided a certain rationale for the Warsaw Pact, especially in the cases of Poland and Czechoslovakia); between Bulgaria and Turkey; and between Hungary and Yugoslavia (between whom there was a 'mini-cold war' in the wake of the Stalin–Tito split).

5. **The arms race** – the East–West conflict (in its ideological, power-political and national dimensions) generated a major arms race, which militarized the conflict and created a powerful and influential 'military-industrial complex' in both East and West. Some have argued that this gave another independent and self-sustaining element to the East–West conflict, which reinforced and to some extent superseded the political and ideological antagonism. E.P. Thompson, for example, has propounded the concept of 'exterminism', which is grounded on the belief that, by the late 1970s at least, the cold war was being driven by the imperatives of modern military technology and the arms race. This, argues Thompson, had acquired a logic and dynamic of its own which was not reducible to either class or national interests, and which was propelling human civilisation towards its own inevitable extermination.[12] This is an extreme view, which overlooks other crucial elements which have sustained the East–West conflict over the last forty years.[13] Yet there is still good reason for suggesting that the arms race – and the industrial, financial and bureaucratic interests behind it – have provided an important element in sustaining the conflict between the two blocs over the last few decades.[14]

It has therefore become a significant variable in the post-war East–West conflict, and even though it is not a primary causal factor in this conflict, it is still more than a reflection of other antagonisms.

The relative weight of these five elements within the overall East–West conflict has varied over time. Superpower rivalry was an important factor in the late 1940s, 1950s and 1960s, but its relative importance has declined as the European states have grown in economic power and political self-confidence. Similarly, ideological antagonism was intensive in the late 1940s and early 1950s, but – despite the resurgence of militant anti-communist rhetoric by the Reagan Administration in the early 1980s – has declined in significance since then. The relative importance of the arms race has tended to increase with time, and was felt more acutely in the 1960s (when the talk was of a 'missile gap' and a 'window of vulnerability'), and again in the late 1970s and 1980s (given the Soviet military build-up and the INF deployments). In general, the most important elements in the post-war East–West conflict have been the first two – superpower conflict and ideological antagonism.[15]

Defining the 'European Security System'

The East–West conflict found its expression in Europe in a specific set of political, economic and military structures, which developed in the early years of the cold war period. The specific features of the post-war security order will be described in Chapter 3. At this point, however, it is necessary to clarify what is meant by 'European security system', since this term lies at the heart of this book. Let us consider each of the words in turn.

'Europe'
Otto von Bismarck is reputed to have said, 'He who speaks of Europe is mistaken; it is only a geographical expression'. Geographically, Europe is the north-west peninsula of the Asian land mass. However, this does not suffice as a description of what constitutes 'Europe', because it leaves its eastern border undefined. In other words, the question still remains: does Europe end at the Lübeck–Maribor line (the Polish-Soviet border); along an imaginary line from the White Sea to the Black Sea; or at the Ural mountains?

Given the lack of clear geographical boundaries for Europe, any definition of Europe is inevitably a political one. Although there is a distinctive European cultural and historical identity – which can trace its roots back to the classical civilisations of Mycenean Crete, Hellenic Greece and ancient Rome – there is no clear-cut European political or socio-economic entity.[16] In the 1970s, and particularly in the 1980s, the awareness of a distinctive 'European' identity and of specific 'European' security concerns became ever more perceptible, and the concept of 'Europeanisation' has become a ubiquitous theme in academic and political writings. This has led to the crystallisation of a number of rival definitions of 'Europe', each of which has very different security implications.[17]

The first is the view that Europe can be equated with Western Europe, in particular, with the European Community. This concept is found not simply amongst some West Europeans, but in East Central Europe too, where many of the post-communist elites speak of a 'return to Europe', in the sense of re-establishing their political, economic and cultural ties with the countries of Western Europe. This vision of Europe has its historical antecedents in the ninth century Carolingian Empire. Nevertheless, as a political, economic, cultural or social definition of modern-day Europe, it is patently inadequate, and it is of very limited use when considering security issues in the continent as a whole.

Second, Europe 'from the Atlantic to the Urals'. This concept of Europe has in the past frequently been advanced by the Soviets – as well as by General de Gaulle – as a way of drawing a political and security distinction between the 'Europeans' (including the Soviets west of the Urals) and the North Americans. Although there is a certain geographical logic to this definition, it again makes little sense from a security perspective, or in political, economic, cultural or value terms.

Third, Europe 'from Poland to Portugal'. This concept of Europe was popular in some sections of the European peace movement in the 1980s, and in parts of the nationalist right. Culturally speaking, its historical antecedents lie with the old medieval notion of 'Christendom', ie, Catholic and Protestant Europe. It is a concept of Europe which excludes both the superpowers, and tends to define 'security threats' to Europe as coming from outside of this politically defined region. However, it ignores the important impact of both the North Americans and the Soviets on Europe, in political, economic, cultural and – above all – security terms.

Finally, there is the concept of Europe used in the Helsinki CSCE protocols and documents, which speak of the 'European security area'. This is a pragmatic and flexible definition, which recognises the power-political and geostrategic realities of post-war Europe, and which eschews the more reductionist and politically motivated definitions based on history, culture, religion and politics. Moreover, it is a definition with particular utility for the purposes of this study, given its concern with the security issues of the 34 CSCE participating states, plus Albania (which until very recently chose to stand apart from this pan-European gathering). Nonetheless, as a definition of 'Europe' it too has its limitations, for it includes by implication San Francisco as well as Vladivostock.

Any definition of 'Europe', therefore, is inevitably a political one, in which history and geography are reinterpreted to suit specific policy prescriptions.[18] With the disintegration of the 'socialist community' in the East, the notion of Europe has become an even greater source of symbolic associations and identification. As we shall see in Part III of this book, differing conceptions of Europe play an important role in contemporary discussions about the continent's future security 'architecture'.

'Security'

As Barry Buzan has remarked, security is an essentially 'underdeveloped' and 'contested' concept.[19] In the field of international relations and strategic studies, there are a number of different definitions of, and methodological approaches towards, 'security', none of which is really able to capture the full richness of this elusive notion. For this reason, therefore, rather than attempting to add to these definitions, we shall adopt a more eclectic and 'holistic' approach to the analysis of contemporary security problems.

The first point to note when considering the nature of security is that it is a condition which incorporates a number of different aspects. It is generally agreed that at the core of any 'security' consideration is the military factor. The question of military forces remains at the heart of any strategic assessment of security relationships. Nevertheless, as Richard Ullman argues, 'defining national security merely (or even primarily) in military terms conveys a profoundly false image of reality'.[20] In the modern world, security problems have become more and more complicated, as military threats to a state's political and territorial integrity have increasingly been accompanied – and to some extent, superseded – by economic and social challenges to a society's viability.[21] At the same time, the relationship of military force to other forms of power has become more complex than in earlier times, given the growing interdependence of the modern world, and the impact of nuclear deterrence.[22]

The military dimension of security, therefore, must be considered in the context of other important elements of security. These include political, economic, societal and environmental factors. The political sphere plays a vital role because it mediates between the economic, social, cultural, technological and military factors in any human endeavour. It is particularly important in that it plays a decisive part in regulating interdependencies between societies and the broader international system, and because it is through the political processes that societies articulate and integrate the many interests they contain.

The economic dimension is also crucial to security, because it determines access to resources, markets and finances, and because it provides the decisive basis for political influence and military power.[23] Societal factors (including cultural values) are less tangible, but no less significant for that. They are important because they affect the stability and character of a state's political system; the military capability of the state; its economic performance and capacity to generate scientific and technological innovation; and because they provide the atmosphere in which the values which affect the behaviour of states in the international system develop and mature. Finally, there are environmental factors. In the past, they were not so important and politically controversial, but in the age of Chernobyl, acid rain, river pollution, deforestation, global warming, the greenhouse effect, contamination of the seas, and dangerous toxic emissions, they are becoming increasingly more significant.[24] Indeed, environmental and ecological concerns are likely to become a major security issue – in the broadest sense of the term – by the early part of the twenty-first century.[25]

These five dimensions are all intimately connected, and constitute an intricate nexus of factors which affect the nature of security – at all levels (individual, state, system) – in the global system.[26] It is for this reason that an eclectic, integrated and holistic analysis of security offers the most promising approach to the study of security problems in the modern world.

The second point to note is that security is a **relative**, not absolute concept: a state is neither simply secure or insecure.[27] Indeed, the search for absolute security is ultimately self-defeating, in that the attempt by individual states or groups of states to achieve more security for themselves tends automatically to feed the insecurities of others. This in turn is likely to provoke counter-balancing actions, leading to a decrease in security for all. It is this which constitutes the 'security dilemma'.[28]

Third, security is linked to power, and the nature of power: it is therefore a **relational** concept. Power never exists in a vacuum, it only exists in a relationship between two or more subjects.[29] It is not a simple quantitative entity or substance that one can possess. Similarly, security is a function of a relationship between two or more subjects.

Finally, the concept of security is linked to other values, concerns and interests. Enjoying security (however relative) means a society is free to pursue a chosen way of life, and to determine its own course of action free from internal or external threats – of whatever nature (economic, political, military, societal or environmental).[30]

'System'

Our concern in this book is not with the specific national security strategies of individual states, nor is it with the security problems of any of the military alliances in the European security area. Rather, it is with the overall structure of the overlapping and interacting security relationships, commitments and institutional networks in Europe. Together, they form a complex configuration of military and non-military factors, with different levels and instances (global, regional, sub-regional, national or local), each with different degrees of effectiveness. This structure has its own internal logic and dynamic, and is not amenable to control by any one actor or group of actors: rather, change within the ensemble must be **overdetermined**, in the Althusserian sense of the term.

Describing the post-war security order in Europe as a 'system' has a number of connotations. Firstly, it implies that the European security system is more than the sum of its constituent parts, ie, more than just the aggregate of the national security measures of its participants, and more than just a specific conjunctural security situation. Secondly, that the security system is more than an anarchic, unstructured 'state of nature'. Its different elements combine to form a pattern of relationships and an identifiable structure of interactions which provide the system with a degree of predictability and relative stability, at least in terms of its core relationships. At the same time, however, the notion of a security system should not be taken to imply the existence of a fixed and inflexible structure, incapable of evolution or change; in other words, it does not imply the continuation or stabilisation of the status quo.[31]

The essential dynamics of the European security system are provided by the intensity of the internal relationships and cross-cutting patterns of conflict and cooperation within the European security area. Nevertheless, it is an open-ended rather than closed system, which is susceptible to influences of other global regions (the Middle East, North Africa, the Pacific) and other international actors (China, Japan). The involvement of the two superpowers in the European security system provides a set of important points of contact (political, economic, cultural and strategic) between Europe and other regions and continents, and establishes a link between the stability of the European security system and security problems in other regions, such as East Asia, the Middle East and southern Africa.

There has been some debate in the past as to whether the European security system is simply the localised version of an East–West security system, or whether it exhibits sufficient regional specificities to distinguish it from other regional security systems. Anton Deporte, amongst others, has argued that the European state system disintegrated from the 1870s onwards under the strain of rising German power, and that since 1945 it has been replaced by a new East–West security system established by the two superpowers: '... for the European states, the new system is basically worldwide and therefore no longer theirs'.[32] However, a clear trend since the early 1960s has been the growing 'Europeanisation' of the European security system, in the sense that the interdependencies within Europe itself have increasingly gained in importance in relation to the influence of the two superpowers. This is a trend which has become even more evident in the 1980s, and which has been reflected in an emerging 'European' identity. The European security system can therefore be seen as a regional example of what Barry Buzan has called a 'security complex', ie, 'a group of states whose primary security concerns link together sufficiently closely that their national securities cannot realistically be considered apart from one another'.[33]

Beyond Yalta – Towards a New Understanding of European Security?

After nearly forty years of remarkable stability and incremental change, Europe has entered a period of fluidity, characterised by uncertainty and transitional instability. The residual bipolar structures of the post-war era have been shattered by the winds of change from the East, and a new security system is now in the offing. The collapse of communism in Eastern Europe has ended the East–West conflict in its traditional, post-war form, and the boundaries between 'East' and 'West' are becoming increasingly blurred. In this new situation 'beyond Yalta', a more complex pattern of economic, political, cultural and strategic relationships is now beginning to emerge.

As a consequence of the final demise of the cold war, the nature of both East–West relations and the European security system has fundamentally changed. Many old assumptions and expectations no longer apply, whilst new patterns of conflict and cooperation are beginning to take shape. New and unforeseen security issues are coming to the fore, partly in response to the changing character of international relations in the late twentieth century. Others, however, derive from earlier quarrels between nations and ethnic groups in Europe. As the nature of the security in Europe changes, we need both to draw on some older ideas from the past (such as collective security and European concert), and to develop existing concepts (such as common security, complex interdependence and regime theory). Only then can we begin to grasp the enormity of the changes which have recently shaken the continent.

Indeed, the challenges to our traditional understanding of European security have become so great, and the limitations of our existing conceptual framework so apparent, that we could be on the verge of a major 'paradigm shift',[34] in the study of European security. The changing structure of international relations (with the deepening of complex interdependence, the development of international regimes and the declining utility of military force as a currency of power); the transformation of the East–West relationship in recent years; and the changing security agenda in Europe – all these developments have placed considerable strain on the existing conceptual framework which has governed the study of European security for much of the post-war period. If, as seems increasingly likely, it proves impossible to stretch or alter the existing neo-realist, power-politics model to accommodate the changing nature of European security, then a 'paradigm shift' – comparable to that which occurred over thirty years ago as a result of the impact of nuclear deterrence on the international system – will become inescapable.[35]

The limitations of the dominant, neo-realist paradigm have become increasingly evident. Existing concepts in international relations appear to be less and less able to explain the contemporary dynamics of the European inter-state system. The old narrowly focused concept of security is of declining utility; a new definition and content of the concept is required – one that is more comprehensive and which includes a political, economic, environmental and cultural dimension. A concept of security, in other words, which is capable of comprehending the complexities of the contemporary world.

The idea of states as coherent, undifferentiated units and 'rational utility maximisers' has been further weakened by the events of 1989, which have underlined the importance of the dialectic between domestic developments and external international behaviour. These events have demonstrated that the neo-realist logic (which suggests that it is the structure of the international system, not human nature or domestic political characteristics, which determines the nature of international power politics) **can** be counteracted by social and political forces beneath the level of the state.[36] At the same time, the existence or otherwise of democratic political structures can have an important impact on the resolution of contemporary security problems, particularly in terms of war and peace. Indeed, there is little to refute the Kantian notion that states with liberal-democratic systems are unlikely to wage war on each other.[37]

The notion of states as undifferentiated 'rational utility maximisers' has been losing credibility for some time now. Robert Jervis's work on perceptions and misperceptions in international politics has helped focus attention on a richer set of psychological variables than those assumed by the simple rational actor model.[38] This model of state behaviour in the international system needs to be further tempered by an awareness of the impact of bureaucratic politics and the nature of decision-making in large, complex organisations.[39] Indeed, given the role of political, bureaucratic, economic and other elites, to conceive of the 'state' as a coherent actor is a gross simplification of an infinitely more complex and multifaceted reality. Similarly, the notion of the 'national interest' is really little more than a rarified abstraction, given the diversity of socio-economic interests in the modern nation-state.

Furthermore, the traditional, state-centric, power-political paradigm (which gives rise to the 'billiard balls' analogy, in which only the hard exteriors of states touch, the heavier or faster moving ones pushing the others out the way) is less and less able to explain the workings of a global system increasingly characterised by interdependence, international regimes and new patterns of cooperation and integration.[40] The existence of a network of international institutions and intergovernmental forums has increased the ability of states to communicate with each other and reach mutually beneficial agreements, and this in turn has added to their repertoire of strategies and policy-options. In this way, states might acquire new approaches to their understanding of their 'national interest', and develop new patterns of interests, in ways not conceivable within the traditional, realist, balance of power theory.[41] At the same time, the emergence of 'international regimes' helps stabilise expectations, and allow cooperation to develop in some parts of a relationship on the basis of rules and norms governing behaviour, and this is a trend which traditional realist theory has difficulty accommodating.[42]

Finally, the growing complexity of interdependence in world affairs has eroded the traditional hierarchies of the international system, and helped diffuse power (especially economic power) more broadly than in the past. The rise of transnational corporations and continental-wide mergers, acquisitions and take-overs has meant that economic power is increasingly diffused throughout (Western) Europe, and accrues less and less to individual nation-states. This trend is complemented by the process of supranational integration through the EC, which is also part of one of the most important and significant trends in post-war Europe – the demilitarisation of international relations in Western Europe. The diffusion of economic power and the development of the Community of Twelve means that the nation-state is increasingly losing its saliency as an organisational focus in contemporary Western Europe. The substance of foreign policy issues for government leaders has changed in the modern period, as the international system has changed: consequently, the nature of its policy inputs and outputs is very different than earlier in the century.

Thus, as we have seen, these changes in the substance and nature of international relations in Europe suggest that a new conceptual framework for the study of European security is required. In this search for a new conceptual framework, the old 'realist–idealist' dichotomy is likely to prove of little help. What is required is a new synthesis and a broader and richer conceptual framework – one which is able to cope with the complexities of security in Europe in the late twentieth century. This new paradigm is likely to draw heavily on concepts associated with the notions of 'complex interdependence', international regimes and 'pluralistic security communities'.[43] The theoretical elaboration of such a new paradigm is beyond the scope of this book, but it is important to be aware that the approach to the study of European security is itself facing a period of conceptual turbulence and uncertainty.

Suggestions that a 'paradigm shift' in the field of international relations is both necessary and imminent have been growing for some time now.[44] Whether or not a completely new paradigm is needed is not yet clear. What does seem evident, however, is that the processes of change set in motion by the events of the late 1980s have given added weight to calls for a radically new conceptual understanding of international security in Europe.[45] From this perspective, therefore, the seismic upheavals in the political-strategic landscape of Europe in 1989 can be seen as heralding an 'epistemological break' in our conceptual approach to the study of European security. Of course, it is a truism that every period contains elements of transition, and that every 'successor generation' tends to regard itself as the harbinger of a new era – this part of the arrogance of youth. However, this book has been written in the belief that something fundamental **has** changed in Europe over the last few years, and that the European security system of the 1990s and beyond will be radically different from that of the past four decades.

Notes

1. Much of the argument of this section is constructed from three key sources: Paul Kennedy, *The Rise and Fall of the Great Powers* (London: Fontana, 1988), pp. 21–38; Anton Deporte, *Europe Between the Superpowers* (London: Yale University Press, 1979), pp. 1–8; and Jenö Szücs, 'The Three Historical Regions of Europe: An Outline', in *Civil Society and the State. New European Perspectives*, edited by John Keane (London: Verso, 1988), pp. 291–332.

2. The nature of the 'German problem' in its historical dimension was well summarised by a British writer in 1906: 'Suspicious of all sentimentalities in foreign affairs, we have always acknowledged that from the German point of view the aims of German foreign policy are entirely justified. The only objection to them is that in no point of the world can they be realized without threatening the security and independence of existing states or destroying their present order. That is not the fault of the German nation, it is its misfortune.' Quoted by Gerhard Ritter in *The German Problem* (Columbus: Ohio State University Press, 1965).

3. As Anton Deporte argued in 1978, '... I think the postwar system, built over a decade and more of acute tensions sometimes threatening war, can yet be given high marks for providing stability, even if in a sense inadvertently, and at least fair marks for the kind of stability. In any case this system, like all that prove viable, has been well rooted in power realities. If not an inevitable outcome of history, it was at least a natural one .... I suggest that the system which has lasted from 1955 until today – 1978 – may well last as long again, that is, until 2001'. Deporte, *op. cit.*, pp. xii–xiii.

4. Given the complex nature of the East–West conflict, and its different dimensions and elements, Gerd Krell makes an eloquent and timely plea for a *Kultur des Theorienstreits* (a 'culture of theoretical disputes'), which

rejects any simple or monocausal explanation of the East–West conflict, or any vigorous hierarchical ordering of its constituent parts. See *Ost-West-Konflikt: Wissen wir, wovon wir Sprechen?* (Baden-Baden: Nomos Verlagsgesellschaft, 1987), edited by Christiane Rix, p. 104.

5. Dieter Senghaas, *Konfliktformationen im internationalen System* (Frankfurt: Suhrkamp, 1988). See also Ole Wæver, 'Conflicts of Vision: Visions of Conflict', in *European Polyphony: Perspectives beyond East–West Confrontation* (London: Macmillan, 1989), p. 298.

6. It is in this sense that Michael Cox speaks of the cold war 'system': see his article, 'The Cold War as a System', *Critique*, no. 17 (1986), pp. 17–82.

7. See the essay by Louis Althusser, 'Contradiction and Overdetermination', in *For Marx* (London: NLB, 1977), pp. 87–128.

8. See Bowker and Williams, *Superpower Detente: A Reappraisal* (London: Sage, 1988), p. 11.

9. Fred Halliday describes this as a 'globalized social conflict' or 'systemic' struggle between two rival social systems (capitalism and communism); see his influential work, *The Making of the Second Cold War*, 2nd edition (London: Verso, 1984), pp. 9–10.

10. R.J. Vincent, *Human Rights and International Relations* (Cambridge: Cambridge University Press, 1986), pp. 61–62.

11. 'Indeed, a direct comparison has been drawn between Helsinki and the Treaty of Osnabrück (1648), which created the "detente" between Catholics and Protestants among the German states, and provided, in particular, for the rights of individuals who were the subjects of Princes of another religion'. *Vincent*, p. 74.

12. For the full text of E.P. Thompson's seminal essay, and a critical discussion of it from within the ranks of the international peace movement, see E.P. Thompson et al., *Exterminism and the Cold War* (London: Verso, 1982).

13. It is also a view which ignores the simple truism which Hans Morgenthau proclaimed in 1948; 'men do not fight because they have arms' – rather, 'they have arms because they deem it necessary to fight'. Quoted in J. Mueller, 'A New Concert of Europe', in *Foreign Policy*, no. 77 (Winter 1989–90), pp. 3–16.

14. As Barry Buzan has argued, '... weapons possess an independent, or at least a semi-independent, dynamic of their own'. He also refers to the 'institutionalisation of militarisation. The large production and administrative bodies necessary to pursue an arms race naturally tend to take on a life and momentum of their own: and since their survival and welfare as organisations depend on the continuance of the arms race, they become a significant political force in its favour'. This is the root of what is often described as the 'military-industrial complex'. See Barry Buzan, *People, States and Fear* (Brighton: Wheatsheaf, 1983), pp. 186 and 197.

15. Professor Werner Link, one of the most influential theorists of the East–West conflict, argues that it is a conflict constituted by the convergence, on the one hand, of the clash of two rival social systems, and, on the other, a struggle for hegemony between the USA and the USSR. See his study, *Der Ost-West-Konflict. Die Organisation der internationalen Beziehungen im 20 Jahrhundert*, 2nd revised edition (Stuttgart: Kohlhammer, 1988).

16. See Hugh Seton-Watson, 'Thoughts on the Concept of West and East in Europe', *Government and Opposition*, vol. 20, no. 2 (Spring 1985), pp.

156–65. See also his lecture to the Royal Institute of International Affairs, 'What is Europe, Where is Europe?', reprinted in *Encounter*, July–August 1985, pp. 9–17.

17. For an informative and well-argued discussion on the implications of the different definitions of 'Europe', see E. Jahn, P. Lemaitre and O. Wæver, *European Security – Problems of Research on Non-Military Aspects*, Copenhagen Papers No.1, (Copenhagen University: Centre of Peace and Conflict Research, 1987).

18. See Chapter 2 of William Wallace's Chatham House Paper, *The Transformation of Western Europe* (London: Pinter, 1990).

19. B. Buzan, *op. cit.*, pp. 1–8.

20. R. Ullman, 'Redefining Security', in *International Affairs*, vol. 8 (Summer 1983), p. 129.

21. 'Security is far more than a military matter. The strengthening of political consultation and economic cooperation, the development of resources, progress in education and public understanding, all these can be as important for the protection of the security of a nation, or an alliance, as the building of a battleship or the equipping of an army.' From the Report of the Committee of the Three on Non-Military Cooperation in NATO, December 1956; quoted in *The North Atlantic Treaty Organisation: Facts and Figures* (Brussels: NATO Information Service, 1989), p. 301.

22. Robert O. Keohane and Joseph S. Nye, *Power and Interdependence* (Boston, MA: Little, Brown, 1977), and their subsequent article on the same theme, '*Power and Interdependence* Revisited', in *International Organisation*, vol. 41, no. 4 (Autumn 1987).

23. This is the central thesis of Paul Kennedy's influential book, *op. cit.*, pp. xxiv–xxvii.

24. Gwyn Prins, 'Politics and the Environment', *International Affairs*, vol. 66, no. 4 (October 1990), pp. 711–30.

25. See Paul Eavis, *Security After the Cold War: Redirecting Global Resources*, A Saferworld Report (Bristol: Saferworld Foundation, 1990), pp. 2–3.

26. See Barry Buzan, *op. cit.*, p. 247.

27. Security is 'the *relative freedom* from harmful threats', John E. Mroz, *Beyond Security* (New York: International Peace Academy, 1980), p. 105; 'Security itself is a relative freedom from war, coupled with a relatively high expectation that defeat will not be a consequence of any war that should occur', Ian Bellany, 'Towards a Theory of International Security', *Political Studies*, vol. 29, no. 1 (1981), p. 102.

28. John Herz, 'Idealist Internationalism and the Security Dilemma', in *World Politics*, vol. 2 (1950), pp. 157–80.

29. S. Lukes, *Power: A Radical View* (London: Macmillan, 1974).

30. '... a nation is secure to the extent to which it is not in danger of having to sacrifice core values if it wishes to avoid war, and is able, if challenged, to maintain them by victory in such a war', Walter Lippman: '... security, in an objective sense, measures the absence of threats to acquired values, in a subjective sense, the absence of fear that such values will be attacked', Arnold Wolfers. Quoted in Buzan, *op. cit.*, p. 219.

31. See Hassner, *Change and Security in Europe. Part 1: The Background*, Adelphi Paper no. 45 (London: Institute for Strategic Studies, 1968), Part II, pp. 4–5.

32. Deporte, *op. cit.*, p. 116. See also L. Dehio, 'The Passing of the European System', in *Germany and World Politics in the Twentieth Century* (London: Chatto & Windus, 1960), p. 124; and C. Fisher, 'The Changing Dimensions of Europe', *Journal of Contemporary History*, July 1966, p. 3.
33. B. Buzan, *op. cit.*, p. 106.
34. The concept of a 'paradigm change' has been elaborated by Thomas Kuhn in his seminal work, *The Structure of Scientific Revolutions* (Chicago: University Press of Chicago, 1972), p. 68.
35. For an accessible introduction to the literature on, and issues in, contemporary international relations theory, see Ray Maghoori and Bennett Ramberg (eds), *Globalism Versus Realism: International Relations' Third Debate* (Boulder, Co.: Westview, 1982), and Michael Smith, Richard Little and Michael Shackleton (eds), *Perspectives on World Politics* (London: Croom Helm, 1981).
36. Despite Barry Buzan's suggestion to the contrary: see his contribution, 'The Future of Western European Security', in *European Polyphony*, p. 18. The classic statement of realist theory is Kenneth Walz's, *Theory of International Politics* (Reading, MA: Addison-Wesley, 1979).
37. See Michael Doyle, 'Kant, Liberal Legacies and Foreign Affairs', in *Philosophy and Public Affairs*, vol. 12, no. 3 (Summer 1983), pp. 205–35, and Part II of the articles in no. 4 (Fall 1984), pp. 323–53; M. Doyle, 'Liberalism and World Politics', in *American Political Science Review*, vol. 80, no. 4 (December 1986), pp. 1151–69; and Jean-Baptiste Duroselle, 'Western Europe and the Impossible War', in *Journal of International Affairs*, vol. 41, no. 2 (Summer 1988), pp. 345–61.
38. Robert Jervis, *Perception and Misperception in International Politics* (Princeton, NJ: Princeton University Press, 1976).
39. This is a point made by J.L. Gaddis in his article, 'The Emerging Post-Revisionist Synthesis on the Origins of the Cold War', *Diplomatic History* (Summer 1983), pp. 171–204 (pp. 184–85).
40. Richard L. O'Meara, 'Regimes and Their Implications for International Theory', in *Millennium*, vol. 13, no. 3 (Winter 1984), pp. 245–64. See also Joseph S. Nye, 'The Contribution of Strategic Studies: Future Challenges', in *The Changing Strategic Landscape, Part 1*, Adelphi Paper 235 (London: Brassey's for the IISS, 1989), pp. 20–34.
41. In his article, 'What's the matter with Realism', Justin Rosenberg argues that 'the interlocking of the emphasis on anarchy with the restrictive definition of sovereignty forms a kind of stranglehold on the development of international relations theory'. See the *Review of International Studies*, vol. 16, no. 4 (October 1990), pp. 286–304 (p. 299).
42. Stephen Krasner defines an international regime as a set of implicit or explicit 'principles, norms, rules, and decision-making procedures around which actor expectations converge in a given issue-area'. See his edited volume, *International Regimes* (Ithaca, NY: Cornell University Press, 1983), p. 1.
43. See for example Arend Lijphart, 'Karl W. Deutsch and the New Paradigm in International Relations', in *From National Development to Global Community: Essays in Honor of Karl W. Deutsch*, edited by R. Merritt and B. Russett (London: George Allen & Unwin, 1981), pp. 233–51.
44. 'As with nuclear deterrence 30 years ago, strategic studies may be poised

for what Thomas Kuhn would call a "paradigm change": the adoption, within an academic community, of a new corpus of knowledge and ideas.' Neville Brown, 'Climate, Ecology and International Security', in *Survival* (November–December 1989), pp. 519–32 (p. 531). See also his article, 'New Paradigms for Strategy', in *The World Today*, vol. 46, no. 6 (June 1990), pp. 115–18, and the articles already referred to by O'Meara, 'Regimes and their Implications for International Theory', and Nye, 'The Contribution of Strategic Studies'.

45. '... the changing European political order requires that the field of international security enriches its rather limited repertoire of Hobbesian theories with borrowings from the fields of comparative politics and international political economy', Jack Snyder, 'Averting Anarchy in the New Europe', *International Security*, vol. 14, no. 4 (Spring 1990), pp. 5–41.

PART I
The Post-war Security System

2

'From Yalta to Malta': Europe, 1945–89

In 1945, Europe lay exhausted and enfeebled after six years of modern, mechanised warfare. Vast swathes of the continent were in ruins, and the political and economic structures of much of central and eastern Europe had largely disintegrated. Having effectively torn itself apart in the most vicious of its perennial 'civil wars', the 'old continent' had lost its pre-eminent place in the international system. The experience of war and resistance generated new political and social forces, and it was clear that post-war Europe – along with other parts of the world caught up in the maelstrom of global war – would be a very different place than it had been before 1939.

The security order which emerged from the devastation of total war and Nazi barbarity was one which represented a dramatically new constellation of power relations in Europe. The collapse of the old balance of power system (largely as a result of its inability to accommodate the strength of a unified German state at the heart of Europe), left the way open for the creation of a substantially new pattern of strategic and political relations on the continent. The post-war security system was thus based on a new set of political and economic relationships, and involved different protagonists and institutional arrangements. This meant that many of the diplomatic practices, methods of conflict-resolution and forms of power projection developed in the old multipolar, Europe-centred system, were less and less relevant to the bipolar nuclear world of the cold war. As the East–West conflict unfolded, therefore, and as the new European security system took shape, new 'rules of the game' had to be developed by the principal protagonists.

The purpose of this chapter is to sketch the evolution of the European security system from the Yalta conference of the 'Big Three' to the Malta summit of Presidents Bush and Gorbachev in November 1989. Despite the element of historical exposition that this necessarily entails, the main concern here is not to give a precise chronological survey of the post-war period, but to consider the underlying trends and key events which have shaped the formation of the post-war security order in Europe.

This involves considering a crucial cluster of questions at the heart of the political and historical controversy over the nature of the cold war: namely, why did it begin in the first place? Who or what was primarily responsible for causing it? And why did it continue? The answers to these questions are many and varied. Responsibility for the cold war division of Europe is usually ascribed to one of the following: (i) innate Soviet expansionism; (ii) US imperialism; (iii) the global clash of antagonistic class forces; (iv) mutual misperception and misunderstanding (the cold war as a ghastly mistake); or (v) the implicit 'collusion' of Atlanticism and Stalinism,[1] 'an imperialist bargain, a pact between Anglo-Saxon and Soviet imperialism'.[2]

My concern here, however, is not to offer a definitive assessment of the causes of the cold war, still less to evaluate the merits and weaknesses of the competing explanations for its outbreak and development – this is the task of the specialist historians of the subject. Moreover, trying to date the cold war from a specific cause or event is not particularly productive. Nor is there much to be gained by attempting to reduce its complexities and ambiguities to a simple *Schuldfrage* – a 'question of guilt'. Instead, my aim in this chapter is, first, to illustrate the complex motives and interests of the principle actors involved; and second, to illuminate the impact of the unfolding cold war on the formation and early development of the European security system. In doing so, it is hoped that some light will be shed on both the nature of the East–West conflict and the structural dynamics of the post-war security order.

Implicit in the following arguments is the view that the East–West relationship – of which the cold war constitutes one manifestation – must be seen as an intricate pattern of relationships, embodying a peculiar dialectic of confrontation and detente. Instead of seeing the cold war as a Manichaean struggle between the forces of light and darkness, therefore, this chapter will seek to highlight the complexities and ambiguities of this unfortunate period of post-war history.

'Yalta' and the Birth of a New Security Order in Europe

The post-war devastation of Europe left a power vacuum which the two superpowers were quickly drawn into. The continental heartland of Europe was particularly weakened: the power of Germany had been decisively crushed; the old regimes in Eastern Europe and the Balkans had collapsed; and France, the other main continental great power, was a shadow of its former self. Great Britain itself emerged victorious but badly enfeebled. Into the vacuum that was left stepped the two flanking powers, the USA and the USSR. It was these two great nations that were to become the decisive arbiters of the post-war future of Europe, as de Toqueville had predicted in the 1830s.[3]

At the same time as the 'Big Three' were beginning their conference in Potsdam (16 July 1945), news reached President Truman of the first successful testing of a new and terrible weapon of immense power, the atomic bomb. The subsequent atomic bombing of Hiroshima and

Nagasaki brought to a close the war in Asia, and marked the birth of the 'nuclear age'. A number of revisionist historians have argued that the American use of the bomb in August 1945 was designed not only to force the Japanese to surrender, but also to put political pressure on the Soviet Union in Europe.[4] Whatever the truth of these controversial allegations (and the evidence in their favour is not very convincing[5]), the dawning of the nuclear age was to have a profound effect on the future evolution of the post-war security order in Europe.

The foundations of the post-war world were laid at the summit meetings of the wartime coalition allies (the 'Big Three') at Teheran, Yalta and Potsdam. It was these three meetings – rather than the Paris Conference of 1946 – which shaped the broad outlines of post-war Europe. Nevertheless, the conferences themselves, particularly the Yalta meeting (4–11 February 1945), have become burdened with a symbolism they do not deserve. Yalta is frequently painted as the conference at which the Great Powers divided Europe up amongst themselves.[6] This, however, is a myth, and one largely propagated by the French, given their exclusion from Yalta.[7] The Yalta conference was **not** a grand exercise in Great Power geopolitical engineering. On the contrary, it dealt with immediate, short-term issues, such as Germany, Poland and the UN: as Wojtech Mastny notes, 'Contrary to Yalta's later reputation, an agreement to partition Europe was not reached there. It was rather the deplorable lack of any clear consensus on this and other matters that explains the summit's notoriety'.[8] Despite Churchill's attempt to reach an agreement with Stalin in Moscow in October 1944 on spheres of interest in the Balkans and south-east Europe (the so-called 'percentages agreement'[9]), there was no machiavellian division of the globe in the closing stages of the war. Instead, the partition arose from the military disposition of the victors' forces in 1944–45 (as Stalin observed to Milovan Djilas[10]), in accordance with the seventeenth-century principle of *cujus regio, ejus religio*.

The attempt by the wartime allies to agree to a common approach to the post-war reconstruction and reordering of Europe – especially of Germany – ran aground on the divergent interests of the leading protagonists. Their varying national priorities led them to pursue differing policies in Europe, and even when they could agree on common goals (for example, 'democratisation', 'decentralisation' and 'denazification' in Germany, or 'free elections' in Eastern Europe), their different national perspectives and ideological assumptions led them to pursue diverging policies.

The Onset of the Cold War and the Division of Europe

By 1945, America was the undisputed hegemon of the world.[11] At this uniquely favourable conjuncture in its history, its enormous economic, financial, industrial and military power meant that it could play a decisive role in shaping the key institutions of the Western world – including NATO, the IMF, the World Bank and GATT. Having ended its isolationism, therefore, it was almost inevitable that the USA would come to play a central role in post-war Europe.

In view of their immense economic potential, the Americans were keen to establish an open international economic system, based on free trade and private enterprise. With this in mind, they initially expressed considerable sympathy towards anti-colonial movements in India, Indochina and elsewhere, and sought an end to European colonialism (and the 'imperial preference' that went along with it).[12] At the same time, American foreign policy exhibited tendencies towards an idealistic universalism – a belief in its 'Manifest Destiny' – based on a belief in the worldwide applicability of US values and the 'American way of life'. Americans tended to believe that an international system founded on Wilsonian principles and incorporating an open economic system and the international rule of law would be good for America, and at the same time, good for the world. Many Americans therefore believed that, in contrast to the hegemonies of the past, that of the USA would be in the interests of all peoples and nations, in that it would produce a peaceful and prosperous world, founded on free trade, open markets and political democracy.

Given these assumptions, US thinking towards Europe was often ambiguous in the mid-1940s. One element of American thinking tended to reject what it saw as the old 'European' system of spheres of influence and balance of power politics, and looked to a new era of international relations based on Wilsonian principles. On the other hand, the US was keen to ensure that the European continent did not fall under the domination of any one power. When in the late 1940s the Americans began to perceive a growing Soviet threat to the European equilibrium, however, they quietly dropped the anti-colonial elements of their policy, and rallied to the defence of what they chose to describe as the 'free world'.

Moreover, the United States tended to regard any restrictions on access to global markets and resources as a challenge to its vital interests, and this – combined with America's visceral hatred of communism – led its political elite to view Soviet policy with considerable suspicion, if not outright hostility. American policy-makers tended to equate the communist system with the militaristic neo-mercantilism of the 1930s, and therefore saw it as a challenge to the peace, stability and prosperity of the whole global system.[13] Consequently, from late 1946 to early 1947 the USA began to mobilise its awesome resources and capabilities in order to 'contain' what it regarded as the 'threat' emanating from the USSR.[14] The result of this was a self-fulfilling prophecy: from the autumn of 1947 onwards, communist policy in Europe hardened, and Moscow began a policy of *Gleichschaltung* which was to culminate in the Titoist witch-hunts and show trials of the late 1940s-early 1950s. At the same time, however, the US was able to assert its position as the undisputed leader of the 'free world', and to exercise its (largely benign) hegemony to construct its global 'empire'.[15]

Soviet policy towards post-war Europe was guided by Stalin's conception of the USSR's security interests in central and eastern Europe. The victory of the Red Army in the 'Great Patriot War' ended the enforced isolation of the Soviet Union, and allowed Soviet power to expand into central and eastern Europe – previously a region dominated by German influence and anti-communist, nationalistic, clerical and authoritarian dictatorships. Having suffered 27 million dead in the course of the war, the Soviets wanted both to exact substantial reparations from Germany in order to restore their shattered economy, and to ensure that their country would never again have to face such an onslaught from the West. Stalin therefore worked to obtain a drastic weakening and containment of German power, and a collective security arrangement in Europe in which the USSR would play an influential role. He was also keen to establish some sort of hegemony in East Central Europe in order to create a protective glacis in the region, and to control the elements of discord which had so often threatened the security interests of the Soviet (and before that the Russian) state. The problem with this was that – faced with the attractive pull of US economic power – this ultimately involved systemic changes in Eastern Europe, and the imposition of new communist elites there. This in turn galvanised West Europe and the USA, resuscitating traditional European conservatism and American hatred of Bolshevism. Given the economic weakness of the USSR and Russian traditions of imperial dominance and control, Soviet control of its 'sphere of interest' was frequently little more than a brutal exercise in Realpolitik, whatever the ideological trappings of the 'Peoples Democracies' and 'national roads to socialism'. As a result of this heavy-handed and ruthless approach, the Soviet Union squandered the political and moral credit it had acquired in the 'Great Patriotic War': the image of the USSR as a nation of valiant partisans and courageous civilians led by an avuncular 'Uncle Joe' was transformed into that of a brutal police state terrorised by a paranoid dictator.

Despite the dominant role played by the two superpowers in Europe in the post-war years, the other key powers, notably Britain and France, were also active participants in the formation of the new security system. The release of official papers in Britain has allowed scholars to re-evaluate the significant role played by the UK in the development of the cold war,[16] and to appreciate the full extent of British endeavours to secure an American commitment to Europe in order to counter what it perceived to be a growing Soviet threat to the European balance of power.[17] Similarly, the

French under De Gaulle pursued their own distinctive agenda for Europe (focusing in particular on the future role of Germany) which diverged on a number of points from that of the other two major Western powers. The early cold war therefore has a distinctive 'European dimension' which should not be overlooked, even though its significance is often underestimated in the literature on the subject.[18]

Another important aspect to the development of the cold war was the domestic political situation in post-war Europe. The foreign policy manoeuverings of the wartime allies were conducted against the background of a turbulent and unstable social and political scene in much of Europe, and this had a significant impact on the emerging East–West conflict. In some parts of the continent, important elements in the traditional political and economic elites had been discredited by their collaboration with fascism and the German Reich. The experience of war and occupation engendered a wave of radicalism in much of Europe, and a yearning for a socially just, economically fairer and politically democratic way of life. This was manifested in growing support for social-democratic, socialist and communist parties throughout Europe, and the creation of centre-left governments in many West European countries (frequently with communist participation). In the East, the Soviets and their communist allies sought to direct these aspirations into channels compatible with their interests – with some success at first, given the popularity of the initial land reform and nationalisation measures.[19]

However, the widespread aspirations for 'a continent both democratic and at peace'[20] were frustrated by the onset of the cold war. In Western Europe, communists were expelled from coalition governments, and pressure was put on trade unions and socialist parties not to cooperate with the communist left. In the 'Peoples' Democracies', the communist parties moved rapidly to concentrate power in their hands, and the process of social and economic transformation was forced into the strait-jacket of Stalinist orthodoxy. Later these two trends were to degenerate into the McCarthyism and militant anti-communism of the West, and into the nightmare of the 'Titoist witch-hunts' and show trials of the East. In this way the cold war helped serve the domestic political purposes of local elites through much of Europe, and contributed to the stabilisation of social and political structures in the post-war world. This had a debilitating effect on domestic developments, in that radical domestic opposition groups within either system found it almost impossible to escape identification with the rival system. The political prejudices generated by the cold war meant that, in the West, demands for greater social justice and redistributive welfare measures were often equated with calls for Eastern-style socialism, whilst in the East, socialism became incompatible with democracy and individual civil liberties.[21]

The unfolding East–West conflict therefore took place against the background of acute social and political struggles in Europe, which were fuelled by severe economic dislocations and growing industrial difficulties. Britain had already had to confront this problem in Athens in December 1944, when its residual imperial concerns in the eastern Mediterranean led British forces to engage communist-led antimonarchist partisan forces. The Greek civil war, which simmered on for the remainder of the decade, represented the 'hottest' point of the cold war in Europe. However, it was the dispute between the Western powers and the Soviet Union over Iran in 1946 that played a key role in fuelling mounting suspicion between East and West.[22]

At this stage American policy towards the Soviet Union and Europe still displayed significant elements of ambiguity. Consequently in March 1946, at Fulton, Missouri, Winston Churchill gave a key-note speech in which he sought to convince the Americans of the reality of the 'Soviet threat'. The speech was at the time disavowed by President Truman,[23] although it was subsequently to provide one of the most striking political images of the early cold war period:

> A shadow has fallen upon the scenes so lately lighted by the Allied victory
> .... From Stettin in the Baltic to Trieste in the Adriatic, an iron curtain
> has descended across the Continent. Behind that line lie all the capitals of
> the ancient states of Central and Eastern Europe. Warsaw, Berlin, Prague,
> Vienna, Budapest, Belgrade, Bucharest and Sofia, all these famous cities and
> the populations around them lie in what I must call the Soviet sphere, and
> are all subject in one form or another, not only to Soviet influence but to a
> very high and, in many cases, increasing measure of control from Moscow
> .... Whatever conclusions may be drawn from these facts – and facts they are
> – this is certainly not the Liberated Europe we fought to build up. Nor is it
> one which contains the essentials of permanent peace.[24]

Churchill's words, which seemed premature in 1946, appeared to be vindicated by the events of the next few years. 1947 was the decisive year in the cold war division of Europe, and by 1949, the central features of the bipolar world order were in place. Events in this period followed each other with dizzying rapidity. The Truman Doctrine (12 March 1947)[25] was followed by Marshall Aid (5 June 1947)[26], and given political and conceptual form in Kennan's famous article on 'containment' (July 1947[27]). Communists were expelled from governments in the West in the spring of 1947, and the Soviets responded by establishing the Cominform in September 1947 (with its theoretical underpinnings provided by the 'Two camps' theory of Andrei Zhdanov) and the CMEA on 25 January 1949. In February 1948 Czech Communists seized power in their 'elegant coup',[28] and from late 1948, Stalin's heavy-handed attempt to regiment the 'Peoples' Democracies' behind the banner of the CPSU led to the rift with Tito and the Yugoslav communists. The formation of NATO in April 1949 and the establishment of two separate German states in

May and October 1949 signalled the completion of this initial period of bloc-building. By the end of the decade the crucial structures of the post-war bipolar European security system had been laid.

The fact that the division of Europe ran directly through the heart of Germany was of tremendous political and symbolic significance for the subsequent dynamics of the cold war. It gave the East–West conflict a national dimension, and therefore linked it to one of the most powerful and enduring political forces in the modern age – nationalism. It was the Promethean struggle over Germany which shaped the character of the two alliance systems, and through which the two sides reached some sort of implicit understanding about the means and limits of the East–West struggle. Through the conflict over Germany, therefore, both sides began to develop the unspoken rules of the game.

The Cold War and Europe: from the Berlin Blockade to the Cuban Missile Crisis

The Berlin blockade – Stalin's clumsy attempt to coerce the Allied powers into shelving their plans to establish a separate West German state – provided the 'founding myth' of the FRG and NATO.[29] A central element of Western policy at this time was the integration of German power into the West European and Atlantic Alliance structures – both to defend the FRG, and to control it. This became the overwhelming priority, and consequently previous allied commitments to 'de-Nazification' were quietly overlooked as German strength was harnessed to the military and political defence of the 'Free World'.[30] For this reason, Stalin's note on Germany in 1952 (described by one commentator as 'probably the most intriguing Soviet proposal of the entire cold war period in Europe'[31]) was ignored by the West, and in 1955, the FRG was admitted to NATO and subsequently rearmed – to which the Soviets responded by creating the Warsaw Treaty Organization in May 1955.

At the start of the cold war, there were two perceived threats to Western Europe: first, external – the fear of military invasion by the battle-hardened and numerically superior armoured divisions of the Red Army (this danger – although greatly exaggerated[32] – seemed more credible after the outbreak of the Korean War in 1950). Second, internal – the fear of domestic communist subversion (particularly given the strength and influence of communist parties in France and Italy and the economic problems of post-war reconstruction in Western Europe). For the Soviet Union and its East European allies, the threat appeared to come from the economic and financial strength of the USA (and the challenge that this represented to Soviet and communist control of Eastern Europe); the American monopoly of the atomic bomb (and, perhaps more importantly, the means of delivering them); the string of

US bases around the perimeters of the Soviet Union; and the declaratory policies of 'roll-back' and 'liberation' espoused by the likes of J.F. Dulles and Konrad Adenauer. As the 1950s wore on, and the situation in Europe became increasingly more stable, these perceived threats began to recede. However, the mutual mistrust which had been built up in the late 1940s and early 1950s left a bitter legacy from which it was hard to escape, and which continued to shape East–West relations for many years to come.

In the early 1950s, the focus of the cold war shifted from Europe to Asia. The victory of Mao and the PLA (People's Liberation Army) in China in 1949, the communist-led nationalist insurgency in French Indochina, and the outbreak of the Korean War, all gave an added sense of urgency to American fears of a world-wide communist offensive. Henceforth the development of the European security system was to be affected, albeit indirectly, by events in the Third World. The struggle of the Western powers against communism in Asia signified a globalisation of the East–West conflict, and its intertwining with North–South issues. This has had two important aspects. Firstly, it has meant that many regional conflicts in the Third World, with their own indigenous roots, have been complicated and exacerbated by the involvement of the super-powers and their European allies, who have tended to view these conflicts as one aspect of the global contest between East and West. The relative stabilisation of the East–West conflict in Europe has thus encouraged a series of proxy wars in the Third World. Secondly, the search for a lasting detente in Europe has been made more difficult because of impact of these 'out-of-area' regional conflicts on the overall East–West relationship (as the experience of the 1970s was to demonstrate).

By the early 1950s, Europe was solidly frozen within the cold war structures that had emerged in the crucial years 1947–49. The communist victory in China, the successful Soviet explosion of an atomic bomb in 1949 and the outbreak of the Korean War all contributed to the icy East–West relationship. Diplomatic intercourse between the superpowers virtually ceased, and their public dialogue consisted of little more than a crude trading of insults and propaganda jibes. This in turn stimulated a dramatic arms race and a very real fear of the imminence of war. The result was the 'militarisation' of the cold war as both sides prepared for all-out war, conventional and nuclear. The systemic-ideological dimension of the East–West conflict was therefore supplemented by growing military confrontation, a development which gave a further twist to the East–West conflict.

A limited thawing of the cold war took place in 1953–55, following the death of Stalin, the Korean armistice and the ending of the McCarthyite hysteria in the USA. East–West diplomatic activity increased and a summit was held in Geneva in July 1955. The limited improvement in the international climate allowed for a temporary settlement of the Indochina war, and more significantly, the signing of the Austrian State Treaty and the withdrawal of Soviet troops from occupied Finnish territory. The Soviet–Allied agreement on Austria was particularly significant, as it created a model of a neutral and independent state which was a very attractive one for many others in Central Europe – it was this model which helped inspire the Hungarians in 1956, and which many Germans in both East and West believed offered the best prospect of achieving a reunited, neutral and demilitarised German state.

By this stage, Western Europe had largely recovered from the diffi-culties of the immediate post-war years, and the perceived threat from internal communist subversion or imminent Soviet invasion was receding. The sense of beleaguerment therefore declined, although a defensive and highly suspicious attitude remained. The European colonial powers (primarily Britain and France) experienced some traumas associated with the disengagement from Empire, but the domestic political problems that this generated were largely contained by the early 1960s. Nevertheless, the American humiliation of the UK and France over Suez clearly demonstrated the limits of independent European power in international affairs. At the same time, however, the Suez crisis gave a boost to the process of West European integration, which developed under the protective shield of NATO and the US nuclear guarantee. This process received a major fillip in 1957, with the signing of the Treaty of Rome and the establishment of the EEC.

The period of the late 1950s and early 1960s, therefore, was a period of transition in the European security system. The cold war lost some of its bitter intensity from the mid-1950s onwards, whilst both Western Europe and the countries of the East had largely recovered from the privations of the immediate post-war years. The security relationships and alliance structures that were to characterise the European security system were in place by 1955, and this gave the post-war order on the continent a growing sense of stability and predictability.[33] Moreover, after the upheavals of 1956, it was evident that the post-war strategic and political status quo in Europe was not likely to change as a result of war or violent revolution.

At this time of growing stability in the European security order, two developments took place which were to have an indirect, though nonethe-less important, long-term impact on European security. First, in October 1957 the Soviets announced the successful launch of the first Sputnik. The 'Sputnik shock' came as a grave blow to the Americans, because it spelt the end of the USA as a 'sanctuary': henceforth, the Soviets would be able to attack American cities with their nuclear weapons. This was a prospect which necessitated a fundamental rethink of the entire problem of NATO's defence posture and strategy. The Europeans felt fairly secure as long as they were certain that the American threat to use their strategic nuclear weapons against the USSR was credible enough to deter a Soviet attack. However, the American nuclear guarantee seemed less credible once the Soviets could threaten US cities with a retaliatory atomic strike (ie, would the Americans sacrifice Chicago for Hamburg?). The dilemmas that this posed for the West Europeans were to lead both to the adoption of 'flexible response' in 1967, and to the search for an independent nuclear deterrent in Europe itself.[34]

Second, at the end of the 1950s, it was clear that all was not well in the 'fraternal' alliance of the two communist giants, the USSR and the People's Republic of China. National and great-power rivalries were intensifying, and this was leading to increasingly bitter ideological controversies. By the early 1960s Sino-Soviet relations had completely broken down, and by the end of the decade armed clashes had taken place along the Ussuri river. The rift between the Soviet Union and China was the USSR's most serious foreign policy set-back in the post-war period, and it fundamentally transformed the dynamics of global politics. This was to have a significant impact on European security – not least because it encouraged the Soviet Union to seek a reduction of tension along its Western borders, in order to be able to contain the growing threat from the East.

1961–62: the Stabilisation of the European Security System

The 1950s in Europe ended with renewed tension over Berlin – that beleaguered city, described by Khrushchev as 'the testicles of the West'. Khrushchev's ultimatum of November 1958 sparked off a crisis which was not resolved until 13 August 1961, when the East Germans sealed off the inner-German border and erected the mis-named 'Anti-fascist Defence Wall'. A year later, in October 1962, the world held its breath as the US and the USSR confronted each other, 'eyeball to eyeball', over planned Soviet missile deployments in Cuba. These two events were to have a profound impact on the European security system, and together constitute a watershed in the post-war development of East–West relations.

The building of the Berlin Wall in August 1961 permanently changed the German conception of East–West relations.[35] It underlined the limitations of Adenauer's 'policy of strength', and encouraged Willy Brandt and others to develop a new approach to the socialist community – the result was the eventual abandonment of the 'Hallstein doctrine' and the development of *Ostpolitik*. The Berlin Wall itself, as Khrushchev acknowledged in his memoirs, symbolised the failure of socialism in the East to compete effectively with Western-style 'welfare capitalism'. It nevertheless gave a sense of physical permanency to the post-war division of Europe, and underlined that this division could not be overcome by 'roll-back' or the speedy internal collapse of the 'Soviet bloc'. In this way it contributed to the formulation of a new approach to East–West relations in both parts of Europe.

The Cuban missile crisis of October 1962 was also to contribute to this new approach to East–West relations. It was this dramatic event which really brought home to people in East and West the full significance of the existential threat posed by nuclear weapons.[36] It therefore highlighted the chilling implications of the onset of the 'nuclear age' for international security, especially for Europe. The US–Soviet confrontation in the Caribbean was the last major case of superpower conflict involving the traditional pre-Second World War type of politico-military confrontation: 'Henceforth in Europe more measured reactions to crises were evident and it seemed clear that both security systems were developing codes of behaviour and reaction to minimise friction and to defuse dangerous situations'.[37] The new climate that subsequently emerged between Moscow and Washington resulted in the 'hot-line' agreement of 1963, the 1963 Partial Test-Ban Treaty,[38] the 1968 Non-Proliferation Treaty and ultimately, the search for a durable superpower detente.

By the early 1960s therefore, Europe possessed a fairly stable and predictable security framework. The two military and economic alliance systems were locked into a managed, albeit abrasive 'cold peace', involving an armed stand-off and intense ideological rivalry. Two stable military-political alliances faced each other, with a small but clearly defined group of neutral and non-aligned states occupying the middle ground between them. The two superpowers continued to play a dominant role within what was still primarily a bipolar world order; and the whole system was underpinned and reinforced by nuclear deterrence. There were some attempts in both alliances to modify the relationships within the existing framework (ie, by France[39] and Romania), but there was no significant attempt at fundamental change. In Western Europe, integration was proceeding apace, and the 1963 Elysée Treaty between France and the FRG symbolised the new spirit of friendship and trust that was developing between these two long-time enemies. In the 'socialist community' there was also a greater sense of security and stability, and the building of the Berlin Wall allowed the GDR (itself a key link in the Soviet Union's alliance system in the East) to develop its own limited *Wirtschaftswunder*.

On the basis of the relative stability and growing confidence in East and West, there was a new willingness to achieve some sort of rapprochement and understanding between the two alliance structures in Europe. From 1966 the Americans reversed their view that German reunification must be the point of departure for the resolution of the East–West conflict, and began arguing that gradual change in East–West relations would have to precede the resolution of the German problem.[40] At the same time, Lyndon Johnson began speaking of 'bridge-building' and 'peaceful engagement', and in 1969, Vice-President Nixon visited Romania. There was growing recognition in the United States in the late 1960s that American power had passed its zenith, and that the US needed to develop a more cooperative relationship with the USSR in order to establish a new equilibrium in an increasingly polycentric and conflict prone world.[41] The change of government in Bonn in 1966 led to the adoption of the policy of Ostpolitik, which was made possible by the FRG's firm anchorage in the West and its reconciliation with France. In 1967, these changes in Western thinking towards the East found their expression in the Harmel Report (which called for both defence and detente[42]), whilst in the Warsaw Pact countries, the search for 'peaceful coexistence' was embodied in the Bucharest Declaration of July 1966.[43]

Thus in the 1960s there was a steady movement towards a lessening of East–West tension in Europe, and a growing desire on both sides to reach a *modus vivendi* with the other. This process gathered momentum towards the end of the decade, and was reinforced by the commitment of Willy Brandt and the social-liberal coalition in West Germany to Ostpolitik, and that of Henry Kissinger and President Nixon to developing a superpower detente with the USSR. The crushing of the Prague Spring by the Warsaw Pact in 1968, and the escalating American military involvement in Vietnam, did not seriously delay progress along the road to detente. Indeed, it has been argued that the Soviet intervention in Czechoslovakia 'can be understood as a prerequisite for the further progress of detente. Although the immediate impact of the intervention was to increase East–West tension and to postpone the opening of talks on strategic arms control, the reassertion of Soviet control over the bloc made possible the further development of Soviet detente policy'.[44] In other words, stability within the two military-political alliances had become a prerequisite for stability between them. The end of the 1960s, therefore, marks the transition from cold war (or cold peace) to detente; however, the differing expectations associated with detente and continuing East–West conflicts prevented the resolution of Europe's underlying security problems and the development of a durable peace order in the region.

Detente in the 1970s

In the early 1970s, the European security system entered a new phase in its development. After a decade in which the two hostile alliances in Europe, chastened by the Berlin and Cuban crises, groped for a new and less adversarial relationship, came a period of rapid political developments and raised expectations. The emergence of detente in Europe took place at a specific conjuncture in global politics. The improvement in East–West relations coincided with a further disintegration of the bipolar world order, and the consequent rise of new regional centres of power.[45] The

Sino-Soviet conflict also put pressure on the Soviet Union and its Warsaw Pact allies to try and resolve some of the outstanding problems still plaguing its relationship with the NATO countries. In this increasingly polycentric world, Western Europe itself was beginning to emerge as an international actor in its own right, by dint of its economic prowess and emerging political identity. The flowering of detente, therefore, both reflected and encouraged new developments in the post-war order in Europe.

There were two main dimensions to the detente process in the 1970s: US–Soviet and pan-European. US–Soviet detente manifested itself in a number of bilateral agreements, including the 1972 Moscow Basic Principles Agreement, the SALT 1 Treaty, the ABM Treaty, the June 1973 Agreement on the Prevention of Nuclear War, and the Vladivostock understanding on limiting the number of strategic nuclear weapons. Detente in Europe was centred on the series of *Ostverträge* signed by the FRG with its Eastern neighbours, such as the treaty with the USSR in August 1970, the Polish treaty of December 1970, the Basic Treaty with the GDR in May 1972, and the Munich Treaty with Czechoslovakia in 1973. The Four Power Agreement on Berlin of 1971, whatever its legal and political ambiguities,[46] also helped defuse what had been one of the cardinal flashpoints of the cold war. These two dimensions of the detente process converged in 1973, with the opening of both the Mutual and Balanced Force Reduction negotiations and the 35-member Conference on Security and Cooperation in Europe.

The highpoint of the detente process came in 1975, with the signing of the Helsinki Final Act: although this had no binding force in international law, it was a document of great political importance, and it served as a *de facto* peace treaty. Its three baskets – covering security, economic cooperation and humanitarian issues – met WTO aspirations by enshrining the principle of the inviolability of frontiers in Europe (whilst providing for their change through peaceful means and by agreement), and met Western concerns by embodying a series of principles on human rights which has given the West a dynamic point of reference for pressing for improvements in this area in Eastern Europe.[47] Indeed, the Helsinki process, with its follow-up conferences and specialist forums, has been one of the most important and enduring fruits of the detente of the 1970s.

The precise meaning of detente (or 'peaceful coexistence' as it was known in the socialist camp) is an issue of considerable controversy. Detente itself was characterised by a relaxation of tension between East and West, and search for compromise solutions to the problems arising from the lack of a peace treaty after the end of the Second World War. It involved a mutual acceptance of the territorial status quo in Europe, the renunciation of force as a means of settling disputes, a commitment to developing cooperation in certain limited areas, and a search for non-violent forms of competitive struggle.

At this time of change in the East–West relationship, there were three main visions of detente. For Willy Brandt, one of its foremost European architects, detente was a dynamic process within existing structures, which would gradually lead to a qualitative change involving the development of a new system – an *europäische Friedensordnung* (a 'European peace order'), in which the gradual convergence of social and political systems in Europe would take place. This in turn would provide the context for the resolution of the German question.[48] For Henry Kissinger on the other hand, inspired as he was by the example of Metternich and the Concert of Europe, detente was essentially a contemporary manifestation of traditional balance of power politics: it was regarded as a convenient method of regulating the superpower conflict, and of developing new codes of conduct and limited forms of cooperative endeavours. This view was close to the Soviet conception of 'peaceful coexistence', which was defined as a specific form of the class struggle. For Brezhnev and his fellow Warsaw Pact allies, detente comprised both competing and cooperative modes of behaviour. They also maintained that it would provide the most felicitous conditions for the ultimate victory of socialism on a global scale.

These divergent concepts of detente, reflecting as they did differing interests and concerns, are one of the principle reasons why the period of East–West understanding in the early and mid-1970s was to give way to a renewed period of tension by the end of the decade. There was no consensus on what detente meant, or what codes of conduct it involved. Was it global and indivisible, or regional and divisible? The military component of detente (ie, the balance between detente and defence – to use the Harmel Report's formulation of the problem) was not clarified. Consequently, the 1970s witnessed a steady build-up in Soviet military strength, both conventional and nuclear, whilst at the same time, NATO (and the USA in particular) continued to lead the way in many of the qualitative aspects of the arms race.[49] Furthermore, East–West cooperation in Europe was limited by the Soviet refusal to recognise the EEC. Above all, real East–West understanding was severely inhibited by the East's concern to restrict the development of political and social links between the peoples of the continent – a policy symbolised most starkly by the East German pursuit of *Abgrenzung* ('delimitation') from the West.

Nevertheless, despite its obvious limitations, detente succeeded in putting down firm roots in Europe. It was a development which corresponded to the growing desire for pan-European economic and political cooperation. It also went some way towards meeting the deep-seated aspirations of many on the continent for a more relaxed and cooperative

East–West relationship. This aspiration has found its clearest expression in the CSCE process, which has provided an institutional forum for continuing dialogue and consultation between East and West.

The CSCE process had a number of important – and positive – effects on the subsequent development of the European security system in the 1970s and 1980s. First, by acting as a *de facto* peace treaty, it helped to take the heat out of the territorial and political disputes resulting from the post-war settlement. Second, it gave the small and medium-sized states (especially in Eastern Europe) a larger voice in the discussion on European security, and this encouraged them to articulate their own specific national interests. Third, it allowed the neutral and non-aligned states in Europe to play a more prominent and constructive role in the European security system, as mediators between the two military alliances. Fourth, it contributed to the development of a growing body of international law regulating East–West relations in Europe, including the sensitive area of human rights. Fifth, it helped reinforce a sense of a common European identity, especially in East Central and South-Eastern Europe, despite deep-seated cultural, social, ethnic and political differences. And finally, in the 1980s it remained a powerful symbol of the commitment of all 35 participating states to the lowering of tension and promotion of cooperation across the ideological and political divide. In this way it helped the European members of NATO and the WTO to press on their respective alliance leaders the need for restraint and moderation, and provided opportunities for maintaining intra-European dialogue at a time of heightened East–West confrontation.[50]

The success of the Helsinki process, with its follow-up meetings and specialist forums, however, was not enough to prevent a steady deterioration in East–West relations in the second half of the 1970s. The primary reason for this was superpower rivalry in the Third World: the 1970s witnessed the success of a number of national liberation movements and insurrectionary struggles in Indochina, southern Africa, the Horn of Africa, Central America, Afghanistan and Iran. This presented the Soviet Union and its WTO allies with the opportunity of expanding their military and political influence in the Third World, thereby shifting the 'correlation of forces' further in the direction of the communist world. The USA, still smarting from its ignominious defeat in Indochina and the shame of Watergate at home, found itself on the defensive and blamed the Soviet Union for its set-backs. Superpower involvement in Third World regional conflicts contributed to the growing East–West mistrust and tension at the end of the 1970s, and this adversely affected the political climate in Europe. By this stage, however, many Europeans themselves had learnt to appreciate the benefits to be gained from detente, and had developed a vested interest in its continuation. This in turn contributed to growing intra-alliance tensions. Thus although the problems generated by the 'Euromissiles' dispute and the Polish crisis should not be overlooked, the roots of what has been called the 'Second Cold War'[51] are to be found primarily in the superpowers' involvement in Third World regional conflicts (and the impact of this on the domestic political debate in the USA), rather than in indigenous conflicts in Europe itself.

Euro and the 'Second Cold War': From 'Dual-Track' to 'Double Zero'

Hopes for a continent united and at peace with itself which the early experience of detente engendered in Europe were to prove ill-founded. The Soviet deployment of SS-20s, NATO's 'double-track' decision on INF, the Soviet intervention in Afghanistan, the US Senate's failure to ratify SALT 2, and the Polish crisis, all contributed to the steady erosion of detente. President Reagan launched his militantly anti-communist crusade against the 'Evil Empire',[52] whilst the ailing gerontocracy in the Kremlin was unable to respond any more creatively than to step up the arms race and threaten a 'new ice age' in East–West relations. By 1983–84, East–West relations had reached their nadir, and there was a growing fear of the possibility of war.

Amongst many of the superpowers' European allies, however, there was a strong interest in the preservation of as many of the fruits of detente as possible, and a desire partially to insulate East–West relations in Europe from the chill winds of US–Soviet confrontation. This was nowhere more apparent than in the two Germanies: both the FRG and the GDR (despite the latter's original suspicions about the domestic political implications of Bonn's Ostpolitik) made considerable efforts to preserve good relations, even at the cost of more conflictual relations with their superpower patrons. The differences between the superpowers and their European allies at this time reflected their different geostrategic and power-political interests: the USA and the USSR were superpowers with global concerns, and their antagonism was reinforced to some extent by the nature of the bipolar world order which had helped shape their evolving post-war relationship. The European states, on the other hand, were primarily regional powers, with more limited and specific concerns: at the same time, 'If the superpowers were natural adversaries in a bipolar system, Europe was a continent which had been artificially and arbitrarily divided.'[53] This meant that the detente of the 1970s had developed an organic dynamic of its own, 'involving countries and people more than political acts and institutions' (as was so frequently the case with the superpowers),[54] and so was not as vulnerable to 'out-of-area' regional conflicts as was the superpower relationship.

The re-emergence of East–West tension in the early 1980s, therefore, had the effect of generating intra-alliance controversies on both sides of the 'iron curtain'. In the West there were disputes over, *inter alia*, 'out-of-area' disputes and US policy in the Third World (ie, the invasion of Grenada and the bombing of Libya); over East–West trade, economic sanctions, COCOM and technology transfer; over SDI, INF, burden-sharing and 'discriminate deterrence'; and over growing trade disputes (given the US twin-deficits). In the socialist bloc, there were bitter disputes concerning the necessity for further missile deployments, and over the role of small and medium-sized states in maintaining an East–West dialogue at a time of superpower confrontation.

However, the conflicts and tensions unleashed by the 'Second Cold War' not only manifested themselves in disputes between the superpowers and their allies, but also and perhaps as significantly, in growing controversies **within** the European states themselves. The deterioration in East–West relations coincided with a period of economic depression and intensifying social unrest in Western Europe. This led to a polarisation of left and right throughout much of Europe, and, given the growing fear of war, this had a powerful impact on the defence and foreign policy debates in a number of European states. The growth in support for peace movements throughout much of Europe led to certain 'democratisation' of the security debate in many countries. At the same time, the elite consensus on security issues in many West European countries began to disintegrate. In this highly charged situation, many of the basic post-war assumptions of defence policy in Western Europe (particularly nuclear deterrence and the American role in Europe) were no longer taken as axiomatic by significant parts of the population.

Nevertheless, NATO survived the traumas of the INF deployments, and by 1985–86, the war scare was beginning to recede. The lessening of East–West tension at this time was linked to a number of developments. First, Gorbachev's election to the post of CPSU General-Secretary; second, a less dogmatically anti-communist President Reagan in his second term; and third, persistent and growing West European pressure for an improvement in East–West relations, symbolised above all by the positive role played by the 'Iron Maiden' herself, in league with her uncharismatic but competent Foreign Secretary of the time, Geoffrey Howe. This favourable conjuncture of trends ultimately led to the Stockholm CSBM Agreement of September 1986, the Reykjavik summit of October–November 1986, and the INF Treaty of December 1987. Although Reykjavik was initially met with alarm and outright hostility in the capitals of Western Europe, the global double-zero came to symbolise the new spirit in East–West relations, which President Reagan and General-Secretary Gorbachev did so much to foster.

By the end of the following year (1988), there was a widespread sense that the cold war era was finally drawing to an end.[55] It was only in late 1989, however, that it became clear that Europe had reached a watershed in its post-war history. The collapse of communist rule in Eastern Europe, and the opening up of the Berlin Wall, signalled the end of the East–West conflict in its traditional form. When Presidents Bush and Gorbachev met in the stormy waters off Malta from 2 to 3 December, their meeting provided the symbolic last rites for four decades of East–West antagonism. At the same time, the Malta summit demonstrated the extent to which Europe had changed since the mid-1940s. Although change in Europe had been stimulated by the reform programme in the USSR, it was now apparent that the initiative in European affairs was increasingly the prerogative of the Europeans themselves, rather than the two superpowers (as had been the case in the 1940s).[56] The seaborne summit off Malta, therefore, can be seen as symbolising the end of a period in European history which began at the time of the Yalta summit in 1945.

Notes

1. Mary Kaldor in *The New Detente: Rethinking East–West Relations*, edited by M. Kaldor et al. (London: Verso, 1989), p. 13.
2. Konrad, *Antipolitics* (London: Quartet Books, 1984), p. 1.
3. 'There are now two great nations in the world which, starting from different points, seem to be advancing toward the same goal: the Russians and the Anglo-Americans.

   Both have grown in obscurity, and while the world's attention was occupied elsewhere, they have suddenly taken their place among the leading nations, making the world take note of their birth and of their greatness almost at the same instant ....

   Their point of departure is different and their paths diverse; nevertheless, each seems called by some secret design of Providence one day to hold in its hands the destinies of half the world.' Alexis de Tocqueville, *Democracy in America*, trans. George Lawrence (New York: Harper & Row, 1966), pp. 378–79.
4. Gaz Alperovitz, for example, has argued that Truman's major preoccupation during the summer of 1945 was not the final defeat of Japan but the use of the American possession of the bomb as a means of coercing the Soviet Union into adopting American policies in Eastern Europe and elsewhere - *Atomic Diplomacy: Hiroshima and Potsdam. The Use of the Atomic Bomb and American Confrontation with Soviet Power* (New York: Simon and Schuster, 1965).
5. Barton J. Bernstein, 'Roosevelt, Truman and the Atomic Bomb 1941–1945: A Reinterpretation', in *Political Sciences Quarterly* (Spring 1975), pp. 23–69.
6. 'To find the main reason for today's threat of war, we must go back to the year 1945, to Yalta. It was there that a helpless Europe was divided; it was there that agreements were reached for military zones of occupation that would become political spheres of interest as well. Yalta gave birth

to a system of international relations based upon a state of rivalry and equilibrium between the Soviet Union and the United States. Whether the three old gentlemen who met there knew it or not, the idea of the Iron Curtain was born at Yalta, a symbol of great-power logic.' George Konrad, *op. cit.*, p. 1.

7. Alfred Grosser, *The Western Alliance. European–American Relations Since 1945* (London: Macmillan, 1978), p. 40.

8. W. Mastny, 'Europe in US–USSR Relations: A Topical Legacy', in *Problems of Communism*, vol. 37, no. 1 (January–February 1988), pp. 16–29 (p. 17).

9. This gave the Soviet Union 90 per cent influence in Romania, the British (and Americans) 10 per cent; in Greece, 90 per cent Western influence, 10 per cent Soviet; in Bulgaria, 75 per cent Soviet influence, the rest Western; whilst in Hungary and Yugoslavia, it was to be 50–50 per cent. See Fernando Claudin, *The Communist Movement: From Comintern to Cominform* (London: Peregrine, 1975), p. 752.

10. Stalin is reputed to have told Djilas that 'this war is not as in the past; whoever occupies territory also imposes his own social system as far as his army can reach. It cannot be otherwise.' M. Djilas, *Conversations with Stalin* (New York: 1962), p. 114.

11. See for example Paul Kennedy, *The Rise and Fall of the Great Powers* (London: Fontana, 1989), pp. 460–62.

12. This was apparent from both the 'Atlantic Charter' of August 1941 and the Lease-Lend agreement of February 1942.

13. See Anton Deporte, *Europe between the Superpowers* (London: Yale University Press, 1979), p. 81.

14. Michael Cox, 'From the Truman Doctrine to the Second Superpower Detente: The Rise and Fall of the Cold War', in *Journal of Peace Research*, vol. 27, no. 1 (February 1990), pp. 25–42 (p. 31).

15. The use of the term 'empire' does not imply that American foreign policy was 'imperialist' in either the Leninist sense or in the way suggested by US revisionist writers. Rather, as John Lewis Gaddis has argued, 'the aspect of New Left historiography that postrevisionists are likely to find most useful – and the point upon which their work will depart most noticeably from orthodox accounts – is that there was in fact an American "empire" .... Washington's experience in projecting first its interests and then its power on a global scale does bear a striking resemblance to the experiences of other great imperial powers in history; from these resemblances, it would seem, revealing comparative insights might be derived.' See his seminal article, 'The Emerging Post-Revisionist Synthesis on the Origins of the Cold War', *Diplomatic History* (Summer 1983), pp. 171–204 (p. 181). For an excellent example of this sort of historical comparison of the American 'empire' with other empires (particularly that of the British), see David P. Calleo, 'NATO and Some Lessons of History', in *Nato at Forty: Change, Continuity and Prospects*, edited by James R. Golden et al. (London: Westview, 1989), pp. 155–78.

16. R. Smith, 'A Climate of Opinion: British Officials and the Development of British Soviet Policy, 1945–47', *International Affairs*, vol. 64, no. 4 (Autumn 1988), pp. 631–47, and A. Shlaim, 'Britain, the Berlin Blockade and the Cold War', *International Affairs*, vol. 60, no. 1 (Winter 1983–84), pp. 1–14.

17. N.J. Wheeler, 'British nuclear weapons and Anglo-American relations,

1945–54', *International Affairs*, vol. 64, no. 1 (Winter 1985–86), pp. 71–86.

18. Jan Melissen and Bert Zeeman, 'Britain and Western Europe, 1945–51: Opportunities Lost?', *International Affairs*, vol. 63, no. 1 (Winter 1986–87), pp. 81–95 (p. 81–82).

19. This is apparent, for example, from the popular support enjoyed by the communist-led partisan forces in Yugoslavia and Albania, and the 38 per cent vote for the Czechoslovak Communist Party in relatively free elections in 1946. Communist parties also enjoyed significant support in many other European countries at this time. See Bogdan Szajkowski, *The Establishment of Marxist Regimes* (London: Butterworth, 1982), p. 58, and Martin McCauley, ed., *Communist Power in Europe, 1944–49* (London: Macmillan, 1977).

20. E.P. Thompson, *Beyond the Cold War* (London: Merlin Press, 1982), p. 5.

21. Gian Giacomo Migone, 'The Decline of the Bipolar System, or A Second Look at the History of the Cold War', in *The New Detente*, ed. by M. Kaldor, p. 160.

22. 'The Iranian crisis, besides representing a setback for the Soviet Union in an area on its own borders, was also the occasion of the first public breach between the former wartime allies'; S.R. Ashton, *In Search of Detente: The Politics of East–West Relations since 1945* (London: Macmillan, 1989), p. 14.

23. Michael Dockrill, *The Cold War 1945–63* (London: Macmillan, 1988), pp. 35–36.

24. Quoted in Louis Halle, *The Cold War as History* (London: Chatto and Windus, 1967), pp. 103–4.

25. President Truman appealed to Congress for economic and military aid for Greece and Turkey, arguing that 'it must be the policy of the United States to support free people who are resisting attempted subjugation by armed minorities or by outside pressures': see John Lewis Gaddis, *Russia, The Soviet Union, and the United States: An Interpretive History* (New York: John Wiley and Sons, 1978), pp. 185–86.

26. The Speech of Secretary of State George Marshall at Harvard on 5 June 1947, in which he proposed a long-term American undertaking to grant aid in support of a cooperative European regional effort to achieve economic self-sufficiency – as he said, 'a cure, rather than a palliative'.

27. 'Mr. X', 'The Sources of Soviet Conduct', *Foreign Affairs* (July 1947), pp. 566–82.

28. Pavel Tigrid, 'The Prague Coup of 1948: The Elegant Takeover', in Thomas Hammond (ed.), *The Anatomy of Communist Takeovers* (New Haven: Yale University Press, 1975), pp. 399–432.

29. Diana Johnstone, *The Politics of the Euromissiles* (London: Verso, 1984), p. 36.

30. Tom Bower, *Blind Eye to Murder. Britain, America and the Purging of Nazi Germany – A Pledge Betrayed* (London: Granada, 1981).

31. S.R. Ashton, *op. cit.*, p. 43.

32. Matthew Evangelista, 'Stalin's Postwar Army Reappraised', *International Security*, vol. 7, no. 3 (1983), pp. 110–38.

33. Mike Bowker and Phil Williams, *Superpower Detente: A Reappraisal* (London: Sage for the Royal Institute of International Affairs, 1988), p. 17.

34. Alfred Grosser, *op. cit.*, pp. 166–67.
35. For an excellent study of the impact of this event on German post-war political consciousness, see Peter Siebenmorgan, *Gezeitenwechsel: Aufbruch zur Entspannungspolitik* (Bonn: Bouvier Verlag, 1990), p. 331ff.
36. Cuba, according to Dean Rusk, was the 'most dangerous crisis the world has ever seen'. It was the one occasion when the USA and the USSR viewed each other 'through a barrel of a gun'. Quoted in Blight et al., 'The Cuban Missile Crisis Revisited', *Foreign Affairs*, vol. 66, no. 1 (Fall 1987), p. 170.
37. Richard Vine, ed., *Soviet–East European Relations as a Problem for the West* (London: Croom Helm, 1987), p. 17. See also L. Halle, *op. cit.*, p. 408.
38. For an analysis of the significance of this treaty see the series of articles in the UN journal *Disarmament*, vol. XXII, no. 2.
39. In March 1959, de Gaulle gave a major speech on the need for detente and cooperation, heralding the reunification of Europe 'from the Atlantic to the Urals'. From 1964 onwards, he sought to engage France in cooperation with the socialist states, and launched a series of vehement attacks on what he chose to describe as 'American hegemony'.
40. G.R. Urban, ed., *Detente* (London: Temple Smith, 1976), p. 264.
41. Kissinger has written that 'the late sixties coinciding with Vietnam, marked the end of the period when America was overwhelmingly more powerful than any other nation'. See his book, *For the Record. Selected Statements, 1977–1980* (London: Weidenfeld and Nicolson, 1981), p. 73. It is also significant that a number of influential 'realist' analysts were speaking of the need to move 'beyond the cold war' at this time. See for example Hans Morgenthau, *A New Foreign Policy for the United States* (London: Pall Mall, 1969).
42. The Report 'The Future Tasks of the Alliance' was prepared by the then Belgian Foreign Minister, Pierre Harmel, and approved by the North Atlantic Council in 1967. See Guido Vigeveno, *The Bomb and European Security* (London: C. Hurst and Co., 1983), p. 59.
43. L.C. Kumar, *The Soviet Union and European Security* (London: Sangam Books, 1987), pp. 69–75.
44. Williams and Bowker, *op. cit.*, p. 27. Monsieur Debre, the French Foreign Minister at the time, compared the Czech crisis to a road accident that need not lead to the permanent closure of the road.
45. Helga Haftendorn calls this 'fragmented bipolarity with features of partial cooperation'. See R. Juette, *Detente and Peace in Europe* (Frankfurt: Campus Verlag, 1977) p. 102.
46. See I.D. Hendry and M.C. Wood, *The Legal Status of Berlin* (Cambridge: Grotius Publications, 1987).
47. See K. Dyson, ed., *European Detente: Case Studies of the Politics of East–West Relations* (London: Frances Pinter, 1986), p. 63.
48. 'A European peace structure should not only be conceived of as merely confirming the legacy of the Second World War for Europe. A European peace structure would have to overcome the effects of existing borders, and it should encourage new forms of cooperation, e.g. it might include an all-European law of minorities. It ought to realize human rights in the most essential areas, and in concrete and practical terms rather than just proclaiming them. A European peace structure would then have to represent a greater degree of community in economic terms, i.e. the bilateral trade

relations between East and West would have to be transcended towards meaningful relationship between the EC and COMECON.' Quoted in Juette, *op. cit.*, p. 103.

49. As Roy and Zhores Medvedev have argued, 'Successive administrations have made the preservation of a clear US military-technological lead over the USSR the precondition to any serious negotiation. Looking at this from another angle, every significant new technology of nuclear warfare – nuclear missile submarines, MIRVs, cruise missiles, the neutron bomb, and so on – has been introduced into the arms race by the United States.' See E.P. Thompson et al., *Exterminism and the Cold War*, p. 162.

50. Karl Birnbaum and Ingo Peters, 'The CSCE: A Reassessment of its Role in the 1980s', in *Review of International Studies*, vol. 16, no. 4 (October 1990), pp. 305–19.

51. Fred Halliday, *The Making of the Second Cold War* (London: Verso, 1983).

52. Strobe Talbot, *The Russians and Reagan* (New York: Vintage, 1984), pp. 94–95, 117–18.

53. Bowker and Williams, *op. cit.*, p. 86.

54. R. Garthoff, *Detente and Confrontation: American–Soviet Relations from Nixon to Reagan* (Washington, DC: The Brookings Institution, 1985), p. 122.

55. Even the old Bavarian anti-communist Franz Josef Strauss was to declare, 'The post-war period has now ended. A new chapter has opened up'; quoted in the *Süddeutsche Zeitung*, 31 December 1988.

56. For details of the summit see *Keesing's Record of World Events*, vol. 35, no. 12 (1989), pp. 37110–12.

3
Europe at the Crossroads?

There are recurrent moments in international affairs, when the pattern of
relationships and alliances which has been prevalent is transformed into a
new one. It is something similar to what happens when, by a sudden tap,
the pieces in a kaleidoscope are reassembled to form a different shape. The
moments recur at long intervals and are separated by periods during which
the existing pattern comes to be venerated as if it were a dictate of the laws
of nature .... We are witnessing the dissolution of that dual pattern of North
Atlantic Alliance versus Warsaw Pact which anyone alive today under the age
of 40 was born into, regarding it as only slightly less pre-ordained than the
solar system.

Enoch Powell[1]

From Lisbon to Leningrad, Europe is experiencing a process of profound
change. After decades of gradual, incremental evolution, a period of
accelerated political and strategic development has taken place, which
has transformed the very nature of post-war Europe. In the preceding two
chapters we considered what was meant by the term 'European security
system', and explored the salient features of post-war European history.
In this chapter, we shall assess the nature of the changes which are
currently transforming East–West relations in Europe. To begin with,
we will consider the distinctive characteristics of the post-war order
in Europe. We will then identify the secular trends which have been
eroding its foundations over recent years. One interesting issue to be
considered briefly here is whether the passing of the bipolar cold war
era is a regrettable and worrying development, as some commentators
have suggested. Finally, we shall end by indicating the key elements of
the new security agenda which is beginning to take shape in a Europe
'beyond containment'.

The Determining Characteristics of the European Security System

The post-war European security order was the product of a specific period
in modern history – the cold war years of the late 1940s and early 1950s.
Whatever underlying hostilities it incorporated, the cold war represented
a unique conjuncture in world politics – a period when Europe lay

exhausted and enfeebled by total war; when the USA was the only real global superpower, with a prodigious economic and financial strength to complement its awesome military potential; when the USSR emerged as a major military and political force in Europe and parts of Asia, and communism seemed to be on the offensive throughout the globe; and before the rise of other significant regional power centres within the international political system. It was this specific conjuncture which gave birth to the contemporary European security system, a security system which – despite the profound international changes that have taken place over the last four decades – remained intact until the very end of the 1980s.

Five unique features distinguished post-war Europe from other international security systems, either past or present: these were as follows:

1. The Decisive Role of the Superpowers

This is a function of the historic decline of Europe since its heyday in the nineteenth century, when it stood at the very centre of world affairs. The Great War of 1914–18 was a milestone in this decline, but the crucial watershed was the Second World War. The devastation of the continental heartlands of Europe in 1939–45 created a power vacuum which was filled by the two flanking states, the USA and the USSR. Post-war Europe was consequently to bear the unmistakable imprimatur of the two superpowers. The creation by the USA and the USSR of, respectively, the 'Atlantic alliance' and the 'socialist community' ruptured the traditional patterns of association and exchange in Europe, and produced an entirely new security environment. Henceforth, the future of Europe was to be decided not by its traditional great powers – the French, Germans and British – but, as Alexis de Toqueville had predicted in the 1830s, by the two great nations on the periphery of the continent, America and Russia. Despite the relative decline of the two superpowers in an increasingly polycentric and interdependent world, their interaction – confrontational or cooperative – has, until relatively recently, been the preponderant influence on the development of the post-war European security system.

2. Nuclear Deterrence

The success of the Manhattan project and the subsequent atomic destruction of Hiroshima and Nagasaki heralded the dawn of the nuclear age.[2] Although the full implications of the existential threat posed by nuclear weapons only became apparent after the Cuban missile crisis, their very existence from 1945 onwards began a process of fundamental change in the nature of the international system. Nuclear deterrence has negated Clausewitz's central precept of war as the continuation of politics by other means, and imposed a new and terrifying discipline on both the superpowers and their European allies. In doing so it has effectively removed the option of war in Europe as a credible means of international statecraft. At the same time, it tended to reinforce the bipolar dynamics of the post-war world, and for many decades seemed to slow down the pace of historical evolution in Europe.[3] Despite the changes that have occurred in the doctrine and practice of deterrence, the existence of nuclear weapons has remained a central feature (some would say the central feature) of the post-war security order.

3. The Division of Germany

The cold war division of Europe into two opposed alliance systems was symbolised above all by the division of the former German Reich into the FRG and the GDR in 1949. The *Spaltung* of Germany was subsequently to imbue the East–West conflict in Europe with a powerful national dimension, whilst the disputed status of Berlin was to generate some of the most serious cold war conflicts in this part of the globe. Nevertheless, for many years the post-war division of Germany seemed to provide a workable solution to the perennial 'German problem'. The creation, by 'blood and iron', of the Bismarckian Reich at the centre of Europe generated enormous security problems for Germany's neighbours, and was one of the principle factors leading to the outbreak of war in 1870, 1914 and 1939. Richard Vine's comments reflected the unspoken views of many Europeans, East and West, throughout much of the post-war period:

> The division of Germany has provided reassurance in Eastern and Western Europe; it has provided stability in large measure by removing the spectre of a security threat to the Soviet Union or to other European countries. There are few determined rooters for a politically reunited Germany, not even in the two Germanies. A divided Germany, with one part 'hostage' in the Eastern security system, may be an indispensable condition to continued system stability for the foreseeable future.[4]

In the end, of course, the division of Germany was to prove a source of instability in Europe: nevertheless, for over forty years it was a central feature of the post-war European security system.

4. The Neutral and Non-aligned Countries

The existence of a block of neutral and non-aligned states was another significant feature of post-war European security, and one frequently overlooked in the literature. Their existence, wedged in between the two military blocks, contributed to the overall stability of Europe, and they have been seen as an integral part of the strategic balance.[5] These countries were always a very heterogeneous group, their neutral status deriving from different historical backgrounds and political contexts.[6] Nevertheless, they played a not insignificant mediating role in a number of international forums (such as the CSCE), and have made a distinctive contribution to the overall management of East–West security affairs. Furthermore, they played a passive but still significant role as models for reformists in the East. Austria, for example, with its neutral status, was attractive to some Germans in both East and West, whilst for reformers in the Soviet Union and East Central Europe, Sweden (with its 'active neutrality' and impressive social welfare system) provided the ideal example of a democratic socialist society.

5. The Intra-Alliance Regulatory Function of the European Security System

The alliance structures of post-war Europe served not only to provide a stabilising framework for East–West relations, they also created an important means of regulating and managing intra-alliance disputes.[7] NATO explicitly defined for itself such a role in regulating conflicts between countries within the Alliance.[8] Indeed, Josef Joffe was to argue that the American presence in Europe played a vital role in suppressing many traditional intra-European disputes, thereby making possible the process of West European integration.[9] A similar argument has been advanced in the case of the 'Soviet bloc': Soviet domination of the Warsaw Pact and the CMEA, it is sometimes suggested, created a *pax Sovietica* in Eastern Europe – an area riddled with deep-seated national, ethnic and political conflicts.[10] The existence of the broader East–West conflict, therefore, and the alliance structures it generated, helped contain – although not to remove – more localised conflicts (such as the Hungarian–Romanian or Greco-Turkish disputes).

The Sources of Change in Europe Today

The security structures which emerged in the early cold war years proved remarkably durable for nearly four decades. Despite a series of incremental and evolutionary changes, which modified some of the security relationships in the continent (ie, between France and NATO, or Romania and the Soviet Union), the structure as a whole remained intact until the late 1980s. Indeed, it seemed to some commentators that the post-war system was likely to continue until at least 2001, because it reflected 'the true balance of power in the Europe that has emerged from the crises of the twentieth century'.[11]

For all its apparent stability and durability, however, this security order began unravelling at an accelerating pace in the late 1980s, producing a veritable 'bonfire of the certainties'. The reason for this was that, despite its surface appearance of calm and stability, the foundations of this security order had steadily been eroded by a series of powerful secular trends. The gradual erosion of the underlying structures of the bipolar system, by a barely perceptible process of subterranean change, radically altered the power relationships underpinning the post-war order. The foundations of the post-war security system had therefore become increasingly fragile and 'structurally unsound'. Gorbachev's programme of 'revolutionary reforms' in the USSR acted as a catalyst, producing a far-reaching process of qualitative change in the very structures of the post-war order itself.

These subterranean processes of change were as follows:

1. The Stagnation of the Soviet Economy and the Crisis of 'Developed Socialism'

By the mid-1980s, it was clear to many people in the USSR that 'developed socialism' was in need of fundamental reform. The bureaucratic structures of the command economy and authoritarian one-party rule had seriously undermined the international prestige of the Soviet Union, and were frustrating both individual initiative and technological innovation. The USSR, it was feared, was fast becoming 'Upper Volta with missiles'. Moreover, the military policies of the Brezhnev era had proven increasingly counterproductive in terms of guaranteeing the security of the Soviet state. Its foreign policy adventures had also led to a series of culs-de-sac – in Afghanistan, Indochina, Africa, Europe and the Middle East.[12]

The systemic failure of Soviet-style communism was therefore a major reason for the disintegration of the foundations of the post-war order. The election of Mikhail Gorbachev to the post of General-Secretary of the CPSU in April 1985 amounted to a recognition by the country's political elite of the structural weaknesses of the Soviet system. The reform programme which he subsequently initiated then provided the catalyst for broader changes in the post-war international system.[13]

2. The Failure of Authoritarian State Socialism in Eastern Europe

If 'developed socialism' has been a disappointment in the Soviet Union, its catastrophic consequences have been even more apparent in Eastern Europe. Despite the dream that many East Europeans harboured of an escape from economic backwardness and political instability through a process of communist-led modernization, the communists were never able to develop economically viable and politically legitimate socialist regimes in the East. After 40 years of authoritarian rule in Eastern Europe – a period punctuated by intermittent crises and upheavals – the illusion that 'developed socialism' and 'proletarian internationalism' could solve the region's deep-seated problems has incontrovertibly been exposed as a hollow sham. Whatever the early industrial successes and social achievements of at least some of the 'Peoples' Democracies', the authoritarian and bureaucratic structures of orthodox communist rule have proved inadequate to the demands of the late twentieth century. By the 1980s, Eastern Europe had become a zone of incipient crisis and instability – caught between the conflicting pressures of perestroika in the East and economic prosperity in the West.

3. The Growing Economic Prosperity and Political Cohesion of Western Europe

Over the past four decades, Western Europe has evolved from post-war devastation and weakness to prosperity and political stability. This has been accompanied by a process of deepening integration, primarily – though not exclusively – through the European Community. This post-war renaissance of Western Europe has had important consequences for the continent's security relationships. By virtue of the intensity of economic and social interactions in Western Europe, the area has emerged as the core of the wider Europe. Within Western Europe, it is the EC which has become the institutional core of the European integration process.[14] Indeed, as a result of the energies and dynamism unleashed by the '1992 project', the EC has become a magnet for other European countries, both in EFTA and the CMEA. At the same time, integration in the EC has been accompanied by closer West European security cooperation through a variety of bilateral and multilateral forums, such as the WEU and Franco-German defence cooperation. Moreover, given its economic prosperity, welfare provisions, rule of law and limited government, West Europe has become a 'model' for countries to its east and south, and a powerful source of attraction to the relatively poor and underprivileged peoples on the region's periphery.[15] Finally, the growing self-confidence and cohesion of Western Europe has led it to become more and more assertive in its dealings with other world powers, including its former patron and close strategic ally, the United States.[16]

4. The Changing Transatlantic Relationship

In the immediate post-war years, the USA bestrode the world like a mighty hegemon, seeking to reshape the international system in its own image, and to bestow the advantages of the 'American way of life' on the peoples of the 'Free World'. In the late 1940s–early 1950s, American power was artificially high, given the wartime boom of the US economy and the devastation of much of Europe and Asia. It was in this period, however, that many of the key institutions of the post-war international order were established, ie, the UN, NATO, GATT, the IMF and the World Bank – all of which bore the decisive imprint of American thinking.

Since then, however, the very success of US policies has led to the relative decline of American power, given the recovery of Western Europe and Japan, the containment of the Soviet Union, and the development of at least parts of the Third World. The consequent break-up of the bipolar global order, and the emergence of a more pluralist and interdependent world, has forced the US and its allies to rethink their relationships, and this has been nowhere more apparent than in the Atlantic community.

The 1980s were a troubled decade for US–West European relations. Conflicts between the Reagan Administration and the West Europeans developed over East–West relations, 'out-of-area' regional conflicts, arms control policy and strategic nuclear issues. These conflicts reflected more fundamental problems arising from shifts in the underlying power relationship: namely, the relative decline of US power and the growing economic weight of Western Europe with the Atlantic alliance.

As Europe moves 'beyond containment', the institutional lynchpin of the Atlantic alliance – NATO – will face growing pressures for major change, and its relative importance will tend to decline. New institutional ties between the Europeans and the Americans are therefore required, if the relationship is to stay healthy and vital. An agenda for a 'new Atlanticism' was sketched by Secretary of State James Baker in Berlin in December 1989,[17] but progress in this area has been slow – particularly given US–EC differences over trade policy (as the dispute over agricultural subsidies at the 1986–90 Uruguay GATT Round illustrated).

These four trends were part and parcel of a broader process of change in the global system, which developed gradually from the mid-1950s onwards: namely, the fragmentation of the bipolar world order, and the emergence of a more polycentric world characterised by patterns of 'complex interdependence'. The underlying cause of this is to be found in the changing nature of the global economy, with the growing internationalisation of the world market and the developing of new transnational modes of production, commerce and information exchange. It was also linked to the uneven nature of economic modernisation, which created new foci of economic activity in different parts of the world (such as Latin America and the Pacific rim). The more polycentric world order of today is characterised by deepening interdependence and a diffusion of economic power beyond the borders of the traditional nation-state. These developments in the global system have changed the parameters of the East–West relationship, and contributed to the process of transformation currently underway in Europe.

The Changing East–West Relationship in Europe

In the summer of 1989, Valery Giscard d'Estaing, Yasuhiro Nakasone and Henry Kissinger declared that, 'East–West relations have entered a new phase'.[18] After decades of cold war belligerency, and after the disappointments generated by the failure of successive attempts at a durable detente, Europe had finally entered a new period of East–West detente. This new phase of detente was qualitatively different from that of the 1970s, and was constructed on much firmer foundations. It also possessed a dynamic which was to lead to a fundamental transformation of the post-war security order in Europe. This became apparent from 1987 onwards, thanks particularly to the Washington INF Treaty – a treaty of tremendous political and symbolic importance. With the steady improvement in superpower relations in the late Reagan years and the unfolding of the reform process in the Soviet Union, East–West relations moved from confrontation to detente, and from there to something without precedent in the post-war period. With the dramatic and largely unexpected events of late 1989, it has become evident that Europe has entered a qualitatively new stage in its history – and that it had moved decisively 'beyond Yalta'.

Europe and the 'End of History'

The passing of forty years of military confrontation and ideological enmity, however, has not been met with universal acclaim. Indeed, in some quarters there seems to be a marked sense of nostalgia for the old certainties of the cold war. Some seemed to think that, whatever its faults, the cold war was at least predictable, stable and orderly.[19] As attributes of the international system, these are characteristics which tend to be highly valued by diplomats and statesmen. This mood of nostalgia for the simplicities and certainties of the bipolar world has been especially prevalent in some quarters of the USA. This is because, even at its darkest moments, the antagonisms of the US–Soviet relationship were less dangerous and more controlled than they appeared to be on the surface. The rivalry never amounted to a bitter fight to the death, and it increasingly became a carefully controlled contest with commonly agreed rules. In many ways, such a carefully managed, albeit abrasive conflict with a weak and unattractive competitor had much to recommend it to the US foreign policy establishment. It provided a popular theme around which to build a foreign policy consensus; it facilitated and legitimized US leadership of the 'Free World'; it united the Western world after centuries of conflict; and it helped consolidate the post-war 'welfare capitalist' system.[20]

It was perhaps for this reason that some prominent Americans appeared to be, in the words of George T. Mitchell (the Senate majority leader), 'almost nostalgic about the cold war and the rigid superpower relationship that divided the world into two hostile and isolated camps'.[21] Indeed, Lawrence Eagleburger (Deputy Secretary of the State Department) favourably compared the cold war years, 'characterized by a remarkable set of stable and predictable set of relations among the great powers', to the late 1980s, 'in which power and influence is diffused among a multiplicity of states', and where the danger existed 'that change in the East will prove too destabilizing to be sustained'.[22] At the same time, in his oft-quoted article, Francis Fukuyama equated the passing of the East–West conflict with the 'end of history' (in the Hegelian sense of 'history'), and commented that this will be 'a very sad time', in which 'daring, courage, imagination and idealism will be replaced by economic calculation, the endless solving of technical problems, environmental concerns'.[23]

Given this sense of nostalgia for the certainties and stability of the cold war, it is perhaps worth reminding ourselves of the costs of the Manichaean division of the world into two hostile camps. Firstly, the division of both Europe and Germany (not to mention that of China, Vietnam and Korea) entailed enormous economic, political, social, cultural and, not least, human costs. The Berlin Wall itself (or at least, what remains of it), whatever stability its erection might have brought to the East–West conflict, stands as a grotesque concrete and steel monument to man's inhumanity to man.

Secondly, the cold war placed severe limits on national sovereignty within the two alliances. This is most apparent in the East, given the Soviet invasion of Hungary in 1956 and Czechoslovakia in 1968, as well as the threat of intervention in Poland in 1956 and 1981. However, as Gian Giacomo Migone has argued, US hegemony in NATO also resulted in a 'benign limited sovereignty' in Western Europe, particularly as regards national defence and security policy. Furthermore, although more subtle methods of superpower influence were used in the West, especially in the North Atlantic region,

> In the Mediterranean countries, whenever any real or potential threat to the status quo has emerged, American intervention has been more blatant, even to the point of supporting existing dictatorships (Franco, Salazar, Metaxas), promoting new ones in the face of political and social change (more recently, Greece and Turkey), or manipulating and curtailing democratic systems (Italy).[24]

Thirdly, the cold war tended to foster a concentration of power in the national security apparatuses within individual states. This has at times led to both limitations on some individual and collective liberties, and restrictions on what would otherwise be considered legitimate social and political activities.[25] Again, this has been most apparent in the East (particularly in the Stalinist period), but one should not forget McCarthyism and the Rosenberg trial in the USA; the *Berufsverbot* and the ban on extremist political parties in West Germany;[26] and the Official Secrets Act and various nefarious activities of MI5 and the Special Branch in Britain.[27]

Fourthly, it generated an arms race which has had enormous social and economic costs for the Europeans and Americans, and which has stimulated the growth of what Dwight Eisenhower was to call the 'military-industrial complex'.

And finally, it exacerbated regional conflicts in Korea, Indochina, the Middle East, southern Africa, central America, the Horn of Africa and Afghanistan. Given the bipolar stalemate in Europe, and the high stakes involved there, the superpowers and their allies tended to transfer their hostilities to the Third World. Throughout the post-war period, most regional conflicts in the Third World were seen by analysts in Washington and Moscow as part of the global machinations of the other side, and this stimulated the search for pawns in the 'Great Contest' between East and West. The cold war therefore gave almost every local Third World conflict an international dimension, as one side or the other sought to win the sponsorship (and with it, the weaponry) of one or the other superpower.[28]

The passing of the bipolar cold war era should thus not be mourned, given its considerable human, economic and social costs. The stability and predictability it provided was founded on an unacceptable, threatening and thus ultimately unstable division of the continent into antagonistic military blocs. At the same time, the bipolar nuclear structures of the cold war era produced a 'deceleration' of history in Europe, as long-standing national, ethnic and political rivalries were submerged by the broader East–West conflict. In this sense, Fukuyama's thesis is fundamentally flawed, particularly when applied to Europe.[29] What he describes as the 'end of history' is in a very real sense the re-awakening of historical development in Europe. As the East–West conflict recedes, traditional patterns of cooperation are reasserting themselves – ie, between the two Germanies, Austria and Hungary, and in the Baltic region – but at the same time, older disputes and historical animosities are resurfacing, and new antagonisms developing. The demise of what Michael Cox has called the 'cold war system'[30], has thus opened up a Pandora's box of ancient conflicts, historical antagonisms and new tensions.[31]

The New Security Agenda in Europe

The recent changes in Soviet security policy and in Eastern Europe have profoundly transformed the nature of the security agenda in Europe.

The 'Soviet threat' – the threat posed by the forward deployment of large numbers of Soviet and Warsaw Pact armoured units capable of executing a large-scale, short-warning offensive in central Europe – no longer appears credible. The old bipolar structure of European security has disintegrated (given the *de facto* collapse of the Warsaw Pact), and more complex patterns of political and economic relationships are developing across the wider Europe.

Despite the ending of the traditional East–West conflict, however, Europe still faces potential challenges to its peace and stability. In the immediate future, there is the danger of 'transitional instability' arising from the rapid pace of change in Eastern Europe and the Soviet Union today. This could make peaceful adjustment more difficult, and sow the seeds of future discord. In the longer term, many fear that a polycentric world will be more conflict-prone than a bipolar one. The problem is that no-one really knows the answer to one simple but crucial question: what will the winding down of the East–West conflict mean for the European security system and the broader international system? On the one hand, it has removed some of the obstacles preventing the resolution of regional conflicts in Afghanistan, Indochina, central America and southern Africa, and improved the prospects for greater cooperation through the aegis of the UN (as the Gulf crisis of 1990 has shown). On the other, it seems to have exacerbated some of the tensions in the Middle East (given the influx of Soviet Jews into Israel, for example), and done little to resolve major problems of poverty and underdevelopment in other parts of the globe.

In Europe itself, the demise of the East–West conflict has not meant the end to all disputes, tensions and security challenges. It is unrealistic to assume that the collapse of communism will remove all sources of conflict in the continent. The potential risks to the security of the European continent may no longer be as 'black-and-white' as they were in the cold war years, but they are no less real for that. The urge triumphantly to celebrate the victory of liberal ideology in Europe as the 'end of history' should, therefore, be resisted: the dawn of a Europe at peace with itself and its neighbours is, alas, not yet in sight.

The challenges – potential or actual – to the stability and peace of the continent are of two types: those deriving from tensions and disputes *within* Europe, and those arising on the peripheries of the continent, or through its interaction with other regions of the world. Within Europe, there are four main problems:

1. *A Residual Soviet Threat.* Even after its unilateral troop cuts and its strategic reversal in Eastern Europe, the USSR still possesses enormous conventional and nuclear forces. It will therefore continue to cast a long geopolitical shadow across the continent, even though it is becoming more democratic and pluralist. One fear is that a future post-Gorbachevian

leadership might seek to use the Soviet Union's considerable military assets for limited political or strategic aims, perhaps in south-eastern Europe, south-west Asia, or at sea. Another source of concern is that instability in the Soviet Union may spill over into Eastern Europe. Finally, there is the nightmare scenario of civil war breaking out in the Soviet Union – a country possessing enormous numbers of strategic and theatre nuclear weapons. This is a worry which has recently been exercising the minds of NATO planners.

2. *Social Turmoil and Political Instability in the East.* The reform process in the Soviet Union and most of Eastern Europe is generating severe domestic problems. The tensions of economic restructuring are placing tremendous pressures on the fragile democratic institutions in the East. This means that there is a real danger of the break-down of social order in parts of eastern and south-eastern Europe. In this context, the rise of new forms of authoritarian nationalism cannot be discounted. The financial and economic disruption which would result from these sorts of developments would give rise to serious concerns in the West, not least because of the wave of emigration to Western Europe it would inevitably provoke.[32]

3. *Ethnic and Nationalist Disputes.* Eastern Europe and the Balkans are riddled with ancient quarrels, ethnic tensions and nationalist irredentia. Unlike the *pax Americana* in Western Europe, which at least did attempt to give these problems an airing in order to resolve them, the *pax Sovietica* in the East simply suppressed them. With the disintegration of the 'socialist community', and the intensifying economic crisis in the region, the danger of resurgent nationalism is becoming ever more real.[33] This has two aspects: first, the question of national minorities, and second, that of borders. The fear here is that nationalist conflicts could become a challenge to the territorial or political status quo in the region, which in turn could draw in other major powers, spill into contiguous geographical areas (perhaps in NATO's Southern region) or degenerate into a 'Lebanon-type' situation of incessant conflict.

4. *The Problem of a More Assertive Germany.* As Michael Howard notes, this is something which is seldom mentioned in polite society (except by the likes of Nicholas Ridley): nevertheless, 'There *is* a German Problem. It may be only a problem of perception, but it exists none the less'.[34] Germany's history, its strength and its geographical centrality mean that it is a potential security concern to many other Europeans. The desire to contain the power of a resurgent Germany within broader European and Atlanticist structures is tempered by the recognition that the Germans might find special constraints on their freedom of action increasingly irksome, thereby fuelling nationalist resentment. The next generation of German leaders, it is feared, may not be willing to accept the structural constraints of the Western alliance. This could lead to a

number of unsettling developments: for example, Germany might leave
NATO, or ask allied troops to leave its territory; alternatively, a united
Germany might decide that it wanted to acquire nuclear weapons, a
prospect which would probably not be welcome in many of Europe's
capitals.[35] Germany is of particular concern to some of the East European
nations: some fear that a nationalist government might aggressively raise
issues such as Germany's 1937 borders, German ethnic minorities or the
'rights' of expellees. Similarly, future German economic dominance in
the lands to their East may cause resentment amongst the East Europeans,
who might come to feel that 'they have exchanged one kind of hegemony
for another; a more beneficent and benevolent hegemony, certainly, but
one they would nonetheless cordially resent'.[36]

As regards the security challenges arising on Europe's periphery or
'out-of-area', there are five main concerns:

1. *The Proliferation of New Weapons Technologies.* The spread
of ballistic missile technology in the Third World, combined with the
proliferation of both chemical and nuclear weapons capabilities, poses a
potential risk to the security of Europe. This danger has been highlighted
by the Gulf crisis of 1990: Saddam Hussein's ruthless and unpredictable
regime has already shown its willingness to use chemical weapons against
its own citizens. The Iraqi regime, it seems, is also attempting to acquire
its own nuclear weapons capability – a prospect which horrifies many
in the region, and in the wider international community. One worrying
aspect of this is the environmental dangers of inter-state conflict in the
Middle East, especially in the light of chemical and nuclear weapon
proliferation.

2. *Economic, Social and Financial Problems.* The problems of
underdevelopment and indebtedness are not only creating more volatile
societies in the Third World, they are also potentially threatening to the
financial and economic stability of the global economy. In an increasingly
interdependent world, the worsening problems of poverty in many parts of
Africa and Asia pose a possible risk to the well-being and security of the
developed world.

3. *Immigration and Demographic Trends.* Western Europe is facing
the growing problem of a huge influx of unskilled migrant workers from
the Mediterranean, North Africa and the Maghreb. There are already
estimated to be 13 million migrant workers in the EC – some of them
from inside the Community – with perhaps 4 million illegals. As the EC
plans to remove internal frontiers and create a unified internal market,
stemming the flow of these economically motivated and culturally diverse
people from the Third World (as well as Eastern Europe and the Soviet
Union) will be the major task of European police forces in the 1990s.[37]

4. *International Terrorism.* Europe has its own home-grown terrorist

groups – the IRA, ETA, the Red Brigades, the RAF, etc. But the problem of international terrorism – often linked to the intractable problems of the Middle East – is of growing concern. In part, it has been stimulated by the resurgence of Islamic fundamentalism.[38] A further dimension of this problem is state-sponsored terrorism: Libya, Iran, Syria and Iraq are alleged to be amongst some of the worst offenders in this respect. Given technological advances and more open national frontiers in Europe, international terrorism is a problem which could become of increasing concern in the not-too-distant future. The development of more culturally and ethnically diverse societies in Western Europe – including the existence of substantial minorities of Muslim immigrants in some countries – gives the problem yet another dimension, as the Salman Rushdie affair illustrates.

5. *Access to Natural Resources and Markets.* Of major concern to the industrialised countries is their ability to ensure regular supplies of the raw materials and mineral resources essential to the functioning of modern, developed societies. In this respect, oil and gas are particularly important, but other metallic minerals (such as manganese, vanadium, chromium and cobalt) are of strategic importance too.[39] Supplies of such vital natural resources – or the sea-lanes along which they must travel – could be interrupted by war, revolutionary chaos, 'anti-imperialist' blockades or outbreaks of 'economic nationalism'.[40]

Conclusion

The winding down of the East–West conflict, therefore, and the disintegration of important elements of the post-war security order, have fundamentally changed the security agenda in Europe. In the cold war years, threat perceptions on both sides were relatively clear-cut. Today, in contrast, the potential security challenges are increasingly less straightforward: in the words of a recent French study, everything 'has turned global, diffuse and multiform'.[41] We are now facing a more differentiated set of potential 'threats' than in the bipolar days of bloc confrontation. Indeed, it is perhaps better to talk of security 'risks' and 'challenges' rather than 'threats', because the latter implies a degree of directness and immediacy which no longer applies. Many of these new security challenges are economic in character. This is not surprising, for as Lawrence Freedman has argued, 'this is the critical form of power in Europe at the moment'.[42] Military responses to such security challenges – and to the political, social and demographic challenges linked to them – are not always appropriate. The changing nature of the security agenda will undoubtedly necessitate a different system of European security than that which has existed for the last 40 years.

The evolving character of European security has stimulated a lively debate on the future 'architecture' of the continent. As Europe moves 'beyond containment', security arrangements developed in the 1950s and 1960s have become increasingly anachronistic. In this situation, the competences and powers of existing bodies – such as NATO, the EC, the CSCE, the WTO, etc. – are being rigorously examined, whilst proposals for radically new structures of European security are proliferating. At this moment in its history, therefore, Europe stands at a crossroads. We are faced with a number of difficult questions: what institutional ensemble or pattern of security relations will best be able to cope with the changing security agenda in Europe? What will be the role of the superpowers in this new Europe? What sort of military forces are necessary, and what will be the balance between military power, on the one hand, and economic and political instruments of diplomacy on the other?

In the second part of this book, we shall consider in greater detail the key determinants of change in the European security system. These key determinants are: the revolutionary upheavals in the USSR; political and economic developments in the post-communist regimes of Eastern Europe; the process of integration in Western Europe and the future evolution of transatlantic relations; the role of a united Germany in the new Europe; and the restructuring of military forces and alliance systems in the continent. It is developments in these five crucial areas that will determine the nature of European security in 2010. By assessing their possible trajectories and interactions, as well as the relationship between domestic change and international behaviour, we can arrive at more informed judgements about the likely direction of change in the European security system.

Notes

1. E. Powell, 'Return to an Older Pattern of Europe', *The Guardian*, 7 December 1987.
2. On the history of nuclear weapons and their impact on international relations, see John Newhouse, *The Nuclear Age: From Hiroshima to Star Wars* (London: Michael Joseph, 1989), and Lawrence Freedman, *The Evolution of Nuclear Strategy* (London: Macmillan, 1983).
3. '... the existence of nuclear weapons has tended to slow down the normal evolution of events, to prevent revolutions and wars, to freeze what would have otherwise been considered unacceptable situations'. Pierre Hassner, *Change and Security in Europe*, Part I (London: the Institute for Strategic Studies, 1968), p. 6. Raymond Aron also argued that nuclear weapons led to the 'deceleration of history' in Europe; see Alastair Buchan, *Europe's Futures, Europe's Choices* (London: Chatto & Windus, 1969), p. 155.
4. R.D. Vine, ed., *Soviet–East European Relations as a Problem for the West* (London: Croom Helm, 1987), p. 33.
5. Binter, 'In Search of Peace and Security: The Potential of Neutrality', in *Europe: Dimensions of Peace*, edited by Björn Hettne (London: Zed Books for the United Nations University, 1988), pp. 235–48.

6. See Bo Huldt, ed., *Neutrals in Europe: Austria* (Stockholm: The Swedish Institute of International Affairs, 1987).

7. As Anton Deportes has argued, 'the superpowers not only eventually managed to define their own mutual relations in Europe but in the process, and as a by-product of it, also established a system of relationships with and among the countries of Europe, their own allies and dependants, and those of the other'; *Europe Between the Superpowers* (New Haven, CT: Yale University Press, 1979), p. 116.

8. More significantly perhaps, the Report of the 'Committee of the Three' on non-military cooperation in NATO (which was approved by the North Atlantic Council on 13 December 1956), recommended that any dispute between member countries which has not proved capable of direct settlement should be submitted to good offices procedures within the NATO framework, before resorting to any other international agency (except for economic and legal disputes). They also advised that the Secretary General should be empowered to offer his good offices to the countries in dispute and, with their consent, to initiate or facilitate procedures of enquiry, mediation, conciliation or arbitration. See *The North Atlantic Treaty Organization, Facts and Figures*, published under the auspices of the Secretary General (Brussels: Nato Information Service, 1989), p. 187.

9. J. Joffe, 'Europe's American Pacifier', *Foreign Affairs*, vol. 54 (Spring 1984), p. 178.

10. Although the two alliance systems are symmetrical in terms of their structural functions in the post-war security system, they are asymmetrical in that the Western alliance has rested primarily on consent, the Warsaw Pact largely on coercion.

11. Anton Deporte, *op. cit.*, p. 244.

12. Robert G. Kaiser, 'The USSR in Decline', *Foreign Affairs*, vol. 61, no. 2 (Winter 1988/89), pp. 97–113.

13. As President Gorbachev said at the November 1990 CSCE Summit in Paris, the major changes in international relations in previous year were due in no small part to the historic turn in the Soviet Union 'from totalitarianism to freedom and democracy, from the administer-by-command system to a law-governed state and political pluralism, from state monopoly in the economy to diverse and equal forms of ownership and market relations, and from a unitary country to a union of sovereign states based on the principles of a federation .... While remaining a great country, my country has become different and will never be its old self again. We have opened up to the world, and the world has opened up to us. This predetermined the radical turn in international relations, a turn towards a fundamentally different perception by states of one another'. Quoted in *Soviet News*, Wednesday, 21 November 1990, p. 385.

14. William Wallace, *The Transformation of Western Europe* (London: Pinter for the RIIA, 1990), Chapter 6.

15. See A. Hyde-Price and William Wallace, 'Specific West European Contribution to the Shaping of East–West Relations', in *Inside the European Pillar: Integration and Security in Western Europe*, edited by M. Jopp et al. (forthcoming).

16. Robert Hormats, 'Redefining Europe and the Atlantic Link', in *Foreign Affairs*, vol. 68, no. 4 (Fall 1989), pp. 71–91.

17. On 12 December 1989, James Baker gave a speech in West Berlin calling for a new political role for NATO, and proposed that the USA and the EC should try to achieve 'a significantly strengthened set of institutional and consultative links'; see *Keesing's Record of World Events*, vol. 35, no. 12 (1989), p. 37108.

18. Giscard d'Estaing, Y. Nakasone and H. Kissinger, *East–West Relations: A Task Force Report to the Trilateral Commission* (New York: The Trilateral Commission, 1990), p. 1.

19. In his seminal book on post-war Europe, Anton Deporte, whilst acknowledging the 'high cost and many victims' of the post-war security system, argued that it is not clear that 'it would have been possible to bring about a state of affairs in Europe that would have been better than the one we have known since 1945 – better for peace, which was preserved despite tensions threatening war; better for the states of Europe as such, whose independence could no longer be maintained in the old European state system but has been preserved, in however limited a way, in the new; better, even, for the "greatest good of the greatest number" of the peoples of Europe in terms of the liberal democratic values which I hold.' *op. cit.*, p. xi.

20. Michael Cox, 'From the Truman Doctrine to the Second Superpower Detente: The Rise and Fall of the Cold War', *Journal of Peace Research*, vol. 27, no. 1 (1990), pp. 25–41.

21. Peter Tarnoff, 'Why All this Sudden Nostalgia for the Cold War', in the *International Herald Tribune*, 20 September 1989, p. 4.

22. From a speech at Georgetown University, 13 September 1989; quoted in the *New York Times*, 13 September 1989, pp. 1, 6.

23. Francis Fukuyama, 'The End of History', in *The National Interest* (Summer 1989), pp. 3–18.

24. Gian Giacomo Migone, 'The Decline of the Bipolar System, or a Second Look at the History of the Cold War', in *The New Detente*, edited by M. Kaldor et al. (London: Verso, 1989), p. 162.

25. The existence of weapons of mass destruction created a national security bureaucracy and an ideology which strengthened the state at the expense of individual rights; see Barry Buzan, *People, States and Fear* (Brighton: Wheatsheaf, 1983), pp. 21–34, and Philip Lawrence, 'Nuclear Strategy and Political Theory: A Critical Assessment', in *Review of International Studies*, vol. 11, no. 2 (1985), pp. 105–21.

26. The primary significance of the 1956 ban of the KPD (the Communist Party of Germany) was that it illegalised many of the issues and campaigns that the KPD had been associated with. For a critique of the *Berufsverbot*, see Claudia von Braunmuhl, 'The "Enemy Within" – The Case of the *Berufsverbot*', in *The Socialist Register 1978*, edited by R. Miliband and J. Saville (London: Merlin Press, 1978), pp. 56–70.

27. See for example Peter Wright, *Spycatcher: The Candid Autobiography of a Senior Intelligence Officer* (London: Viking, 1987).

28. See the excellent study by Roy Allison and Phil Williams (eds), *Superpower Competition and Crisis Prevention in the Third World* (Cambridge: Cambridge University Press, 1990).

29. For a more sustained critique of Fukuyama's 'end of history' optimism, see Samuel Huntington, 'No Exit: The Errors of Endism', in *The National Interest*, vol. 17 (Fall 1989), pp. 3–11.

30. M. Cox, 'The Cold War System', *Critique*, no. 17 (1986), pp. 17–82. Michael Cox's notion of the cold war as a 'system' can rightly be criticised for understating the degree of contestation and rivalry which existed between East and West throughout the cold war years. These issues are discussed at greater length in the debate between Edward Thompson and Fred Halliday on 'The Ends of the Cold War', in the *New Left Review*, no. 182 (July/August 1990), pp. 139–50.

31. Professor Lawrence Freedman has suggested that, with the winding down of the East–West conflict, the danger is that the 'traditional patterns of European politics, which managed to produce two world wars this century, will reassert themselves and take over from the straightforward alliance confrontation. The question of German reunification – producing a pre-eminent power in Central Europe – will have to be addressed and mechanisms will have to be developed for handling disputes between European states that had hitherto been managed through the alliance system; see *Nuclear War and Nuclear Peace*, edited by G. Segal, E. Moreton and L. Freedman, second edition (London: Macmillan, 1988), p. 123.

32. In 1989, for example, approximately one million people moved from the East to the West – the biggest shift in the continent's population since the immediate post-war years. The majority were ethnic Germans from the Soviet Union and Eastern Europe, but the figure includes 320,000 'Bulgarian Muslims', who fled to Turkey. These shifts in population produced some adverse reactions for the host nations, particularly in West Germany. See Edward Steen, 'East Europe votes with its feet', *The Independent*, 2 September 1989, p. 1.

33. See Zbigniew Brzezinski, 'Post-Communist Nationalism', *Foreign Affairs*, vol. 68, no. 5 (Winter 1989/90), pp. 1–25.

34. M. Howard, 'The Remaking of Europe', *Survival*, vol. XXXII, no. 2 (March/April 1990), pp. 99–106 (p. 105).

35. A process of 'controlled nuclear proliferation' (to include Germany) has actually been advocated by John Mearsheimer, in his article, 'Back to the Future: Instability in Europe after the Cold War', *International Security*, vol. 15, no. 1 (Summer 1990), pp. 5–56. Unfortunately the author shows little understanding of the political realities of post-cold war Europe, or of the nature of interdependence in the continent.

36. M. Howard, *op. cit.*, p. 103.

37. The countries most affected so far are France, Spain and Italy, where racial tensions have been escalating. A new form of 'boat people' is now crossing the Straits of Gibraltar, and as the Iron Curtain comes down in parts of Europe, a part of the border between France and Italy is being sealed off with barbed wire, armed patrols, torch squads and undercover policemen, in an effort to staunch a rising tide of illegal immigration from the Third World; *The Sunday Correspondent*, 24 September 1989, p. 13. See also 'The Would-be Europeans', *The Economist*, 4 August 1990, pp. 12–13.

38. The chilling reality of this threat was demonstrated in Paris at the trial of 10 Islamic fundamentalists charged with plotting the bombing which killed 13 people and wounded 255 in the city. The leader of the gang opened the court proceedings by proclaiming, 'I am called Death to the West'. He went on to announce that 'I am a terrorist. The Koran says, "Terrorise the enemies of God". Our children are dying of hunger while you eat caviare. Muslims arise!

Strike at the nuclear power stations and the chemical weapons factories!'. In reply to the prosecution's questions, he replied, 'Your questions don't interest me. What interests me are the crimes of the West for which you will be punished without pity right up to the extermination of the last white man from the planet. Judeo-Christians, Greco-Romans, whites and Westerners .... You will find no refuge!'. See 'Politics and the Bombers', Patrick Marnham, *The Independent*, 3 February 1989, p. 17.

39. A study on the strategic requirements of the US Army notes for example that, 'The heavy reliance of the United States and other industrial democracies on minerals imported from the region of Africa southward from Zaire is undisputed'. Quoted by Mariano Aguirre, 'Looking Southwards', in *European Security in the 1990s*, edited by Dan Smith (London: Pluto, 1989), p. 135.

40. See William Gutteridge, *The Case for Regional Security: Avoiding Conflict in the 1990s*, Conflict Studies 217 (London: The Centre for Security and Conflict Studies, 1989), pp. 18–25.

41. Claude Nigoul and Maurice Torrelli, *Menaces en Méditerranée* (Paris: Fondation pour les Etudes de Défense Nationale, 1987), p. 27.

42. L. Freedman, 'Architecture with Eurovision', *The Independent*, 8 March 1990.

PART II
The Determinants of Change

4

Soviet *Perestroika* and the 'New Political Thinking'

There is no doubting the historic importance of Soviet *perestroika*. Nor of the extraordinary role played by Mikhail Gorbachev in transforming the face of contemporary Europe. Gorbachev's programme of *perestroika*, *glasnost* and *demokratizatsiya* – along with its foreign policy corollary, the 'new political thinking' – has had a profound and irrevocable impact on all aspects of Soviet society and its relations with the outside world. An attempt has been made to drag the Soviet people from the lethargy of the Brezhnev 'years of stagnation' towards a breath-taking venture in societal rejuvenation. With a deteriorating economic situation, growing political instability and resurgent nationalism, the very future of the Soviet state is now in doubt. Indeed, the Soviet Union's accelerating slide into chaos is currently the major source of concern and instability in post-cold war Europe.

The purpose of this chapter is to consider the possible impact of the Soviet reform process on the European security system. We shall begin by considering the role of the USSR in post-war Europe, and will then go on to assess the nature of the domestic reform package, and the implications for Europe of the 'new political thinking'. Finally, we will consider a range of scenarios for the future development of the USSR.

Russia, the USSR and Europe

Since the eighteenth century, Russia has played an important part in the European balance of power system – as Russia's defeat of Napoleon's armies in 1812 underlines. The Tsarist Empire had long-standing geopolitical interests in the Baltic, Eastern Europe and the Balkans. With the success of the Bolsheviks in October 1917, however, Soviet Russia began to play a qualitatively new role in European politics. The USSR emerged as the bastion of a new international political movement – the Comintern – based on an all-encompassing ideological *Weltanschauung*, and committed to the revolutionary transformation of the prevailing world order. This gave an ideological dimension to the new state's conflict with its traditional and more contemporary rivals, and meant that, initially at least, the Soviet Union was unwilling to accept the traditional rules of international diplomacy and power politics.[1] Soviet foreign policy has thus been driven by two distinctive motivations – geostrategic interests and Marxist-Leninist ideology – which have often coexisted in an uneasy dialectical tension, given that they tend to set different agendas for the conduct and goals of foreign policy.[2]

The Red Army's defeat of Nazi aggression in the 'Great Patriotic War' fundamentally transformed the situation of the Soviet Union in Europe. By virtue of its military success, the USSR acquired a decisive say in the politics of east-central and south-eastern Europe. The strengthening of communist parties in many West European countries – itself stimulated by the often heroic role played by communists in the wartime resistance – further amplified Moscow's influence on European affairs. The break-down of the wartime alliance of the 'Big Three' was undoubtedly a set-back for Stalin's hopes of a period of international cooperation in which the Soviets could rebuild their shattered society and economy. Nevertheless, as a result of the Second World War, the USSR achieved a number of historic gains: firstly, secure frontiers within what the Soviet leadership regarded as its legitimate and natural borders; secondly, the ending of its international isolation, and the creation of a belt of 'friendly' states across its new western borders; thirdly, a neutering of German power and an influential voice on the future of the German nation; and finally, the subsequent creation of a 'socialist community' based on the CMEA and the Warsaw Pact.

Soviet behaviour in the post-war international system has been the subject of considerable controversy. In order to illustrate the range of mainstream Western analyses of Soviet foreign policy in Europe, we can refer to four broadly drawn typologies.[3] First, that of the '**Great Beast of the Revelation**', in which the Soviet Union is seen as deeply purposeful, devious and expansionist; an aggressive and amoral 'evil empire', motivated, in Angela Stent's words, by 'one basic desideratum: to divide and influence, if not conquer, Europe'.[4] Second, the Soviet state as a '**Mellowing Tiger**': a post-revolutionary regime gradually losing its ideological fervour and messianic drive, and evolving into a status quo, rather than revisionist, power. This interpretation of Stalinism underpinned George Kennan's thinking in 1947, when he argued that the contradictions within the Soviet Union would eventually lead to a 'mellowing' of Soviet power.[5] Third, the USSR as a '**Neurotic Bear**', its neuroses being rooted in centuries of turbulence and geographical exposure – 'a dark, bloody, and tumultuous tapestry of success and failure, conquests and staggering defeats, occupations and losses of blood and land'.[6] In the immediate post-war years, the economic weakness of the Soviet Union and its strategic vulnerability to US nuclear forces gave a further twist to the historically grounded neuroses of the Russian bear.[7] Finally, there is the revisionists' and apologists' view of the Soviet Union as an **'Injured lamb'**, the innocent victim of unrelenting imperialist aggression. Like the 'Great Beast of the Revelation' image (of which it is the mirror twin), that of the 'Injured Lamb' fails to capture the complexities and ambiguities of the Soviet Union's position in the post-war international system.[8] Perhaps the most appropriate way of conceiving of the foreign policy behaviour of the Soviet state is as a mellowing – but understandably neurotic – bear.

By the 1980s, it seemed as if this mellowing but neurotic bear was undergoing a nervous break-down, as a result of its exertions in attempting to compete with a healthier and more dynamic set of rivals. Indeed, the very sources of Soviet post-war strength in Europe (its hegemony in Eastern Europe and its massed concentration of forward-deployed armoured forces in the region) were proving more of a liability than an asset. Soviet domination of Eastern Europe and its substantial investment in offensive armoured divisions – coupled with the repression of its domestic critics – gave substance to Western perceptions of a 'Soviet threat'. In the end, Soviet policy proved counter-productive: it promoted cohesion in the Atlantic Alliance; it stimulated closer West European integration and security cooperation; and it hindered access to Western markets, technology and know-how. Eastern Europe itself – the 'jewel in the crown' of the Soviet empire – proved to be neither economically effective nor politically stable. In the Third World, Soviet advances in the 1970s brought only limited political gains at considerable economic cost, and further complicated relations with the West. With the INF deployments and the SDI initiative, along with growing US assertiveness around the world (embodied in the 'Reagan doctrine'), Soviet foreign policy-makers were forced to undertake a major reassessment of the substance and assumptions of their *Westpolitik*. By the mid-1980s, in other words, the USSR was coming to realise that it had effectively lost the 'Great contest' with the capitalist world, and had therefore to devise a new approach to the West.

From *Uskorenie* to *Perestroika*

In March 1985, after a debilitating interregnum, Mikhail Sergeyevich Gorbachev was elected General Secretary of the CPSU. His accession to power amounted to a recognition by the Soviet elite of the urgent need for structural reform of 'developed socialism'. Without major reform, it was feared, the Soviet Union would fast become 'Upper Volta with missiles'. Gorbachev's brief, therefore, was to reverse the pattern of decline, and to initiate a programme of reform designed to reinvigorate Soviet society.

Gorbachev began by introducing an Andropov-style package of economic *uskorenie* ('acceleration') and greater social discipline. As he consolidated his power base, however, and became aware of the enormity of the problems facing the Soviet Union, his reform programme became increasingly radical and comprehensive. By the time of the 27th CPSU Congress in February 1986, two key themes had emerged: *perestroika* ('restructuring') and *glasnost* ('openness').[9] In January 1987 at the Central Committee Plenary meeting, a new front was opened - *demokratizatsiya* ('democratisation'). Another landmark was the XIX Extraordinary Party Conference in June 1988 which resulted in radical political and constitutional reform.[10] Since then, events have developed with startling rapidity, as the process of political and economic transformation has acquired an accelerating momentum of its own. Previously constrained centrifugal and disintegrative forces have been unleashed, which are threatening to overwhelm the very process of restructuring itself. The effect of *perestroika* has been fatally to undermine central planning and the one-party system, but to date, no politically legitimate or economically effective structures have emerged to take their place. Indeed, Yuri Bondarev has compared *perestroika* with 'a plane that had taken off without any idea of where it was going to land'.[11]

Economic Reform

At the heart of the Gorbachev reform programme is the attempt to achieve economic *perestroika*. On this hangs the success or failure of all other aspects of the reform programme. Without a visible improvement in the living standards of the Soviet people, the Soviet Union is doomed to sink further into political turmoil and nationalist unrest. One does not have to be a Marxist to realise that the economy is, 'in the last instance', the determining factor in the outcome of the reform process.

The problems of the Soviet economy are as intractable as they are many. Basically, the 'command-administrative system' has failed to cope with the demands of intensive growth and the 'scientific and technological revolution'. Decades of forced industrialisation created 'a giant with enormous bone and muscles but with the circulation and nervous system of an infant'.[12] The system of fixed prices has produced what the economist Nikolai Shmelev calls a 'kingdom of distorting mirrors',[13] and the lack of a market mechanism has resulted in a costly squandering of resources. The USSR's failure to participate in the growing internationalisation of economic life has further stunted its development: the Soviet economy has been slipping further and further behind the capitalist West, and is in danger of being overtaken by the East Asian NICs.

The long-term aim of the *perestroika* project is to develop a functioning 'regulated market economy', fully integrated into the global economy, and capable of generating intensive patterns of growth on the basis of higher labour productivity. This necessitates – at the very least – price liberalisation and currency convertibility; enterprise autonomy and self-financing (*khozrashchet*); the break-up of large monopoly producers and substantial privatisation; an expansion of the private sector (especially in service industries); agricultural reform (involving an extension of the leasing system, *arendnye podryady*); and the development of a functioning capital market, banking system and financial infrastructure.[14] The problem which has prevented effective reform to date, however, is this: how to move from central planning to a market-orientated economic system, without thereby producing a total collapse of the economy and widespread political unrest?

By late summer 1990, two main schools of thought had crystallised on this question within the Soviet Union: the radical Shatalin '500-Day Plan' which followed the Polish example of a 'short, sharp shock'; and the rival plan, favoured by the Soviet Prime Minister Nikolai Ryzhkov, which proposed a more gradual and 'administered' transition to capitalist market relations.[15] A compromise document was presented to the Soviet Parliament in October 1990, but by then the country's precipitate economic collapse and political fragmentation had made a coherent plan for economic reform increasingly academic. There is, unfortunately, no simple solution to the Soviet Union's economic problems, as the joint report by the IMF, World Bank, OECD, EBRD and the EC Commission in November 1990 made painfully clear. Economic reform will be even more difficult to achieve in the Soviet Union than in other CMEA countries given the sheer size of the USSR, and the impact of seven decades of 'socialist construction' on the attitudes and assumptions of Soviet citizens. Soviet economic reform is in danger of being overwhelmed by both inertia and spontaneity: inertia from ingrained habits and vested interests (above all, those of the bloated *apparat*) and spontaneity from the popular unrest which economic reform is provoking (particularly from industrial workers and the trade unions[16]). Soviet workers are being asked to change their attitudes to work and remuneration in exchange for promises of a better life tomorrow – yet to date, *perestroika* has only meant declining living standards, higher prices, greater job insecurity and lengthening queues.

Economic reform has been made much more impossible by the political and constitutional impasse that has arisen between the central government and the republics. The political fragmentation of the Soviet Union has generated growing dislocations in the economy, and has contributed to the steadily worsening conditions facing Soviet consumers. The economic prospects for the next 5–10 years are thus not good: at best, the government can hope to slow the trend towards economic decline and begin a process of industrial recovery; at worst, economic dislocation and disruption will intensify, with all the attendant social and political problems that

that implies. The appalling economic problems of the USSR therefore constitute a bleak and unpromising back-drop for Soviet reformers as they struggle to democratise their political system and contain the centrifugal tendencies unleashed by rising nationalism.

Glasnost and Demokratizatsiya

Political reform has become the most dynamic element of the Soviet reform process. Although initially regarded as a tool for facilitating economic modernisation, it has acquired a momentum of its own. *Glasnost* itself was originally seen as a way of exposing the errors of the past and of mobilising social forces (in the first place, the intelligentsia) behind the reform process. Given the innumerable grievances of the Soviet peoples, however, it has unleashed a flood-tide of pent-up frustration and criticism, which now threatens to engulf the whole *perestroika* project.

Linked to the policy of *glasnost* is *demokratizatsiya* ('democratisation'). Having recognised the problems of bureaucracy, authoritarianism, arbitrariness and corruption, Gorbachev has attempted a more fundamental reform of the political system. The aim has been to shift power from the communist *apparatchiki* to the soviets and other elected bodies. The middle-level bureaucracy (the main obstacle to reform) was to be squeezed from two sides: from above by a reformist leadership, and from below by an increasingly assertive populace. A watershed in this respect was the June 1988 IX Party Conference. This prepared the way for competitive elections to a revamped Congress of Peoples Deputies. This body in turn has quickly developed into a lively forum for vigorous debate and discussion.[17]

The consequence of these reforms for the Soviet political system has been growing political turbulence. *Glasnost* and democratisation have fatally undermined the old bureaucratic-authoritarian structures – based on the leading role of the CPSU and democratic centralism. But they have not yet created a functioning parliamentary democracy based on the rule of law – indeed, they have not yet established an institutionally coherent and effectively functioning political system of any kind. Instead they have greatly confused the decision-making process, not least because of the proliferation of competing power centres (including the Federation Council, the Congress of Peoples Deputies, the Party apparatus, the Union Republics, the local soviets, etc.). Civil society has sprung into life, and a nascent pluralist system has been created, but the result to date has been growing confusion over institutional competences and responsibilities. The necessary rules and regulations, codes of behaviour and underlying societal consensus for a flourishing pluralist democracy have not yet evolved. In this situation, there is a very real danger of the sort of 'praetorian politics' characteristic of Weimar Germany or Taisho Japan:

in other words, of strong political groupings and assertive social forces, but weak and ineffectual institutions.[18] Indeed, there is a growing body of opinion – both within the Soviet Union and without – which believes that the country is 'poised between coup or chaos'.[19] Given the immaturity of the evolving forms of interest articulation and integration, a period of sustained and acute political instability in the Soviet Union is inevitable – with all the uncertainty that this implies for Europe's evolving security structures.

Nationalism

It now seems chillingly apparent that Gorbachev's biggest single mistake since 1985 has been to underestimate the emotive appeal and political importance of nationalism. It is a problem that, in President Gorbachev's own words, will determine 'the fate of *perestroika* and the destiny of our state'.[20] The USSR is the last great multinational empire in the World: of its 286 million inhabitants, just under 50 per cent are non-Russian. It contains 15 Union Republics, constituted along national lines, but is in fact a mosaic of over 170 ethnic groups and several hundred language and dialect groups. President Gorbachev has proposed a new Union Treaty, aimed at establishing a new set of federal relations between Moscow and the republics.[21] But economic crisis has fuelled the national tensions which *glasnost* has aired, and as the process of *demokratizatsiya* gathers pace, demands for secession are growing. Indeed, the 'Soviet Union' has become a contradiction in terms, as the 'prison-house of the nations' teeters on the brink of becoming the 'battlefield of the nations'.[22] One by one, the republics have declared their independence from Moscow. The country has begun to split into autarkic fragments, worsening the economic crisis. In the early 1990s, therefore, the decisive political issue facing President Gorbachev will be maintaining the integrity of the Soviet Union as a federal state, whilst defining the future status and responsibilities of its constituent republics and autonomous regions.

The nationalities problem in the USSR has three distinct dimensions to it. Firstly, a 'vertical' dimension: the nationalism of the non-Russian peoples, which expresses itself in opposition to perceived domination by Moscow.[23] This is evident in most of the Union Republics to varying degrees, and has acquired a political expression in the various 'Popular Fronts': it is most developed in the three Baltics, Georgia, the western Ukraine, Moldova and the Central Asian republics of Azerbaijan and Uzbekistan. Secondly, a 'horizontal' dimension: between neighbouring non-Russian peoples. Examples here include the simmering civil war between the Armenians and the Azeris over the disputed enclave of Nagorno-Karabakh; the bitter conflicts between the Georgians and minority groups like the Abkhazins and Ossetians in Georgia (an otherwise fairly homogeneous Republic);[24] and in Moldova, where in October 1990 ethnic Romanians clashed with the Gaugauz, a small Christian Turkic community of 150,000.

The third dimension of the nationalities problem in the Soviet Union is Russian nationalism itself: this is a complex phenomenon, which is evolving rapidly in the face of non-Russian nationalism. As the British know only too well, every once mighty nation facing a retreat from empire suffers a crisis of identity: this is particularly traumatic for a nuclear superpower, which for decades has believed that 'history' is on its side. In recent years, an intense struggle for the political soul of Russian nationalism has been developing – between the more democratic and 'enlightened' elements of the nationalist movement (who would like to see Russia give up its imperial pretensions and concentrate on the spiritual, ecological and economic renaissance of the Russian people), and the more chauvinistic, anti-Western, anti-semitic and conservative elements (of which the *Pamyat'* and *Otechestvo* societies are the most extreme manifestation).[25] The crucial question is where the centre of gravity of Russian nationalism will form as a result of these controversies, and how Russian nationalism will relate to the rest of the political spectrum. Indeed, the future evolution of Russian nationalism has become one of the most important factors determining both the future of the Soviet state, and the nature of East–West security relations in the new Europe.

Given the historical legacy of centuries of Russian domination, and the worsening economic crisis, demands for secession are bound to grow. Some now believe that Moscow may even consider allowing some of the non-Russian nations to leave the USSR. A new Law on Secession has been passed to give substance to the constitutional right to secede (under Article 72 of the 1977 Constitution). A complicating factor, however, is the presence of over 25 million Russians in the other non-Russian Union Republics, and the existence of a further 40 million non-Russians who live outside of their ethnic territories. This raises the danger of not simply the 'balkanisation' of the Soviet Union, but its 'lebanonisation' (ie, protracted inter-communal, ethnic strife).

In the end, the future viability of the Soviet state depends above all on the way nationalism develops in its Slavic heartlands – Russia, Byelorussia, Ukraine and Kazakhstan (which, despite its Central Asian location, has a Slav majority). Even without Georgia and Armenia, the Baltic Republics and the other Central Asian SSRs, the Slavic rump of the Soviet Union would remain a mighty industrial, agricultural and military power. If, however, the Ukraine (with its 50 million citizens and vast agriculture and natural resources) and Byelorussia were to secede, the Soviet state would no longer be viable. Russia would still be an important European great power, but it would no longer be the global superpower the USSR once was. The future of the Soviet state as a significant international actor will therefore depend on the developing relationship between the various nationalist forces in its Slavic core.

Novoe Myshlenie ('New Political Thinking')

The depth of the domestic crisis facing the Soviet leadership has resulted in a profound reassessment of the goals and methods of Soviet foreign policy. The theoretical expression of this foreign policy *aggiornamento* is the 'new political thinking'. The roots of this *novoe myshlenie* lie more with nineteenth-century Russian universalist thinking, Scandinavian social democracy, Christian liberation theology and Western international relations discourse than they do with traditional Marxism-Leninism – which itself symbolises how fundamental has been the Soviet re-evaluation of its relations with the outside world.[26]

Central to the 'new thinking' is the emphasis on global interdependence, common security and the need for a more cooperative international approach to common problems (such as Third World underdevelopment, AIDS and environmental pollution). This has involved a radical reassessment of the relationship between class interests and 'all-human' issues, and a redefinition of 'peaceful coexistence'(which is no longer seen as a 'specific form of the class struggle').[27] At the same time, Gorbachev has stressed the need to rethink the nature of security in the nuclear age, and to demilitarise East–West relations.[28]

The *novoe myshlenie* has been associated with a series of important developments in Soviet foreign policy. There have been a number of significant institutional[29] and personnel changes in the foreign policy establishment, and a plethora of new international initiatives. These include, *inter alia*, the February 1988 Geneva accords on Afghanistan; the Soviet Union's more positive approach towards international organisations like the UN,[30] UNESCO, GATT, the IMF and the World Bank; the formal recognition of the EC; new approaches to regional disputes in Indochina, southern Africa and the Middle East; a series of compromises on arms control issues; and finally, Sino-Soviet rapprochement.[31] Of particular interest, however, is the Soviet Union's new approach to Europe. Here, the shift in Soviet policy was linked to Gorbachev's adoption of the concept 'Common European House'.

Gorbachev and the 'Common European House'

When Mikhail Gorbachev became General-Secretary, there were indications that Western Europe would be accorded a higher priority than in the past, and that Soviet relations with the West Europeans would not simply be viewed as an appendage of US–USSR relations. These hopes were bolstered by personnel changes,[32] and the establishment of a new foreign policy think-tank, the 'Institute for Europe'. Despite this, however, Soviet *Westpolitik* continued to exhibit its traditional American focus during Gorbachev's first two years in office. It was only in 1987 – Moscow's 'Year of Europe' – that Soviet policy towards Western Europe became more dynamic and innovative.[33]

Gorbachev's more active *Europapolitik* is associated above all with his description of Europe as 'our common house' (*nash obshchii dom*[34]) – a notion first used by Leonid Brezhnev in 1981.[35] Initially, it seemed that this notion was little more than an ill-thought out slogan – a thin veneer covering traditional anti-American 'wedge-driving', combined with a renewed 'peace offensive'. From 1987 onwards, however, Gorbachev's European policy began to acquire more substance. Soviet negotiators became increasingly more amenable to compromise, and Moscow's position on a whole range of issues – including the role of the US in Europe, nuclear deterrence and East–West economic relations – shifted considerably over a relatively short period of time, as the Gorbachev leadership responded to many West European concerns.[36]

Gorbachev's use of the concept of a Common European House reflects a number of contemporary Soviet preoccupations. To begin with, the desire to reduce the level of military confrontation in Europe, in order to free resources for domestic restructuring and improve prospects for pan-European cooperation. Second, the wish to expand economic and trade links with Western Europe, in order to avoid being further marginalised by the '1992 process', and to facilitate the eventual integration of the USSR into the global economy. Finally, to ensure that – despite its geostrategic set backs in Eastern Europe in late 1989 – it remains a full participant in the political life of the European continent. The Soviets are particularly keen to avoid being marginalised by the integration process which is currently reshaping the contours of Europe. Both Gorbachev and former Foreign Minister Shevardnadze have stressed the importance they attach to the Council of Europe and the CSCE as a means of fostering pan-European dialogue and cooperation. The Soviets have also been amongst the foremost advocates of institutionalising the CSCE process, of giving it a more important role in Europe's post-cold war security 'architecture'.[37] Indeed, despite the continued haziness about the programmatic content of the Common European House idea, it does reflect a pressing Soviet concern: namely, not to be excluded from the new pattern of economic, political and security relationships that are developing across the continent as the East–West conflict fades away. This is a legitimate Soviet worry, and one which many Europeans – especially the Germans[38] – are increasingly aware of.

Soviet relations with Europe in the 1990s will be complicated by a number of unresolved issues. To begin with, is the USSR willing to give up its pretensions to being a global superpower, and, like

Britain before it, return to its European roots? Second (and related to the first question), can a country the size of the Soviet Union, with its very different heritage and *samobytnost* (its 'own way of being'), be included in the process of European integration in the same way as the countries of East Central Europe? Third, what are the Soviet Union's legitimate security interests in Europe, and how should they be accommodated? What are Moscow's residual security concerns in Eastern Europe? Would the Soviets feel threatened by a process of closer West European security cooperation? This problem would become particularly acute if the European Community were to develop a security and defence dimension, whilst at the same time offering Community membership to former Warsaw Pact and neutral countries. Finally, how will Soviet policy towards Germany develop? Already in the 1980s, it was clear that the FRG had come to play a pivotal role in Soviet policy towards Western Europe. A united Germany will undoubtedly become the central focus of Soviet *Europapolitik* in the 1990s and beyond.[39] Nonetheless, Soviet–German relations are likely to remain highly ambiguous and complex: on the one hand, there is the bitter memory of two World Wars; on the other, there are common strategic and political interests which have manifested themselves in centuries of Russo-German (especially Prussian) cooperation.[40] Indeed, some Europeans fear a 'new Rapallo' between a united Germany and a weakened Soviet Union. Whatever form the Soviet–German relationship takes, it will without doubt be of decisive importance for the overall security 'architecture' of the new Europe (and is an issue we will return to in Chapter 7).

Whither the Soviet Union?

The future of the USSR now depends on the outcome of the domestic struggles which Gorbachev's reform programme has brought to the surface. *Perestroika* and *demokratizatsiya* have generated a fierce struggle for power within the Soviet Union between a variety of competing political forces, from convinced Marxist-Leninists to Western-style liberal democrats, and from Catholic nationalists to Islamic fundamentalists. The fissures in Soviet society run not only between different groups – like the army or the intelligentsia – but through them: the CPSU, for example, is deeply divided between, *inter alia*, orthodox communists, Marxist reformers and social-democrats. Similarly, the army can be divided into a loose group of conservative generals, a mass of disaffected conscripts and an increasingly assertive group of junior officers and NCOs.[41] At the same time, social groups like the working class and peasantry are increasingly divided along national and ethnic lines, and by narrower sectional interests. As we have seen, these fissiparous political groupings are competing for influence within a political system which, as a result of the creation of new centres of decision-making, is suffering from worsening institutional confusion. In this situation, the process of interest articulation and integration is becoming more and more difficult.

The political spectrum in the USSR can be summarised in terms of five broad categories, corresponding to the evolving political tendencies within Soviet society. These are, first, the **'radicals'**: they consist of democratically minded and cosmopolitan liberals, who tend to look to the West for inspiration. They are currently organised in the Inter-Regional Group in the Soviet Parliament and in the 'Democratic Platform' within the CPSU. Both Moscow and Leningrad city councils are now dominated by radicals, who tend to regard Boris Yeltsin as their leading representative. Second, the **'modernisers'**: this group encompasses reformist Marxists and social-democrats, and includes Gorbachev himself.[42] Third, **'Russian nationalists'**: this is perhaps the key group, and also the most interesting but ambiguous. As we have seen, Russian nationalism is a very diverse and confusing phenomenon, which is currently in the throes of crystallising into a number of distinct tendencies. The political role of Russian nationalism will depend on where its centre of gravity comes to lie, and what sort of political alignments it forms. Fourth, **'communist conservatives'** – those who continue to draw their inspiration from the 'Great October Socialist Revolution', and who wish to retain a distinctly socialist system in the Soviet Union. This group has been represented in the CPSU leadership by Ligachev, and is organised in the 'Marxist Tendency' within the CPSU and in the 'Russian Communist Party' (formed in Leningrad in April 1990). Finally, there are the **'empire loyalists'**: ie, those who want to preserve the political and territorial integrity of the Soviet Union, for nationalist as much as ideological reasons. This group is particularly strong in sections of the army and KGB, and amongst the Russian minorities in the non-Russian Union Republics. It is represented in the Supreme Soviet by the *Soyuz* ('Unity') group, who claim 100 members: they claim to be against 'separatism, chauvinism and nationalism', and to support the rights 'of all groups, regardless of their place of residence'.[43]

Some interest groups and social forces in the Soviet Union are more represented in one category than another – e.g., the intelligentsia, who are over-represented amongst the radicals and modernisers, or the party/state *apparatchiki*, who incline more towards the conservative communists or empire loyalists. Nonetheless, in general, the political divisions increasingly cut across the various groups in Soviet society. The future development of the USSR will therefore depend on the evolving balance of forces between these competing tendencies, and on the alignments and coalitions that develop between them.

Using this rough analytical framework, one can envisage five alternative futures for the USSR:

1. *The Soviet Union evolves into a liberal-democratic, market-orientated Commonwealth of nations.* This, unfortunately, appears to be the least likely outcome of the current political struggles in the USSR: it assumes a successful outcome of *perestroika* and *demokratizatsiya*, the dominance of westernisers and modernisers within the Soviet political class, and a benign evolution of Russian nationalism.

2. *The secession of the peripheries, and a continuation of economic and political reform in Russia (or the Slavic heartlands as a whole).* This would involve an alliance of modernisers with an (externally) benign form of Russian nationalism. It is possible that this might entail a period of authoritarian rule in Russia, as a way of ensuring a stable transition to a new political and territorial reality.[44] Indeed, some proponents of reform (such as Andranik Migranyan) advocate a period of authoritarian presidential rule by Gorbachev as a way of implementing radical economic restructuring.[45] On the other hand, if liberals and westernisers develop as a strong and influential political force, then a democratic RSFSR could emerge, willing to establish normal diplomatic relations with newly independent republics on its borders – this seems to be the policy currently advocated by Boris Yeltsin.[46]

3. *A long and inconclusive period of continuing stagnation and limited reform.* This would be the likely result of a political stalemate between the forces of reform on the one hand (radicals and modernisers), and conservatism on the other (conservative communists and empire loyalists), in which neither side was able to prevail. In this context of political impasse, it might be able to stave off the complete collapse of the Soviet system for many years by marginal improvements to the economic system,[47] and a strengthening of central authority by a greater reliance on authoritarian means of rule. However, such a long and drawn-out period of gradual decline would be inherently unstable, and would be prone to intermittent crises and upheavals.[48]

4. *Authoritarian Russian nationalism at home, and the suppression of national unrest on the peripheries of the USSR.* This would signify a dramatic defeat for the radicals and modernisers, and the ascendancy of the conservative communists and empire loyalists, in league with a more authoritarian and chauvinist elements of Russian nationalism (such as *Pamyat'*). There are a number of possible variations within this scenario: (a) Gorbachev could be retained as a Bonapartist figurehead, in order to reassure the West; (b) Gorbachev could be deposed by another political leader; (c) a military coup could establish a period of martial law. It is also possible that an authoritarian nationalist regime in Moscow would allow some of the more peripheral SSRs to secede (such as Lithuania or Armenia), whilst intensifying repression of nationalist movements in other parts of the Soviet Union (especially in the Slavic heartlands and parts of Central Asia).[49] This new authoritarian regime would probably

rely on a pan-Slavic, anti-Western ideology, in which the alleged plots of 'Western imperialism' would merge with the supposed machinations of the international 'Judaeo-masonic conspiracy'. As one Russian writer has suggested, the prospect of such a 'brutal counter-reformist dictatorship' is even more chilling because it would be 'fascist nuclear dictatorship'.[50]

5. *The collapse of the Soviet Union into a protracted period of chaos, political instability and civil war.* In its most pessimistic version, this modern version of the 'Time of Troubles'[51] would involve the 'lebanonisation' of the USSR, a succession of weak governments punctuated by palace intrigues or military coups, and foreign intervention (perhaps in Central Asia). It would probably be accompanied by pogroms against the Jews and other scapegoats, and would conjure up the nightmare scenario of a break-down of civil order in a nuclear-armed state. Such grim visions of the future are becoming increasingly prevalent in the Soviet Union itself. One particularly depressing example of this genre is Alexander Kabakov's 'anti-utopian' story 'The Man Who Wouldn't Come Back', published in the journal *Art of the Cinema*. In this bleak tale, a man discovers how to travel through time, and the KGB bullies him into travelling to 1993 to assess the prospects for *perestroika*:

> Not good. After the 1991 civil war the only relic of Mikhail Gorbachev is that money is now called Gorbatti, but you need ration coupons anyway. The new boss is General Panayev who travels around in a tank while petrol shortages have put his cavalry escort on horse-back. Pamyat′ is hunting down the Jews: the skinheads are hunting down the heavy metal fans; a political group called the Levelling Committees is hunting down the bureaucrats, and the Afgantsi are hunting down everybody.[52]

Conclusion

The future of the European security system is increasingly dependent on the fate of Soviet *perestroika*. The most intractable problem facing post-cold war Europe is neither the 'German question' nor the fate of the East Europeans (important as these issues undoubtedly are), but the 'Soviet question', ie, the future of the USSR, and its role in the new Europe. Indeed, as Sergei Karaganov has argued, 'If *perestroika* fails, it is hard to conceive of the possibility of creating a peaceful order in Europe, whatever happens elsewhere'.[53]

Gorbachev has set in motion an open-ended and irreversible reform process which promises to make the USSR less like the country forged by Stalin, and less distasteful and menacing to the rest of the world. The agenda for reform that Gorbachev presented to the Soviet people is highly ambitious – perhaps impossible – and will preoccupy the Soviet leadership for many years to come. In the 1990s, the Soviet

Union faces a potentially explosive cocktail of economic decline, ethnic strife, class conflict, political polarisation and a growing sense of social injustice. It is possible that what Seweryn Bialer has called, 'the strength and the hidden reserves of the forces' defending the Soviet system will ensure that the USSR – in some form at least – survives its present convulsions.[54] Nevertheless, it seems almost certain that Soviet society will continue to experience recurrent crises for a long period to come.

The deepening crisis of Soviet society has become an issue of growing concern to the West, and a major factor of strategic uncertainty.[55] There are some fears that an embattled leadership in Moscow might seek to divert the population's attention from domestic problems by embarking on an adventurist and aggressive foreign policy. It is more likely, however, that Moscow will strive to preserve and foster a benign external environment so that it can concentrate on domestic restructuring. Nonetheless, the domestic problems in the USSR could affect the stability of Europe in a number of ways. First, there is a danger of ethnic and national conflict spilling over into surrounding countries, thereby fuelling irredentist ambitions – for example along the Romanian–Moldovan border, or between Poland and the western Ukraine. Even more alarming is the spectre of political instability and ethnic strife in Soviet Central Asia, which would bring another element of uncertainty to an already volatile region – this could ignite larger regional conflicts in Central Asia.[56] Second, social disintegration in the Soviet Union would be destabilising for the West in both economic terms (given the loss of markets, investments and financial instability this would entail) and demographically (given the inevitable surge forward in emigration by Jews, ethnic Germans and others).

If a durable peace order in Europe is to develop, it is essential that the Soviet Union does not feel excluded from the evolving patterns of economic and political exchange in the continent. The Gorbachev leadership has placed great emphasis on developing a more open and cooperative relationship with the West – especially in Europe – and if the impression were to be given that the capitalist world was simply shifting the boundaries of the East–West conflict eastwards from the River Elbe to the Bug, this would only strengthen the nationalist and conservative opposition to the reform programme. It would be equally short-sighted to take advantage of the USSR's current weakness in order to force disadvantageous settlements on the Soviet leadership: this would only generate a 'Versailles syndrome' in Moscow, and as the experience of the inter-war years shows, a stable European order cannot be constructed which includes major revisionist powers harbouring national resentments.

Nevertheless, incorporating the Soviet Union in the new Europe will not be an easy task, given the sheer size of the country and its historically ambivalent relationship to the European heartland (a function of its geographical location on Europe's periphery and its distinctive cultural traditions). Whatever the outcome of its current reform endeavours, the USSR will remain a major military power, and, as Michael Howard has suggested, 'at least for the time being, an alien power .... it may take a generation of sustained reciprocal effort before we can really treat them in the same fashion as we do one another'.[57] This, however, demands positive, concerted and sustained Western support for the Soviet reform process. Although the success or failure of Soviet *perestroika* depends primarily on the Soviet people themselves, the effects of external stimulants and supports are by no means insignificant.

The West can help establish a more conducive and supportive international environment for the Soviet reforms in a number of ways. First, by adopting a constructive approach to arms control negotiations; developing a comprehensive verification regime based on military transparency; and considering very carefully before introducing new weapon systems or military doctrines that seem to threaten the Soviet Union's legitimate security concerns. Second, by facilitating the USSR's gradual integration into the global economy and international institutions like GATT, the World Bank and the IMF, and by closer association with the European Community. In this respect, the announcement in December 1990 that the World Bank and the IMF have proposed a 'special association' for the USSR is to be warmly welcomed.[58] Third, by helping to develop an institutional framework for multilateral negotiation and diplomacy on a broad range of political and security questions: both the UN and the Council of Europe have a useful role to play here, but an organisation of growing importance in this respect will be the CSCE, which, after the November 1990 Paris Summit, can begin to provide an ideal framework for pan-European dialogue and cooperation. Finally, by expanding contacts and cooperation at all levels. This could include, *inter alia*, the involvement of the USSR in international research and development projects; exanding academic and student exchanges; facilitating travel and international communications; and by encouraging the diffusion of management skills, 'know-how' and specialist training. By such means, it might be possible to enmesh the Soviet Union in a web of deepening interdependencies, in ways which provide positive encouragement for domestic restructuring. Given the historic importance of the transformations currently under way in the USSR, a policy of excessive 'prudence', 'caution' and 'restraint'[59] would not necessarily be the wisest approach. On the contrary, the historic opportunity for a radical improvement of the situation in Europe and the wider international system, opened up by the democratic renovation of Soviet society, demands of Western leaders a policy of vision, generosity and boldness to match that of President

Gorbachev himself.

Notes

1. When Leon Trotsky became the new state's Commissar for Foreign Affairs, he declared that he would simply issue a few proclamations, and then shut up shop. But as Klaus von Beyme remarks, '"The Shop" which Trotsky … promised to shut up, has grown into the most powerful foreign policy apparatus in the world'!; see his study, *The Soviet Union in World Politics* (Aldershot: Gower, 1987), p. 22.

2. Adam B. Ulam has argued that Marxism-Leninism has not so much given Soviet leaders a plan for changing the world as a prism for looking at it. This, in itself, is of great importance, in that perception is a crucial factor in determining the goals and methods of policy-makers; *Expansion and Coexistence: The History of Soviet Foreign Policy, 1917–67* (New York: Praeger, 1968), p. 30. For a more recent discussion of the relationship between theory and practice in Soviet foreign policy see Margot Light, *Soviet Theory of International Relations* (Brighton: Harvester-Wheatsheaf, 1988), p. 13.

3. These typologies are derived from Anton Deportes' book, *Europe Between the Superpowers* (London: Yale University Press, 1979), p. 63. Typologies such as these inevitably simplify a broad spectrum of opinions, and overlook the change of perceptions over time (ie, from the 1950s to the 1970s). Nevertheless, I have included them here because they do provide a series of striking images which help illustrate a number of main approaches to the study of Soviet foreign policy.

4. A. Stent, 'The USSR and Western Europe', in R. Laird and E. Hoffmann (eds), *Soviet Foreign Policy in a Changing World* (Berlin: De Gruyter, 1986), pp. 443–56. A similar conception of the Soviet Union as 'The Great Beast of the Revelation' can be found in Ray Chine et al., *Western Policy in Soviet Global Strategy* (London: Westview, 1987).

5. Michael Cox, '"Hoist the White Flag" – Soviet Foreign Policy in an Era of Decline', *Critique*, no. 22 (1990), pp. 68–86 (p. 85).

6. Deportes, *Europe Between the Superpowers*, p. 64.

7. As Ken Booth notes of the Soviet leadership, 'They appreciated the terrifying destructive power of the US nuclear strike forces, the creation and expansion of NATO, the development of British nuclear power, the relative invulnerability of the US homeland until the late 1950s, the growth of tactical nuclear forces in Europe; the revival of German military power, and the complete encirclement of the USSR by a ring of US military bases and a series of hostile military alliances – there was even talk about roll-back and the liberation of Eastern Europe. All this maintained the spectre of surprise nuclear attack on the Soviet Union as a possible if increasingly improbable scenario'. See J. Baylis and G. Segal, *Soviet Strategy* (London: Croom Helm, 1981), p. 84.

8. As Edwina Moreton and Gerry Segal note in their edited volume, *Soviet Strategy Toward Western Europe* (London: George Allen & Unwin, 1984), 'while other analysts might suggest with great confidence that Soviet policy is clear cut and unchanging, we have found no such certainty. What emerges from our analyses is several themes of Soviet policy, many of which are

characterised by dilemmas, while others have been seen to change over time. To suggest that there is a Soviet code of behaviour ... is to simplify a far more complex reality' (p. 3).

9. For an informative discussion of the 27th Congress, see the collection of papers edited by R.F. Miller et al., *Gorbachev at the Helm: A New Era of Soviet Politics?* (London: Croom Helm, 1987). Also of interest is Martin Walker, *The Waking Giant: The Soviet Union Under Gorbachev* (London: Michael Joseph, 1986); Martin McCauley (ed.), *The Soviet Union Under Gorbachev* (London: Macmillan, 1987); and Gordon B. Smith, *Soviet Politics: Continuity and Contradiction* (London: Macmillan, 1988).

10. Boris Meissner argues that the XIX Party Conference represented 'a far-reaching watershed'; 'Gorbachev in a Dilemma: Pressure for Reform and the Constellation of Power', *Aussenpolitik*, vol. 41, no. 2 (1990), pp. 118–34 (p. 118). See also Baruch A. Hazan, *Gorbachev's Gamble. The 19th All-Union Party Conference* (London: Westview, 1990).

11. *Pravda*, 1 July 1988, p. 3.

12. S. Bialer, 'The Passing of the Soviet Order?', *Survival*, vol. XXXII, no. 2 (March/April 1990), pp. 107–20 (p. 118).

13. Quoted in *The Economist*, 'Survey of the Soviet Economy', 9 April 1988, p. 16.

14. Margie Lindsay, *International Business in Gorbachev's Soviet Union* (London: Pinter, 1989). See also 'A Survey of Perestroika', *The Economist*, 28 April 1990.

15. The Shatalin Plan was published in summarised form in the government newspaper *Izvestia*, on 5 September 1990. It called for rapid privatization and the break-up of state monopolies, combined with an austerity programme and a devolution of power to the republics. Ryzhkov's plan proposed 'stabilisation' measures first (in other words, price rises and budget cuts), followed by 'structural reforms' (ie, the break-up of monopoly producers). For further details see '500 Days to Shake the World', in *The Economist*, 15 September 1990, pp. 125–26.

16. With the Mezhdurechensk miners' strike of July–August 1989, which quickly spread to the Kuzbass, Donbass and Vorkuta regions, the Soviet working class has begun flexing its considerable muscles and has entered the political stage as a distinctive social force. For an informative account of the Kuzbass strikes, see Yu. Anenchenko's report in *Znamya*, no. 10 (1989). In May 1990, the new head of the official trade unions, Gennady Yanayev, expressed support for 'market relations', but called for indexation of all wages and a guarantee of full employment: if these demands were not met, he warned 'we will use all available means to oppose decisions that are in direct conflict with the interest of the Soviet people'. *Pravda*, 17 May 1990.

17. Zhores Medvedev, 'Soviet Power Today', *New Left Review*, no. 179 (January–February 1990), pp. 65–80.

18. 'In a praetorian system, social forces confront each other nakedly; no political institutions, no corps of professional political leaders are recognized or accepted as the legitimate intermediaries to moderate group conflict. Equally important, no agreement exists among the groups as to the legitimate and authoritative methods for resolving conflicts .... Each group employs means which reflect its peculiar nature and capabilities. The wealthy bribe;

students riot; workers strike; mobs demonstrate; and the military coup': Samuel Huntington, *Political Order in Changing Societies* (New Haven: Yale University Press, 1968), p. 196.

19. Professor Anikin of the Moscow Institute of World Economy has compared Gorbachev's Moscow to the last days of the Kerensky regime in 1917 – a vision increasingly shared with US officials and other Western officials. In a gloomy assessment of the prospects for the USSR in the early 1990s, Mr David Roche of Morgan Stanley argued that, 'Perestroika is likely to fail shortly and be replaced by one of four options: a radical national salvation government backed by the younger military officer corps, a conservative coup by senior officers, a military-backed, half-hearted economic reform government under an increasingly "bonapartist" President Gorbachev, or "chaos"'. Quoted in the *Financial Times*, 19 December 1990, p. 2.

20. *Pravda*, 2 July 1989, p. 1.

21. *Pravda*, 23 November 1990.

22. Zbigniew Brzezinski, 'Post-Communist Nationalism', *Foreign Affairs*, vol. 68, no. 5 (Winter 1989/90), pp. 1–25.

23. See B. Nahaylo and V. Swoboda, *Soviet Disunion: A History of the Nationalities Problem in the USSR* (London: Hamish Hamilton, 1990), p. 354.

24. See Dominic Lieven, 'The Dissolution of an Empire', *The Independent*, 15 November 1989.

25. Stephen K. Carter, *Russian Nationalism: Yesterday, Today, Tomorrow* (London: Pinter, 1990).

26. See Neil Malcolm, 'De-Stalinization and Soviet Foreign Policy: The Roots of "New Thinking"', in *Perestroika: Soviet Domestic and Foreign Policies*, edited by Tsuyoshi Hasegawa and Alex Pravda (London: Sage for the RIIA, 1990), pp. 178–205; and Allen Lynch, *The Soviet Study of International Relations* (Cambridge: Cambridge University Press, 1987), and his shorter but more recent study, *Gorbachev's International Outlook: Intellectual Origins and Political Consequences*, IEWSS Occasional Paper 9 (New York: Institute for East–West Security Studies, 1989).

27. See Stephen Shenfield's excellent study, *The Nuclear Predicament: Explorations in Soviet Ideology* (London: Routledge & Kegan Paul for the RIIA, 1987). For a less sanguine view of the 'new thinking', see Edward L. Warner III, 'New Thinking and Old Realities in Soviet Defence Policy', *Survival*, vol. XXXI, no. 1 (January–February 1989), pp. 13–33.

28. 'Clausewitz's dictum that war is the continuation of policy only by different means, which was classical in his time, has grown hopelessly out of date. It now belongs to the libraries. For the first time in history, basing international politics on moral and ethical norms that are common to all humankind, as well as humanizing interstate relations, has become a vital requirement.' Mikhail Gorbachev, *Perestroika: New Thinking for our Country and the World* (London: Fontana-Collins, 1988), p. 141.

29. Jeffrey W. Legro, 'Soviet Crisis Decision-making and the Gorbachev Reforms', *Survival*, vol. XXXI, no. 4 (July–August 1989), pp. 339–58.

30. Jonathan Haslam, 'The UN and the Soviet Union: New Thinking?', *International Affairs*, vol. 65, no. 4 (Autumn 1989), pp. 677–84, and Thomas Weiss and Merly Kessler, 'Moscow's UN Policy', *Foreign Policy*, no. 79 (Summer 1990).

31. Joachim Glaubitz, 'Rapprochement Between China and the Soviet Union

- Background and Prospects', *Aussenpolitik*, vol. 40, no. 3 (1989), pp. 251–63.

32. In this respect, the promotion of Alexandr Yakolev and Valentin Falin in October 1988 (the former Chairman of the new Central Committee Foreign Affairs Commission, the latter as Dobrynin's replacement as Head of the International Department) was seen as particularly significant, given their reputations for being more pro-European and anti-American than, for example, Dobrynin and the other *Amerikanisty*. On these and other changes in Gorbachev's European policy, see Neil Malcolm's excellent study, *Soviet Policy Perspectives on Western Europe* (London: Routledge for the RIIA, 1989), esp. p. 66.

33. See Hannes Adomeit, 'Gorbatchows Westpolitik (I): "Gemeinsames europäisches Haus" oder Atlantische "Orientierung?"', *Osteuropa*, no. 6 (1988), pp. 419–34; 'Gorbatchows Westpolitik (II): Die Beziehungen im "Gemeinsame Haus"', *Osteuropa*, no. 9 (1988), pp. 815–34; and 'Gorbatchows Westpolitik (III): Vorrang für die Beziehungen zu den Vereinigten Staaten', *Osteuropa*, no. 12 (1988), pp. 1092–1105.

34. The Russian word *dom* can be translated as either 'house' or 'home'. For most Russians, however, this means a block of apartment flats; it therefore implies a lesser degree of communality and intermingling than it does in the West.

35. On the occasion of his visit to Bonn; see *Pravda*, 24 November 1981.

36. For a thorough analysis of the changes in the Soviet conception of the Common European House, see Neil Malcolm, 'The "Common European House" and Soviet European Policy', *International Affairs*, vol. 65, no. 4 (Autumn 1989), pp. 659–76.

37. In his speech to the Council of Europe in Strasbourg in July 1989, Gorbachev proposed establishing an all-European ecological centre (which would eventually acquire regulatory powers), a European institute of human rights and a 'European legal framework', along with more familiar suggestions for joint research and development projects and building a 'peoples' Europe' on a continental scale. *Pravda*, 7 July 1989.

38. In the Soviet–German 'Grand Treaty' of November 1990, both sides promised to cooperate closely together in the new Europe. The Germans also promised to promote Soviet interests in Western economic forums.

39. See Horst Teltschik, 'Gorbachev's Reform Policy and the Outlook for East–West Relations', *Aussenpolitik*, vol. 4ᴐ, no. 3 (1989), pp. 201–14 (p. 208); Gerhard Wettig, 'The German Problem in Soviet Policy', *Aussenpolitik*, vol. 41, no. 1 (1990), pp. 38–51; and Gregory F. Treverton, 'West Germany and the Soviet Union', in *Western Approaches to the Soviet Union*, ed. by Michael Mandelbaum (New York: Council on Foreign Relations, 1988), pp. 1–23.

40. See Douglas A. MacGregor, *The Soviet–East German Military Alliance* (Cambridge: Cambridge University Press, 1989), esp. Chapter 1.

41. Quentin Peel, 'Divisions Appear in Soviet Ranks', *Financial Times*, 12 May 1990.

42. For an interesting and illuminating study of prospects for the socialist project in the Soviet Union, see R.W. Davies, 'Gorbachev's Socialism in Historical Perspective', *New Left Review*, no. 179 (January–February 1990), pp. 5–27.

43. *The Independent*, 17 February 1990.

44. The model here would be the French transition from the Fourth to the Fifth Republics, with Gorbachev as the Russian De Gaulle, the Baltic states as Algeria, and the Russian minorities in non-Russian SSRs as the *pied noir*.
45. Migranyan (a senior researcher at the Institute of Economics of the World Socialist System) has argued that 'The Soviet Union is acting like a democracy without really being one .... Maybe we need an authoritarian period of development ... if democracy prevents market mechanisms from developing'; see *Time*, 18 December 1989, p. 19. Migranyan's 'treachery' is criticised by Boris Kagarlitsky, 'The Importance of Being Marxist', *New Left Review*, no. 178 (November–December 1989), pp. 29–36 (p. 32). For the debate about the need for an 'iron hand', see *Literaturnaya gazeta*, 16 August (Igor Klyamkin and A. Migranyan), 20 September (L. Batkin) and 17 September (readers' letters) 1989.
46. Announcing his plans to stand for President of the Russian parliament, Yeltsin called for the RSFSR to have its own constitution, its own tax laws, its own international trade deals, and to sign treaties with the other Union Republics regulating their political and economic relations; reported in the *Financial Times*, 15 May 1990, p. 2.
47. Vladimir Kontorovich has argued that 'Command economy is a viable system. While it cannot solve its immanent problems, it can prevent them from getting out of hand'; see his chapter on the Soviet economy in *Soviet Society under Gorbachev: Current Trends and the Prospects for Reform*, edited by M. Friedberg and H. Isham (London: M.E. Sharpe, 1987), p. 46.
48. Zbigniew Brzezinski has suggested that when people think of *perestroika* failing, they tend to think of a return to Stalinism. 'But', he argues, 'I don't think that it is likely. More likely is something in between, a floundering, a sinking into the morass, with economic conditions getting even worse and political tensions getting sharper, the line of the government getting more zig-zaggy.' Quoted by David Remnick in 'Whither Perestroika? It May Simply be a Matter of Muddling Through', *International Herald Tribune*, 3 November 1989, p. 1.
49. See Brzezinski, 'Post-Communist Nationalism', p. 15.
50. Alexander Yanov, quoted in Stephen Carter, *Russian Nationalism*, p. 129.
51. The 'Time of Troubles' occurred in Russia 1605–13, after Boris Godunov became Tsar. It was characterised by a generation of chaos, involving a succession of dynastic struggles, social upheavals and foreign invasion – including the occupation and burning of Moscow by the Poles in 1610.
52. Quoted in *The Weekend Guardian*, 4/5 November 1989, p. 4.
53. Sergei A. Karaganov, 'The Year of Europe: a Soviet View', *Survival*, vol. XXXII, no. 2 (March–April 1990), pp. 121–28 (p. 128).
54. S. Bialer, 'The Passing of the Soviet Order?', (pp. 111–12).
55. See *Strategic Survey 1989–1990*, (London: Brassey's for the IISS, 1990), pp. 5–8.
56. Mark N. Katz, 'The Decline of Soviet Power', *Survival*, vol. XXXII, no. 1 (January–February 1990), pp. 15–28 (pp. 19–21).
57. M. Howard, 'The Remaking of Europe', *Survival*, vol. XXXII, no. 2 (March–April 1990), pp. 99–106 (p. 105).
58. 'How to Help the Soviet Union', *Financial Times*, 17 December 1990, p. 36.
59. This is the weakness of the 'Z' article, 'To the Stalin Mausoleum', which

appeared in *Daedalus*, in January 1990, and which has been seen as indicative of the perspectives of many in the Bush Administration. Similarly, the limits of the sort of excessive caution and prudence advocated by Sir Geoffrey Howe in his article, 'Soviet Foreign Policy under Gorbachev' (see *The World Today*, vol. 45, no. 3 (March 1989), pp. 40–45), were soon being exposed by the pace of events in late 1989–early 1990, e.g. regarding SNF modernisation, the Berlin Wall and the 'leading role' of the CPSU.

5

Post-Communist Eastern Europe

In the fall of 1989, Eastern Europe became the stage for some of the most heartening events in post-war history. In a dramatic display of 'Peoples' Power', the authoritarian communist regimes of Eastern Europe were finally consigned to the 'dustbin of history'. Since then, much of the debate on the reshaping of Europe has focused on the changing foreign and domestic policies of the post-communist regimes in Eastern Europe. For over forty years, the countries of this diverse region were at the heart of the East–West conflict. It was Stalin's quest for absolute security on his western borders that generated Western concern about Soviet post-war aspirations. It was conflict in east central Europe that triggered the cold war in the late 1940s. Eastern Europe subsequently provided the site of the worst flash-points of the East–West conflict in Europe, and remained a zone of intermittent crisis throughout the post-war period – as is apparent from the events in the GDR, 1953; Hungary and Poland, 1956; Czechoslovakia, 1968; and Poland, 1970, 1976, 1980–81.[1]

In the late 1980s and early 1990s, Eastern Europe has once again become the focus of change in the European security system. This time, however, change in the region could contribute to the healing of post-war divisions in Europe. The revolutions of 1989 promise a transformation of the former communist regimes into liberal-democratic, market-orientated states, free to develop 'organic' relationships with the Soviet Union, Western Europe and each other. But the problems facing the East Europeans are enormous, and the prospects for peaceful and democratic development in the region are – to say the least – uncertain. The purpose of this chapter is to consider the reasons for the implosion of communist power in Eastern Europe, and the prospects for economic and political reform in the region. We will also examine the international dimensions of East European politics, focusing above all on the security implications of the collapse of Soviet hegemony and communist power in the area.

The Collapse of the Communist Utopia

Pre-war Eastern Europe was, with the notable exception of Czechoslovakia and parts of eastern Germany, characterised by economic backwardness, widespread social deprivation, political instability, authoritarian regimes, irredentist ambitions, and ancient but enduring national, ethnic and religious conflicts.[2] Communism – 'the greatest political utopia in history'[3] – promised an escape from this bitter legacy, and a shortcut to industrialisation, modernisation and social justice. With the radicalisation of the war years and the Red Army's victory over Hitler's legions, the political pre-conditions for a process of communist-led modernisation in the region seemed assured.

However, communism in Eastern Europe suffered from a severe congenital defect: with the exceptions of Yugoslavia and Albania, it was largely imposed from above and without.[4] Even though it was to capture the imagination of some elements of the post-war generation,[5] it never succeeded in putting down sturdy indigenous roots of its own. Much of the blame for this lies with the Soviet Union: its failure to develop an 'organic'[6] relationship with its communist neighbours in the Eastern Europe, and its use of the 'Brezhnev doctrine' to prevent internal democratisation and structural reform, prevented the evolution of economically viable and politically legitimate socialist regimes.[7] Post-war East European history has consequently been dotted with turning-points where history failed to turn – 1956, with the 20th CPSU Congress, Gomulka in Poland and Imre Nagy in Hungary; 1968 and the 'Prague Spring'; and 1980, with *Solidarnosc* in Poland.

By the 1980s, it was clear that the communist experience in Eastern Europe had failed – economically, politically, and perhaps more importantly, spiritually.[8] In the late 1980s, both communist reformers and their anti-communist critics were united in their belief that Eastern Europe was ripe for either radical transformation or revolutionary upheavals.[9] The systemic problems of the region were compounded by the fact that it found itself caught between the conflicting pressures of growing integration and prosperity in the West and *perestroika* in the East.[10] When it became apparent that the 'Brezhnev doctrine' had been replaced by the 'Sinatra doctrine',[11] and that Eastern Europe's geriatric communist leaderships lacked the political will to repeat a 'Tiananmen' massacre in Berlin, Prague or Sofia, the stage was set for the 'Springtime of the Nations'.

The implosion of communist power in Eastern Europe was thus a result of the communists' inability to develop economically viable and politically legitimate structures in these societies. Communism's attempt to 'leap-frog' history and to pioneer a new road to human emancipation proved a dismal failure. Nevertheless, although communism failed to solve the region's deep-seated legacy of backwardness and underdevelopment, by creating industrialised and urbanised societies with literate and increasingly enlightened citizens, it generated the pre-conditions for its own demise. History has played a cruel trick on Marxism-Leninism: instead of the capitalist 'relations of production' acting as a 'fetter' on the further development of the productive forces in the West, it was the 'social relations' of communism that acted as the fetters on the further development of East European societies. In an ironic vindication of Marx, this led to a popular uprising which swept away the historically anachronistic structures of an authoritarian system.

1989: the 'Springtime of the Nations'?

The elemental upsurge of 'People's Power' in late 1989 in Eastern Europe resulted in a major shift in the strategic balance in Europe. It effectively ended the East–West conflict in its traditional form, and further blurred the bipolar structures of post-war Europe. Independent and democratic states in East Central Europe promise to be one of the principal building blocks of a new European peace order. For the first time in its long and troubled history, therefore, the prospect of a Europe 'whole and free' seems a realistic and attainable goal.

There is, however, a darker side to the revolutions of 1989. The spectacular disintegration of communist power has released many pent-up frustrations and deep-seated historical animosities in a region renowned for its ethnic, national, religious and political rivalries. The reassertion of past values and political traditions risks reopening old conflicts in countries riven with barely suppressed antagonisms. Against a background of worsening economic problems, social unrest and political fluidity, the transition to democratic and market-orientated societies will be far from easy. On top of this, the collapse of the *pax sovietica* has left the countries of Eastern Europe in a 'security limbo' – with regard to a weakened Soviet Union, a united Germany and each other.

The long-term consequences of the 1989 revolutions are thus far from clear. Nonetheless, the outcome of the reform processes in the countries of Eastern Europe will be of considerable significance for the future evolution of the European security system. One feature of the region which has become increasingly apparent over recent years is the very diversity of 'Eastern Europe'. In terms of economic and industrial structures; politics and culture; social, ethnic, national and linguistic composition – the countries of this part of Europe are exceedingly heterogeneous.[12] The biggest political and cultural divide, however, is between the countries of East Central Europe (the GDR, Poland, Czechoslovakia, Hungary) and south-east Europe and the Balkans (Bulgaria, Romania and Albania), with the fracture running through the heart of Yugoslavia. In East Central Europe, the dominant theme of post-communist politics is the ill-defined notion of a 'return to Europe'. In south-eastern Europe, the specificities of Balkan politics seem to be reasserting themselves, in ways that do not necessarily bode well for the future stability of this part of the continent.

I: DOMESTIC DEVELOPMENTS

Economic Reform

As the countries of Eastern Europe begin the process of market-orientated reform, the sheer enormity of the economic problems they face is becoming apparent. Four decades of centralised planning have produced distorted economies, large parts of which are unable to withstand the rigours of international competition. The command-administrative structures of the Comecon states resulted in economies characterised by bureaucratic control of investment and production; monopolistic structures of industrial production; prices which bore no relation to the true value of resources used; inefficient agricultural sectors; restrictive if not autarkic trade policies; an underdeveloped service sector; and an omnipresent black market.

On top of this, however, bureaucratic planning has generated environmental destruction on a scale unmatched in the Western liberal-democracies. The industrial centres of Polish Silesia, northern Bohemia and Saxony are amongst the most environmentally polluted areas in the world. In Poland, water from 95 per cent of the length of the Vistula (the country's longest river) is unfit for human consumption, whilst 75 per cent of it cannot even be used for industrial purposes, because it is too corrosive. The south-west of Poland used to be one of the nation's most fertile areas, but today a third of the land cannot be used for root crops because of the level of heavy metal contamination. In Czechoslovakia, the Academy of Sciences has admitted that 50 per cent of the country's drinking water does not meet its own low standards. Small wonder, then, that life expectancy in these countries is falling.[13]

The aim of the post-communist regimes in Eastern Europe (especially in East Central Europe) is the transition to a 'social market economy', fully integrated into European and global markets. This involves a huge transformation of structures and practices, for which there is no theoretical model or practical experience. The task is daunting: the East Europeans need to create – virtually from scratch – institutions and attitudes which are taken for granted in the West (eg, financial, legal and institutional frameworks; accounting procedures involving notions of profit and loss; social security systems, etc.).[14] As in the Soviet Union, economic reform involves a choice between two strategies – either a crash-programme or 'Big Bang' approach (adopted by Poland in early 1990), or a more gradual and administered transition (currently adopted by the new democratic governments of Hungary and Czechoslovakia). The arguments revolve around the pace of reform, and the social and political costs entailed. Indeed, one of the central problems facing these post-communist regimes is how to achieve economic reform (with the costs and hardships that inevitably involves) without destabilising their fragile structures of political democracy.

The prospects for successful economic reform in Eastern Europe are better than in the USSR. Traditions of entrepreneurship and enterprise have survived more in Eastern Europe than in Soviet Russia; Eastern European countries are smaller and therefore easier to restructure with Western aid; and the region has much to offer the West in terms of a skilled and relatively cheap labour-force, high levels of science and technology, and a proximity to German and other West European markets. Nevertheless, it will be difficult to overcome the relative economic backwardness of Eastern Europe. Indeed, many East Europeans speak of their fear of 'Mexicanisation' – in other words, of their becoming economically dependent on the stronger countries to their West. In this situation, a new division of Europe may arise, between the prosperous West and the underdeveloped East. As Timothy Garton Ash notes, the 'return to Europe' in Eastern Europe

> ... may end in a new version of Giselher Wirsing's 'Zwischeneuropa' or the intermediate zone identified by Hungarian writers and historians, its economies exporting tin saucepans, bottled fruit, cheap shoes, and cheap labor, importing German tourists and Japanese capital. A zone, that is, of weak states, national prejudice, inequality, poverty, and *shlammessel*.[15]

A 'Third Way'?

One interesting question is whether the reform process in the East will result in the complete adoption of democratic capitalism, or whether or not some sort of 'Third Road' is possible. The notion of a 'Third Way' between capitalism and socialism has a long intellectual pedigree, yet is notoriously hard to define. Basically, it embodies a desire to avoid the worst excesses of competitive capitalism – such as unemployment, social inequalities, consumerism and rampant individualism – whilst benefiting from the advantages of a market system.

This desire to 'have one's cake and eat it too' does not seem feasible in the conditions of economic adversity in Eastern Europe. There is no way these countries can escape from the painful austerity that structural economic readjustment will bring. At the same time, forty years of communism has permanently poisoned the concept of 'socialism' in Eastern Europe, and there is no desire for anything that smacks of planning or socialist regulation.[16] East Europeans have no interest in new experiments in large-scale societal engineering, and want a 'democracy' without adjectives, and a 'social market economy' that owes more to Ludwig Erhard rather than to Ota Sik.[17] Indeed, if there are any ideological illusions left in the east, it is that the 'market' provides a simple answer to all their problems, and that Hayek and Friedman are in some significant way relevant to the dilemmas of late twentieth-century Europe.

Nonetheless, there is no reason for assuming that the East Europeans are simply going to embrace the neo-liberal economics of Thatcherism or Reaganism. In the 1990s, the old dichotomy between 'capitalism' and 'socialism', between central planning and the market, is less and less helpful in understanding the choices and dilemmas facing modern industrialised societies. As Marshall Shulman has written, all countries now need to find the optimum balance between 'the free enterprise market sector that provides yeasty growth and innovation, and the political state sector that establishes priorities, regulates economic abuses and provides for social needs sufficiently to maintain the legitimacy of the system'.[18] The pragmatic experimentation that this involves by no means implies that a new synthesis between the market and state regulation is likely to emerge. In other words, a distinctive 'Third Way' between capitalism and socialism (concepts which themselves are of declining analytical utility), with its own specific political economy, is unlikely to emerge. Rather, each country is likely to find its own specific answers to problems such as environmental destruction, bureaucratism and social injustice, on the basis of its own political culture, history and socio-economic structure.

The sort of societies and economic systems that develop in East Europe will therefore tend to reflect these countries' specific history and traditions. There is still widespread support for a relatively egalitarian distribution of wealth, and a strong and comprehensive welfare system. The state will also tend to play a larger role in East European societies than in Western Europe, for both practical and historical reasons: these societies tend to be more *etatist* than in the West, and enjoy much stronger traditions of community solidarity and state-regulated equality.[19] There is therefore good reason to suppose that the dominant political forces in the region are more likely to be nationally specific forms of social-democracy[20] or Christian-democracy (drawing extensively on Catholic teachings of social justice), rather than the neo-liberalism of Reagan's America or Thatcher's Britain. Post-communist Eastern Europe is thus likely to provide a distinctive addition to the rich diversity of liberal-market societies currently found on the continent – from Scandinavian welfarism to the market liberalisation of the Iberian countries.

The Politics of Post-Communism

The future political evolution of Eastern Europe will be a major influence on the sort of security structures which develop in the continent. If democracy succeeds in laying firm roots in these countries, then it will become more possible to develop cooperative structures of mutual security in

Europe. On the other hand, if the region experiences sustained bouts of political instability, or a reversion to pre-war patterns of authoritarian nationalism, then the security environment will remain inclement for bold experiments in pan-European security cooperation.

The peaceful nature of the 1989 revolutions (with the notable exception of Romania) bodes well for the immediate prospects for democratic transition. One interesting feature of the transitional period in most East European countries (with the exception of East Germany, which – because of the unification process – remained a *sui generis* case) has been the prevalence of broad and diverse movements leading the opposition to communism. The forerunner of this type of 'popular front' organisation was Solidarity, which 'pioneered a new kind of politics in Eastern Europe (and not only there): a politics of social self-organisation aimed at negotiating the transition from communism'.[21] In Czechoslovakia it is Civic Forum and its Slovak ally, Public Against Violence; in Hungary, this role was initially played by the Hungarian Democratic Forum, although even before elections of March 1990, the anti-communist opposition had already fragmented into two main parties, which have subsequently come to dominate the political scene. In Bulgaria and Romania, reformist elements in the old communist parties also established broad front organisations which have attempted – with some success – to mobilise a wide range of social forces. As the need for a broad anti-communist front recedes, and as the political systems mature, these conglomerate organisations are likely to fragment and disintegrate – a trend clearly apparent in both Solidarity and Civic Forum/Public Against Violence.

The development of functioning liberal-democracies in Eastern Europe requires the establishment of the necessary constitutional and legal framework, a stable party system, and open mechanisms for interest articulation and integration. It also demands the existence of a flourishing civil society. However, the problem for the East Europeans is that it takes a long time for democratic polities to evolve from inchoate political forces. Furthermore, a high degree of social calm and political consensus is essential for new parliamentary structures to take root. The example of Weimar Germany highlights the vulnerability of fragile democratic institutions in conditions of acute economic crisis, political polarisation and weak democratic traditions.

Thus the transition to democracy in Eastern Europe will be difficult and uncertain. Although many in Eastern Europe look optimistically to the **Spanish experience** as a model of democratic transition,[22] the problems of transition in the region are much more intractable than in southern Europe. Indeed, the future of Eastern Europe might well resemble a number of other less desirable examples. One such example is what Adam Michnik has dubbed, the **'Iranian model'**: in other words, a reactionary clerical-nationalist backlash in countries in which former repressive regimes had employed slogans of modernity to justify their unpopular rule. A second is the **East Asian model** (ie, South Korea or Taiwan) of benign technocratic absolutism, in which authoritarian governments implement harsh programmes of economic reform and market liberalisation, whilst crushing all signs of domestic political resistance.[23] Finally, there is the example of the **Chilean** or **Turkish** model, in which the army seizes power in order to stabilise what it perceives as a deteriorating political and social situation, whilst promising to lead the country towards democracy in the future, once law and order have been restored.

The politics of the transition to market-based democracies are therefore likely to be far from smooth. The danger of authoritarian nationalism remains a very real one, especially in those countries where the economic crisis is most severe. Once again, the East Germans will be in a relatively privileged position in this respect, in that they are simply to be absorbed into a functioning parliamentary system. Czechoslovakia is perhaps the next best placed country, given its pre-war traditions of parliamentary government, and its relatively good economic prospects. Nonetheless, in both Czechoslovakia and Poland, the nature of the transitional politics – with broadly based catch-all popular movements and charismatic leaders – could impede the development of a parliamentary democracy based on institutionalised decision-making and a multiparty system. In Hungary, the traditional political cleavages of the pre-war period seem to be re-emerging – between 'urbanists' and 'populists', nationalists and cosmopolitans, liberals and conservatives. If the economic situation continues to deteriorate and social tensions mount, then a reversion to the nationalist demagogy, anti-semitism and political intolerance typical of the inter-war period cannot be discounted. Even if this deeply pessimistic scenario is avoided, the political divisions in the country could lead to political paralysis and a failure to contain the social strains of marketisation and privatisation. In Bulgaria, Romania, Serbia and – more recently – Albania, there are disturbing signs of the re-emergence of the internecine struggles and political intolerance that have been a feature of Balkan politics for many centuries.

Having considered some of the domestic problems facing post-communist Eastern Europe, let us now turn to the wider security implications of the 1989 revolutions.

II: EAST EUROPEAN SECURITY ISSUES

The security concerns of the newly independent and democratising states of East Europe revolve around three factors, all of which stem from the geopolitical position of these countries and their specific cultural and historical traditions. The first is their proximity to the USSR; the second is their proximity to Germany; and the third is the extraordinary national, ethnic and communal diversity of the region. The first two factors are closely connected: it seems to be a geostrategic fact that as Soviet/Russian influence on the region declines, that of Germany increases, and vice versa. The East European experience of either has not been a particularly happy one. Moreover, for countries like Poland or Czechoslovakia, their worst fear involves the possibility of a new Soviet–German 'Rapallo', in which they would become the pawns of this bilateral relationship between the regional great powers (see pp. 150–52).[24]

The disintegration of the *pax sovietica* has left the countries of Eastern Europe in a security limbo, and it is this which poses some of the most intriguing but difficult questions of the post-cold war order in Europe. How can conflicts in the region be peacefully managed? Who will guarantee the security of these countries? How can armed clashes in the region be prevented, or if necessary, contained? How should NATO respond if the East Central European countries request security guarantees, or even membership of the alliance? What are the Soviet Union's residual security concerns in Eastern Europe, and how legitimate are they? The answer to these questions will determine the future evolution of the security system in Europe.

Eastern Europe and the USSR

Gorbachev's 'new thinking' and the 1989 revolutions have ended postwar Soviet domination of Eastern Europe. Whatever happens now, there can be no return to the pre-Gorbachev pattern of Soviet–East European relations. Nevertheless, the Soviet Union, by virtue of its sheer size and its geostrategic weight in Eastern Europe, still has a great capacity to influence the course of developments in the region. To begin with, although direct military intervention by the Soviet Army is unlikely in the foreseeable future, the USSR's huge military forces could be used for purposes of political intimidation and leverage. Secondly, the countries of the region are likely to remain dependent on the Soviet Union for supplies of fuel and raw materials for many years to come, and will remain closely linked to the vast and promising market of the USSR: this will give the Soviet leadership scope for utilising various forms of economic statecraft in order to influence political developments in these countries. Finally, the Soviet Union may attempt to influence the domestic politics of these countries by intervening in their political struggles in support of one side or the other. Despite this possibility, however, its should be recognised that the political influence of the Soviet Union on Eastern Europe is likely to decline steadily over the next decade or so.[25]

The diminishing influence of the Soviet Union on developments in

Eastern Europe raises doubts about the future viability of the two institutional expressions of the 'socialist community', the Warsaw Pact and the CMEA. The former body has already ceased to function as an effective military alliance of like-minded countries, and its days are clearly numbered.[26] The Warsaw Pact now survives as an instrument of political consultation and multilateral diplomacy until new security structures (perhaps based on an institutionalised CSCE) can be created. Nevertheless, given the common concern of many East Europeans with the 'German question', and the need for arms control negotiation and verification, the East Europeans themselves may find some utility in the continued existence of a demilitarised and democratised WTO.[27] At the same time, the Soviet Union may seek to restructure its security relationships with the East Europeans along pre-1955 lines, by developing a network of bilateral security links, especially with countries like Bulgaria, Poland, Czechoslovakia and Romania.

The prospects facing the CMEA are no less certain. Since its establishment in 1949, the organisation has failed to provide an effective mechanism for supranational economic integration, or to promote dynamic growth within its member states.[28] Most of the East European states are now seeking to deepen their economic relations with the EC, as a prelude to full Community membership. Nonetheless, there might be a role for a reformed CMEA as a sub-regional economic bloc in the East, at least in the medium term. Intra-bloc trade will remain important for most CMEA states, partly because they will not be strong enough to compete in Western markets for many years to come, and partly because they share common tasks of economic restructuring. A reformed CMEA, based on convertible currencies and market relations, could therefore play a positive role in contributing to the formation of a common 'European Economic Space'.[29] It might also facilitate a more coordinated 'return to Europe' by the countries of East Central Europe.

Eastern Europe and Germany

Relations between the Eastern Europeans and the other regional great power – Germany – are likely to be as complex and ambiguous as those with the Soviet Union. Whereas the power of the USSR is in decline, however, that of Germany is unmistakably in the ascendant. Indeed, with its prodigious economy, a united Germany will undoubtedly be the single most powerful external influence on developments in the region.

As the countries of Eastern Europe attempt to restructure their societies, they are looking increasingly to the FRG as a major supplier of investment, aid, technological expertise and 'know-how'. Germany is set to become the major economic actor in the area, especially in Czechoslovakia, Hungary and Poland.[30] This is already generating mixed feelings in these countries. On the one hand, German investment is welcomed as a means of modernising their moribund economies: on the other hand, however, there are fears that this will turn the region into an indebted and underdeveloped appendage to Germany.

These fears of economic dependency tend to be mixed with residual feelings of resentment about past German expansionism in the region (the *Drang nach Osten*). The shadow of the Third Reich continues to haunt German relations with the peoples to their east. Some in the East bitterly resent the thought that Germany – by virtue of its economic prowess – is achieving in peacetime what it failed to achieve by military means in two World Wars: namely, the creation of a German-dominated *Mitteleuropa*, which serves as a provider of cheap goods, labour, land and markets to the German Fatherland. Such feelings are particularly prevalent in Poland and Czechoslovakia, and to a lesser extent, Hungary.

Despite this, there is another dimension to Eastern Europe's relationship with Germany which is of growing importance, and which mitigates these feelings of resentment. As reformers east of the Elbe seek to restructure their societies, they tend to look to the West for inspiration, and along with Sweden and Austria, it is West Germany which provides an attractive model of a prosperous and democratic country, particularly given its 'social market economy'. At the same time, many West German organisations – private and public – have proved generous providers of practical advice, moral encouragement and material support in facilitating the reform process in the East. German influence on the region is thus not necessarily malign, and if German policy towards the lands to its east continues to be characterised by tact and sensitivity, then the East Europeans may be able to develop balanced and cooperative relations with their more powerful neighbour in the West.

One final point to note is that the incorporation of the GDR into the FRG can provide valuable lessons for East European countries seeking to integrate with the West – especially in terms of economic restructuring. Furthermore, the successful integration of East Germany into the EC might facilitate the future entry of other East Central European countries into the Community. If the GDR can make the adjustments necessary to join the EC, the argument goes, why not Czechoslovakia, Poland and Hungary? In this way, German unification could contribute to the overcoming of the East–West divide in Europe.

National and Ethnic Conflicts: Forward to the Past?

Eastern Europe has long been the site of nationalist and inter-communal strife, given the kaleidoscopic diversity of its peoples. The region is a complex mosaic of different national, ethnic, linguistic and religious groupings, and contains a host of unresolved territorial irredentia. Some of the complexities of the region have been brutally eroded as a result both of the Holocaust and of the post-war expulsion of ethnic Germans from East Central Europe.[31] Nevertheless, Eastern Europe remains a tangle of ancient rivalries and historical disputes.

For four decades, these traditional disputes were suppressed beneath the bipolar nuclear structures of the cold war. In contrast to Western Europe, however, where the East–West conflict and American leadership facilitated a far-reaching process of rapprochement between historical enemies (symbolised above all by the 1957 Treaty of Rome and the 1963 Elysée Treaty), the *pax sovietica* merely put these conflicts on ice.[32] With the thawing of the East–West conflict, these ancient rivalries are threatening to re-emerge with a vengeance.

This is apparent from the rising tensions in Transylvania, where the problems of the Magyar minority continue to sour Hungarian–Romanian relations; in Bessarabia (now Soviet Moldova) and north Bukovina, a potential source of Soviet–Romanian conflict; in Kosovo, between Serbs and ethnic Albanians; in Macedonia, an area which contains a volatile cocktail of disputes involving Yugoslavia, Bulgaria and Greece; and in Slovakia, where there is a small Magyar minority. National, ethnic and religious conflicts have complicated relations between Bulgaria and Turkey, given Bulgarian treatment of its Muslim minority; between Poland and the western Ukraine, given the substantial Polish minority in what was formerly East Galicia; and between Poland and Lithuania, given the Polish minority in the latter. There have also been long-running border disputes between Poland and the former GDR over the coastal waters off Swinoujscie, and between Romania and Bulgaria at Dobrogea.[33]

One of the primary tasks facing whatever new security arrangements are created in Europe must be to ensure that the resurgence of nationalism in Eastern Europe does not lead to a repeat of the all-too-familiar patterns of outright conflict over territory and minorities. One fear is that unscrupulous nationalist demagogues might seek to distract attention from domestic economic difficulties by stirring up national and ethnic antagonisms.[34] This was one of the themes raised at a conference of Central Europeans in Bratislava in April 1990.[35] Adam Michnik and Gyorgy Konrad both warned that national bigotry and inter-communal violence represented the biggest threat to the peaceful and democratic evolution of these countries. Indeed, Michnik has argued that the central political cleavage in Eastern Europe is not between left and right, but between those – primarily urban-based, secular, liberal-progressive groups – who speak of a 'European potential' and who favour an outward-looking and liberal approach, and proponents of an inward-looking and parochial obscurantism who emphasise the need for a revival of pre-communist, national traditions and cultures (often linked to the more conservative trends in Catholicism).[36] The latter may well lead to xenophobism and chauvinism, and has already been painfully evident from an increase in anti-gypsy and anti-semitic prejudice in Poland and Hungary.

In this potentially volatile situation, the role of Western nations could have a significant impact on the evolving politics of the region, and it is to this that we now turn.

III: EASTERN EUROPE AND THE WEST

International Economic Organisations

With the demise of communism in the East, the countries of Eastern Europe are now seeking a much closer set of economic, political and cultural relations with the West. They have expressed considerable interest in participating in international economic organisations (IEOs), as a means of moving beyond the bloc framework and reintegrating themselves into the global economy. Some of the East European countries and the Soviet Union are already involved, to varying degrees, in a number of IEOs, including the GATT, the Economic Commission on Europe (ECE) at the United Nations in Geneva, the IMF/World Bank and the OECD.[37] In addition, they will participate in the newly formed European Bank for Reconstruction and Development (EBRD)[38] and the European Environment Agency.[39] The European Investment Bank is also granting loans to Hungary and Poland under the PHARE programme coordinated by the European Commission, and this is to be extended to other East European countries.

The development of closer links between East European countries and IEOs is a process which deserves the fullest support of Western nations. One of the most effective ways of ensuring that the disintegration of the Soviet bloc does not produce a zone of chronic instability and authoritarian nationalism on the eastern borders of Western Europe is by enmeshing these newly democratising states in a web of ever-deepening interdependencies. In this way, it may be possible to create a favourable and supportive international environment for the reform process in the East. By providing positive incentives and an institutional framework for pan-European cooperation, it may be possible to give practical encouragement to liberal and reforming coalitions in the East, and to prevent the emergence of autarkic, repressive and excessively nationalistic policies in these fragile polities.[40]

A key role in this respect can be played by the European Community. The EC has already emerged as the central Western actor in the region, since the decision by the OECD World Economic Summit in July 1989 to give the Commission the responsibility for coordinating Western aid to Poland and Hungary.[41] Although this has placed some strain on the machinery of the Community by giving it tasks for which it was not initially designed, the EC remains the best institution for coordinating Western economic assistance to Eastern Europe.[42] The Community already has some experience in facilitating the democratic transition in Spain and Portugal, and as the immediate neighbour of Eastern Europe, it has a direct interest in the outcome of the reform processes there. The Community is already exploring the possibility of developing new forms of 'Association' with the East Europeans, but in the long term, it is likely to be faced with a growing list of membership applications from former CMEA states. This will pose a whole series of difficult problems for the Community, given that it will challenge the very assumptions underlying the process of West European integration through the EC – an issue to which we will return in Chapter 6.

The Council of Europe

There are a number of other multilateral organisations which can play a positive role in Eastern Europe. One such is the Council of Europe, with which a number of East European countries already have developing relations. The Council of Europe was established in 1949 to further aims of political union, social progress and the protection of human rights, and one of its advantages is that it already possesses a small secretariat, a European Convention on Human Rights and a court of appeal (the European Court of Human Rights at Strasbourg). The Council of Europe has already helped with the construction of legal systems and pluralist democracies in Spain and Portugal during their transitions from dictatorship to democracy, and has begun playing the same role in Eastern Europe. It also provides another means of putting international pressure on those countries that renege on democracy, such as Greece during the Colonels' rule (1967–74), and more recently, Turkey since the 1980 coup. Membership of the Council would be a highly prized certificate of acceptance as a fully fledged democracy by the East Europeans, and a valuable safeguard against subsequent backsliding.[43]

The CSCE

Neither the European Community nor the Council of Europe, however – still less NATO or the WEU – provide an adequate institutional mechanism for dealing with the security problems of Eastern Europe in the wake of the effective disintegration of the Warsaw Pact. There is therefore scope for developing a new institutional framework for managing, and if possible, resolving, the national and political tensions that are likely to emerge in the region. The most suitable body in this respect is the CSCE. Although the CSCE cannot be expected to provide a comprehensive solution to all the security problems of Europe,[44] it could possibly provide a more limited framework for conflict prevention and crisis management in Eastern Europe. Since its inception in 1975, the CSCE has proved an invaluable forum for pan-European consultation and cooperation. It has developed a particular legitimacy and importance in the eyes of the smaller countries of Eastern Europe. The collapse of communist power in Eastern Europe in late 1989 was followed almost immediately by calls from the new democratic governments for an expanded international role for the CSCE. The government of Vaclav Havel led the way in calls for institutionalising the CSCE and developing it as a framework for common security in Europe, in close cooperation with the governments of Poland and the GDR.[45]

Since the November 1990 Summit in Paris, the CSCE has acquired a more institutionalised structure – with a Conflict Prevention Centre in Vienna, an Office of Free Elections in Warsaw, a secretariat in Prague and regular meetings of Heads of State (every two years) and Foreign Ministers (twice a year). It is therefore better equipped to function as a forum for pan-European dialogue and cooperation. Many in Eastern and Central Europe, however, favour going beyond this and envisage giving the CSCE an institutional mechanism for conflict prevention and crisis management. If the CSCE were to assume responsibility for managing the security problems of Europe and providing a form of collective security for even part of the continent, however, the decision-making procedures of the CSCE (which are currently based on the unanimity principle) would have to be revised in order to facilitate some form of majority voting. The 34 CSCE-participating nations will also need to develop a more robust normative framework for regulating human rights (including the rights of minority groups) and inter-state relations. The difficulties in developing this sort of CSCE security regime, therefore, are enormous: however, with the necessary political will, and if the CSCE is not hastily over-burdened with major new responsibilities, they are not insurmountable. If the CSCE were to be encouraged to evolve and grow, it could provide an important element in a new security framework in Europe, one which would be particularly well suited to managing the security problems of Eastern Europe and the Balkans. In this way, it might be able to avoid the mistakes of both Sarajevo in 1914 and Munich in 1938.

Alpe-Adria, Danubian Cooperation and the 'Pentagonale Initiative'

One particularly interesting development in recent years has been the emergence of regional and sub-regional forms of cooperation, which overlap the old East–West divide. The cold war severed many historical ties between nations and countries in Europe – especially central Europe – and imposed a new network of relations corresponding to the bipolar bloc structure. As the initial intensity of cold war lessened, however, many of these traditional patterns of relationships re-emerged. One early example of this was the creation in 1955 by the Austrians of the *Forschungsinstitut für den Donauraum*, which was dedicated to finding areas of common interest between the Danubian states: the link here being the Danube river itself.[46]

More recently, the idea of regional cooperation in the *Mitteleuropäische* lands of the old Habsburg Empire has found its expression in the Alpe-Adria organisation. This body, established in 1978, embraces the provinces and counties of western Austria, western Hungary, southern Germany (Bavaria), northern Italy and northern Yugoslavia (Croatia and Slovenia), which comprises an area larger than the FRG, with a population of 37 million. The aim is to promote regional cooperation in the fields of tourism, trade, transport, environmental protection, sport and culture.[47] The Hungarians have also become enthusiastic proponents of inter-regional cooperation in the Danubian-Central European area.[48]

The disintegration of the 'iron curtain', however, has opened up major new opportunities for regional cooperation in central Europe. Indeed, one of the key features of the new post-cold war Europe is likely to be the growing importance of regional and sub-regional cooperation – not only in central Europe, but in the Baltic region and the Balkans. The most recent example of this is the creation of the 'Pentagonale initiative'. This grew from an agreement to begin quadripartite cooperation between Italy, Austria, Hungary and Yugoslavia, which resulted from a meeting of foreign ministers in Budapest on 11 November 1989. The four were later joined by Czechoslovakia on 20 April 1990, and on 27 April, the 'Pentagonale Initiative' was formally launched. The initiative includes projects in the fields of environmental protection; cooperation between small and medium-sized enterprises; transport links; information and telecommunications; culture; and education and youth exchanges. The five have already begun coordinating their foreign policy initiatives in forums such as the UN, the Council of Europe and the CSCE Human Rights meeting in Copenhagen in June 1990 (where they presented a joint proposal on minority rights). The first heads of government meeting took place in July 1990, where a formal declaration setting out the objectives of the 'Pentagonale' was adopted.

These initiatives have no direct military or security dimension. Hungary proposed the creation of a 'zone of confidence' between the original four, in which offensive weapons would be withdrawn from a zone of 50 km (initially along the Austrian–Hungarian–Yugoslav borders), but this received a very cool reaction from its partners. Since then, security issues have not figured prominently on the agenda of the 'Pentagonale'. Nevertheless, the 'Pentagonale Initiative' (and similar forms of cooperation, for example in the Nordic area) are of tremendous significance for European security. They further erode the foundations of post-war military alignments and force dispositions, and create new centres of economic and political cooperation which – in the case of the five – embrace one EC and NATO member, one neutral EFTA country, two Warsaw Pact/CMEA states, and one non-aligned socialist state. This *Kleinmitteleuropa* can be seen as a partial counterweight to German hegemony in central and north-eastern Europe, and a reflection of Italy's growing regional importance. It also brings together countries who see the European Community as a central focus of their international aspirations in the future – Italy, of course, is a founder member, whilst the other four all aspire to future membership. Such forms of regional cooperation can make an important contribution to the re-linking of Europe, and thereby to the process of pan-European integration and cooperation.[49]

Conclusion

Eastern Europe has embarked on a fascinating but uncertain process of far-reaching change, which will have profound implications for the future development of the European security system. The transformations sweeping the lands between the Elbe and the Bug are pregnant with promise, but also with grave danger. The promise is that democratic states in Eastern Europe will provide a key building-block for a less militarised and more cooperative security structure in Europe. The danger is that the disintegration of the 'socialist community' will produce a region of impoverished and politically unstable states, economically dependent on the West – especially Germany – and plagued by endemic national and ethnic conflicts. The current period of uncertainty and transition will probably endure for many years to come. Whatever the outcome of the reform process in individual East European states, however, the revolutions of 1989 have irrevocably transformed the assumptions underpinning West European integration and European security. In this situation, the policies of the European Community and of NATO will be of considerable importance to the future of the European security system, and it is to Western Europe and the Atlantic Alliance that we now turn.

Notes
1. George Schöpflin has argued that Eastern Europe has lived through a constant state of 'unstable equilibrium' for over forty years; *Soviet–East European Dilemmas*, edited by K. Dawisha and P. Hanson (London: Heinemann

for the RIIA, 1981), p. 82. For some useful studies of post-war East
European developments, see L.P. Morris, *Eastern Europe Since 1945*
(London: Heinemann, 1984) and Olga A. Narkiewicz, *Eastern Europe,
1968–1984* (London: Croom Helm, 1986).

2. See for example Joseph Rothschild, *East Central Europe between the Two
   World Wars* (Seattle: University of Washington Press, 1974) and Antony
   Polonsky, *The Little Dictators* (London: Routledge and Kegan Paul, 1975).

3. Norberto Bobbio, 'The Upturned Utopia', in the *New Left Review*, no. 177
   (September–October 1989), pp. 37–39 (p. 37).

4. See Thomas T. Hammond, ed., *The Anatomy of Communist Takeovers* (New
   Haven, Conn.: Yale University Press, 1975), and Bogdan Szajkowski, *The
   Establishment of Marxist Regimes* (London: Butterworth, 1982).

5. Lesek Kolakowski, as a young man attracted to the Communist Party in
   post-war Poland, reflected the views of others of his generation; 'We ...
   saw Communism as a continuation of the revolutionary, humanist, socialist
   tradition – of the spirit of the enlightenment ... We were very hostile to a
   certain kind of cultural, somewhat obscurantist tradition – a tradition of
   bigotry. We believed Marxism to be an intellectual instrument to oppose this
   tradition, and one which would give us a large, internationalist, rationalist,
   view of the world.' Quoted in Michael Charlton, *The Eagle and the Small
   Birds* (London: BBC Publications, 1984), p. 88.

6. The phrase was coined by a State Department Counsellor Helmut
   Sonnenfeldt at a closed meeting in London of American ambassadors in
   Europe in December 1975; see Lincoln Gordon et al., *Eroding Empire:
   Western Relations with Eastern Europe* (Washington, D.C.: The Brookings
   Institution, 1987), pp. 80–81.

7. The classic statement of the 'Brezhnev doctrine' is S. Kovalev, 'Suverenitet
   i internatsional'nye obyazannosti sotsialisticheskikh Stran', *Pravda*, 26
   September 1968, p. 4.

8. Jim Seroka and Maurice D. Simon, *Developed Socialism in the Soviet Bloc:
   Political Theory and Political Reality* (Boulder, Co.: Westview, 1982).

9. In 1987, Mieczyslaw Rakowski, Poland's Prime Minister of the time, wrote
   that 'symptoms of crisis are becoming apparent in all socialist countries'.
   If they did not reform themselves, he continued, 'the further history of our
   [socialist] formation will be marked by shocks and revolutionary explosions,
   initiated by an increasingly enlightened people'; quoted by T. Garton Ash
   in 'Reform or Revolution?', *New York Review of Books*, 27 October 1988,
   p. 47. Zbigniew Brzezinski also argued that Eastern Europe was in a
   pre-revolutionary situation, and that 'It is not an exaggeration to affirm
   that there are five countries now ripe for revolutionary explosion': talk
   given at the Hugh Seton-Watson Memorial Lecture at the Centre for Policy
   Studies, January 1988.

10. Christoph Royen, *Osteuropa: Reformen und Wandel. Erfahrungen und
    Aussichten vor dem Hintergrund der sowjetische Perestrojka* (Baden-Baden:
    Nomos Verlag, 1988), and Karen Dawisha et al., *Change in Eastern Europe:
    Soviet Interests and Western Opportunities* (Washington: The Atlantic
    Council of the United States Occasional Paper, 1989).

11. After Gennady Gerassimov's reference to the Frank Sinatra song, 'My Way',
    when speaking of Eastern Europe.

12. Two excellent volumes in this respect are David Turnock's *Eastern Europe:*

An Economic and Political Geography (London: Routledge, 1989), and his companion study, *The Human Geography of Eastern Europe* (London: Routledge, 1989).

13. See Flora Lewis, 'Eastern Europe: A Heritage of Marxist Grime', in the *International Herald Tribune*, 11 April 1990, and 'The West Wakes up to Eastern Nightmare', in the *Financial Times*, 14 May 1990, p. 25. For an assessment of the economic wastage involved in this ecological pollution, see 'Clearing up after Communism', *The Economist*, 17 February 1990, pp. 62–63.

14. See the special edition of *The Annals*, vol. 507 (January 1990), 'Privatizing and Marketizing Socialism', edited by Jan S. Prybyla (London: Sage, 1990).

15. T. Garton Ash, 'Reform or Revolution?', p. 56.

16. Adam Michnik has said, 'the language of socialism is dead in Eastern and Central Europe'; *The Guardian*, 8 March 1990, p. 24. Similarly, Vaclav Havel has argued that socialism has lost all meaning in 'the Czech linguistic context' over the last fifteen years, even though he favours social justice and a plural economy, with different forms of ownership; quoted in T. Garton Ash, 'The Revolution of the Magic Lantern', in *The New York Review of Books*, 18 January 1990, pp. 42–51 (p. 45).

17. Timothy Garton Ash is one of the strongest proponents of the view that the East European revolutions simply sought 'not Utopian new models but tested old ones'; see 'The Bitter Legacy of 40 Lost Years', in *The Independent*, 8 December 1990, p. 19, and his collection of essays, *The Uses of Adversity* (Cambridge: Granta, 1989), esp. pp. 281–82. For a contrasting view, see John Palmer, 'Eastern Bloc in Search of a Third Way', in *The Guardian*, 22 November 1989, p. 23.

18. Marshall Shulman, 'Can Change be Sustained?', in *The Strategic Implications of Change in the Soviet Union*, Adelphi Papers no. 247 (London: Brassey's for the IISS, 1990), pp. 29–40 (p. 40).

19. George Schöpflin, 'Why Communism Collapsed: The End of Communism in Eastern Europe', *International Affairs*, vol. 66, no. 1 (1990), pp. 3–16 (p. 12).

20. See the Mori poll published in *The Independent*, 19 February 1990, p. 14, and the articles by Peter Kellner, 'Social Democracy Has Yet to Earn Its Inheritance', *The Independent*, 19 February 1990, and Isabel Hilton, *The Independent*, 22 February 1990.

21. T. Garton Ash, 'Eastern Europe: The Year of Truth', in the *New York Review of Books*, vol. 37, no. 2 (15 February 1990), pp. 17–22 (p. 17).

22. On the Spanish model as a classic example of evolutionary and consensual regime transition, see Geoffrey Pridham, 'When the partying stops', *The Times Higher Education Supplement*, 16 March 1990, p. 17. It is tempting to extend the Iberian paradigm by drawing out the parallels between the Portuguese case of revolution and disruption with the Romanian experience. Nevertheless, as the Spanish Prime Minister said in his *Financial Times* interview (published on 17 December 1990), 'there has never been a Spanish model'. Developments in Spain, he insisted, occurred through mutual tolerance, moderation and extraordinary improvisation. 'Also, Spain had a personal dictatorship, not a totalitarian system. Franco, and, later, Pinochet, showed us that market economies are perfectly compatible with

dictatorships. But the last thing I tell visitors from eastern Europe is usually the most bitter – things are going to be bad. And I can say this from my Spanish experience. Franco died in 1975 and the whole world rejoiced ... but we went through a terrible economic crisis and we discovered that international solidarity did not translate into economic aid or a flow of investment.'

23. For an analysis of this model of authoritarian state capitalism, see Gordon White (ed.), *Developmental States in East Asia* (London: Macmillan, 1988).
24. See Arthur Hajnicz, 'Poland within its Geopolitical Triangle', in *Aussenpolitik*, vol. 40, no. 1 (1989), pp. 30–40, and Andrzej Karkoszka, 'Transition of the East – a New Beginning for Europe?', in *The Strategic Implications of Change in the Soviet Union, Part 1*, Adelphi Paper 247 (London: Brassey's for the IISS, 1990), pp. 81–91 (p. 90).
25. Renee De Nevers, *The Soviet Union and Eastern Europe: The End of an Era*, Adelphi Paper 249 (London: Brassey's for the IISS, 1990). Somewhat dated, but still of considerable interest, are the studies by Richard D. Vine, *Soviet–East European Relations as a Problem for the West* (London: Croom Helm, 1987), and Karen Dawisha, *Eastern Europe, Gorbachev and Reform* (Cambridge: Cambridge University Press, 1988).
26. An excellent recent study of the impact of the *novoe myshlenie* on the WTO is Gerard Holden's *The Warsaw Pact: Soviet Security and Bloc Politics* (London: Blackwell, 1989).
27. See Adam Roberts, 'Does the Warsaw Pact have a Future?, in *Samizdat*, no. 8 (January–February 1990), pp. 6–7. Two Soviet analysts, Mikhail Bezrukov and Andrei Kortunov, have proposed a similar role for the WTO: see their article, 'What Kind of Alliance do we Need?, in *Novoe Vremya*, no. 40 (1 October, 1989). As regards the role of the 'German question' in cementing the Warsaw Pact together, Bakunin's remarks are of relevance; 'if there were no Germans we should have to invent them, since nothing so successfully unites the Slavs as a rooted hatred of Germans'. Quoted in Walter Laqueur, *Russia and Germany* (London: Weidenfeld and Nicolson, 1965), p. 13.
28. Joszef van Brabant, *Socialist Economic Integration: Aspects of Contemporary Economic Problems in Eastern Europe* (Cambridge: Cambridge University Press, 1980). For more recent analyses, see the papers by Michael Kaser and Laszlo Lang on 'The Economic Dimension of East–West Relations', in *The Strategic Implications of Change in the Soviet Union*, pp. 92–103, and pp. 104–16.
29. See Jürgen Nötzold, 'Several European Economic Blocs? The Future Significance of the COMECON', in *Aussenpolitik*, vol. 40, no. 3 (1989), pp. 277–92, and Christian Meier, 'COMECON – a Follow-on Organization is Planned', in *NATO Review*, vol. 38, no. 5 (October 1990), pp. 22–26.
30. See Laszlo Lengyel, 'Europe through Hungarian eyes', in *International Affairs*, vol. 66, no. 2 (1990), pp. 291–97, and Horst Teltschik, 'The Federal Republic and Poland – A Difficult Relationship in the Heart of Europe', *Aussenpolitik*, vol. 41, no. 1 (1990), pp. 3–14.
31. As Ernest Gellner notes, the map of Eastern Europe now bears a closer resemblance to a picture by Modigliani than to one by Kokoschka; quoted in T. Garton Ash, 'Eastern Europe: Year of Truth', p. 20.
32. See Teresa Rakowska-Harmstone, 'Nationalism and Integration in Eastern Europe: The Dynamics of Change', in her edited volume, *Communism in*

Eastern Europe, second edition (Manchester: Manchester University Press, 1984), pp. 360–81.

33. See Neal Ascherson, 'Old Conflicts in the New Europe', *The Independent on Sunday*, 18 February 1990, pp. 3–5, and 'Flood danger after thaw', *The Independent*, 3 April 1990, p. 19. For an analysis of some of the security implications of these national-ethnic conflicts, see Jonathan Eyal's edited volume, *The Warsaw Pact and the Balkans: Moscow's Southern Flank* (London: Macmillan for RUSI, 1989).

34. The so-called 'Macedonian syndrome', in which in the past weak, modernising states in Eastern Europe have been captured by different political factions – including the military and ethnic groupings – exploiting nationalist themes for their parochial purposes. See Myron Weiner, 'The Macedonian Syndrome: An Historical Model of International Relations and Political Development', *World Politics*, vol. 23, no. 4 (July 1971), pp. 665–83.

35. See Ian Traynor, 'Ideal of Europe Meets Reality of Nationalism', *The Guardian*, 7 April 1990, and Patricia Clough, 'Time of Truth for Central Europe', *The Independent*, 10 April 1990.

36. Adam Michnik, 'The Two Faces of Europe', in the *New York Review of Books*, 19 July 1990, p. 7.

37. 'Theodore Malloch on Eastern Europe and International Economic Organisations', *Meeting Report*, 30 January 1990, Institute for East–West Security Studies, New York.

38. For the relevant details, see 'The BERD's in Hand', *Time*, 4 June 1990, p. 81.

39. The decision to establish the European Environment Agency was taken at a conference of EC environment ministers and their East European counterparts in Dublin in June. This will be the first EC institution with participation of East European countries, including the Soviet Union. See the *Financial Times*, 18 June 1990, p. 4.

40. Jack Snyder, 'Averting Anarchy in the New Europe', *International Security*, vol. 14, no. 4 (Spring 1990), pp. 5–41.

41. Frans H.J.J. Andriessen, 'Change in Central and Eastern Europe: The Role of the Community', *NATO Review*, vol. 38, no. 1 (February 1990), pp. 1–6.

42. J.M.C. Rollo et al., *The New Eastern Europe: Western Responses* (London: Pinter for the RIIA, 1990), pp. 130–31.

43. Catherine Lalumiere, 'The Council of Europe in the Construction of a Wider Europe'; talk given at the Royal Institute of International Affairs, 28 February 1990. See also Isabel Hilton, 'Specifications for Building a New Europe', *The Independent*, 1 March 1990, and Edward Mortimer, 'Springtime for Euro-institutions', in the *Financial Times*, 12 June 1990.·

44. 'The Dream of Europax', *The Economist*, April 7 1990, pp. 14–15.

45. See the addresses by Jiri Dienstbier, Minister of Foreign Affairs of the Czechoslovak Federative Republic, and Markus Meckel, Minister of Foreign Affairs of the GDR, at the Royal Institute of International Affairs, 3 April and 20 June 1990.

46. See Lincoln Gordon, *Eroding Empire: Western Relations with Eastern Europe* (Washington, D.C.: The Brookings Institution, 1987), pp. 277–78.

47. For details, see 'East is East and West is West, and What is in the Middle?', *The Economist*, 26 December 1987, pp. 31–32.

48. See Laszlo J. Kiss, 'Chances of the Interregional Danubian-Central European scheme of Cooperation', a paper presented at the international scientific conference on *The Danube: River of Cooperation*, Belgrade, 28 September –2 October 1989.
49. See Heinz Gaertner's stimulating paper, 'The Role and Perspectives of the Neutral Countries in a New European Security Order', presented at the CeSPI-Friedrich Ebert Foundation work-shop on *'The New European Security Order'*, Rome, 19–20 July 1990.

6

West European Integration and the 'New Atlanticism'

Although it is Eastern Europe and the Soviet Union which have recently been the site of dramatic – indeed, revolutionary – changes in post-war Europe, Western Europe itself has been undergoing a process of profound transformation no less far-reaching in its consequences. From the devastation of the 1940s, Western Europe has experienced a veritable renaissance. Today, it is one of the most dynamic and prosperous regions of the global economy.[1] The post-war recovery of Western Europe is in no small part due to the benevolent self-interest of the Americans. The subsequent emergence of the transatlantic community in the second half of the twentieth century has been one of the decisive features of the contemporary international system. It has provided a strategic safeguard for Western Europe, which has facilitated the stable development of the region. At the same time, the economic recovery of Western Europe has been accompanied by a process of growing cooperation and integration, which has helped overcome the national and historical enmities of its peoples. This remarkable integration process has been led by the European Community, which has both doubled in size from its original membership of six, and deepened and expanded its forms of integration. Furthermore, the 1980s witnessed renewed efforts to develop a distinctive West European security identity, through a variety of bi- and multilateral forms of cooperation.

Western Europe is therefore engaged in a historical process of transforming the dynamics of its internal relationships, and in doing so, it is changing its relations with the USA, the Soviet Union and Eastern Europe, and other parts of the global system, including the expanding economies of the Pacific rim and the Third World.[2] In this chapter, we will consider the implications for the European security system of West European integration and the evolving transatlantic relationship. This involves assessing three sets of issues: the EC and the process of European construction; the future of NATO and the Atlantic community; and the prospects for the WEU and closer West European security cooperation.

I: WEST EUROPEAN INTEGRATION AND
THE EUROPEAN COMMUNITY

Western Europe's recovery after 1945 has been astounding. Not only
was Western Europe able to overcome its wartime destruction, it was
also able to put behind it the bitterness and social divisions of pre-war
laissez-faire capitalism. Although many countries in the region face difficult problems of unemployment, social deprivation, regional disparities
and environmental pollution, these 'contradictions of capitalism' pale into
insignificance when compared with the unenviable legacy of 'developed
socialism' in the East.[3] As a consequence of its post-war achievements,
Western Europe – with its welfare states, limited governments, social
market economies and vibrant civil societies – has emerged as a powerful
pole of attraction for those to its east and south. Indeed, many of Western
Europe's problems today derive from its very successes – from the
environmental costs of an affluent society, to the pressures of immigration
from less developed societies on the region's borders.[4]

After the trauma of the Second World War, Europeans like Jean
Monnet, Robert Schuman and Winston Churchill[5] felt that nationalism
and the nation-state should be transcended in a European federation
or union. This was the thinking behind both the European Coal and
Steel Community (ECSC) and later, the European Economic Community
(EEC) and Euratom.[6] The integration process, however, has not taken
the unilinear form envisaged by some of its early pioneers. Instead,
cooperation and integration have assumed a variety of institutional
forms. The institutional landscape of Western Europe has subsequently
become highly complex and diverse, with a whole array of functionally
and geographically distinct bodies, including the EC and EFTA; the
Council of Europe; the Western European Union (WEU), Independent
European Programme Group (IEPG) and the Eurogroup; EUREKA,
EURATOM, and the European Space Agency (ESA); the Pompidou,
Trevi and Schengen[7] groups; and the Nordic Council and Pentagonale.

This 'Euro plethora' (as it has been dubbed by Michel Rocard), with
its institutional and functional diversity, certainly leaves Western Europe
prone to a degree of political incoherence and fragmentation. But its
flexibility and pragmatism is also a source of considerable strength. It
permits integration to proceed at different paces through different forums,
and corresponds to the richness and diversity of Europe's historical
traditions and experiences. As Karsten Voigt has argued, 'The various
degrees of integration and the diversity of institutions' functions and
boundaries are not something negative. Indeed, they are uniquely and
historically European. A mechanical expression of past state-creating
processes to the pan-European integration process would be historically

inappropriate and politically counterproductive.'[8]

In the 1980s, the pace of West European integration perceptibly quickened. Security cooperation acquired a new momentum as a result of both European differences with the Reagan Administration, and a renewed sense of the 'Soviet threat'. In the EC, Eurosclerosis was replaced by Europhoria, as the adoption of the Single European Act in 1986 released a surge of energy and political dynamism.[9] As a consequence of the southern expansion of the Community and the Single European Act, the EC has acquired a new significance and importance, reaching far beyond the borders of the Twelve themselves. Within an institutionally diverse Western Europe, the EC is pioneering an integration process which increasingly has far-reaching implications for the whole post-war security architecture of Europe.

At the same time, the process of West European integration now stands on the threshold of profound change, in both its direction and dynamic. The parameters of post-war integration in Western Europe were defined by two key factors: the protection of the US strategic nuclear umbrella within the transatlantic community, and the division of the continent into two distinct and antagonistic blocs. Western Europe – 'OECD Europe' – defined itself in opposition to the communist East. With the collapse of communism in Eastern Europe, however, and Gorbachev's reforms in the Soviet Union, the comfortable assumptions underpinning four decades of West European construction no longer hold. Western Europe – and the EC in particular – now needs to redefine its relations with democratising and independent states in Eastern Europe, and with a reforming USSR. Western Europe is thus faced with the demanding task of integrating two historic processes – West European integration and the healing of the division of Europe. In both processes, the European Community will play a central role, and in doing so, it will be taking decisions which are of great significance for the future development of the European security system.

'1992' and Beyond: the Future of the European Community

After decades of incremental development and despite intermittent periods of institutional stagnation, the EC has emerged as **the** central body in the new Europe. Today, it stands at the heart of the restructuring of economic and political relations in Europe. The Community represents the institutional embodiment of the effective demilitarisation of security relations amongst former enemies in Western Europe. Whatever conflicts may divide them – from disputes over bans on British beef to differences over sanctions against South Africa – war has become unthinkable between the countries of Western Europe. What Francis Fukuyama (bemoaning the passing of the cold war as the 'end of history') dubs the 'common marketisation of international relations' is in fact the Community's greatest achievement. By pioneering new forms of regional economic integration, the EC has developed into a novel experiment in supranational integration and cooperation, involving a pooling of sovereignty amongst nation-states.

In the 1950s, the driving force behind integration was political. By the late 1970s and early 1980s, by contrast, it was primarily economic and social. Western Europe is without doubt the pre-eminent regional example of 'complex interdependence' – which, as we have seen, is becoming a key feature of the contemporary international system (see Chapter 1). Patterns of economic, financial and industrial interaction in Western Europe no longer coincide with the boundaries of individual nation-states. An integrated regional economy has emerged in Western Europe, characterised by transnational corporations, continental-wide business mergers and strategic corporate alliances. Technological pressures (above all the communications and information revolution, and the spread of micro-chip technology) – and business requirements in an increasingly competitive global economy – have led to cross-border corporate networking, Europe-wide production systems and integrated European markets.[10] By the 1980s, the intensity of informal forms of economic and social interaction had given rise to the emergence of a West European social and economic space, centred on the West German economy. Indeed, by this time, the West European economy was moving beyond the interdependence of distinct national economies, and was becoming more and more an integrated regional economy.[11]

The Single European Act is in one important sense the Community's adjustment to the surge in economic and social integration which took place in the 1970s, independently of government action. It is a response to the disjuncture between the needs of modern economies, and the limited means at the disposal of nation-states. In order to facilitate and regulate the social and economic flows and informal patterns of interaction in a region marked by particularly high forms of complex interdependence, there is a need to provide a set of commonly agreed rules and regulations. This in turn requires an institutional framework for devising, adjusting and enforcing these rules.[12] In the experience of the Twelve, this can best be done at the Community level, rather than by the individual nation-states.

This clearly has important conseqences for the exercise of national sovereignty by the twelve, and therefore, for security relations in Europe. Critics of a more integrated Community point to the loss of national sovereignty that the creation of such an 'identikit' Europe would involve.[13] Nevertheless, the autonomy of the nation-state has long been undermined by the developing patterns of regional economic integration in

Europe, whilst traditional concepts of national sovereignty are increasingly becoming anachronistic in an era of deepening economic and political interdependencies. Over the last thirty years or so, individual West European states have been less and less able to control economic developments within their own boundaries, given the transnational character of modern economic and social life.[14] Formal political and economic integration is a way of overcoming this, by pooling sovereignty on a supranational basis.[15]

Furthermore, counterposing 'national sovereignty' to 'supranational integration' is too simplistic: the experience of the EC suggests that it is possible to achieve a pooling of sovereignty in some areas of policy, whilst retaining a strong national or regional identity, and considerable national authority over other important policy-issues. The key to this is the notion of 'subsidiarity' (ie, nothing should be decided at Community level that is better done at national or local level), which is emerging as a guiding principle of EC construction.[16]

The debate over sovereignty has intensified in recent years as the process of European integration through the EC has accelerated. This acceleration has three principal causes. First, logic of the '1992 project', which has given a powerful impulse towards economic and monetary union (EMU), and which has highlighted the need for further reform of the Community's decision-making mechanisms. Second, German unification, and the associated desire to integrate German power into broader pan-European structures. And third, the upheavals in Eastern Europe, which have underlined the need for a strong and coherent Community as a dependable bulwark in a period of acute transitional instability.[17]

The Community is thus engaged on a bold and potentially far-reaching process of adaptation and integration, as it seeks to respond to a rapidly changing external environment. The Community's full agenda reflects the demands that history has now placed on it: whilst seeking to complete the building of the unified internal market by 1992, the EC is now exploring the next steps along the road towards both economic and monetary union, and political union. At the same time, it is engaged in complex negotiations with both EFTA and GATT; it is absorbing eastern Germany within the Community; it is seeking to establish a new set of relationships with the reforming countries of Eastern Europe and the Soviet Union; and it is recasting its relations with the USA.

The two Inter-Governmental Conferences which opened in December 1990 focused on two of the key issues facing the Community in the early 1990s – EMU ('Economic and Monetary Union') and 'Political Union'. The debate on EMU centres around the Delors Committee proposal for the creation of a European System of Central Banks and a single currency.[18] This would facilitate trade and investment in the single market, but is a highly sensitive political issue, because it directly impinges on a crucial area of national sovereignty. It is also widely regarded as a way of institutionalising the existing hegemony of the Deutschemark and the Bundesbank – a prospect which might provide reassurance to some (given the Bundesbank's political independence and firm anti-inflationary policy), but which causes acute alarm in other quarters. Nevertheless, given the powerful constituencies in favour of EMU (especially in industrial and financial circles), it seems inevitable that some form of intensified monetary cooperation in the Community will emerge, even if the Delors plan is not accepted in its entirety.

The debate on political union is even more controversial. The problem here is that there is no clear definition of what this emotive phrase means: as Sir Leon Brittan has said, the term 'political union' is understood differently in different languages and in different countries.[19] 'Political union' actually means something much more prosaic than the creation of a federal Europe – namely, institutional reform, along with some new policy tasks (primarily in the area of foreign and security policy) and a greater political commitment to the notion of 'European integration'. One thing is certain: US-style federalism – a 'United States of Europe' – is **not** on the agenda.[20] Instead, guided evolution towards tighter forms of political cooperation is feasible, possibly leading to quasi-confederation in the long term.

Proposals for institutional reform include extending majority voting in the Council of Ministers (perhaps to include taxation and 'Green' issues); redressing a perceived 'democratic deficit' by increasing the powers of the European Parliament and involving national parliaments in decision-making; expanding the powers of the Commission; and strengthening the powers of the European Court of Justice in Luxembourg.[21] One of the central issues in the debate is the relationship between the Commission and the Council of Ministers – the Community's twin-headed executive – and their relative powers and responsibilities.[22] At the same time, European political union involves a discussion of a common foreign and security policy. This takes us on to the issue of the Community's impact on the evolving European security system.

The EC and European Security

The Community's greatest impact on the European security system has already been mentioned – it institutionalises economic and social inter-dependence within the core nations of Western Europe, thereby making a major contribution to the demilitarisation of security relations between former rivals. By providing institutional mechanisms for the pooling of sovereignty, the Community has helped overcome the legacy of national enmity which has so disfigured modern European politics. This is particularly relevant in the case of Germany: indeed, the EC provides one key to resolving the centuries old problem of accommodating German power in the heart of Europe. The existence of the Community – with its supranational integration – provides an indispensable institutional framework for absorbing the substantial power of a united Germany within broader West European structures. In this way it helps provide a peaceful solution to one of the most sensitive issues of contemporary European security.

The Community's other vital contribution to European security can be its role as an active supporter of the reform process in post-communist Eastern Europe, and in the Soviet Union itself. As we have already seen, East European aspirations for closer relations with the EC are forcing a re-evaluation of the assumptions underlying West European integration, by raising the issue of the future widening of the Community's membership. This, however, is an issue for the next century: given the scale of the economic and political problems facing Eastern Europe, these countries will not be in a position to apply for full membership of the Community in the 1990s. The immediate question, therefore, concerns the restructuring of the EC's relations with the countries to its east. By providing a supportive international environment for the reform processes in Eastern Europe, the Twelve can play a vital role in the reshaping of security relations in the new Europe – as we saw in Chapter 5.

This reflects the changing nature of security in Europe: as the military confrontation eases, the non-military aspects of security are acquiring greater prominence. Given its 'civilian' character, the Community is well placed to take the lead in establishing a new pattern of economic and political relationships in Europe. This was recognised by the G7 Summit in Paris in July 1989, when the Commission was assigned the role of coordinating aid by the OECD countries to Poland and Hungary. This meant that for the first time in post-war history, the lead for the West in East–West relations was being taken by the Europeans, rather than by the Americans. It is also significant that – amidst a wide-ranging debate on European 'architecture' – the first institution to see the light of day was an economic one – the EBRD (European Bank for Reconstruction and Development), the purpose of which is to facilitate market-orientated economic reform in the East. Moreover, two new bodies have been proposed within the framework of the European Community: a European Environmental Agency is to be established, with which the Soviet Union and East European states will be associated;[23] and a European Energy Community.[24] This latter body was proposed by the Dutch at the Dublin meeting of the European Council in June 1990, and ideas for such a European energy initiative are now being canvassed, both within the EC and in the USSR.[25] Such proposals could help to strengthen and institutionalise the interdependencies between East and West, thereby serving an analogous function to the ECSC in the 1950s (which made war between France and West Germany economically and politically untenable).

In the medium to long term, however, the magnetic pull of a unified internal market of over 350 million consumers means that the Community will face a growing queue of prospective members. Turkish, Austrian, Cypriot and Maltese applications are already on the table.[26] In October 1990, Sweden announced its intention to apply for full EC membership. If the complex negotiations with EFTA over the creation of a 'European Economic Space' come to naught, then the Community could find itself faced with membership applications from Norway, Switzerland, Finland and Iceland.[27] The case for opening the EC up to the 'four Mediterranean orphans' (Turkey, Yugoslavia, Cyprus and Malta) is weaker on both economic and cultural grounds, although rejecting the Turkish application could cause complications for NATO and political unrest in Turkey.[28] It would be particularly difficult (on political grounds) to reject applications from democratic and market-orientated countries in East Central Europe – such as Czechoslovakia, Poland and Hungary – if they were willing to accept the costs of the *acquis communitaire* (which would be even higher after EMU and 'Political Union'). The case for Community membership for the East Europeans has been persuasively argued – not least, because it would provide a means of fostering cooperation between former communist countries which otherwise might find themselves divided by national, political and ethnic conflicts.[29] The expansion of the Community beyond its existing Twelve members, however, would require further institutional reform, in order to ensure effective decision-making and implementation in a much larger Community. Before the end of the 1990s, therefore, the Community may be forced to confront the issue of how to combine 'widening' with 'deepening'.[30]

The debate on 'widening' versus 'deepening' has been brought sharply into focus over the question of whether the EC should develop a common security and defence policy. In December 1990, the Rome meeting of the European Council (which established the broad framework for the negotiations in the two subsequent inter-governmental conferences) declared that,

> As regards common security, the gradual extension of the union's role in this area should be considered, in particular with reference, initially, to issues debated in international organisations: arms control, disarmament and related issues; CSCE matters; certain questions debated in the United Nations, including peace-keeping operations; economic and technological co-operation in the armaments field; co-ordination of armaments expert policy, and non-proliferation.

Furthermore, the European Council emphasises that, with a view to the future, the prospect of a role for the union in defence matters should be considered, without prejudice to member states' existing obligations in this area, bearing in mind the importance of maintaining and strengthening the ties within the Atlantic alliance and without prejudice to the traditional positions of other member states.[31]

These two sections raise a series of complex issues for the EC and for the future security architecture of Europe. Those who advocate the development of a defence dimension for the Community argue that there is a logical line of progression from a single market with supranational decision-making institutions, to a common external policy, and from there to a common security and defence policy. The Community might also acquire a greater international standing, it is suggested, if it assumed responsibility for its own defence.[32]

On the other hand, the Twelve will face a number of serious – perhaps insurmountable – problems if they attempt to go beyond their current concern with the 'economic and political' aspects of security (which the Single European Act assigns to EPC), to the 'hard' issues of military defence. First, the European Commission has no experience in the defence area, and giving it such responsibility might lead to institutional overload. Second, developing a common foreign and security policy in the 1980s has been difficult enough because of the reluctance of Ireland (a neutral country), Greece and Denmark to go down this road. Given the potential differences within the Twelve on questions such as nuclear policy and the future significance of the NATO alliance, it is hard to imagine how a common West European defence policy could be based on anything more than the lowest common denominator. Third, and perhaps most importantly in the long term, if the EC were to emerge as a distinctive security entity with its own military defence policy, it would make it much more difficult – if not impossible – for neutral and non-aligned countries (like Austria and Sweden) and former Warsaw Pact members to join.[33] It would also complicate relations with the Soviet Union, particularly if East European or neutral countries were to develop even closer links with such a Community.

For these reasons, the Twelve may decide to leave military security cooperation to existing bodies (such as NATO or the WEU) and to other forms of bi- and multilateral security cooperation. On balance, the disadvantages of the EC developing a military competence in this sensitive area seem to outweigh the advantages – at least in the short to medium term. Although there is no pressing need to foreclose future options, it may be in the EC's best interests to leave defence policy to other organisations, and to concentrate on the broader (mainly non-military) aspects of security – a task of tremendous importance in the post-cold war period, and one for which the Community is eminently suited.

II: NATO AND THE TRANSATLANTIC COMMUNITY

Whilst the prospects for the European Community in the new Europe appear to be bright, those of the cold war's other Western offspring – NATO – appear much less rosy. Indeed, with the collapse of communism in the East and the effective disintegration of the Warsaw Pact, NATO is now facing the dreaded question: is there life after 40?

For over four decades, NATO has been the bed-rock of Western security. An alliance of sixteen (mostly) democratic nations, it has provided Western Europe with a shield against aggression, ultimately through the strategic umbrella of American extended nuclear deterrence. The linking of American and European military capabilities has meant that Western Europe's security requirements could be met without excessive defence expenditure and the militarisation of their societies, allowing them (in the words of President Truman), 'to get on with the real business of achieving a fuller and happier life for all our citizens'.[34] Although prone to perennial 'crises' and bouts of agonising soul-searching, NATO has survived to become the longest lasting multilateral peacetime alliance in history – thanks in no small part to its collective decision-making procedures (NATO has over 400 committees which meet every year to discuss a wide variety of issues, thereby providing the Alliance with a permanent and extensive consultation process).

With the fading of the cold war, however, NATO faces its most serious challenge to date. In 1968 Pierre Hassner wrote that cold war alliances are perhaps even less easily converted to the uses of detente than war industries to civilian production.[35] Guided by the strategy of the Harmel Report, NATO survived the detente period in remarkably good shape. But can it survive the end of the cold war? What justification can there be for an alliance whose purpose was, in the words of NATO's first Secretary General, Lord Ismay, to 'keep the Russians out of Europe, the Americans in, and the Germans down'? Alan Clarke, the British Minister for Defence Procurement, has argued that NATO has achieved its original function and is now 'obsolete, ill-suited to present circumstances and urgently in need of adaptation'. He has also challenged what he regards as 'increasingly bizarre suggestions for its future function'.[36]

There is little doubt that NATO will change, and change fundamentally, as a result of the disintegration of the 'iron curtain'. But NATO is still likely to remain a significant element of the strategic landscape of the European security area – at least, for the remainder of the decade. Although the threat of a large-scale, short-warning offensive by Warsaw Pact armoured units (the traditional concern of NATO's commanders) is no longer plausible, NATO will continue to serve a number of important functions for its sixteen member nations in the short to medium term.

NATO's Functions in the New Europe

To begin with, NATO will remain an important element of stability in a period of rapid and unpredictable change in Europe. The strategic and political situation in Eastern Europe, the Soviet Union, the Balkans and the wider Mediterranean is potentially volatile.[37] As a functioning alliance committed to collective defence, NATO contributes to the preservation of a stable security climate, thereby facilitating peaceful reform in the East. At the same time, NATO could further improve the security environment in Europe by developing political and diplomatic links with the Soviets and East Europeans. NATO's London Declaration of July 1990 recognised that the Alliance should extend 'the hand of friendship' to its former adversaries in the WTO, and proposed a Joint Declaration of non-aggression between the member states of the two alliances; the establishment of 'regular diplomatic liaison' between NATO and individual WTO countries; an invitation to Gorbachev and other East European leaders to address the North Atlantic Council; and a visit by Manfred Wörner (NATO's Secretary-General) to Moscow. The North Atlantic Assembly can also help here, by developing contacts with parliamentarians in the East.[38] If Soviet and East European diplomats are accredited to NATO, and political contacts between NATO and Warwaw Pact countries continue to develop at the highest levels, then, as William Taft (the US Ambassador to NATO) has suggested, NATO 'would become one of the places where east European nations, including the Soviet Union, would come to discuss security issues'.[39] In this way, NATO could provide the 'scaffolding' for a new security system in Europe.[40]

Second, NATO will continue to have an important military function as a residual security guarantee against renewed confrontation in Europe. NATO's integrated military structures and collective defence planning constitute the heart of the alliance, and their preservation and development will remain central to its continued efficacy. Whatever the outcome of Gorbachev's plans for military restructuring, the Soviet Union will remain the strongest conventional and nuclear power on the Eurasian continent. It is also the only country strong enough to defend itself without allies. Furthermore, despite the improved military balance in central Europe, the strategic situation on NATO's flanks (in both the eastern Mediterranean and the Nordic area) has changed much less. NATO's military strategy and force structure has already begun to change under the pressure of events in Germany and the East, but (as we shall see in Chapter 9) NATO is likely to continue with its strategy of collective deterrence based on 'an appropriate mix of conventional and nuclear forces, at the lowest levels consistent with our security needs' (to use the time-honoured language of NATO communiqués).

Third, NATO remains the only forum in which like-minded North American and European democracies can discuss the political, economic and military dimensions of security policy.[41] This is especially important in terms of the US–West European relationship, but there is also scope for developing NATO as a forum for intra-alliance consultation and dialogue on a whole range of security issues – from the proliferation of ballistic missile technology to chemical weapons. Moreover, the Alliance could continue to provide a tried and tested framework for conflict prevention and mediation between countries like Greece and Turkey, or Britain and Iceland (in the event of another 'cod war').

Fourth, NATO remains indispensable as a mechanism for coordinating the policy of the 16 nations in arms control and confidence building negotiations. This will no doubt be a task of considerable importance in the 1990s. The 16 are already engaged in complex negotiations on conventional arms reductions in Vienna, and in the parallel CSBM talks. By 1991, the Alliance countries are also likely to be involved in negotiations on sub-strategic nuclear weapons. Furthermore, NATO could provide a forum for broader Alliance consultation on the START negotiations and the chemical weapon talks, and could facilitate coordinated support for existing specialised organisations such as the Missile Technology Control Regime. There are proposals for an arms control and verification agency within an institutionalised CSCE framework: in this case, NATO could cooperate with such a body, thereby fulfilling one of its other roles as the 'scaffolding' for a new security structure in Europe.

Fifth, the Alliance can contribute to managing the external dimensions of German unification, and minimise the dangers of a 'renationalisation' of defence policy in Europe. By integrating a united and sovereign German state into a collective defence body, it may be possible (to use the words of Secretary of State Baker) to provide a security arrangement which can 'satisfy the aspirations of the German people and meet the legitimate concerns of Germany's neighbours'.[42] There are few in Europe who would like to see Germany neutral and non-aligned, pursuing its *Sonderweg* in Central Europe. Integration of a united Germany in a defensively structured NATO, with special arrangements for East German territory, would provide reassurance to many of Germany's neighbours, whilst avoiding the danger of 'singularisation' of the Germans inherent in some other proposals. At the same time, integrating Germany into a reformed NATO may help prevent what the FRG Defence Minister Dr Stoltenberg has called the 'renationalisation' of defence policy in Europe – which would encourage individual countries to seek security in shifting (but potentially unstable) coalitions.

The Limits to NATO's Competency

Having considered some of the reasons why – in the short and medium term at least – NATO might remain relevant to the the security requirements of a Europe 'beyond containment', it is essential to specify what tasks NATO would not be suited for.

First, NATO cannot feasibly be expected to 'police the world',[43] or to play a major role in dealing with 'out-of-area' disputes and regional conflicts in the Third World. The Alliance can provide a forum for consultation on such issues among the 16, and could perhaps provide some logistical support for 'out-of-area' operations.[44] But for NATO to become militarily involved in the Middle East or the Gulf – let alone Africa or Asia – would be most inappropriate. The authority of the UN is only grudgingly accepted in some parts of the world: there would be very little international support for NATO if it tried to act as a self-appointed global policeman. To do so would also place major strains on the fabric of the Alliance, by eroding the domestic support for NATO within its member nations. Similarly, NATO cannot be expected to take on new responsibilities for combating drug trafficking or international terrorism.[45]

Second, NATO cannot play a significant role – beyond its function in preserving the necessary security climate – in solving the problems of economic and political transition in Eastern Europe, let alone contribute in any meaningful way to solving global social, economic and environmental problems.[46] NATO is not a 'supranational ministry of commerce or a credit bank',[47] and has limited expertise in economic, financial, social or environmental issues. The non-military aspects of security in Eastern Europe and elsewhere are better left to organisations like the EC, OECD, GATT, the World Bank and specialist agencies of the UN.

Third, NATO cannot solve the security problems of Eastern Europe. Again, it would not be 'prudent' (to use a word popular in NATO circles) to extend security guarantees to the East Europeans, or to entertain the idea of accepting former Warsaw Pact members into the Alliance (despite the provisions for this in Article 10 of the 1949 Washington Treaty).[48] The security requirements of the East Europeans should best be left to the East Europeans themselves, or, ideally, to new mechanisms for conflict prevention and crisis management within an institutionalised CSCE. The West should confine itself to providing economic and political support – to do otherwise would risk provoking confrontation with the Soviet Union, and would also threaten the cohesion of the Alliance itself.

Despite these cautionary words on the limits of the Alliance's competences, however, reports of NATO's imminent demise are greatly exaggerated. For the next five or ten years at least, NATO is likely to continue to play an important role in the new security system in Europe – as an insurance against unforeseen eventualities; as a means of negotiating and verifying arms control agreements; as a framework for addressing – without singularisation – some of the security dimensions of German unification; and as the scaffolding for a new security arrangement in a less divided continent. In fulfilling these tasks and responsibilities, NATO will in effect be completing the strategy laid down in the Harmel Report – of maintaining deterrence and adequate defences, whilst seeking 'a more stable relationship in which the underlying political issues can be resolved'.

The danger facing NATO, therefore, is not of collapse, dismemberment or abolition. Rather, it is of the Alliance becoming increasingly irrelevant and anachronistic to the changed strategic and political landscape of Europe – hence the importance of reforming both its structure and strategy. The overall significance of NATO in terms of European security is bound to decline as the non-military aspects of security become increasingly more prominent. It will never again play the central role it did in the 1950s and 1960s, and its importance vis-a-vis organisations like the EC – and perhaps the CSCE and even the WEU – will probably decline in future years. Nevertheless, they are unlikely to develop to such an extent that they render NATO redundant – at least, not before the next century.

However, this relative decline in NATO's importance will place the transatlantic relationship under even greater stresses and strains. It is therefore to the future of the Atlantic community that we now turn.

Transatlantic Relations in a Changing World

One of the most important developments in the post-war world was the emergence of the Atlantic community – a strategic alliance between the 'old' and 'new' worlds, based on shared values and common interests. Although the transatlantic relationship was clearly coloured by the hegemonic role of the USA in the immediate post-war period,[49] it provided the West Europeans with a number of benefits: it gave them a strategic guarantee; it allowed their economic recovery to take place within the stability of a US defined global economic system; and American leadership provided a broader community within which the historic rivalries amongst the West Europeans could be transcended – in this way, the USA acted as 'Europe's American pacifier'.[50] For the Americans, the transatlantic relationship has created a balance in Europe which has made possible America's post-war global predominance. In other words, for the USA, NATO has provided the essential bulwark upon which the post-war *pax Americana* could be constructed.[51]

As Western Europe recovered from its wartime devastation and the perception of an immediate 'Soviet threat' lessened, however, the Atlantic Alliance began to suffer increasing tensions. A major cause of this has been structural change in the world economy and the global balance of power, which have shifted the balance of power relations between the USA and Western Europe. In 1945, American power was overwhelming (see Chapter 2, pp. 25–26). Virtually all the institutions of the post-war world reflected the hegemony of the USA – none more so than NATO itself. Since then, however, the institutions of the *pax Americana* have come under increasing strain as a result of two trends: the relative decline of US power (with the associated signs of what Paul Kennedy has called 'imperial over-stretch'), and the growing economic importance and political cohesion of Western Europe.

The 1980s were a particularly troubled decade for the transatlantic relationship.[52] Differences between the Reagan Administration and Western Europe arose over a number of issues, including East–West relations; policy towards regional conflicts; and trade disputes. At the same time, there was even greater perception of the dilemmas of extended nuclear deterrence, as a result of NATO's 'dual-track' decision of December 1979; SDI; the Reykjavik summit (when President Reagan endorsed the notion of 'a safer world without nuclear weapons'); and the Washington 'double zero' Treaty of 1987.[53] Furthermore, the long-running 'burden-sharing' dispute continued simmering away, threatening a major rift in US–West European relations. On balance, therefore, the European experience of the Reagan Administration has not been a happy one, and President Reagan's attempt to 're-establish American leadership in NATO has simply intensified anxieties in Europe about the nature of that leadership'.[54]

Towards a 'New Atlanticism'?

In contrast to the more ideologically motivated and aggressively assertive Administration of President Reagan, that of President George Bush promises to be more adept at managing the complexities of the trans-atlantic alliance. The Administration seems to have reached two important conclusions: first, that West European integration is compatible with US global interests;[55] second, that Germany is the key to the new Europe. Indeed, in May 1989 in Mainz, Bush spoke of Washington and Bonn as 'partners in leadership'. At the same time, the US has been happy to see the EC take the lead in East–West relations in Europe (especially in terms of economic aid and technical assistance), but would like NATO to remain the bed-rock to Western security in a Europe 'whole and free' – with the CSCE playing a complementary rather than competitive role.

Nonetheless, a number of unresolved problems in transatlantic relations remain. To begin with, there are dangers of growing US–West European friction over security issues. On the one hand, Western Europe is becoming a more cohesive international actor, willing and able to assert its own economic and political interests – for example, in the Middle East, or in terms of relations with the USSR and Eastern Europe.[56] On the other, the Gulf crisis has led to renewed complaints on Capitol Hill that the Europeans are not doing enough to protect their own interests, and that America has been left to carry the main burden of enforcing UN Security Council resolutions on Kuwait. At the same time, a growing number of voices in the USA are beginning to question the need to maintain a substantial military commitment to Europe following the passing of the cold war, especially in the light of US strategic and economic interests in the Pacific. Associated with this are the continued dilemmas of extended nuclear deterrence. The potential for a significant divergence between the perceived security interests and strategic philosophy of Europe and the United States is therefore a very real one.

Second, there are very real dangers of serious US–European disputes over trade issues. US–EC disagreements over agricultural subsidies proved a major problem at the Uruguay GATT Round, and there are residual American fears of a 'Fortress Europe' emerging as a result of the 1992 project. The problem here is that differences over trade issues (involving perhaps a more aggressive use by Washington of the provisions of the 1988 Omnibus Trade Act) could lead to retaliatory action by the Community, and that such trade disputes could spill over into other areas of the transatlantic relationship – such as NATO. 'The net result could be that trade disputes would drive a wedge between Europe and America on political and security matters.'[57]

Thus the critical issue facing NATO and the Atlantic community in the 1990s will be 'the structure and management of the political alliance in the West', rather than 'the management of defence against the East'.[58] The problem here, however, is that for the last four decades, the chief institutional buckle of the Atlantic Alliance has been NATO. But with the relative decline in the importance of NATO in a Europe where non-military aspects of security will be of growing significance, NATO may become too weak to act as the anchor and focal point of the transatlantic relationship. It is for this reason amongst others that Secretary of State Baker (in a speech on 12 December 1989 in Berlin) proposed a 'New Atlanticism', involving 'a significantly strengthened set of institutional and consultative links' between the USA and the EC.[59] Since then, closer institutional ties between the two have been agreed, including twice-yearly meetings of the Presidents of the US and the European Council; between the US President and the President of the EC Commission; and between the US Secretary of State and EC foreign ministers.[60] Nonetheless, the question of what character and form the new transatlantic relationship will assume in the 1990s remains open.

The new partnership between the USA and the West Europeans will inevitably be less marked by the power asymmetries that characterised NATO and its corollary, 'extended deterrence'. This will place great demands on the American political system. The Gulf crisis has shown that America is the only country with the political will and the military capability to take the lead in major international crises. But within Europe itself, the USA needs to adapt to a new role – one which will no longer be defined in terms of 'leadership', but rather of 'partnership'. The USA may still be regarded as a senior partner within the NATO Alliance, but it tends to be regarded as no more than *primus inter pares*. The Americans also need to appreciate that they can no longer use their security relationship with the Europeans as a form of political or economic leaverage (ie, during trade disputes). There is a worrying tendency in American foreign policy thinking to oscillate between a desire for hegemony ('leadership') on the one hand, and isolationism on the other: the requirement of a Europe 'beyond containment', however, is that the Americans retreat from the role of hegemon within Western Europe to that of reserve ally – acting as a backstop to the coalition rather than insisting on running the show the whole time. As David Calleo suggests in a delightful historical analogy, this would mean America's role in the Atlantic Alliance coming to resemble that of Britain and the *pax Britannica* during the reign of Queen Victoria, rather than that of the Rome of Augustus during the *pax Romana*.[61]

In the new, post-cold war Europe, therefore, the transatlantic relationship is facing a new set of pressures. For four decades, the Atlantic community has been an important factor of stability in the international system. It has given an American dimension to Europe, and a European dimension to the USA, thereby broadening horizons and deepening mutual understanding between the 'new' and 'old' worlds. Although the immediate prospect of a 'Europe without America'[62] is not yet in sight, there is some risk of an 'agonising reappraisal' of America's European commitments (first raised by J.F. Dulles after the failure of the EDC in 1954). If this is to be avoided, then there is a need for some hard thinking on two closely related questions: what are US interests in a Europe 'beyond containment'? And what role do the Europeans themselves envisage for the USA in a Europe 'whole and free'?[63] Only through addressing these difficult questions can a durable 'new Atlanticism' be built.

III: WEST EUROPEAN SECURITY COOPERATION

The evolution of transatlantic relations is closely bound up with another issue of crucial importance to the future of the European security system – West European security cooperation. Since the failure of the Pleven Plan and the European Defence Community in the early 1950s, NATO has remained the bed-rock of West European security. Nevertheless, the 1980s have witnessed some significant new developments in Western European security. The failure of the Genscher–Colombo initiative in 1981 (which sought to develop a security component within the EPC by adding to it Defence Ministers and their respective substructures) was followed in 1984 by the reactivation of the WEU. At the same time the 1963 Elysée Treaty has been given a new lease of life since 1982 by the opening of Franco-West German defence and security cooperation: this has resulted in the establishment of a joint brigade and a Security and Defence Council.[64] Security cooperation in the Western Mediterranean has developed through the thickening of bilateral relations between Spain and Portugal, France and Spain, and to a lesser extent, Italy and France. The IEPG has entered a take-off period following the establishment of a secretariat and the adoption of an action plan at Luxembourg in November 1988, and it is now developing as the focus for new initiatives on arms technology cooperation and the gradual creation of a European armaments market. Title III of the SEA has, for the first time, given the EPC a responsibility for the economic and political aspects of security. These initiatives have complemented the already existing multilateral and bilateral forms of West European security cooperation (such as the NATO Eurogroup or Anglo-Dutch military cooperation), and have fuelled the debate on both the desirability and utility of a more pronounced Western European security identity.

There is, however, considerable ambiguity surrounding the purpose of such security cooperation in Western Europe. There are two competing approaches: one – the 'Atlanticist' school – seeks to improve the balance within the Atlantic Alliance; the other – the 'Europeanist' school – regards security cooperation as an integral part of the development of growing political cohesion within a more autonomous Europe. As we shall see, this means that the process of West European security cooperation is characterised by a high degree of institutional pluralism and policy ambiguity.

There is already a burgeoning literature on West European security cooperation. The questions to be addressed here, however, are twofold: what are the prospects for such cooperation in the new Europe; and second, if it is to develop, within which institutional strucuture is it likely to emerge – NATO, the EC or the WEU?

The Changing Dynamics of West European Security Cooperation

The development of an autonomous West European security entity faces two major problems. First, the existence of NATO, which provides a functioning framework for collective defence. Whilst it remains as a viable alliance, there is a powerful disincentive for giving up a tried and tested security organisation for untried forms of European cooperation. Second, intra-West European security differences, between nuclear and non-nuclear powers, small and large countries, and between countries in Central Europe, the Balkans and the Nordic region. A particular difficulty here is the 'triangular asymmetries' between the 'big three' – Germany, France and Britain – over such issues as the relationship to NATO, and nuclear deterrence. If these structural impediments to West European security cooperation are to be overcome, strong incentives are needed to develop the necessary dynamic behind the project of closer security cooperation.

In the 1980s, the dynamics underlying closer West European security cooperation were provided by five main factors: the continuing military build-up of the Soviet Union; growing tensions between the Reagan Administration and America's European allies; the perceived need – especially in France – to anchor the FRG within the Western alliance, in the light of what were interpreted as growing neutralist and anti-nuclear sentiments; the British and German desire to involve France more closely in the West European defence efforts; and the spiralling costs of weapons and their development.

With the watershed in East–West relations which occurred in the late 1980s, the dynamics of West European security cooperation have fundamentally changed – especially as regards the first three factors. The Bush Administration's more pragmatic and moderate policies have led to an improvement in transatlantic relations; the perception of a 'Soviet threat' has evaporated in the era of 'Gorbymania'; and the main means of anchoring Germany in the West are now deemed to be the EC and NATO.

On the other hand, there are three factors which may in the future promote closer West European security cooperation: political union in the EC; the changing nature of the European security agenda, with the growing saliency of North–South and 'out-of-area' issues; and the economic pressures already mentioned. Budgetary restraints in Europe might force Western countries to rationalise their armed forces further through a process of standardisation and defence integration. At the same time, the burden-sharing debate and transatlantic trade disputes might become intertwined, strengthening the punitive trend in congressional thinking about burden-sharing. This – together with the spill-over effect of the single market on the European armaments industry – could give renewed emphasis to West European cooperation in defence procurement, leading to a more integrated European armaments industry.[65] This is turn could stimulate renewed interest in developing a more autonomous

European security entity.

However, it is doubtful whether any of these factors are powerful enough to overcome the structural impediments to closer West European security cooperation. 'Out-of-area' problems (in the Mediterranean or the Gulf), for example, affect West European states differently, and may in fact lead to a further regionalisation of European security policy – if not, indeed, to a 'renationalisation' of defence policy. Similarly, the Europeans may find it cheaper to buy some military hardware 'off-the-shelf' from America, rather than committing themselves to costly projects in European armaments collaboration (such as the European Fighter Aircraft). A qualitative leap-forward in West European security cooperation is thus only likely to occur if two conditions are fulfilled: first, a significant weakening of America's military commitment to Europe (combined with a new period of US isolationism); and second, the appearance of a major security threat to West European security interests – either from a collapse of Soviet *perestroika* (with the attendant danger of a recidivist backlash there), or from a serious out-of-area security challenge from beyond Europe's borders.

If such a combination of circumstances were to appear, there are three possible locations for a European security entity: a 'European pillar' within NATO; security and defence cooperation within the EC; or the WEU, a security body standing in a somewhat ambiguous position between NATO and the EC. Let us consider these three options in turn.

A 'European Pillar' within NATO?

The notion of a 'European pillar' can be traced back to President Kennedy's Independence Day speech in Philadelphia, on 4 July 1962, and was implicit in American conceptions of NATO from the start.[66] As the balance of economic and political power between the USA and Europe has shifted, and as the burden-sharing debate has intensified, proposals for constructing a 'European pillar' have grown. Henry Kissinger has called for a European SACEUR,[67] and there have been other proposals for more senior NATO commands for Europeans, a strengthening of the Eurogroup, a European division, a European 'security assessment' and increased task specialisation.[68]

As the number of US military forces stationed in Europe decreases, NATO will inevitably become a more 'European' organisation. However, the scope for developing a 'European pillar' is limited by the very nature of the Atlantic Alliance. Since its inception, NATO has been an American-led organisation, despite its elaborate consultative and collective decision-making machinery. This is because West European security has rested, at the end of the day, on the US strategic nuclear guarantee. Accordingly, 'the structure of the Alliance is one of US leadership, not one of European–American co-management; it is one of hierarchy, not of equality'. For this reason, it is argued, the Atlantic Alliance can never resemble a 'dumb-bell' with two equal weights, but only a pyramid.[69] Furthermore, it is suggested, any peacetime military alliance tends to require a single, hegemonic leader (especially in the nuclear age) – from this perspective, therefore, American pre-eminence within NATO thus guarantees a modicum of coherence and stability in the Alliance.

Nevertheless, if NATO is to remain relevant to the security concerns of the new Europe, it must be clear that the Alliance adequately represents the security concerns of the West Europeans themselves. A new political balance between the US and Europe is thus essential, with – as we have already seen – the Americans increasingly acting as a back-stop to the Alliance, rather than as its leader. This will place a special responsibility on the USA, who will have to accept that the price of burden-sharing is greater decision-sharing.

The consequent Europeanisation of NATO would have a number of benefits: it would increase the public legitimacy of the organisation in the eyes of West European public opinion, and might make it possible for the French to associate ever more closely with the military command structure of the Alliance. Indeed, a French SACEUR could be the price of French reintegration into NATO's military structures. The danger, however, is that in seeking to reform NATO and strenghten its European pillar, the Americans might lose interest in an Alliance they no longer dominated; the Soviets might feel more threatened; and yet the French might still maintain their nationalistic stance outside of the Alliance's military command structures.

Defence Cooperation in the European Community

The desire to build a defence dimension within the EC is at odds with the 'Atlanticist' model of a European pillar, and derives from a very different political conception of the future of Europe. In recent years, it has been pushed by the French, Italians and Spanish, and its purpose is to develop the cohesion of Europe as an international actor. The French Defence Minister, for example, has argued that, 'without doubt, a European system of defence will crown the process of European construction ...'. In a similar vein, President Mitterrand has suggested that, 'In 1992–93, all our familiar assumptions will change. Among them, our assumptions about the common defence of Europe. Then it will be understood that Europe will not exist unless it can take responsibility itself for its own defence.'[70]

At present, the EPC (which has been formally associated with the

EC through the Single European Act) is limited to a consideration of the 'political and economic' aspects of security. As we have already seen, there are major institutional and political problems in seeking to give the Community responsibility for the 'hard' issues of military security. Above all, it is wrong to assume that the process of European construction through the EC will automatically spill over into the area of defence cooperation. As Berndt von Staden has argued, the concept of a European Union incorporating a defence policy component is ahistorical, and rests on a profound misunderstanding of the nature of Community integration;

> Once again it is based on the concept of the nation-state of the 19th century. It cannot be deduced from the experience of that period, however, that the European Community should follow this pattern. In the foreseeable future it will not possess a structure comparable to that of a nation-state. Even in its further development into an economic and monetary union, or even political union, it will remain a structure with its own special character, an "unfinished federation" as Walter Hallstein said, an "exemplary order" as Willy Brandt called it. It will remain an entity which will only find the guarantee for its security in the backing of the Atlantic alliance.[71]

Security Cooperation outside of NATO and the EC: the WEU

Given the structural impediments to a 'European pillar' within NATO, and the political difficulties involved in defence integration within the EC, many people are looking to the WEU to provide the institutional locus of West European security cooperation.

As we have already seen, the Western European Union was reactivated in 1984. It failed to provide a coordinated response to SDI, but subsequently notched up a number of successes, including the Gulf mine-sweeping operation of 1987–88; the Platform on European Security Interests of 27 October 1987; and its Iberian expansion in 1988. From 1988 until the 1990 Gulf crisis, however, the WEU experienced a period of stagnation, due to differences amongst its leading members on the organisation's role in the European security system.

Saddam's invasion of Kuwait in August 1990 has given the WEU a new lease of life. Once again, the organisation has shown its utility as a forum for West European governments to coordinate their political and military responses to out-of-area crises. The WEU lacks NATO's integrated military command structures, but proposals are now being discussed which could lead to the establishment of a WEU Rapid Deployment Force and a greater degree of military cooperation between its member states.[72]

Indeed, the debate on the future role of the WEU in European security is well underway. For some – namely the British, Germans and Dutch – the WEU should be developed as the 'European pillar' of the Atlantic Alliance, supplementing rather than replacing NATO. For others, such as the French, Italians and Spanish, it provides the nucleus of a more autonomous West European defence body, which should be closely associated with a more politically integrated Europe. At present, the role of the WEU is surrounded by considerable ambiguity, arising from these different perceptions of its future status. Such ambiguity was demonstrated at the December 1990 meeting of WEU Foreign and Defence Ministers, which declared that the nine-member body had a key role to play in both the construction of a more integrated Europe, and in the development of a 'European pillar' within NATO.

Despite the problems facing the WEU in the early 1990s (given the different assumptions and aspirations of its member states), its overall importance within the European security system seems bound to grow. The WEU provides a convenient forum for like-minded West European governments to discuss security issues, and it can play a useful role in coordinating West European responses to 'out-of-area' security challenges. Given the problems inherent in developing a military-defence dimension to the EC, the WEU provides a more suitable forum for West European defence and security cooperation. Unlike the EC, which has no experience of defence matters, the WEU has a long experience of defence and security questions, and has shown its utility in the Gulf crisis. Moreover, if the WEU were to be developed as the locus for West European defence and security cooperation, then the issue of expanding the Community's membership to include neutral or former Warsaw Pact members would be made somewhat less complicated.

The long-term future of West European security may indeed lie in West European defence cooperation.[73] But it is too early to dispense with NATO and to sunder Western Europe's military strategic bonds with the USA.[74] In this situation, the ambiguity surrounding the role of the WEU is an advantage, because it means that West European governments can get on with the practical concerns of strengthening their defence cooperation, without immediately having to confront the more divisive issue of the WEU's place within Europe's future security architecture. In this way, therefore, the WEU may be able to play a key role in bridging the transition between an Atlantic-based system of West European security, to a more autonomous West European defence and security alliance.

Conclusion

Developing a more pronounced West European security and defence identity is an issue which is likely to assume growing importance in the

1990s – due in no small part to the Gulf crisis. Yet we are unlikely to see the emergence of a coherent and autonomous West European security entity before the turn of the century. The present internal dynamics of West European security cooperation are too weak to overcome the triangular asymmetries, institutional pluralism and policy ambiguities which plague efforts to develop a more distinctive West European security entity. Furthermore, there is at the moment little synergy between the various incremental forms of West European security cooperation, and they are thus unlikely to coalesce into a more coherently structured security body. Only if there is a strong external stimulus – involving a significant weakening of NATO and a major new security threat – is a common West European security and defence policy conceivable. In this situation, the existing forms of security cooperation could provide a 'political reservoir of cooperation' for statesmen to draw upon as required.[75] Until then, the existing *de facto* institutional division of labour in Western Europe is likely to continue, with NATO providing the overall defence and strategic guarantees; the EC and EPC dealing with the non-military aspects of security; the WEU providing a convenient forum for security discussions and limited 'out-of-area' coordination between the 'inner-core' of West European NATO members; the IEPG facilitating the formation of European armaments market and a more coordinated procurement strategy; and bi- and multilateral relationships developing to deal with specific regional security concerns. The exact balance between these different forms of security cooperation in the 1990s and beyond is likely to change in response to the specific needs and requirements of the West Europeans, rather than as a result of grand schemes for an new institutional 'architecture'. As the French Prime Minister Michel Rocard has argued, 'A European defence identity cannot be developed as a rigid and comprehensive framework; it is more of a network of particular instances of cooperation and solidarity, case by case.'[76]

Notes

1. In terms of levels of production and trade, Western Europe is today the world's foremost economic power. From the end of the 1960s until 1987, the American share of world production fell from 36 to 25 per cent, whilst that of Western Europe increased from 23 to 28 per cent; at the same time, that of Japan and the four East Asian NICs grew from 3 to 15 per cent. As regards international trade, the US share fell from 20 per cent in 1960 to 15 per cent in 1988; over the same period, Western Europe's share of global trade increased from 41 to 44 per cent, and that of Japan and the 'four little dragons' from 3 to 17 per cent (Sources: GATT, OECD, CEPII).
2. The EC is the leading partner in economic cooperation with developing countries, with a gross contribution of $12 billion in 1986; see Giovanni Jannuzzi, 'European Political Cooperation: Moving Towards Closer Integration', *NATO Review*, vol. 36, no. 4 (August 1988), pp. 11–16 (p. 11).

3. See Josef Joffe, 'After Bipolarity: Eastern and Western Europe', in *The Strategic Implications of Change in the Soviet Union, Part 1*, Adelphi Paper 247 (London: Brassey's for the IISS, 1990), pp. 66–80 (pp. 68–69).

4. 'To us', Karsten Voigt has said (speaking of the Germans), 'success looks very much like failure. We are a frontline state with poor countries next door. This is our new security problem.' Quoted in *Time*, 8 October 1990, p. 25.

5. In his speech at the Albert Hall on 14 May 1947, Winston Churchill called for the creation of a 'United States of Europe'.

6. The purpose of the ECSC was seen by its founders as being no less than 'to substitute for age-old rivalries the merging of their essential interests; to create, by establishing an economic community, the basis for a broader and deeper community among peoples long divided by bloody conflicts; and to lay the foundations for institutions which will give direction to a destiny henceforth shared'. Six years later, the preamble of the Treaty of Rome declared that the aim of the EEC was 'to establish the foundations of an ever closer union among the European peoples'.

7. The Pompidou group was established in 1971 within the framework of the Council of Europe to combat the drugs trade. The Trevi group was established in 1976 within the framework of the EPC to coordinate national efforts in combating terrorism. After five years of negotiations, France, Germany and the Benelux countries signed the Schengen Treaty on 19 June 1990: it created a free travel zone between the five, without border controls, and with a common visa and asylum policy, a giant computer to pool their crime data, and an agreement to allow hot pursuit by the police into each others' countries (see David Buchan, 'Five go off to Schengenland', *Financial Times*, 19 June 1990). Italy signed the Schengen accords in November 1990, becoming the group's sixth member, whilst Portugal and Spain applied to become observers later that month (making clear their intention to become full members at a later date).

8. *Draft General Report on Alliance Security*, for the North Atlantic Assembly, Defence and Security Committee, May 1982, paragraph 138.

9. See Jacques Pelkmans and Alan Winters, *Europe's Domestic Market* (London: Routledge for the RIIA, 1988).

10. Albert Bressand, 'Beyond Interdependence: 1992 as a Global Challenge', *International Affairs*, vol. 66, no. 1 (1990), pp. 47–65.

11. William Wallace, *The Transformation of Western Europe* (London: Pinter for the RIIA, 1990), p. 54.

12. Claus-Dieter Ehlermann, 'The Institutional Development of the EC Under the Single European Act', *Aussenpolitik*, vol. 41, no. 2 (1990), pp. 135–46.

13. See for example Margaret Thatcher's speech on 'Britain and Europe' to the College of Europe at Bruges, 20 September 1988. This speech inspired the creation of the 'Bruges Group' by right-wing proponents of an unfettered free market economy, opposed to supranational integration in the Community; see *'Good Europeans?'* by Alan Sked, Bruges Occasional Paper 4 (London: The Bruges Group, 1989).

14. For an informative discussion of these issues as they pertain to Britain, see William Wallace, 'What Price Independence? Sovereignty and Interdependence in British Politics', *International Affairs*, vol. 62, no. 3 (Summer 1986), pp. 367–90, and Sir Geoffrey Howe, 'Sovereignty and Interdependence: Britain's Place in the World', *International Affairs*, vol. 66, no. 4 (October

1990), pp. 675–96. For a contrary view, see Stephen Haseler et al., *Is National Sovereignty a Big Bad Wolf?*, The Bruges Group Occasional Paper 6 (London: The Bruges Group, 1990).

15. In a speech calling for a United Europe at the Hague in the late 1940s, Winston Churchill addressed the fears of those who worried about the loss of national sovereignty by propounding the notion of a 'larger sovereignty': 'It is said with truth that this involves some sacrifice or merger of national sovereignty, but it is also possible and not less agreeable to regard it as the gradual assumption by all the nations concerned of that larger sovereignty, which can alone protect their diverse and distinctive customs and charac-teristics, and their national traditions'. Quoted by Michael Heseltine in *The Challenge of Europe. Can Britain Win?* (London: Weidenfeld and Nicolson, 1989), p. 210.

16. Marc Wilke and Helen Wallace, *Subsidiarity: Approaches to Power-Sharing in the European Community*, RIIA Discussion Paper No. 27 (London: RIIA, 1990). For a less sanguine view of 'subsidiarity', see Andrew Adonis and Andrew Tyrie, *Subsidiarity – as History and Policy* (London: Institute of Economic Affairs, 1990). They argue that subsidiarity – 'the ultimate institutional elixir' – is a potential 'federalist Trojan horse'.

17. As Felipe Gonzalez said in his interview with the *Financial Times* (27 April 1990), 'The most stable element in Europe as a whole now is the European Community; it would be a grave error not to try and reinforce it'.

18. See Niels Thygesen, 'The Delors Report and European Economic and Monetary Union', *International Affairs*, vol. 65, no. 4 (Autumn 1989), pp. 637–52, and Norbert Kloten, 'The Delors Report: a Blueprint for European Integration?', *The World Today*, vol. 45, no. 11 (November 1989), pp. 191–94.

19. Quoted in *The Independent*, 27 April 1990, p. 19. An agenda for political union was spelt out by President Mitterrand and Chancellor Kohl in their joint letter of 19 April 1990; the objective should be, they argued, 'to strengthen the democratic legitimacy of the union, to make the institutions more efficient, to ensure united and coherent action in the economic, monetary and political fields, and to bring about a common foreign and security policy'.

20. It was clearly stated by the meeting of EC Foreign Ministers in County Kerry in May 1990 that full federal political union was not a viable goal; 'No one is talking about a federal structure for tomorrow', as one spokesman said. 'What we are talking about is a second stage of the Single European Act'. Quoted in the *Financial Times*, 21 May 1990.

21. On the changing role of the European Court of Justice, see Robert Rice, 'Europe Learns to Love its Court', *Financial Times*, 6 June 1990. The importance of this body was underlined in June 1990 when it ruled that United Kingdom courts could set aside a national law if it conflicted with a European one; in terms of British parliamentary tradition, this is of major significance.

22. See Ian Davidson, 'Motor of EC Integration Shifts into Another Gear', *Financial Times*, 28 June 1990; Rene Foch, 'The 12 Must Beware a Shaky House of Government', *International Herald Tribune*, 25 June 1990; and David Buchan and Edward Mortimer, 'Europe on the Drawing Board', *Financial Times*, 16 May 1990.

23. An agreement to create a European Environment Agency was reached in Dublin on 17 June 1990, at a meeting of EC Environmental Ministers and their Eastern counterparts. It is likely to be based in either Copenhagen or Madrid. See the *Financial Times*, 18 June 1990, p. 4.

24. This was proposed by the Dutch Prime Minister at the EC Summit in Dublin in June 1990, and was designed to give Western Europe access to the huge fossil fuel reserves in the Soviet Union in return for credits and economic aid. Reported in the *Financial Times*, 26 June 1990, p. 2.

25. See Peter Ludlow and Heather Ross, 'EC–Soviet partnership – An Energy Model for the Future Europe', in the *Financial Times*, 24 October 1990.

26. Austria applied for full membership in July 1989. See Heinrich Schneider, *Austria and the EC*, RIIA Discussion Paper No. 24 (London: Royal Institute of International Affairs, 1989), and Helen Wallace, 'The External Implications of 1992 II: Austria in the Wings', *The World Today*, vol. 45, no. 2 (February 1989), pp. 31–32. Cyprus applied for membership on 4 July 1990.

27. Discussions between the EC and EFTA on the creation of a 'European economic space' have been underway since April 1984. See Helen Wallace, 'The European Community and EFTA: One Family or Two?', *The World Today*, vol. 44, no. 10 (October 1988), pp. 177–79; and Helen Wallace and Wolfgang Wessels, *Towards a New Partnership: the EC and EFTA in the Wider Western Europe*, EFTA Occasional Paper (March 1989).

28. The Turkish application for EC membership was placed in April 1987. For a discussion of the issues it raises (for both Turkey and Western Europe), see Udo Steindbach, 'Turkey's Third Republic', *Aussenpolitik*, vol. 39, no. 3 (1988), pp. 234–51 (p. 248).

29. See for example Michael Howard, 'The Remaking of Europe', in *Survival*, vol. XXXII, no. 2 (March/April 1990), pp. 99–106 (p. 102); Jack Snyder, 'Averting Anarchy in the New Europe', *International Security*, vol. 14, no. 4 (Spring 1990), pp. 5–41; and Jim Rollo, *The New Eastern Europe: Western Responses* (London: Pinter for the RIIA, 1990), p. 113.

30. For a clear and informative analysis of the issues in this debate, see Helen Wallace, *Widening and Deepening: The European Community and the New European Agenda*, RIIA Discussion Paper No. 23 (London: Royal Institute of International Affairs, 1989).

31. Quoted in the *Financial Times*, 17 December 1990.

32. Evan Luard, 'A European Foreign Policy?', *International Affairs*, vol. 62, no. 4 (Autumn 1986), pp. 573–82.

33. Edward Heath explicitly calls for the exclusion of neutral members from the EC so that it can deepen its integration and develop a military and foreign policy; 'European Unity over the Next Ten Years: from Community to Union', *International Affairs*, vol. 64, no. 2 (Spring 1988), pp. 199–207 (p. 206).

34. Harry Truman, 4 April 1949, on the occasion of the signing of the North Atlantic Treaty in Washington: quoted in Don Cook, *Forging the Alliance: NATO, 1945 to 1950* (London: Secker & Warburg, 1989), p. 222.

35. Pierre Hassner, *Change and Security in Europe, Part I*, Adelphi Paper 45 (London: The Institute for Strategic Studies, 1968), p. 8.

36. Quoted in *The Independent*, 11 December 1990. Similarly Richard Perle, the former Assistant Secretary of State and the Pentagon's 'Prince of Darkness' in the Reagan years, has argued that, assuming there is no

abrupt change in the pattern of events in Eastern Europe and the Soviet Union, 'NATO is essentially finished. I don't think NATO will remain a significant organisation in the conduct of relations among the allies.'

37. As President George Bush has said, 'Our enemy today is uncertainty and instability' (*US Policy Information and Texts*, 7 May 1990, p. 7). In this situation, the British Foreign Minister Douglas Hurd has argued, 'NATO offers us the prospect of stability in a world which to the south and to the east of our part of Europe will certainty remain turbulent' (address at the Konrad-Adenauer-Stiftung, 6 February 1990).

38. See Simon Lunn, 'Alliance Parliamentarians Develop Contacts with the East: 35th Annual Session of the North Atlantic Assembly', in *NATO Review*, vol. 37, no. 6 (December 1989), pp. 19–23.

39. Quoted in the *Financial Times*, 31 May 1990, p. 3. President Bush proposed the creation of Warsaw Pact 'permanent liaison missions' to NATO prior to the NATO Summit in July 1990; see the *International Herald Tribune*, 3 June 1990, p. 1. Strong opposition to such proposals has come – not surprisingly, given their desire to see a Europe without the 'blocs' – from the French.

40. Edward Mortimer, 'Building the European House', *Financial Times*, 21 November 1989.

41. Peter Corterier, the Secretary-General of the North Atlantic Assembly, has suggested that 'NATO's nearly invisible forum, the Economics Committee', could be developed as a mechanism for consultation by holding meetings at 'ministerial level, perhaps concurrently with the NAC ministerial', and by giving it three new tasks. These are: (i) as a forum for discussions on conversion; (ii) as a link between North America and the EC on trade issues; and (iii) as the 'missing connection' between NATO and COCOM. See his excellent article, '*Quo vadis* NATO?', *Survival*, vol. XXXII, no. 2 (March/April 1990), pp. 141–58 (p. 153).

42. G. Baker's Berlin Speech. The official text was published by the US Information Service, London, 13 December 1989.

43. As Margaret Thatcher seemed to suggest in her speech to NATO Foreign Ministers at Turnberry in Scotland, 7 June 1990 (the headline in the London *Evening Standard* that evening was, 'Let NATO police the world'). The NATO SACEUR, General John Galvin, has also called for a review of NATO's Charter inhibitions of 'out-of-area' operations, arguing that NATO strategy needed to take account of 'crisis management', such as in response to the Gulf: see the *Financial Times*, 10 September 1990.

44. NATO's Secretary-General, Manfred Wörner, has proposed that 'the assets of the Alliance' should be available 'for co-ordinatioin and support' for member states involved in crises outside the NATO area. This would mean that NATO countries involved in such crises would have automatic access to all NATO air and sea bases, as well as ammunition and supplies. *The Independent*, 30 November 1990, p. 13.

45. Sir Michael Alexander, 'NATO's Role in a Changing World', *NATO Review*, vol. 38, no. 2 (April 1990), pp. 1–5 (p. 4).

46. In its Summit Declaration of 30 May 1989, NATO spoke of the Alliance committing itself to 'larger responsibilities ... to reduce world tensions, settle disputes peacefully, and search for solutions to those issues of universal concern, including poverty, social injustice and the environment

...' (paragraph 7), and detailed what this meant in a separate chapter entitled 'Global Challenges' (paragraphs 29–34). It also suggested that the Alliance's 'third dimension' (science and environmental matters) should be given more impact through new initiatives (paragraph 35). In a similar vein, Peter Corterier has suggested that NATO's Committee on the Challenges on Modern Life (established in 1969) should undertake fact-finding and advisory missions to Warsaw Pact countries that request its assistance. *Op. cit.*, p. 155.

47. P. Corterier, *op. cit.*, p. 152.
48. Admiral Sir James Eberle, 'New Role for NATO in a World of Change', *The Guardian*, 1 May 1990, p. 23.
49. Johan Galtung once described NATO as a 'feudal alliance', hierarchically organized with rather limited horizontal interaction among its lower-ranking members: quoted in Cees Wiebes and Bert Zeeman, '"I don't need your handkerchiefs": Holland's experience of Crisis Consultation in NATO', *International Affairs*, vol. 66, no. 1 (1990), pp. 91–113 (p. 93).
50. J. Joffe, 'Europe's American Pacifier', *Foreign Policy*, no. 54 (Spring 1984).
51. See David P. Calleo, 'NATO and Some Lessons of History', in *NATO at Forty: Change, Continuity, and Prospects*, edited by James R. Golden et al. (London: Westview, 1989), pp. 155–78 (p. 156).
52. Christopher Coker, *Drifting Apart? The Superpowers and their European Allies* (Oxford: Brassey's, 1989).
53. Admiral Sir James Eberle, 'Where the Defence Interests of Europe and America Diverge', *The Independent*, 6 January 1988.
54. Phil Williams, 'The Limits of American Power: from Nixon to Reagan', *International Affairs*, vol. 63, no. 4 (Autumn 1987), pp. 575–87 (p. 586). See also Evan Luard, 'Western Europe and the Reagan Doctrine', *International Affairs*, vol. 63, no. 4 (Autumn 1987), pp. 563–74.
55. At Leiden in mid-July 1989, President Bush declared that 'a stronger Europe, a more united Europe, is good for my country. And it is a development to be welcomed, a natural evolution within an alliance, the product of true partnership, 40 years in the making.'
56. See David Allen and Michael Smith, 'Western Europe in the Atlantic System of the 1980s', in *Atlantic Relations: Beyond the Reagan Era*, edited by Stephen Gill (New York: Harvester Wheatsheaf, 1989), pp. 88–110, and their article, 'Western Europe's Presence in the Contemporary International Arena', in *Review of International Studies*, vol. 16 (1990), pp. 19–37.
57. Robert D. Hormats, 'Redefining Europe and the Atlantic Link', *Foreign Affairs*, vol. 68, no. 4 (Fall 1989), pp. 71–91 (p. 79).
58. Ian Smart, 'The Political and Economic Evolution of NATO's Central Region', in *NATO at Forty: Change, Continuity, and Prospects*, pp. 39–59 (p. 59).
59. See Robert McGeehan, 'The United States and NATO after the Cold War', in *NATO Review*, vol. 38, no. 1 (February 1990), pp. 7–13.
60. 'US and EC agree to form closer links', *The Independent*, 28 February 1990. President Bush declared that the US wished to 'improve its ties' with the EC, 'so that a new Atlanticism will be teamed with a new Europe'.
61. David P. Calleo, 'NATO and Some Lessons of History', in *NATO at Forty: Change, Continuity, and Prospects*, pp. 155–78 (p. 157).

62. John Palmer, *Europe Without America? The Crisis in Atlantic Relations* (Oxford: Oxford University Press, 1987).

63. A useful starting-point for considering these issues is the articles by Karl Kaiser, 'A View from Europe: the US Role in the Next Decade', *International Affairs*, vol. 65, no. 2 (Spring 1989), pp. 209–24; Linda B. Miller, 'American Foreign Policy: Beyond Containment?', *International Affairs*, vol. 66, no. 2 (April 1990), pp. 313–24; and Max van der Stoel, *The Future of NATO: A European View*, Occasional paper (Washington: The Atlantic Council of the United States, 1989).

64. Peter Schmidt, 'The Franco-German Defence and Security Council', in *Aussenpolitik*, vol. 40, no. 4 (1989), pp. 360–71 (p. 370). Helmut Schmidt has proposed the creation of a 30 division Franco-German army as the 'European nucleus for Europe's defence', with a French commander-in-chief and French extended nuclear deterrence. See his book, *A Grand Strategy for the West. The Anachronism of National Strategies in an Interdependent World* (London: Yale University Press, 1985), p. 42. Helmut Kohl has also endorsed the notion of a European army.

65. For a discussion of these issues, see Andrew Moravcsik, 'The European Armaments Industry at the Crossroads', in *Survival*, vol. XXXII, no. 1 (1990), pp. 65–85, and Simon Webb, *NATO and 1992: Defence Acquisition and Free Markets* (Santa Monica, CA: The RAND Corporation, 1989).

66. Helmut Sonnenfeldt, 'The European Pillar: The American View', *The Changing Strategic Landscape, Part 1*, Adelphi Paper 235 (London: Brassey's for the IISS, 1989), pp. 91–105.

67. H. Kissinger, 'A Plan to Restore NATO', *Time*, 5 March 1984, pp. 20–24.

68. *European Defence Cooperation: America, Britain and NATO*, Fulbright Paper 7, edited by Michael Clarke and Rod Hague (Manchester: Manchester University Press, 1990).

69. Christoph Bertram, 'Western Europe's Strategic Role: Towards a European Pillar?', in *The Changing Strategic Landscape, Part 1*, pp. 106–15 (p. 109).

70. Quoted in Ian Gambles, *Prospects for West European Security Cooperation*, Adelphi Paper 244 (London: Brassey's for the IISS, 1989), pp. 7 and 12.

71. Berndt von Staden, 'Nothing Less than the Whole of Europe Will Do ...', *Aussenpolitik*, vol. 41, no. 1 (1990), pp. 24–37 (pp. 36–37).

72. See Ian Davidson, 'WEU to Play More Important Role in European Defence', *Financial Times*, 11 December 1990, p. 3.

73. Pierre Hassner, 'Europe Beyond Partition and Unity: Disintegration or Reconstitution?', *International Affairs*, vol. 66, no. 3 (July 1990), pp. 461–75 (p. 468).

74. See Uwe Nerlich, *The Atlantic Alliance at the Crossroad: Possible Political and Military Function in a Changing Europe*, a European Strategy Group paper, 1990.

75. Ian Gambles, *Prospects for West European Security Cooperation*, p. 71.

76. Quoted in Gambles, *ibid.*, p. 5.

7

Germany after the Berlin Wall

Heinrich Heine once said, '*Denk ich an Deutschland in der Nacht, dann bin ich um den Schlaf gebracht*' ('When I think of Germany in the night, then I can't sleep'). With the fall of the Berlin Wall, the Pandora's box of the 'German problem' has been re-opened – and this, for some in both East and West, has meant many a sleepless night. The unification of Germany is the single most important development in post-war European history, and will accelerate the re-shaping of the political, economic and strategic contours of the European continent. The Europe of the 1990s is likely to be greatly influenced by a Germany which is already the strongest economic force in the EC. Once again, Germany will resume its place at the centre of the European interstate system – not only geographically and economically, but also politically and strategically.

The creation of a German nation-state with nearly 80 million citizens at the heart of Europe has rekindled a host of half-repressed fears and historically generated suspicions. Some fear that the new Germany will seek to dominate Europe, and that the Germans will resume their restless wandering between East and West. On the other hand, others have welcomed the creation of a prosperous and democratic Germany at the heart of a reuniting Europe, as a motor of economic recovery and democratic transformation in the East, and as a crucial building-block of a future European peace order. In this chapter, we shall consider the nature of the contemporary 'German problem', and the possible role of a united Germany in the new Europe.

The 'German Question' in History

Historically, Germany has long been the key to the European balance of power, either as the axis around which the other great powers have manoeuvred, or as a great power in its own right. From the 1648 Treaty of Westphalia (when the 'German question' emerged as a wider European issue) to the creation of the Bismarckian Reich in 1871, Germany was a weak and fragmented European actor. The creation – through 'Blood and iron' – of a Prussian-dominated *Kleindeutschland* produced a major challenge to the European balance of power. Thus was born the contemporary 'German problem': the problem, in other words, of how to integrate – or at least contain – the prodigious economic strength

and military potential of a unified German state, situated at the very heart
of the European continent. It was the failure to resolve this conundrum
that led to the two world wars of the twentieth century.

'What is wrong with Germany', A.J.P. Taylor once wrote, 'is that
there is too much of it'.[1] At the same time, Germany's enormously
productive economy and vibrant society has been of such concern to its
neighbours because of its geographically central location – its *Mittellage*.
Indeed, David Calleo has argued that 'The German Problem does not
somehow emanate from some special German "character"', but from its
geography:

> ... unlike Britain, Russia, or the United States, the Germans lacked the space to
> work out their abundant vitality. Moreover, because of geography, Germany's
> vitality was an immediate threat to the rest of Europe. Modern Germany was
> born encircled. Under the circumstances, whatever the lesson of the wars
> between Germany and its neighbours, it cannot be found merely by analyzing
> the faults of the Germans.[2]

The third aspect of the 'German problem' has been the political
character of the German state. Germany has presented a threat to the
stability of Europe, not simply because of its strength and location, but
because of its character. The Germany that Bismarck created, and upon
which Hitler constructed the National Socialist state, was characterised
by a propensity towards authoritarianism, militarism, intolerance and
economic protectionism.[3] For this reason therefore, the political character
of the German state has been an issue of considerable concern to the wider
European comity of states.

The Post-war Division of Germany

Given the fear of a concentration of German power at the heart of the
continent, German unity has been both difficult to achieve and hard to
maintain. With the division of Germany in 1949, the 'German question'
acquired a new meaning, and became caught up in the politics of
East–West confrontation.[4] Indeed, Germany became the focus of the
cold war in Europe – the 'pawn which both sides wished to turn into
a queen' (in the words of a FCO Memorandum of the time).[5] Divided
Germany also served as 'the permanent catalyst for change', thus ensuring
that the division of Europe remained a live issue despite a stalemate of
over 40 years, in a way that it might not have, had the East–West divide
run along the Rhine or the Oder-Neisse, rather than along the Elbe.[6]

Despite the formal commitment of the Western Allies to unification
(enshrined in the May 1955 Paris Treaty and again in the Harmel doctrine
of 1967[7]), there was a feeling in many parts of Europe that the division
of Germany 'provided a solution, inadvertently, to the problem which
the countries of Europe had faced and failed to master since 1870:

the place of a too-powerful Germany in a European system which could not of itself preserve the independence of its members in the face of German strength'.[8] The creation of two separate German states, each integrated into opposed military-political blocs, and each with its own 'special relationship' to its superpower patron, provided an apparent solution to the perennial *deutsche Frage*.[9] Germany, it was sometimes argued, had only been united in a single nation-state for a relatively brief period of its history, and the experience had not been a happy one, either for the German people themselves or the rest of Europe.[10] Many Germans therefore suspected that, despite their formal commitment to unification, their Western Allies tended to share the sentiments of Francois Mauriac, who said: 'I love Germany so much that I rejoice at the idea that today there are two of them.'[11] This suspicion was reinforced in 1984 when the then Italian Foreign Minister declared that 'one has to recognise that pan-Germanism is something that must be overcome. There are two German states and two German states they should remain.'[12]

The problem with such notions, however, was that division was ultimately unacceptable to the German people – especially those in the GDR. Being imposed from without (by the Soviet Union) and from above (by the SED), the attempt to build 'socialism in half a country' stood little chance of success. The erection of the 'Antifascist Defence Wall' on 13 August 1961 was an implicit recognition of the bankruptcy of East German 'state socialism'. The much-maligned 'Pankow regime' may have been able to survive the Hallstein Doctrine and Bonn's policy of *Alleinvertretungsanspruch* (the West German claim that it was the only legitimate state representing the German people), and under Erich Honecker go on to win wide international recognition. But it could not compete with its wealthier and more democratic Western sibling, and never won the loyalty and support of its 16 million citizens. In the end, therefore, the SED regime collapsed like a house of cards, under the irresistible pressure of 'People's power'.

The collapse of the SED was as unexpected as it was rapid. Long regarded as the most stable of the East European regimes, its disintegration was a consequence of the deep malaise that had gripped East German society in the late 1980s. The opening of the Berlin Wall on 9 November 1989 was Egon Krenz's last desperate gamble to stabilise a deteriorating situation, and when it failed, unification became inevitable. As the slogans at the weekly demonstrations in Leipzig changed from '*Wir sind das Volk*' ('We are the people') to '*Wir sind ein Volk*' ('We are one people'), so the aims of the revolution shifted from democratic self-determination to national unity. When Chancellor Kohl announced his 10–Point Plan for reunification on 28 November 1989, his proposal seemed premature and hasty.[13] Within two months, however, his three-stage strategy for unification through confederation had already been 'OBE' ('overtaken by events', to use the Foreign Office parlance of the day). In the elections of March 1990, the East German people voted for the fastest possible route to unification – in doing so, the 'Republic' voted itself out of existence. As the renowned GDR writer, Stefan Heym, bitterly declared, 'There is no more GDR. It will be nothing more but a footnote in world history.'[14]

Germany: No longer a 'Question', but still a 'Problem'[15]

The German 'question' (in its post-war form) is now over: with Economic and Monetary Union on 2 July 1990, Germany effectively became one country. On 3 October 1990, Germany finally became one nation again, as the five east German *Länder* formally acceded to the FRG under Article 23 of the *Grundgesetz*. The 'German question' has thus been settled after 41 years of division. But the German 'problem' in its deeper, historical sense is still very much alive; the problem, in other words, of incorporating a country the size and potential of Germany into the heart of the continent, without threatening the security of other European nations.

There are two pitfalls to be avoided when discussing the role of a united Germany in the new Europe: on the one hand, exaggerating the danger of a 'Fourth Reich'; on the other, pretending that there are no problems associated with the creation of a German nation-state of 79 million people in the centre of Europe. At the heart of this debate is the crucial issue of how the weight of history and geography will affect the character and behaviour of a united German nation-state, in a Europe 'transformed by economic and social integration, and reshaped by the construction of formal institutions' (above all, the EC and NATO).[16]

In this context, talk of a 'Fourth Reich' is needlessly offensive and ignorantly superficial. Conor Cruise O'Brien was guilty of both when he spoke of reunification being 'celebrated with an explosion of nationalist enthusiasm', leading to the 'rehabilitation of National Socialism and of Adolf Hitler', and a 'breaking off of relations with Israel; a military mission to the PLO; a statue of Hitler in every German town ...'.[17] Nicholas Ridley's intemperate outburst against European integration and what he saw as the Germans' desire to 'take over the whole of Europe' was perhaps more worrying, given his position as a Cabinet Minister close to the former Prime Minister, Margaret Thatcher.[18] Such displays of chauvinistic ignorance are not only insulting, they fail to advance the debate on Germany's place in modern-day Europe, and overlook the changes that have taken place over the last 40 years in both Germany and the wider international system.

The nature of the 'German problem' is very different in the closing decade of the twentieth century from what it was in 1933, 1914, or 1871, for four main reasons. First, the power of a united German nation-state will not be concentrated in the hands of a centralised government, because significant state functions and responsibilities have been devolved **downwards**, to the *Länder* and local government level. Second, Germany is integrated into both the European Community and NATO, and this means that some power will be devolved **upwards**, to supranational bodies. Third, the rise of transnational corporations, strategic alliances and cross-border mergers means that economic power no longer accrues directly to the nation-state, but is diffused **outwards**, beyond the confines of the nation-state. And finally, the political culture and social structure of contemporary Germany is fundamentally different from what it was in the first half of the century. Germany today has a democratic and liberal ethos, in which, if anything, pacificism, not militarism, is the concern of its allies. As Alfred Grosser has commented, 'Germans today are different from those who supported Hitler. They have accepted democratic values. They have done everything possible to demonstrate their good faith.'[19]

The absurdity of notions of a 'Fourth Reich' are even more apparent when one considers the nature of the events of 1989–90 themselves. First, the revolution in East Germany was overwhelmingly peaceful. Second, political extremism in Germany did not increase as a result: in fact, both the Republicans and the Greens suffered electoral reverses in West German elections in 1990, whilst the East German elections showed solid support for democratic parties of the centre left and right. Third, unification has not – as many feared – unleashed a tidal wave of nationalist emotion: indeed, voters in West Germany have shown themselves to be guided first and foremost by rather mundane calculations of their own self-interest. Finally, the drive for unification itself came from below, as the people themselves and their organisations (churches, trade unions, private associations, etc.) merged together. In this sense, the revolution of 1989 can be seen as completing the liberal-democratic and humanist agenda of 1848/49, rather than being a re-run of the unification from above of 1871.

But although talk of a 'Fourth Reich' is both ignorant and superficial, one cannot pretend that the emergence of a united Germany – with 79 million people and a prodigiously productive economy – is an event which will not have a profound and possibly unsettling impact on the rest of Europe. The Germans may have changed since 1945, but after Auschwitz,[20] one cannot look with complete equanimity on the re-creation of a German nation-state in Central Europe. German unification raises serious issues for the future political, economic and security 'architecture' of Europe, and will demand new approaches to the process of European integration.

One early problem was that the internal aspects of unification raced ahead of the external aspects. It was always expected that German unification would result from – or come in tandem with – the healing of the division of Europe. Instead, German unification has preceded the emergence of a wider European peace order. Diplomats and strategists concerned with the external ramifications of a united Germany consequently found it hard to keep up with the domestic political momentum which built up behind unification. The '2 plus 4' negotiations agreed at the Ottawa 'Open Skies' conference in February 1990 provided an indispensable forum for discussing some of the external aspects of unification. The fact remains, however, that the very speed at which unification occurred was unsettling for the European security system.

A second problem is that no-one really knows the medium and long-term impact that unification will have on the domestic politics of Germany. In this sense, the 'German problem' is very much a domestic one: how to integrate 16 million East Germans – with their very different traditions, experiences, patterns of socialisation, and expectations – into a liberal market society, after 40 years of division. Germany will face a major regional divide for 10–20 years, if not longer – a problem comparable only to the Italian *mezzogiorno* in its scale and potential intractability. The economic costs of unification have escalated beyond what was originally expected; the political implications of unification for the West German party system are uncertain;[21] and the long-term psychological impact – especially on the East Germans themselves – is unforeseeable.[22] One thing is certain: the German political system will have to cope with a series of mammoth tasks arising from unification and the restructuring of the East – whilst at the same time, defining its place in the new Europe, and reassuring its neighbours, allies and former enemies of its benign intentions. This will present the Germans with a demanding and crowded policy agenda: the institutional overload of the German political system is therefore a potential problem which should not lightly be dismissed.

'*Deutschland über Alles*'?

With the lifting of the iron curtain and national unification, Germany will become an even more important political and economic actor in Europe. A united Germany will have a population of 79 million and a GDP of close to DM2500 bn. Its potent, export-driven economy, with its skilled labour force, high labour productivity, developed infrastructure and strong record in engineering and design, will further reinforce Germany's role as the economic power-house of Europe.[23] If the restructuring of the East German economy is successful, Germany could experience a second *Wirtschaftswunder* before the end of the century. The role of Frankfurt as a major financial centre has already been reinforced by unification, and there are strong pressures for Frankfurt to be the site of the proposed European central bank. West Germany, with 19 per cent of its population, produced 25 per cent of the European Community's GDP: with unification, these figures have risen to 23 per cent and 27 per cent respectively.[24] Nevertheless, it is misleading to speak of Germany as an economic 'superpower': even on the most optimistic forecast of eastern Germany's economic potential, the German economy will only constitute three-quarters of that of the combined French and British economies.[25] At the same time, it is wrong to see Germany's economic power as an unremittingly malign influence: its liberal, free-market views and booming economy could act as the locomotive for growth elsewhere in Europe. Nonetheless, the prospect of an economically dominant Germany is unsettling for many Europeans, in East and West.

With Germany's burgeoning economic might will come growing political assertiveness. For much of the post-war world, the FRG has been what Willy Brandt described as an 'economic giant, but a political dwarf'. This is changing. More than ever before, Germany is an economic giant. But it is also becoming more willing to articulate and assert its specific interests. This is apparent within a whole range of international forums, from NATO and the EC, to the G7 and the OECD. In doing so, however, Germany is simply beginning to act as a 'normal', sovereign country. Nevertheless, for some this is a source of concern. Professor Arnulf Baring, for example, in a book entitled *Our New Megalomania*, has warned his fellow-countrymen that, 'Germany is in danger of over-reaching itself and imagining it can solve all the problems of Europe, East and West'. At the same time, there are worries that a more assertive German nationalism will emerge, as the Germans seek to come to terms with their contradictory cultural and historical legacy. One worrying manifestation of this over recent years has been the *Historikerstreit* (the 'historians' dispute'), which has seen some historians seeking to 'relativise' the Nazi past.[26] Similarly, Chancellor Kohl's reticence on the question of recognising the Oder-Neisse border in early 1990 was seen by many – inside Germany as well as outside – as a use of a legal-constitutional nicety in order to play to the worst chauvinistic elements in German society.[27]

With German unification and the fading of East–West confrontation, the centre of gravity in Europe will shift eastwards, from the Rhineland to Berlin and the historic lands of *Mitteleuropa*. After forty years in which the two German states lay along the front line between two hostile worlds, a united Germany will once again resume its place at the heart of the European continent. It will be the focus of many of the evolving economic, political and security relationships in the continent, and will play a pivotal role in the evolution of a new European security system. But how will Germany – situated as it is at the crossroads of Europe – exercise its new-found economic and political influence? Will Germany become a 'wanderer between the worlds', or will it finally commit itself to any of its 'three possible futures: Atlantic, West European or central European'?[28] As Renata Fritsch-Bournazel has argued,

> The German Question has always been the question of where in Europe the Germans belong: looking Westwards or wandering between East and West; recognising their geographically central position or breaking out of it? This was the vital question for domestic as well as foreign policy in Bismarck's day. Despite the discontinuities in German history in the last hundred years, the same questions were and are continually posed anew and require answers from responsible statesmen, always keeping in view the continually changing patterns in international relations.[29]

As they seek to work out where they belong, the Germans will have to bear in mind the dilemmas arising from their position in the European balance of power. This dilemma was spelt out by Chancellor Kiesinger as long ago as 1967, when he warned that, 'Germany, a reunited Germany, would be of a critically large size. It is too big not to have an effect on the balance of power, and too small to be able to hold the balance with the powers around it.'[30] Germany, in other words, would not be big enough to dominate Europe, but its size and location means that it will have a decisive impact on the new security structures of a Europe 'beyond containment'.

This raises a series of crucial issues for the future of Germany and the European security system:

1. Germany's 'Westbindung'
The outbreak of the cold war forced the newly established FRG to turn unreservedly to the West for its security guarantees, trade links and political allies. *'Westbindung'* ('commitment to the West') became central to the *raison d'être* of the West German state, and determined the very character of post-war West German society. With the democratic revolutions of 1989, however, Germany has been faced with new opportunities to develop its traditional economic, political and cultural relations with the lands to its east. The question this raises is whether Germany's post-war commitment to the West – embodied above all in its 'special relationships' with France and the USA, and its membership of the EC and NATO – will become correspondingly weaker, as Germany reverts to its traditional role as a central European country situated between East and West?[31]

The first point to note is that Germany's economic, financial and trade interests lie overwhelmingly with the West. In 1989, 53 per cent of West German trade was with fellow EC countries, whilst only 4.7 per cent was with the countries of the former Soviet bloc.[32] Secondly, the key political and business elites in Germany seem firmly committed to the values and institutions of the Western world, whilst the dominant cultural norms in German society are all those of the West. Finally, German unification has not weakened the West German government's commitment to further integration within the EC – as Chancellor Kohl and Foreign Minister Genscher's active support for economic and political union indicates.

The European Community itself provides an indispensable mechanism for integrating German power into broader West European structures. Although some fear that the EMS protects German industry and institutionalises the FRG's trade surplus, the truth is that even without the EC and the EMS, Germany (and its mighty Deutschmark) would still play a leading role in the European economy. The Community provides a means of channelling and absorbing German energies into supranational institutions, and serves as a positive focus for German aspirations – indeed, the Germans themselves rank amongst some of the most committed Europeans on the continent.[33] Moreover, 'The integration of the Federal Republic in the European Community has reduced ... some of the uncertainties traditionally associated with Germany's location at the crossroads between East and West. The ties which have developed between the Federal Republic and Western Europe, on ideological, political, economic and military levels, cannot be undone and render extremely unlikely any return to traditional see-saw policies between East and West.'[34]

The FRG's *Westbindung* has also been embodied in its bilateral relations with France and the USA. For Konrad Adenauer, rapprochement with France (which was embodied above all in the 1963 Elysée Treaty) was of decisive importance as a means of anchoring the FRG within the Western commonwealth of nations. For the French, a central purpose of their post-war *Deutschlandpolitik* has been to tie the FRG to the West by enveloping it in a special relationship. In the future, however, a united Germany may be less amenable to French overtures and expectations, particularly given Franco-German differences over French security policy (especially its nuclear doctrine).[35] This in turn is likely to aggravate French perceptions of *les incertitudes allemandes*. Nevertheless, despite recurrent bouts of friction, decades of rapprochement and cooperation have produced close bonds between these former adversaries, and the Franco-German relationship is likely to remain one of the most intimate bilateral relationships in Europe.

West Germany's 'special relationship' with France is rivalled only by its close links with the USA. Indeed, Roger Morgan has argued that 'Bonn's relations with Washington was and still is seen as the most important single element in the Federal Republic's foreign policy'.[36] There has been a strong Atlanticist bent to West German foreign policy throughout the post-war period, and Günter Grass has even suggested that the USA has been a sort of *Ersatzvaterland* for many in the FRG. Relations between Bonn and Washington have strengthened in recent years given strong US support for German unification, and President

Bush's call for Americans and Germans to be 'partners in leadership'.

However, the prospects facing US–German relations in the future are uncertain. In the short term, the Bonn–Washington axis is likely to be strengthened: this may be the cause of some irritation within the broader Atlantic community, if other West European states (notably France) feel that their interests are being marginalised by the two 'partners in leadership'. On the other hand, US–German differences over policy towards the Soviet Union and Eastern Europe, over trade issues, and over security policy[37], could undermine the closeness of the Bonn–Washington axis. German 'nuclear pacifism' is growing, and it is not inconceivable that at some stage in the future, the Germans might ask their NATO allies to withdraw their troops from German soil. This could well provoke a major crisis in US–German relations.

German unification and the fading of East–West confrontation will therefore produce some important shifts in the foreign policy of the enlarged FRG. There will inevitably be some reordering of the priorities and substance of Germany's bilateral relations as the policy agenda responds to the geopolitical changes in Europe. A united Germany in a Europe no longer divided by an 'iron curtain' will clearly be more eastward-looking than the FRG was in the cold war years. But this is not likely to be at the expense of Germany's extensive integration into the institutions and economic interdependencies of the Western world. Rather, Germany's *Westbindung* will be complemented by its *Ostverbindung* (its 'Eastern connections'), as a united German state seeks to develop its economic and political relations with the reforming countries to its East.

2. Towards a New 'Rapallo'?

In the Europe of the 1990s, the Soviet–German bilateral relationship will be of crucial importance for the development of a more cooperative relationship between the eastern and western parts of the continent. Relations between Bonn and Moscow steadily improved in the late 1980s after a slow start, and 'Gorbymania' reached new heights during the General-Secretary's visit to Bonn in June 1989. In the Political Declaration that the two leaders signed on 13 June 1989, both sides stressed that 'a positive development' of their bilateral relations was of 'central importance for Europe and the East–West relationship as a whole'.[38] Nearly one year later, the Kohl–Gorbachev summit in Moscow and Zheleznovodsk (14–17 July 1990) not only removed the final 'external' obstacles to unification, but also produced a commitment to negotiate a comprehensive treaty of non-aggression and wide-ranging cooperation. This treaty – the 'Grand Treaty of Good-neighbourliness, Partnership and Cooperation' – was signed in November 1990 during Gorbachev's visit to Bonn, and reflected Germany's growing importance as the Soviet Union's closest West European partner. The closeness of the Soviet–German relationship was also in evidence in September 1990, when a senior Soviet official floated the idea of Germany joining the UN Security Council as a permanent member.[39]

The 'special relationship' that seems to be developing between Bonn and Moscow has caused some feelings of unease amongst Germany's neighbours, particularly in Poland and France.[40] Over the last 300 years, Russo-German cooperation has often been at the expense of third parties – in the eighteenth century the Swedes, and later the Poles. The memory of the 1922 Rapallo Treaty and the Molotov–Ribbentrop pact of 1939 continues to haunt the imagination of some. This fuels the unspoken fear that Germany may be tempted to repeat Bismarck's old diplomatic game of seeking to act as an 'honest broker' between East and West, and in doing so, constructing a complex set of diplomatic relations centred around Bonn/Berlin.

Talk of a 'new Rapallo' (or 'Stavrapallo', as *The Economist* insists on calling the July 1990 Kohl–Gorbachev summit), however, overlooks the changed nature of the Soviet–German relationship in the late twentieth century. As we have already seen, the balance of German interests lies overwhelmingly with the West, in terms of both its economic and security concerns. In 1989, the FRG's trade with the USSR amounted to only 1.7 per cent of West Germany's total trade (compared to an average of 3 per cent in the 1970s): in fact, the FRG exported three times more to Austria than it did to the Soviet Union.[41] In the security field, the Eight-Point Accord agreed between Gorbachev and Kohl in July 1990 is significant because it implicitly accepts that NATO will be the guarantee of security for a united Germany. Germany is clearly interested in developing a more cooperative relationship with the Soviet Union, and its generous food aid to the Soviet people in December 1990 reflected a very real German concern with the fate of President Gorbachev's reform programme. This, however, cannot be equated with the 1922 Rapallo agreement. Similarly, the worries of the East European states about a Soviet–German condominium are understandable in view of their historical experience, but largely misplaced. A cooperative and close relationship between a united Germany and the Soviet Union remains an indispensable precondition for the stable and peaceful evolution of the European security system.[42]

3. Germany and Eastern Europe

It seems to be a 'law' of power politics in Eastern Europe that as Soviet/Russian influence in the region declines, that of Germany increases, and vice versa. With the steady deterioration of Soviet domination over its former Warsaw Pact allies, therefore, Germany is poised to become the leading economic and political influence in the region. Over the years, the West Germans have assiduously cultivated contacts and nurtured economic links with the East Europeans: with the collapse of communist rule, they are well placed to reap the harvest. Germany's geographical proximity, common traditions and linguistic ties mean that its industry will be best placed to profit from the cheap labour, resources and markets of Eastern Europe. Germany will become the dominant economic power in the region, and with its economic relations will come political influence – which the Germans appear increasingly willing to exercise.[43]

In part, this will amount to the re-establishment of the old *'Mitteleuropa'* of the nineteenth and early twentieth centuries – in other words, an area of German cultural, economic and political influence. As we have seen (in Chapter 5), this is generating some very ambivalent feelings amongst the East Europeans themselves. But in terms of Germany's strategic orientation, this closer economic and political involvement in East Central Europe is not likely to be at the expense of Germany's *Westbindung*. Germany's integration into the European Community will encourage the Community to play an active role in the reform process in the East, whilst at the same time ensuring that much of Germany's involvement in the region will be part of a broader multilateral effort. This will encourage a wider West European concern with the problems of the East Europeans, rather than simply 'leaving it to the Germans' – even though the Germans will be the main paymasters and beneficiaries. Furthermore, Germany's integration within the Community will make this growing German influence in the lands to its east more acceptable, both to the East Europeans themselves and to the Soviet Union. In this way, the EC could provide both a platform and a carapace for the simultaneous projection and containment of German power in the East.

4. German Security Policy in the New Europe

By mid-1990, the outlines of German security policy beyond the cold war had become clear. A united Germany was to be a full member of a reformed NATO, but no NATO structures were to be moved into East German territory, at least for the 3 to 4 year transition period whilst Soviet troops remained there. The East German NVA was to be disbanded and elements of it integrated into the Bundeswehr, which was in turn to be reduced in size to 370,000 within 3 to 4 years. Furthermore, a united Germany was to renounce the right to manufacture or possess nuclear, chemical and biological weapons. At the same time, the number of Allied troops on German soil was to be reduced, military manoeuvres and training exercises would decline in size and number, and the overall level of military infrastructure was to be reduced. In the medium term, Allied stationed forces in Germany may only be acceptable to German public opinion if they are part of multinational integrated forces, and only on the basis of reciprocal stationing rights. The Germans are also likely to pressure NATO into modifying its strategy and force posture even further, so that there is less reliance on nuclear deterrence, and a greater emphasis on defensively structured conventional forces.[44]

In the long term, however, there are a number of possible options for German security policy. Some of the main ones are as follows:

(i) The most dangerous scenario is of the 'renationalisation' of German defence policy, and the decision by an independent German government to build up its conventional forces; acquire a nuclear capability;[45] and revise – or 'reinterpret' – the Constitution to allow 'out-of-area' missions by German armed forces. This, however, is most unlikely, and is certainly unthinkable with the current generation of Germans.[46]

(ii) A neutral and largely demilitarized Germany. This would not necessarily be welcome to many of Germany's neighbours, and may not be in the interests of the Soviet Union either. It would raise the spectre of a reunited Germany wandering between East and West, and would revive memories of the Bismarckian 'nightmare of coalitions'. As Ernest May has argued, 'nothing – *nothing* – could so disturb and endanger international relations as a German state offering to play makeweight in the balance of power'.[47]

(iii) The 'Denmarkisation' of Germany within NATO. This is a much more plausible scenario than either of the above. It assumes that Germany remains within NATO and within its integrated military command, but refuses to have nuclear weapons or Allied forces stationed on its territory in peacetime. This would weaken NATO's cohesion, and could provoke a major crisis within the Atlantic community. Nevertheless, it is a development which should not be discounted, and which may become popular to significant sections of the German electorate if the military and political situation in central Europe continues to improve over the next five to ten years.

(iv) The 'French option' for Germany within NATO. In this scenario, Germany would not only ask foreign troops to leave its territory, but would also leave the integrated military command. This would inevitably mean the disintegration of NATO as an effective military alliance for collective defence, and the 'renationalisation' of defence policy in Germany and elsewhere. This option has been raised by some on the left of the West German SPD.

(v) The integration of Germany in a substantial West European security and defence entity. If NATO were to be eclipsed by a viable 'European Defence Community' (perhaps based on the WEU or established within the ambit of the EC), then Germany could opt to integrate its forces within such a body. This scenario has many adherents in France, and amongst supporters of political union within the European Community.

(vi) The development of a pan-European security structure, based on the CSCE, and capable of meeting Germany's security requirements. The CSCE has figured prominently in the German security debate in recent years, and although most Germans do not believe that an institutionalised CSCE will be able to absorb the functions of existing alliances like NATO for many years, this vision has been endorsed by sections of the SPD and the radical left, and even by Foreign Minister Genscher himself. In this scenario, a slimmed-down Bundeswehr could be used as a European (or UN) peacekeeping force.[48]

As Germany became one nation again in 1990, there was a remarkable degree of domestic political consensus on the broad outlines of German security policy in the early 1990s. However, such domestic consensus could prove fragile once the transitional period (in which Soviet troops remain in eastern Germany) has passed. If East–West relations remain cooperative and stable, then pressures will grow for further reforms within NATO and a strengthening of the CSCE. If, on the other hand, the reform process in the Soviet Union suffers a major set-back, there will be a fierce debate in Germany on the best way to respond. Whatever the outcome, it is Germany that holds the key to the future of NATO, and thus at the same time, to the future strategic contours of the new Europe. The decisions Germany takes concerning its defence and security policies will therefore be crucial to the evolution of the European security system.

5. Berlin, Germany and Europe

In 1973, the historian Allan Bulock argued that no other city has reflected the history of the twentieth century – for better or worse – as Berlin. It has played a symbolic role for the traumas and dramas of modern Europe, and has embodied the restlessness, experimentation and non-conformity of modern industrial culture and politics. It is, therefore, the 'symbolic city of the twentieth century'.[49]

With the Berlin blockade of June 1948–May 1949, Berlin switched from being the symbol of the Third Reich to the symbol of the 'free world'. Berliners were no longer seen as the villains of the Second World War, but as the victims of the cold war. This image was reinforced after 13 August 1961, when the Berlin Wall – the very symbol of the division of the continent – was built. The Quadripartite Agreement of 1971 transformed Berlin from a source of conflict into a keystone of the new detente. Thus throughout the post-war period, Berlin remained a crucial element in both the open German question, and in East–West relations in general.[50]

The fall of the Berlin Wall has given the city a renewed prominence and improved prospects. Once again, it was the opening up of the Berlin Wall which symbolised the end of the cold war in Europe. The debate has now been joined on whether Berlin should become the seat of parliament and government of a united Germany. There are strong arguments both ways. On the one hand, Bonn symbolises the modesty, quiet self-confidence and above all, the *Westintegration* of the FRG: these qualities might be lost amongst the Wilhelmine grandeur of Unter den Linden and the Reichstag.[51] On the other hand, moving the capital to Berlin would correspond to the new geopolitical realities of Europe, and would make unification seem less like *Anschluss* to the East German people. A compromise was reached in the Unity Treaty in which Berlin became the official capital and the seat of the Presidency, whilst the seat of government remained in Bonn.[52] How long this arrangement will last, however, remains to be seen.

Whether or not Berlin becomes the seat of government and home to the Bundestag, the city could become 'the hinge of an enlarged Europe',[53] playing a key role in overcoming the legacy of a divided continent. As President Reagan proposed in 1987, Berlin could become a hub of an aviation network in central Europe, and could also serve as an important venue for East–West conferences. There have also been proposals to site some CSCE institutions in Berlin, which would further reinforce its role as a major **European** city. Moreover, Berlin is well-placed – economically and geographically – to become a bridge for East–West economic cooperation. In such ways, Berlin could use its pivotal position in Europe to act as a major conduit for East–West reconciliation and cooperation.

Conclusion: Germany and the New Europe

An underlying theme of this book is that Europe has recently experienced the end of an era. One chapter of modern European history has just ended, and another one is beginning. In this new era in Europe, a united Germany will be a powerful economic, political and cultural influence. As William Rees-Mogg has written, 'History has put 80 million Germans with their discipline and idealism at the heart of the Europe which is again the rising continent.' Given Germany's economic strength and cultural legacy, the new Europe will have a strong German influence; the new age will therefore be 'a German age, perhaps to the degree that the age of Louis XIV was French, that the age of Queen Victoria was British and that the twentieth century has been American'.[54]

This German influence will not necessarily be malign. As we have seen, a united Germany will not be a 'Fourth Reich'. The spectre of Bismarck and Hitler has been exorcised from modern Germany, which has emerged as the *locus classicus* of the 'European Dream' (the successor to the 'American Dream', which died in the paddy-fields of Indochina and in the ghettos of America). In the 'European Dream' – which has caught the imagination of those in Eastern Europe – everyone lives in a prosperous, liberal-democratic, social market economy, enjoying a high standard of living and a comprehensive welfare state.[55] Germans today are not concerned with *Lebensraum* in the East, but with preserving the environment and the eco-balance, with 'quality of life' issues, with participation and *Bürgerinitiativen*, and with women's equality – all of which will be themes of growing saliency in the new age.

At the same time, a united Germany will be a powerful force for peace in Europe. The commitment to peace has emerged as a decisive element of the modern German consciousness. As Richard Löwenthal suggested back in 1984, 'For the first time in modern history ... what appears as the German Question has taken the form of an almost desperate desire for peace by the German people in East and West.'[56] More recently, Anne-Marie Burley has argued that for a nation with the stigmata of responsibility for two world wars and the cold blooded murder of millions of people, peace is a powerful catalyst. There is a strong current of thinking in modern Germany which sees peace not simply as the absence of war, but as the precondition for turning to 'real' problems such as Third World poverty, the problems of post-industrial societies in the West, and the human costs of reform in East Europe. This conception of peace, it is suggested, could provide the basis for what Otto Schily has termed 'a new German identity', which would at the same time be 'a European, human identity'.[57]

Of course, there is a danger that a united Germany may use its economic power and political influence in selfish and short-sighted ways – in this respect, it is no better than France, Britain or the USA. As Stanley Hoffmann has argued, the most serious concern regarding Germany is not of a militaristic or aggressive 'Fourth Reich', but that Germany may yield – like so many major states in history – to the 'arrogance of power';

> Under these circumstances, Germany might behave less like a wise 'hegemon', understanding the need to take account of the interests of lesser powers, than like a selfish player concerned above all with relative gains and insensitive to the claims and fears of others.[58]

In the end, of course, there can be no foolproof safeguard against this danger, but two points are relevant here. First, as Joseph Rovan said four months after his liberation from Dachau concentration camp, we get *l'Allemagne de nos merites* ('the Germany we deserve').[59] He coined this phrase in order to indicate the need at that time for mutual reconciliation and a shared responsibility for the democratic development of Germany. Today, this means treating the Germans as our allies and partners in a new Europe, working with them, not against them – and not treating them as if they were suffering from 'angst, aggressiveness, assertiveness, bullying, egotism, inferiority complex, sentimentality'.[60]

Second, the best way of managing and containing the tremendous dynamism and productivity of the Germans is through developing and strengthening supranational and pan-European structures in Europe – above all, the EC, NATO and the CSCE. In this way, it may be possible to achieve what Thomas Mann spoke of in 1952 – namely a 'European Germany' rather than a 'German Europe'.[61] A united Germany will inevitably become a powerful actor in the new Europe, but there is little cause for believing that it will not remain peaceful and industrious. A Germany integrated into broader European structures, enjoying good relations with its neighbours, allies and former adversaries, could become a positive engine for pan-European cooperation and East–West rapprochement. In this way, Germany would be able to fulfil both aspects of its constitutional duty laid down in the preamble to the *Grundgesetz*: preserving 'its national and political unity', whilst at the same time, serving 'the peace of the world as an equal partner in a united Europe'.[62]

Notes

1. A.J.P. Taylor, 'German Unity', in *Europe, Grandeur and Decline* (London: Pelican, 1967), p. 21.
2. David Calleo, *The German Problem Reconsidered. Germany and the World Order. 1870 to the Present* (Cambridge: Cambridge University Press, 1978), p. 206.
3. For a provocative discussion of these issues, see David Blackbourn and Geoff Eley, *The Peculiarities of German History: Bourgeois Society and Politics in Nineteenth Century Germany* (Oxford: Oxford University Press, 1984).
4. See Wilhelm G. Grewe, *Die Deutsche Frage in der Ost-West-Spannung. Zeitgeschichtliche Kontroversen der achtziger Jahre* (Herford: BusseWald, 1986), and Günther Wagenlehner (ed.), *Die Deutsche Frage und Die Internationale Sicherheit* (Koblenz: Bernard & Graefe Verlag, 1988).
5. Quoted in Edwina Moreton, ed., *Germany Between East and West* (Cambridge: Cambridge University Press for the RIIA, 1987), p. 32.
6. Z. Brzezinski, 'The Future of Yalta', in *Foreign Affairs*, vol. 63, no. 2 (Winter 1989/90), pp. 279–302 (p. 291).
7. *Europäische Integration und deutsche Frage*, edited by Jens Hacker and Siegfried Mampel (Berlin: Duncker & Humblot, 1988), pp. 17–18.
8. Anton Deportes, *Europe Between the Superpowers* (New Haven, CT: Yale University Press, 1979), p. 116.
9. Joyce Marie Mushaben, 'A Search for Identity: The "German Question" in Atlantic Alliance Relations', in *World Politics*, vol. XL, no. 3 (April 1988).
10. Christoph Bertram, 'Change in Moscow – Continuity in Europe?', *The World Today*, vol. 44, nos. 8–9 (August/September 1988), pp. 137–39 (p. 138).
11. Quoted in Moreton, *op. cit.*, p. 76. See also Walter Kiep, 'The New Deutschlandpolitik', in *Foreign Affairs*, vol. 63, no. 2 (Winter 1984/85),

pp. 316–29; he quotes the words of President Weizsäcker, 'Most Europeans dislike the Wall about as much as they do the idea of a large German state in Central Europe' (p. 320).

12. G. Andreotti at a *L'Unita* festival; reported in *La Republica*, 16–17 September 1984.

13. 'Ausführungen von Bundeskanzler Dr. Helmut Kohl zur Deutschlandpolitik in der Haushaltsdebatte des Deutschen Bundestages', *Pressemitteilung* (Presse- und informationsamt der Bundesregierung), nr. 575/89, 28 November 1989. See also Barbara Donovan, 'Reaction in the GDR to Kohl's Speech on Confederation', *Radio Free Europe*, Background Report 211, 30 November 1989.

14. Timothy Garton Ash, 'East Germany: The Solution', in the *New York Review of Books*, 26 April 1990, pp. 14–20 (p. 17).

15. This is the title of a conference paper by the West German security analyst, Hans-Joachim Spanger, presented at the joint Chatham House–Frankfurt Peace Research Institute conference on 'European Security in the 1990s', held at Wilton Park, Sussex, 8–10 April 1990.

16. William Wallace, *The Transformation of Western Europe* (London: Pinter for the RIIA, 1990), p. 92.

17. Conor Cruise O'Brien, 'Beware, the Reich is Reviving', *The Times*, 31 October 1989. Of the same ilk is Roger Scruton's 'Don't Trust the Germans', in *The Sunday Telegraph*, 21 May 1989.

18. 'Saying the Unsayable about the Germans', interview with Nicholas Ridley, in *The Spectator*, 14 July 1990, pp. 8–10.

19. Quoted in *Newsweek*, 26 February 1990, p. 10. See also the interview with Hans Magnus Enzensberger in the *New Left Review*, no. 178 (November–December 1989), pp. 87–104 (esp. pp. 100–1).

20. Günter Grass has argued that 'anyone thinking about Germany these days and looking for an answer to the German Question must include Auschwitz in his thoughts'. See his collection of essays and speeches entitled *Two States – One Nation? The Case Against German Reunification* (London: Secker & Warburg, 1990). Even Chancellor Kohl, in his speech on German unification to the Reichstag on 4 October 1990, said that, 'If we want to face up to the whole of German history, we must not leave out the darkest chapters. We must never forget, push aside or belittle what crimes were carried out by the Germans this century, and what pain has been inflicted on individuals and peoples. Only if we bear that burden together do we show ourselves worthy of liberty ...'.

21. Meredith Heiser, 'The Unification of East and West German Parties', in *Report on Eastern Europe*, 20 July 1990, pp. 18–22.

22. See A. James McAdams, 'Towards a New Germany? – Problems of Unification', in *Government and Opposition*, vol. 25, no. 3 (Summer 1990), pp. 304–16.

23. As early as 1919 it was recognised by none other than J.M. Keynes that the modern European economy would, quite naturally, be centred on Germany; it was around Germany, he suggested, that 'the rest of the European economic system grouped itself, and on the prosperity and enterprise of Germany the prosperity of the rest of the world depended'. *The Economic Consequences of the Peace* (London: Macmillan, 1919), p. 14.

24. See 'If Two Germanies Became One', *The Economist*, 2 September 1989,

pp. 45–46; 'The Mighty Mark', *The Independent on Sunday*, 29 April 1990; 'Ein Wissenschaftswunder?', *The Economist*, 11 November 1989, pp. 145–52; and 'Frankfurt's Star may be Rising in the East', *Financial Times*, 5 June 1990.

25. See Meinhard Miegel, 'Why a United Germany Would Pose No Threat to its Neighbours', *Frankfurter Allgemeine Zeitung*, 15 February 1990, and 'Reuniting Germany' in *UBS International Finance*, no. 4 (Summer 1990), pp. 1–8.

26. See *'Historikerstreit': Die Dokumentation der Kontroverse um die Einzigartigkeit der nationalsozialistischen Judenvernichtung*, edited by Ernst Reinhard Piper (München: R. Piper & Co., 1987); Hans-Ulrich Wehler, *Entsorgung der deutschen Vergangenheit? Ein polemischer Essay zum 'Historikerstreit'* (München: Verlag C.H. Beck, 1988); and Jochen Thies, 'Germany's History War', in *The World Today*, vol. 44, no. 4 (April 1988), pp. 69–72.

27. See 'Will Germany Rule Europe?', Peregrine Worsthorne, *The Sunday Telegraph*, 12 February 1989, p. 24; 'Dreams and Delusions of Unity', Ralf Dahrendorf, *The Independent*, 13 April 1990; 'A Case of the Jitters', *Time*, 5 March 1990, pp. 10–12; and 'The Politics of the Oder-Neisse Line', Jan B. de Weydenthal, *Radio Free Europe*, Background Report/217, 15 December 1989.

28. Pierre Hassner, 'The Shifting Foundation', *Foreign Policy* (Fall 1982), p. 19.

29. R. Fritsch-Bournazel, *Confronting the German Question: Germans on the East–West Divide* (Oxford: Berg Publishers, 1988), p. 80.

30. K.G. Kiesinger, 'Rede anlässlich des Staatsakts zum Tag der deutschen Einheit', 17 June 1967.

31. This fear was articulated by a Parisian journalist, who wrote that, 'By rediscovering its geography, Germany is reviving the central European side of its character. This turns its back not only on imports from the USA's "cultural stores", but also on its old, close friends, the French'; quoted in F. Stephen Larrabee (ed.), *The Two German States and European Security* (London: Macmillan for the IEWSS, 1989), p. 38.

32. C.H. Flockton, 'The German Economy and the Single European Market', in *Politics and Society in Germany, Austria and Switzerland*, vol. 2, no. 3 (Summer 1990), pp. 54–70.

33. Konrad Adenauer once said that, 'In the lands of the German West, there is a natural longing to escape from the confines of national narrowness into the fullness of the European consciousness'. Quoted in Gordon A. Craig's 'A New, New Reich?', in the *New York Review of Books*, 18 January 1990, pp. 28–33 (p. 29).

34. R. Fritsch-Bournazel, *op. cit.*, p. 141.

35. See 'What's French for Ridley?', *The Economist*, 21 July 1990, pp. 46–47, and Jolyson Howorth, 'France since the Berlin Wall: Defence and Diplomacy', in *The World Today*, vol. 46, no. 7 (July 1990), pp. 126–30. The Germans were also very annoyed by President Mitterrand's unilateral declaration that France would withdraw its 50,000 troops from western Germany, despite Chancellor Kohl's public call for the French government not to do so.

36. R. Morgan, 'West German Foreign and Security Interests', in Edwina

Moreton, *op. cit.*, p. 104. See also Margarita Mathiopoulos, 'The US Presidency and the German Question During the Adenauer to Kohl Chancellorships', in *Aussenpolitik*, vol. 39, no. 4 (1988), pp. 348–64, and Wolfram F. Hanrieder, 'The German–American Alliance at Forty', in *Aussenpolitik*, vol. 40, no. 2 (1989), pp. 148–59.

37. See for example Wolfram F. Hanrieder (ed.), *Arms Control, the FRG and the Future of East–West Relations* (Boulder, CO: Westview, 1987), and Daniel J. Nelson, *Defenders or Intruders? The Dilemmas of US Forces in Germany* (Boulder, CO: Westview, 1987).

38. See Barbara Donovan, 'The Soviet–West German Political Declaration', *Radio Free Europe*, Background Briefing Report/107, 20 June 1989.

39. The proposal came from Nikolai Portualov, a key adviser to President Gorbachev on German affairs, who suggested that 'The new Germany will without doubt have not only a regional/European dimension but also a global dimension – with a bridging function between east and west'. See the *Financial Times*, 17 September 1990.

40. The French High Commissioner, Andre Francois-Poncet, once said that 'We all know that the Germans, whenever they join forces with the Russians, are soon afterwards on the outskirts of Paris.' Quoted by Renata Fritsch-Bournazel, 'The French View', in Edwina Moreton (ed.), *Germany Between East and West*, p. 74.

41. *Financial Times*, 16 July 1990, p. 23.

42. As the Polish analyst, Andrzej Karkoszka, has written, 'With the Federal Republic deeply embedded in the process of West European integration, such increased Soviet–FRG co-operation can only be seen as beneficial to all European states. Only if Western integration were to dwindle while, at the same time, the great powers' involvement in Central Europe waned and the stability of the East European states failed to be established over a longer period, might such close co-operation between these two powerful states be seen as jeopardizing the political balance in Europe. Such a scenario seems, however, rather unrealistic.' See his article, 'Transition in the East – A New Beginning for Europe?', in *The Strategic Implications of Change in the Soviet Union*, Adelphi Papers, no. 247 (London: Brassey's for the IISS, 1990), pp. 81–91, (p. 91).

43. 'We *want* to lead', a top Kohl adviser has said; 'Perhaps in time the United States will take care of places like Central America, and we will handle Eastern Europe.' See 'The New Superpower', *Newsweek*, 29 February 1990, p. 9.

44. See Clay Clemens, 'Beyond INF: West Germany's Centre-right Party and Arms Control in the 1990s', in *International Affairs*, vol. 65, no. 1 (Winter 1988/89), pp. 55–74.

45. In a provocative but misguided article, John Mearsheimer has argued that Germany should be encouraged to acquire its own nuclear weapons; 'Back to the Future: Instability in Europe after the Cold War', *International Security*, vol. 15, no. 1 (Summer 1990), pp. 5–56.

46. It would also be internationally unacceptable: even John Foster Dulles, a good friend of the FRG, warned Willy Brandt that 'we shall never permit a reunited and rearmed Germany to roam around in the no man's land between East and West'. Quoted by Robert Blackwell, 'European Influences and Constraints on US Policy toward the Soviet Union', in *US–Soviet Relations:*

The Next Phase, ed. by Arnold L. Horelick (Ithaca and London: Cornell University Press, 1986), p. 132.

47. Ernest May, 'American Forces in the Federal Republic: Past, Present and Future', in *The Federal Republic of Germany and the United States: Changing Political, Social and Economic Relations*, ed. by James A. Cooney et al. (Boulder, Co: Westview, 1984), p. 170.

48. For a discussion of the constitutional issues involved, see Peter Bardehle, '"Blue Helmets" From Germany? Opportunities and Limits of UN Peacekeeping', *Aussenpolitik*, vol. 40, no. 4 (1989), pp. 372–84.

49. Peter Jelavich, *Berlin and the 20th Century*, Conference Report no. 2/85 (Berlin: Aspen Institute for Humanistic Studies, 1985), p. 1.

50. See I.D. Hendry and M.C. Wood, *The Legal Status of Berlin* (Cambridge: Grotius Publications, 1987), p. xiii., and Robert Hunter, 'Berlin: Forty Years On', in *Foreign Affairs*, vol. 68, no. 3 (Summer 1989), pp. 41–52.

51. As Hans Magnus Enzensberger has argued, Bonn represents 'the very paradigm of a government lacking in aura', and there is much to be said for the 'mediocre sort of government which is embodied in my mind by the city of Berlin'. See his interview in the *New Left Review, op. cit.*, p. 100.

52. Article 2 of the Unity Treaty stated that 'The Capital of Germany is Berlin. The question of the seat of parliament and government will be decided after the unity of Germany has been accomplished.'

53. As proposed by the Governing Mayor of Berlin, Walter Momper, in his Address to the Royal Institute of International Affairs, London, 3 May 1989.

54. William Rees-Mogg, 'Year of Change that Heralds a German Age', *The Independent*, 4 December 1989.

55. R.W. Johnson, 'European Dream Ticket Lures East's Voters to the Right', in the *Independent on Sunday*, 25 March, 1990.

56. R. Löwenthal, 'The German Question Transformed', in *Foreign Affairs*, vol. 63, no. 2 (Winter 1984/85), pp. 303–15 (p. 303).

57. Anne-Marie Burley, 'The Once and Future German Question', in *Foreign Affairs*, vol. 68, no. 5 (Winter 1989/90), pp. 65–83 (p. 74).

58. Stanley Hoffmann, 'Reflections on the "German Question"', in *Survival*, vol. XXXII, no. 4 (July–August 1990), pp. 291–98 (pp. 295–96).

59. Quoted in Moreton, *Germany Between East and West*, p. 67.

60. These were the 'national characteristics' ascribed to the Germans in the confidential Whitehall memorandum drawn up by the Prime Minister's private secretary Charles Powell after an informal seminar at Chequers on Sunday, 24 March 1990. The seminar was attended by Mrs Thatcher and a number of British and American 'experts' on Germany, and the memo was leaked and published in the *Independent on Sunday* on 15 July 1990.

61. 'I reaffirm what Thomas Mann said as early as 1952: we seek a European Germany, not a German Europe. That is our rejection of the power politics of the past'; *Newsweek*, 26 February 1990, p. 10.

62. Dieter Haack et al. (eds), *Das Wiedervereinigungsgebot des Grundgesetzes* (Cologne: Verlag Wissenschaft und Politik, 1989).

8

Military 'Grammar' and Political 'Logic'

War is only a part of political intercourse, therefore by no means an independent thing in itself .... War is nothing but a continuation of political intercourse, with a mixture of other means .... Is not War merely another kind of writing and language for political thoughts? It has certainly a grammar of its own, but its logic is not peculiar to itself.

Accordingly, War can never be separated from political intercourse, and if, in the consideration of the matter, this is done in any way, all the threads of the different relations are, to a certain extent, broken, and we have before us a senseless thing without an object.

Carl von Clausewitz, *On War*, 1832[1]

In his famous work, *On War*, Carl von Clausewitz wrote that whilst military issues had their own grammar, it was politics that gave them their logic. Once military matters became divorced from their wider political context, the result was 'a senseless thing without an object'. With the end of the cold war, the grammar of military forces in Europe has indeed become divorced from the politics of a reuniting continent.[2]

For almost four decades, the structure of military forces in the European security system was primarily determined by the East–West confrontation, in a bipolar world dominated by two antagonistic military-political blocs. This produced the largest concentration of conventional and nuclear forces the world has ever seen, focused above all on the central front in Europe. Despite the political mistrust that this arms build-up engendered, the military balance in Europe appeared remarkably stable. But with the political convulsions that have shaken the continent over the last few years, the prevailing configuration of military forces has become highly anachronistic. As we have seen, Soviet *perestroika*, the democratic revolutions in Eastern Europe, growing West European integration, changing transatlantic relations and above all, German unification, have transformed the political and strategic landscape of Europe. These tremendous changes have made the task of dismantling the military structures left over from the cold war an urgent necessity.

In this chapter, we will assess the effect of the political changes on the military structures of Europe – focusing on the Soviet Union, Eastern Europe and NATO. We will also consider the evolving military-strategic landscape of Europe in the light of the changing security agenda, and the role of nuclear weapons in a Europe 'beyond containment'.

Gorbachev and Soviet Security Policy in Europe

The catalyst for the recent political and strategic changes in Europe has been the Soviet President, Mikhail Gorbachev. When he came to power in March 1985, he found himself responsible for a country suffering from a deepening economic and political malaise, but with a huge military machine. This bloated military apparatus was enormously expensive, and was proving a growing liability. For a start, the steady drain on manpower, resources, expertise and finance was diverting scarce resources from other more worthwhile needs. Second, there were the international political costs: the massive investment in forward-deployed offensively orientated armoured forces in Eastern Europe had become an obstacle to closer relations with the West, which were vital if Soviet industry was to get access to the Western technology and know-how it so urgently needed. Third, this massive military Leviathan was no longer even capable of guaranteeing the security of the Soviet Union itself. The attempt to provide a one-sided security guarantee to the USSR by building up its conventional and nuclear capability in the 1970s and early 1980s had failed: NATO had demonstrated its resolve over the INF deployments issue, and was developing new and threatening military technologies, including the Strategic Defence Initiative and new 'Emergent Technologies' (ETs), such as precision-guided munitions and smart weapons.

Given the economic costs and political disutility of the military machine he inherited from Brezhnev, Gorbachev and his advisers decided to undertake a major reform of the Soviet armed forces. To begin with, Gorbachev has encouraged a radical overhaul of the administrative structures of the Soviet military, and implemented sweeping personnel changes. Second, he has initiated a series of unilateral arms control and disarmament measures, beginning with the 18-month moratorium on nuclear testing (from August 1985 to February 1987), and culminating in the unilateral troop cuts announced in his United Nations speech of 7 December 1988. Third, he has encouraged a switch in resources from the military to the civilian sectors of the economy.[3] Finally, he has encouraged a new Soviet approach to arms control and disarmament policies. Gorbachev has demonstrated that he has no time for the plodding incrementalism of the MBFR, and has sought to underline the USSR's commitment to serious arms control agreements by a judicious mixture of conciliatory gestures and unilateral arms cuts.

Underlying this has been a more fundamental shift in Soviet grand strategy and military doctrine. As Michael MccGwire has argued, a major strategic reassessment was carried out by Soviet military planners in the early 1980s. They believed that the likelihood of war breaking out in Europe was remote, but that conflict with the USA in the region north of the Persian Gulf could not be ruled out. Such a regional conflict, they argued, would not necessarily escalate to all-out world war, and consequently, there would be no point in escalating the conflict horizontally by launching an offensive into Western Europe. Instead, holding operations in the European theatre would suffice.[4] MccGwire's analysis has been criticised on the grounds that he adduces too high a degree of rationality and coherence to strategic decision-making in the USSR than is probably the case, and that he pays relatively little attention to the subtleties of European security politics.[5] Nevertheless, a relative shift of Soviet military thinking away from Central Europe towards the southern Soviet border has been in evidence in the course of the 1980s, and his arguments do seem to provide a convincing rationale for the subsequent changes in Soviet military doctrine and command structure.

The shift in Soviet strategic thinking has made possible a major revision in the country's military doctrine.[6] In the past, the technical-military aspects of Soviet military doctrine have posited the need for forward deployments and large-scale offensive operations against NATO forces in Europe (in order to establish an extended 'defence perimeter' and deny the USA a European 'bridge-head' for operations against the Soviet homeland). At the same time, they hoped to avoid provoking a US nuclear attack on the USSR itself by not attacking North America.[7] The precise relationship between this strategy and nuclear weapons has evolved over the years – to some extent, in tandem with changes in NATO doctrine. In the early 1980s, under the direction of Chief of the General Staff Nikolai Ogarkov, Soviet military doctrine focused more on the ability to wage a 'protracted' conventional war successfully, using fast-moving offensive operations which emphasised surprise, firepower and the concept of 'Operational Manoeuvre Groups'(OMG).[8]

However, the economic and political costs of these offensive doctrinal concepts – along with changes in Soviet strategic thinking and the political leadership's re-evaluation of the military competition with the West – prompted Gorbachev to push for a thorough-going revision of the military-technical elements of Soviet military doctrine. In February 1986 at the 27th CPSU Congress he used the concept of 'reasonable sufficiency' (*razumnaya dostatochnost*) for the first time,[9] and Soviet scholars were subsequently encouraged to investigate the nature and significance of this concept.[10] In Soviet military academies and journals, more attention has been paid to strategic defensive operations, whilst the Warsaw Pact communiqués of June 1986 (Budapest) and May 1987 (Berlin) committed the Warsaw Pact as a whole to a defensive military doctrine.[11] The unilateral cuts of December 1988 also provided the first tangible evidence that Gorbachev was serious about restructuring the Soviet armed forces on a more defensive and non-provocative basis. In the future, therefore, the Soviet Union is likely to possess smaller military forces, which will no longer be deployed in significant numbers in Eastern Europe, and which will no longer be trained and equipped to conduct large-scale offensive operations against Western Europe. The emphasis of Soviet military doctrine will thus shift to concepts of strategic defence of the Soviet homeland.

At the same time, the combat effectiveness of the Soviet army has been weakened by the divisions and turmoil within Soviet society as a whole. There have been calls for the reconstitution of the army along republican lines, and an intense debate is under way on the feasibility of moving to a professional volunteer army. There has also been fierce domestic criticism of the army, both for its privileges and for its role in internal security (after the events in Tbilisi on 9 April 1989 and Baku in late January 1990). Within the army itself, an independent trade union – 'Shield' – has been established, to campaign for better pay and conditions. To cap it all, the internal divisions within the army have been greatly exacerbated by the problems associated with rehousing and relocating Soviet forces returning from Eastern Europe.[12]

As a result of these changes within the Soviet army, the military landscape of Europe as a whole is being transformed. Although the Soviet Union remains the largest conventional and military power on the Eurasian continent, it has already lost the capability of conducting short-warning large-scale offensive armoured operations against Western Europe.

Soviet Thinking on Nuclear Deterrence

One further issue which has been subject to considerable debate in the Soviet Union over recent years has been their attitude to the concept of nuclear deterrence. From the start of the nuclear age, the Soviets have been committed to the goal of abolishing all 'weapons of mass destruction'. Gorbachev initially endorsed this goal, and in January 1986, he proposed a three-stage plan for the elimination of nuclear weapons by the year 2000. However, in a number of speeches since then, he and the former Foreign Minister, Eduard Shevardnadze, have hinted that the Soviet Union was willing to accept the notion of a 'minimum nuclear deterrence'. Soviet civilian security analysts have already explicitly endorsed this notion.[13] There are a number of reasons for believing that the Soviets might be reconsidering their evaluation of the deterrent function of nuclear weapons. Firstly, after a CFE Treaty, the USSR will no longer enjoy a numerical superiority in certain categories of conventional forces. Given NATO's qualitative edge, this will put the Soviet Union at a distinct disadvantage in central Europe. At the same time, with slimmed down conventional armed forces, the Soviet Union will find it even more difficult to defend its territorial integrity on all fronts. In an increasingly polycentric and potentially unstable world, the possession of a minimum nuclear deterrence might provide a relatively cheap security guarantee.

Secondly, the USSR's declaratory commitment to nuclear disarmament is a continuing source of mistrust between the Soviet Union and NATO countries – particularly those members of the 'nuclear club'. The West has long suspected that the Soviet Union has sought to exploit differences within NATO and encourage the breakup of the Atlantic Alliance, thereby increasing the military utility and political influence of its substantial conventional forces. If the USSR were to accept the notion of a 'minimum nuclear deterrence', it would reassure many in the West, and might provide a basis for jointly hammering out a new, mutual security regime in Europe.

Even if the Soviet leadership were to accept the military and political arguments in favour of a minimum nuclear deterrent, it is not clear what this might mean in terms of specific categories of nuclear weapons. Would the Soviet Union accept short-range land-based systems, or only sea-based and air-launched systems? What about nuclear artillery?[14] As we shall see below, the concept of a 'minimum nuclear deterrence' might provide the basis for a new security consensus both within and between the two military alliances, but it does not provide any easy or simple solutions to the dilemmas plaguing nuclear deterrence as a whole.

The Warsaw Pact and East European Security

The disjunction between military 'grammar' and political 'logic' is nowhere more evident than in Eastern Europe. For nearly forty years, the East European countries have been integrated into a military alliance dominated by the Soviet Union. Since its creation in 1955, the Warsaw Pact's military command structures have been dominated by the Soviet Union. Moscow was keen to prevent the development of autonomous national military doctrines amongst its allies, especially in East Central Europe. This was particularly the case in the northern tier countries (Poland, the GDR and Czechoslovakia), who constituted the 'iron triangle' of the Pact. Romania's independent stance was tolerated by the Soviet military largely because of its limited geostrategic significance.[15] Expressions of specific national interests in the formulation of military doctrine in WTO countries – for example Poland in the early 1950s and in 1980, or Czechoslovakia in 1968 – did not long survive the reimposition of communist orthodoxy.

However, the revolutions of 1989 have eroded the political foundations of the Warsaw Pact. It is clear that the Soviet Union has fundamentally reassessed its security interests in Eastern Europe. Moscow no longer defines its security in the region in terms of the leading role of indigenous communist parties and the integrity of the WTO. The 'Brezhnev doctrine' has been superseded by the 'Sinatra doctrine', and the Soviet Union is happy to see non-communist – but friendly – governments on its western borders.

Thus although the Pact was renewed for a further twenty years on 26 April 1985 (with an option for an additional ten), its continued survival until 2005 is most unlikely. With the collapse of East Germany, the Soviet Union has lost its key military and political ally in Eastern Europe. Indeed, the GDR was crucial to the very viability of the Soviet military position in East Central Europe.[16] The future of the Warsaw Pact now hangs primarily on Poland – and to a lesser extent, Czechoslovakia. If the Poles decide that some sort of continued security cooperation with the Soviet Union is in their interests – perhaps given their mistrust of a united Germany – then the WTO may survive in a truncated form.[17] If not, then it will quickly be consigned to the 'dust-bin of history'.

Given the uncertainty surrounding the future viability of the Warsaw Pact, the East Europeans are facing the prospect of being left in a 'security limbo'. The collapse of the *pax Sovietica* has left these countries with no clear framework for managing or containing their security problems, which derive from their unenviable geopolitical situation, and their history – a history 'either of domination by outside powers or conflict among the nations of this region'.[18] In Chapter 6 we considered some of the political dimensions of this problem: at this point we shall consider the military and security options now facing the democratising states of Eastern Europe.

The future security 'architecture' of Eastern Europe will certainly be more complex and diverse than in the days of the WTO. There are, broadly speaking, six possible directions within which the security policies of the East Europeans could develop. These are not necessarily mutually exclusive, but could be combined in different configurations by different countries in the region. They are as follows:

1. A Reformed Warsaw Pact

This was the approach agreed at the crucial WTO summit in Moscow on 7 June 1990.[19] It involves the internal democratisation of the Pact, and its retention as a primarily political forum for consultation and limited cooperation on regional security issues. Some military and defence cooperation (perhaps involving some common training exercises, joint weapons procurement and standardised equipment) might continue, but much of the WTO's military command structures will be dismantled, and

Soviet forces will no longer be stationed in Eastern Europe in significant numbers. Such an arrangement might be attractive to countries like Poland and Bulgaria, and perhaps Czechoslovakia and Romania (Hungary, however, would probably still opt for neutrality[20]). Many East Europeans recognise the temporary utility of a reformed Warsaw Pact for arms control negotiation, tempering long-smouldering ethnic grievances, and addressing Soviet security concerns – for they realise that Eastern Europe can never be truly secure if their giant Soviet neighbour feels insecure.

2. Bilateral Soviet–East European Security Cooperation
If the Warsaw Pact were to cease to exist as a viable organisation, it is possible that some of the East European countries might develop bilateral security relations with the Soviet Union – of the sort which existed in the decade prior to the establishment of the Pact in 1955. This might prove welcome to countries such as Poland and Czechoslovakia (given their residual concerns about a possible resurgence of 'German revanchism'), and to Bulgaria (given its exposed geostrategic position in the Balkans). It might also be attractive to some Eastern European armies given that they are armed with Soviet military equipment, and will remain dependent on the USSR for spare parts and replacements, as well as for training programmes.

3. The 'Renationalization' of Security Policy in Eastern
Europe
It is more than possible that the Warsaw Pact will disintegrate and that few – if any – bilateral security relationships will develop between the Soviet Union and its former Pact allies. In this situation, the East Europeans may simply develop their own national military doctrines and restructure their military forces in the light of their perceived individual security requirements – as they are already beginning to do. This might unfortunately mean some East European states configuring their military forces in ways that generate security concerns amongst their neighbours – a serious danger in a region plagued by ethnic, national and political tensions, and which has proven to be the 'powder-keg' of Europe in the past.

On the other hand, as Gerard Holden has demonstrated, there has been considerable East European interest expressed over recent years in ideas of 'defensive defence' and 'non-provocative defence'.[21] It is therefore possible that these notions – along with the experience of territorial defence developed in Yugoslavia, Sweden and Switzerland – will play an influential part in the doctrinal and structural reorganisation currently underway in post-communist Eastern Europe. Moreover, many East European countries have already begun major cut-backs in their armed forces, and by the mid-1990s, the overall military balance in the region will be greatly reduced.[22] However, if national and ethnic tensions continue to mount in the region, it is extremely doubtful whether ideas of 'defensive defence' and 'non-provocative defence' would receive the necessary political support and encouragement.

4. The Development of East European Security Cooperation

One scenario which is most unlikely at the moment, but which cannot be excluded entirely, is the creation of an East European security entity (a sort of Eastern 'WEU'), perhaps involving the three East Central European countries – Poland, Czechoslovakia and Hungary. There has been some discussion of the possibility of establishing a Polish–Czechoslovakian 'Central European Federation', or of closer political and economic cooperation between the three East Central European countries in order to coordinate their 'return to Europe'.[23] Such efforts have, however, run aground on the national differences and rivalries between them. The problem is that although they have common problems, they do not have common solutions – their relations thus exhibit as much competition as cooperation. Even Western proposals for an East European 'Payments Union' have received a cool reception, given the economic asymmetries between the three.

5. Western Security Guarantees for Eastern Europe

Whilst he was still Foreign Minister of Hungary, Gyula Horn spoke of his hopes for Hungary developing closer ties with NATO's political organisations, and there is some evidence to suggest that many East Europeans would welcome security guarantees from the West.[24] Such security guarantees could be provided either by NATO or by the Western European Union.[25] However, this would be extremely difficult for NATO or the WEU to implement in practice; it would antagonise the Soviet Union; and it would also drag Western countries into the quagmire of national and ethnic tensions in the East.

6. The Emergence of a System of Mutual and Collective Security, based on the CSCE

This vision was initially expounded by Vaclav Havel and Jiri Dienstbier. The original Czechoslovak proposals were subsequently coordinated with Poland and the GDR. The aim of these proposals was the creation of a collective security system which would include all 35 CSCE participating states, and which would ultimately supersede both NATO and the Warsaw Pact. This concept is very popular in East Central Europe, and has been gaining adherents in Germany – especially amongst the opposition Social Democrats, although even Hans-Dietrich Genscher has expressed considerable sympathy with the idea.[26] The problem with this scenario is two-fold: first, the unanimity principle upon which CSCE decision-making is based; and second, the lack of credible mechanisms for the enforcement of collective security.

Eastern Europe as a 'Buffer'?

The precise nature of the security structures that will evolve in Eastern Europe – especially in East Central Europe – can only be a matter of conjecture at this stage. But it is clear that the military landscape of Europe has radically altered as a result of the strategic and political 'earthquake' of late 1989. The foundations of the WTO have been severely weakened, and the Pact is unlikely to survive in its post-war form for very much longer. Although countries like Bulgaria and possibly Poland may want to retain some form of security cooperation with the Soviet Union, others – such as Hungary and Czechoslovakia – are already exploring the possibility of achieving a neutral status within a pan-European system of collective security.[27]

There is good reason for believing that the Soviet Union would be willing to accept neutral and non-aligned countries on its western border – particularly given its positive experience of Finnish neutrality since the last war.[28] What seems to be emerging is an expanded belt of neutral and non-aligned states between a militarily weakened Soviet Union and a reforming NATO – a 'buffer' stretching from the Nordic area, through Eastern Europe and into the Balkans. This would be a development which would in turn greatly improve the security environment facing NATO itself – a subject to which we shall now turn.

NATO in a Changing Europe

The disintegration of the 'Soviet bloc' and the beginnings of Soviet military disengagement from Eastern Europe have profoundly altered the military landscape within which NATO operates. Indeed, a question mark now stands over the role and purpose of NATO in conditions of growing East–West cooperation. In Chapter 6 we considered the broader political options facing NATO: we now need to consider the implications of the changing strategic situation for NATO's military strategy, deployment patterns and force levels.

As regards NATO's military strategy, it has exhibited elements of both continuity and change since the Alliance's inception in 1949. At the time of its creation, neither the presence of substantial numbers of US combat troops nor West German membership were regarded as a *sine qua non* of the future viability of the Alliance. NATO's operational doctrine has changed in response to both the evolving perception of the 'Soviet threat' and the changing capabilities of the Alliance. Thus the early 'Counteroffensive' strategy of MC14/1 was replaced by that of the

'Sword and Shield' (MC14/2) in the early 1950s, and then by MC14/3 – 'Flexible response' – in 1967.[29] Despite these operational innovations, however, there have been important elements of underlying continuity – for example, the enduring commitment to extended deterrence and trans-atlantic coupling; the indivisibility of the threat and the 'seamlessness' of security through the Alliance; and the commitment to defend the territorial integrity of NATO as close to the borders as possible.

The twin pillars of NATO's contemporary strategic thinking – 'flexible response' and 'forward defence' – were in place by the early 1970s. NATO explained its strategy in the following terms:

> The aim of NATO's strategy and military planning is to ensure security through deterrence. The primary aim is to deter an attack before it is launched, by making it clear to any aggressor that any attack on NATO would be met by a strong defence and might initiate a sequence of events which cannot be calculated in advance, involving risks to the aggressor out of all proportion to any advantages he might hope to gain. In an era of broad strategic nuclear parity, deterrence to all forms of aggression cannot be based upon strategic nuclear forces alone; it must be provided by the overall capabilities of all NATO forces. The Alliance must be able to respond in an appropriate manner to aggression of any kind; the response must be effective in relation to the level of force used by the aggressor and must at the same time make him recognise the dangers of escalation to a higher level.
>
> Should aggression occur, the military aim is to preserve or restore the integrity and security of the NATO area by employing such forces as may be necessary within the concept of forward defence and flexibility in response. NATO forces must be prepared to use any capabilities at their disposal (including nuclear weapons) for this purpose. This determination must be evident to the aggressor.[30]

But with the fading of the cold war, a reforming Soviet Union and German unification, these strategic concepts are becoming both increasingly anachronistic and politically unacceptable to many in the Western democracies. As NATO's 'London Declaration' of 6 July 1990 recognised, 'as Europe changes, we must profoundly alter the way we think about defence'.[31] This will affect both NATO's integrated force structure, and its strategy – including the twin concepts upon which NATO's strategic thinking is grounded: flexible response and forward defence.

Flexible Response

This concept was adopted by NATO in 1967, as a means of defining a new strategic synergy between American strategic nuclear weapons and conventional forces in Europe. Henceforth, NATO was to match its response to different levels of Soviet aggression, thereby avoiding undue escalation. 'Flexible response' itself consisted of three stages:

direct defence, deliberate escalation and general nuclear response. This involved the creation of a number of options for the use of theatre nuclear weapons in Europe which would be 'militarily significant and politically credible'. The concept itself has proven to be compatible with a variety of operational strategies, and has provided a workable political and military compromise which has succeeded in papering over many of the dilemmas inherent in extended nuclear deterrence for much of the last two decades. However, growing doubts are now being raised as to the sustainability of the operational dimension of 'flexible response' in the changed political conditions of the 1990s.

This strategy has been criticised on a number of counts. To begin with, it is difficult to operationalise given the problems of maintaining C^3I capabilities in conditions of fast-moving and fluid warfare.[32] Second, this strategy assigns a pivotal role to Theatre Nuclear Forces (which are crucial to the 'coupling' of regional defence with the US strategic deterrence), yet it is here that NATO military thinking is at its most muddled.[33] If TNF were to be used, some would probably be targeted against advancing enemy forces on German soil, causing immense collateral damage in the central European region, and destroying much of what was to be defended. In this way, it has been argued, flexible response risks taking a conventional defeat (affecting Germany) and transforming it into an Alliance-wide nuclear disaster.[34] Morton Halperin has suggested that flexible response is flawed because, 'NATO doctrine is that we will fight with conventional weapons until we are losing, then we will fight with tactical nuclear weapons until we are losing, and then we will blow up the world'.[35]

The dilemmas of 'flexible response', and the growing unacceptability of short-range ground-launched nuclear weapons in central Europe, have contributed to a lively debate on NATO's nuclear doctrine. A number of proposals have been put forward over recent years, including 'no first use' and 'no early first use'.[36] As scepticism of the military utility of nuclear weapons has become more widespread, a new consensus has begun to form on the need to raise the nuclear threshold, reduce NATO's reliance on short-range nuclear weapons, and clearly reject nuclear war-fighting strategies. In its 'London Declaration', NATO acknowledged that it would require fewer nuclear weapons (especially 'sub-strategic nuclear systems of the shortest range'), and officially described nuclear weapons themselves as 'truly weapons of last resort'.

The essence of NATO's evolving nuclear doctrine is therefore a less flexible version of 'flexible response'. Nuclear deterrence is to remain an integral part of NATO thinking – indeed, the London Declaration insisted that 'there are no circumstances in which nuclear retaliation in response to military action might be discounted'. Nevertheless, there will be less reliance on short-range systems, and the burden of flexible response is likely to shift to sea- and air-based systems. Whether this new compromise within NATO will survive for long is not yet clear. There is a deepening mood of nuclear pacifism in Germany and central Europe, and very limited support for new nuclear weapons – such as TASM. On the other hand, the French, British and Americans are unlikely to entertain notions of a denuclearised Europe, or of a non-nuclear NATO strategy. Furthermore, the deterrent quality of nuclear weapons is widely recognised in many parts of Western Europe, and increasingly in the Soviet Union too. NATO's reduced reliance on nuclear weapons could help build greater trust and cooperation in Europe (by addressing some of the security concerns of the Soviets and East Europeans), but revision of its nuclear doctrine is not without its risks. Raising the nuclear threshold – or adopting a strategy of 'no first use' – might expand the range of conventional military options open to an aggressor. At the end of the day, therefore, there are no easy solutions to the dilemmas of nuclear deterrence, and no convincing alternatives to NATO's concept of nuclear weapons as 'weapons of last resort'.

Forward Defence

NATO's commitment to the principle of 'forward defence' was the military cost to be paid for the integration of West German forces into the Alliance. 'Forward defence' in military terms is the commitment to maintain the territorial integrity of NATO, at the expense of concepts like 'defence in depth' and 'trading space for time', which the Soviets employed so successfully in 1941–42. The aim of 'forward defence' has been to tie down advancing enemy forces as far to the East as possible, thereby critically disrupting the Soviet offensive time-table, and saving the maximum amount of allied territory from the worst effects of the fighting. As a strategy, however, it has proven compatible with a wide variety of contingency plans and operational doctrines.

Over the last decade, there has been an extensive discussion of conventional force options on the central front. The Americans have played a key role in developing new operational doctrines, such as the US Army's 'Airland Battle' (FM 100-5) and NATO's 'Follow-on Forces Attack' (FOFA). These call for the integration of nuclear, chemical and conventional capabilities, and advocate 'deep strikes' against the enemy's second echelon forces and logistical infrastructure.[37] Within the British army, the former Chief of the General Staff, Field Marshall Sir Nigel Bagnall, stimulated a debate from 1981 onwards over the balance to be struck between manoeuvre and a more static defence, and this has resulted in a shift towards the former. The development of the 'emerging technologies' (such as smart weapons, precision-guided munitions and expanded C^3I capabilities) seemed to offer another way of raising the nuclear threshold and expanding the range of conventional war-fighting options in Europe.[38] The central thrust here, as with Soviet notions of OMGs and their associated operational concepts, was

> ... the military search for escape routes from the apparent cul-de-sac created by the self-deterring nature of nuclear weapons, and the technological impetus of rapid developments in 'conventional' weaponry which seemed to reopen the possibilities of prolonged (and possibly mobile) conventional combat.[39]

These plans for improving conventional force posture and developing more ambitious – and offensively orientated – operational doctrines are unlikely to be comprehensively implemented, given their cost and political unpopularity. Indeed, the end of East–West confrontation has made many of NATO's traditional military doctrines (including forward defence), and its more recent innovations (such as FOFA and Counterair '90), militarily irrelevant and politically unacceptable. Moreover, the Vienna negotiations on Conventional Forces in Europe (CFE) promise to accelerate a process of unilateral defence cuts already well underway, as Western governments search for the elusive 'peace dividend'.[40]

Given these political pressures, financial constraints and arms control negotiations, NATO in 1990 embarked on the most far-reaching strategic review since that which led to the adoption of MC14/3 in 1967. At the time of writing, the results of this are not yet known, but elements of it are becoming clear:

(i) NATO will field smaller and restructured active forces. The emphasis here will be on more mobile, versatile and flexible forces. This will in turn mean fewer large-scale military exercises, and a lower public profile for NATO forces in Germany.

(ii) The Alliance will shift towards a 'reconstitution strategy'. Thanks to a greatly improved warning-time, the number of in-place units and levels of force readiness can be significantly reduced, and a greater emphasis can be placed on the reserves, mobilisation procedures and reinforcement measures.

(iii) National corps within NATO are likely to be replaced by multinational forces, integrated at the corps level. There are powerful political arguments in favour of such multinational force integration, and potential military advantages to be gained too (in terms of greater inter-operability of national forces and increased incentives for equipment standardisation and joint procurement programmes).

(iv) A shift away from the 'layered cake' arrangement of eight national corps along the 'Inner-German Border', to a 'currant bun' structure. This could involve a covering or 'guard force' comprised of all the region's nations, with a multinational 'rapid reaction force' (of perhaps two divisions) grouped behind it, able to provide quick support where needed. Further back would be the 'currants' in the bun – ie, 'manoeuvre forces', which would be cadre units capable of being reinforced by reservists when they become ready. These would tend to be national or joint groupings.[41]

Negotiating a new strategy for NATO will involve a whole series of compromises between the 16 member nations. But – in the same way that Poland holds the key to the future of the Warsaw Pact – a united Germany will play a central role in reshaping both NATO's nuclear doctrine and conventional force structure. This is inevitable given Germany's geostrategic centrality and its conventional military strength – Germany is, after all, the host nation for the bulk of NATO's stationed forces, and could well be the front line of any future large-scale military conflict in Europe.

'Defensive Defence'

As NATO undertakes the task of restructuring its military forces and revising its strategy, interest in notions such as 'non-provocative defence' and 'defensive defence' is likely to grow. Proponents of ideas like 'defensive defence' and 'mutual defensive superiority' have argued that the adoption of a non-nuclear defensive defence posture would improve crisis stability, reduce the risk of escalation, improve the prospects of successful war termination (if deterrence failed), and create a virtuous circle of arms control agreements (in place of the old arms race). The idea is increasingly popular in Germany and amongst centre-left political forces in Europe and North America, where it is frequently regarded as being the only military policy compatible with the political aim of creating a new European peace order.[42]

The defensive restructuring of military forces in Europe will be an important part of improving the military climate in Europe. Mere parity, even at substantially lower levels, will not automatically enhance stability. This puts the onus on restructuring military forces in ways that contribute to a situation of 'mutual, robust defence dominance'.[43] This would involve fewer main battle tanks, heavy artillery, APCs and attack aircraft, and a greater reliance on anti-tank weapons, barrier units and light divisions. Nevertheless, there are a number of potential problems associated with existing concepts of 'defensive defence', which are likely to impede their wholesale adoption by any major NATO country.

First, it is difficult to categorise any weapon system as either offensive or defensive. Smaller defensive forces, for example, will tend to be 'flexible' and 'mobile': but flexibility and mobility are at the same time important characteristics for successful offensive operations. Second, an effective and credible defence seems to require a viable counter-attack capability, and the forces required for this are virtually indistinguishable from those needed for aggressive offensive operations. Finally, many 'defensive defence' models are designed to repel a particular kind of offensive operation – namely, short-warning *Blitzkrieg*-type armoured offensives, rather than, say, an intentional war of attrition.[44] For these reasons, therefore, any moves towards the adoption of elements of 'defensive defence' are likely to be piecemeal, incremental and partial. As Jonathan Dean has argued,

> ... individual aspects of these proposals – increased use of light infantry, increased attention to rapidly emplacable obstacles, sensors, precision-guided munitions and cheap rocket tubes – are likely to be incorporated piecemeal into existing NATO defences. This process is already under way and may intensify .... In coming decades, step-by-step adoption will create more confidence in the new technology and the theoretical possibility of committing NATO increasingly to this defensive concept. However, strong resistance to complete and exclusive reliance on untried technology will continue; some armoured forces are likely to stay in a mixed system.[45]

The Future of Nuclear Deterrence in Europe

The military restructuring of the two alliances in Europe raises the issue of the role of nuclear weapons in a post-cold war security system. Nuclear weapons pose political, strategic and moral dilemmas that are not easily resolvable. Their almost infinite destructive capacity means that the debate on the future of nuclear deterrence arouses strong feelings on all sides.[46] For some, the new political climate in Europe makes the goal of a denuclearised continent both a desirable and a feasible objective.[47] For others, however, nothing has happened which makes nuclear modernisation and robust strategies of nuclear deterrence any less necessary.

In considering the future role of nuclear deterrence in Europe, three points can be made. Firstly, there is no reason for believing that a denuclearised Europe would be any more peaceful or stable than a Europe with nuclear weapons. Nuclear weapons have provided an element of stability in an otherwise anarchic international system, as many statesmen and analysts recognise.[48] It is also important to remember that they have been the symptom of Europe's security problems, not their cause; the problem is ultimately a political one, and derives from the lack of trust and the legacy of the systemic conflict between the Soviet Union and the West.

Secondly, seeking to rid Europe or the world in general of nuclear weapons would be extremely difficult to achieve. Nuclear weapons technology cannot be abolished, and existing members of the 'nuclear club' – such as France, Britain, the USA and the Soviet Union – are unlikely to give up theirs. It is therefore necessary to find other ways of managing the nuclear weapons dilemma apart from denuclearisation.[49]

Finally, nuclear weapons have an indispensable deterrent function. Given their enormous destructive power, they render the notion of 'war as a continuation of politics by other means' totally absurd. No configuration of conventional forces can fulfil this deterrent function, despite the catastrophic consequences of conventional war in modern-day Europe.[50]

There is, therefore, a strong case to be made for retaining nuclear deterrence in Europe, as a stabilising factor in a period of uncertain transition. In the strategic debate in Europe, a broad consensus is forming around the notion of a 'minimum nuclear deterrence'.[51] A minimum deterrence would seek to build around nuclear weapons a 'war-prevention system that, without surrendering the great stability we have now, will become progressively less costly and less abrasive'.[52] Such a minimum deterrence would be clearly orientated towards restraint and selectivity in response. It would, furthermore, have war-prevention as its sole rationale, and war-termination as its sole objective.

There are, however, two main problems associated with the concept of a 'minimum nuclear deterrence':[53]

1. The Problem of Size

A minimum nuclear deterrence would reduce the number and variety of nuclear weapons to a minimum necessary to deter war: but it is not easy to define what this minimum should be, either in terms of numbers or capabilities. A mix of systems would still be needed, because the threat of employing strategic weapons alone would not be practically feasible or politically acceptable for every scenario. But the mix would not need to be as extensive as that required to operationalise 'Airland Battle 2000' or the recommendations of the 'Discriminate Deterrence' report. In particular, the need for short-range sub-strategic systems (above all, nuclear artillery, which could be abolished) would be greatly reduced. Two important criteria for the size and composition of a minimum nuclear deterrent would be, (i) survivability: the nuclear systems should be invulnerable to a first-strike counterforce attack – this puts the onus on submarine-based systems; and (ii) the ability to inflict 'minimum unacceptable damage' ('MUD') on an aggressor.[54]

2. The Problem of Targeting

A minimum deterrence should be based on a war-prevention and war-termination doctrine, rather than one which assigns war-fighting roles to nuclear weapons (as is the case with the 'Discriminate Deterrence' report already referred to[55]). But what should a minimum nuclear deterrent (especially its TNF component) be targeted against? Against countervalue, or counterforce targets? Or against a mixture of both? A minimum deterrence would only act as a deterrent if they had an evident capacity for effective use; this requires credible employment options. Nevertheless, one should remember that deterrence has an important psychological dimension. Much of the deterrent effect of nuclear weapons rests on the uncertainty and ambiguity surrounding their role and potential employment options, which complicates the military and political calculations of a potential aggressor. Hence, the question of targeting need not necessarily be an insurmountable problem for the development of a minimum nuclear deterrence.

Such a minimum nuclear deterrence designed to deter military conflict in general has been labelled by some (including Sir Michael Quinlan and the late Robert Osgood) as a 'just deterrent'. Uwe Nerlich has suggested that when the two superpowers accept the principle of a 'just deterrence', then it would be possible to move towards a situation of 'cooperative deterrence'. This would involve both sides accepting the deterrence principle as a way of progressively displacing war as a political option, thereby paving the way for a mutually agreed security order in Europe. At this stage, deterrence would be reduced to a mere safeguard in a security regime governed by stability, legitimacy and confidence in the removal of war as an instrument of politics.[56]

The notion of 'cooperative deterrence' is an attractive one. But it contains an inbuilt contradiction: deterrence, by definition, involves the threat of punishment. 'Cooperation' and 'punishment' are very uneasy bed-fellows. It might prove difficult, therefore, to base a durable, cooperative peace order in Europe on concepts of nuclear deterrence.[57] If it is possible to develop a European security system based on political trust and economic interdependence – in which war is as unthinkable as it is between Canada and the USA – then nuclear deterrence in the continent would become both unnecessary and undesirable. This, however, depends on a long process of transformation in the Soviet Union and Eastern Europe, and a steady growth of East–West cooperation. In this lengthy transition period, a minimum nuclear deterrence might provide an important element of stability and war-prevention – at least between nuclear armed countries and alliances. Such a minimum deterrence would not solve all the dilemmas and ambiguities associated with nuclear weapons, but it might provide a more realistic framework for managing them than calls for the early denuclearisation of the European continent.[58]

Conclusion

For forty years, military policy in Europe seemed to follow the course proposed by the ancient Roman general, Flavius Vegetius, who advised, '*Si vis pacem, para bellum*' – 'if you wish for peace, prepare for war'. The result was two highly armed military alliances, locked in an antagonistic relationship, and capable of destroying themselves and the rest of the world many times over. But with the ending of the division of Europe and the fading of the Soviet threat, the political foundations of the prevailing military structures have been fatally undermined. Europe has now entered a transitional period in which military forces are being reduced and restructured. There is now good reason for hoping that this could lead to a 'common security regime', based on a negotiated reduction in force levels, mutual defence dominance and a much higher level of military transparency. In this evolving situation, the role of military policy should be to preserve existing elements of strategic stability and war-prevention, whilst striving to ensure that this deterrent military policy does not at the same time pose major obstacles to closer and more cooperative East–West relations in Europe. Balancing these two requirements – deterrence and cooperation – has never been easy, and will remain a difficult and delicate task in future years.

One problem arising from the current disjunction between military 'grammar' and political 'logic' is that political developments have raced ahead of our ability to implement the consequent military restructuring. This is most clearly evident from the Conventional Forces in Europe (CFE) negotiations in Vienna, which have had a hard task remaining relevant to the rapidly changing political situation in Central and Eastern Europe.[59] Although the CFE Treaty was agreed more quickly than many commentators expected, the difficulties involved in the complex multilateral arms control negotiations have led to calls for a 'RUM' ('Related Unilateral Measures') or 'MUD' ('Mutual Unilateral Disarmament') approach to arms reductions. The problems with this RUM/MUD approach are that (a) it is more difficult to verify; (b) is less controllable; and c) it is more easily reversible.[60] Thus irrespective of possible further unilateral measures, there is a need to press ahead with the follow-up negotiations to the CFE Treaty signed in November 1990, and with the related discussions on CSBMs and military doctrine. The aim should be to develop a stable balance of military forces at considerably lower levels, within a cooperative system of negotiated arms control limitations and verification procedures.[61]

A second problem for the restructuring of military relations in Europe – which also affects the arms control and confidence-building process – is the growing fragmentation of the military-strategic landscape of Europe. As the East–West confrontation declines (with its focus on the 'central front'), other sub-regional and more localised security concerns are coming to the fore. The military balance in central Europe has undoubtedly greatly improved as a result of recent political developments in Eastern

Europe. But in the Nordic area, however, no such improvement has taken place – if anything, the military balance in the region has worsened, given the strength of Soviet forces in the Kola peninsula. Similarly, the fading of the once over-arching East–West conflict has highlighted the localised security problems of Eastern Europe and the Balkans – with their ancient ethnic and national animosities, intra-alliance conflicts (Greece–Turkey, Romania–Hungary), inter-alliance tensions (Bulgaria–Turkey) and cross-cutting disputes (such as the Yugoslavia–Bulgaria–Greece conflict over the 'Macedonian issue'). Furthermore, the security concerns of those countries bordering or neighbouring the western Mediterranean – Italy, France, Spain and Portugal – are very different from those of northern or central Europe. These southern European countries are concerned with the security implications of demographic and economic problems on the North African littoral, international terrorism, and their proximity to the Middle East. Hence the growing 'multilateral bilateralism' of security cooperation in the Western Mediterranean.[62]

With the ending of the East–West conflict, therefore, the European security system no longer has a clear front-line. Instead it is becoming a patch-work of different patterns of conflict and cooperation. The more diffuse and variegated security agenda (which we considered in Chapter 3) is thus contributing to the growing fragmentation of the military-strategic landscape of Europe. The security problems of Greece and Turkey, for example, are very different to those of Norway, or, for that matter, the United Kingdom. A predominantly bipolar security system is thus being displaced by a more multipolar security environment, with different foci of security concerns and relationships. At the same time, the overall importance of military power in Europe is declining. The value of military force as a currency of power is diminishing, in a Europe increasingly characterised by ever-widening networks of inter-dependence, and characterised by growing East–West economic and political cooperation.[63]

A final point to note is that a durable peace order in Europe cannot be achieved simply by technical tools such as arms control and force restructuring. As Secretary of State James Baker said in October 1989, 'We compete militarily because we differ politically. Political disputes are fuel for the fire of arms competition. Only by resolving political differences can we dampen the arms competition associated with them.'[64] The basic problem is that there is no particular balance and configuration of military forces that can guarantee peace and international stability. In the end, the 'security dilemmas' of the European states can only be resolved by developing political trust and economic cooperation on a continental wide basis – as already exists in Western Europe. Until then, the task of the military is to maintain a stable framework of 'common security', within which the new political conditions can ripen and mature.

Notes

1. Carl von Clausewitz, *On War*, 1832, translated by Anatol Rapoport (London: Penguin Classics, 1982), p. 402.
2. See Michael Howard, 'Military Grammar and Political Logic: Can NATO Survive if Cold War is Won?', *NATO Review*, vol. 37, no. 6 (December 1989), pp. 7–12.
3. In his speech to the Council of Europe in Strasbourg in July 1989, for example, Gorbachev called for a meeting of experts from East and West to discuss the problems of 'conversion' under the auspices of the Economic Council of Europe (ECE) based in Geneva. In March 1988, he also called for the defence industries to assist in the retooling of the light industry and food-processing sectors. See Paul Dibbs, 'Is Soviet Military Strategy Changing?', in *The Changing Strategic Landscape*, Part 1, Adelphi Paper 235 (London: Brassey's for the IISS, 1989), pp. 35–47 (pp. 41–42).
4. Michael MccGwire, *Perestroika and Soviet National Security* (Washington D.C.: The Brookings Institution, 1991); 'Undate: Soviet Military Objectives', *World Policy Journal*, vol. IV, no. 4 (Fall 1987), pp. 723–31; and 'Rethinking War: the Soviets and European Security', *The Brookings Review*, vol. VI, no. 2 (Spring 1988), pp. 3–12.
5. For a well-balanced critique of MccGwire's thesis, see Gerard Holden's excellent book, *The Warsaw Pact: Soviet Security and Bloc Politics* (London: Basil Blackwell, 1989), pp. 82–85.
6. For a concise and well-argued analysis of recent Soviet military doctrine, see Christoph Bluth's excellent study, *New Thinking in Soviet Military Policy* (London: Pinter for the RIIA, 1990).
7. MccGwire, *Military Objectives in Soviet Foreign Policy*, Chapter 4.
8. Dennis M. Gormley, *Double Zero and Soviet Military Strategy: Implications for Western Security* (London: Jane's, 1988).
9. *Soviet News*, 26 February 1986, p. 91.
10. In 1987, an interesting change in the Soviet definition of 'military doctrine' occurred, emphasising defensiveness and the primacy of war-prevention. The then Soviet Minister of Defence, Dimitri Yazov, defined Soviet military doctrine as 'a system of fundamental views on how to avert war, develop military capabilities and make a country and its armed forces ready to repel aggression. It explains the method of waging armed struggle in defence of socialism'; see his article, 'Warsaw Treaty Military Doctrine – for the Defence of Peace and Socialism', in *International Affairs* (Moscow), no. 10 (1987), pp. 1–8.
11. The Budapest WTO Communiqué declared that, 'In the interests of security in Europe and the whole world, the military concepts and doctrines of the military alliances must be based on defensive principles', *Pravda*, 12 June 1986. The Berlin Communiqué stated that, 'The military doctrine of the Warsaw Pact, just like that of each of its member countries, is subordinated to the task of preventing war, both nuclear and conventional', *Pravda*, 20 May 1987.
12. William E. Odom, 'The Soviet Military in Transition', in *Problems of Communism*, vol. XXXIX, no. 3 (May–June 1990), pp. 51–71.

13. See, for example, Aleksei Arbatov, 'Parity and Reasonable Sufficiency', in *International Affairs* (Moscow), no. 10 (October 1988), pp. 75–87.

14. For an informative discussion of these and other related issues by Soviet security specialists, see Pavel Bayev et al., *Tactical Nuclear Weapons in Europe: The Problem of Reduction and Elimination* (Moscow: Novosti Press Agency Publishing House, 1990).

15. See, for example, *The Warsaw Pact and the Balkans: Moscow's Southern Flank*, edited by Jonathan Eyal (London: Macmillan for RUSI, 1989).

16. See Douglas A. MacGregor, *The Soviet–East German Military Alliance* (Cambridge: Cambridge University Press, 1989).

17. See Jan B. de Weydenthal, 'Poland and the Soviet Alliance System', *Report on Eastern Europe*, 29 June 1990, pp. 30–32, and Anna Sabbat-Swidlicka, 'Polish–German Relations: Turning Borders into Bridges', *Report on Eastern Europe*, 18 May 1990, pp. 34–38.

18. Henry Owen and Edward C. Meyer, 'Central European Security', in *Foreign Affairs*, vol. 68, no. 3 (Summer 1989), pp. 22–40 (p. 36).

19. Douglas L. Clarke, 'Warsaw Pact: The Transformation Begins', *Report on Eastern Europe*, 22 June 1990, pp. 34–37.

20. Alfred Reisch, 'Hungarian Neutrality: Hopes and Realities', *Report on Eastern Europe*, 30 March 1990, pp. 11–22, and by the same author, 'Hungary to Leave Military Arm of the Warsaw Pact', in *Report on Eastern Europe*, 29 June 1990, pp. 20–25.

21. G. Holden, *op. cit.*, pp. 142 ff. On Polish steps in this direction, see Michael Sadykiewicz and Douglas L. Clarke, 'The New Polish Defense Doctrine: A Further Step Toward Sovereignty', *Report on Eastern Europe*, 4 May 1990, pp. 20–23.

22. Douglas L. Clarke, 'The Unilateral Arms Cuts in the Warsaw Pact', *Report on Eastern Europe*, 2 February 1990, pp. 43–47.

23. Proposals for closer cooperation came from the Bratislava summit of April 1990, and may result in the creation of a permanent secretariat. See Timothy Garton Ash, 'Blindly Smitten by Democracy', *The Independent*, 5 July 1990.

24. See Alfred Reisch, 'The Hungarian Dilemma: After the Warsaw Pact, Neutrality or NATO?', *Report on Eastern Europe*, 13 April 1990, pp. 16–21.

25. Indeed, at a meeting of WEU parliamentarians in Paris in June 1990, the Hungarian Foreign Minister, Geza Jeszensky, formally applied for Hungary to be given 'special guest status' in the WEU Assembly.

26. Timothy Garton Ash, 'The New Continental Drift', *The Independent*, 1 March 1990, p. 27.

27. See Thomas Nowotny on the Future of Neutrality in Central Europe, the *Institute of East–West Security Studies Meeting Report*, 31 October 1989, and Vlad Sobell, 'Austria, Hungary and the Question of Neutrality', *Radio Free Europe*, Background Report no. 156, 24 August 1989.

28. Mikhail Bezrukov and Andrei Kortunov (of the United States and Canada Institute of the USSR Academy of Sciences) have written that, 'while remaining a capitalist and neutral country, Finland has created far fewer problems for the Soviet Union over the entire post-war period than have socialist Poland, Hungary and Czechoslovakia'; see their article, 'Reform of the Warsaw Pact Organisation Is Needed', in *Ekonomika, Politika, Ideologiya* (May 1990), pp. 30–35. On Moscow's use of Northern Europe

as a 'model' for restructuring its security relations with its East European neighbours, see Phillip A. Petersen, 'A New Security Regime for Europe?', *Problems of Communism*, vol. XXXIX, no. 2 (March–April 1990), pp. 91–97 (p. 95).

29. See Phillip A. Karber and A. Grant Whitley, 'The Operational Realm', in *NATO at Forty: Change, Continuity and Prospects*, edited by James Golden et al. (London: Westview, 1989), pp. 122–51.

30. Excerpt from the Communiqué of the meeting of the Defence Planning Committee held in May 1975; quoted in Guido Vigeveno's *The Bomb and European Security* (London: C. Hurst and Co., 1983), p. 11.

31. *London Declaration on a Transformed North Atlantic Alliance*, issued by the Heads of State and Government participating in the meeting of the North Atlantic Council in London on 5–6 July 1990 (NATO Press Communiqué S-1(90)36), 6 July 1990, pt.11.

32. Paul Bracken, *The Command and Control and Nuclear Forces* (New Haven: Yale University Press, 1983), pp. 164–69.

33. On the dilemmas of 'entrapment' versus 'coupling', see Jane M.O. Sharp, 'After Reykjavik: Arms Control and the Allies', in *International Affairs*, vol. 63, no. 2 (1987), pp. 239–58.

34. See John Harris, 'From Flexible Response to No Early First Use' in P. Terrence Hopmann and Frank Barnaby (eds), *Rethinking the Nuclear Weapons Dilemma in Europe* (London: Macmillan, 1988), p. 105.

35. Quoted by John Baylis, 'NATO Strategy: the Case for a New Strategic Concept', in *International Affairs*, vol. 64, no. 1 (Winter 1987/88), pp. 43–60 (p. 45).

36. Frank Blackaby et al. (eds), *No-First-Use* (London: Taylor & Francis for SIPRI, 1984), and John Steinbruner and Leon Sigal (eds), *Alliance Security: NATO and the No-First-Use Question* (Washington, D.C.: The Brookings Institution, 1983).

37. See Lars B. Wallin (ed.), *Military Doctrines for Central Europe* (Stockholm: The Swedish National Defence Research Institute, 1986); Andrew J. Pierre (ed.), *The Conventional Defense of Europe: New Technologies and New Strategies* (New York: Council on Foreign Relations, 1986); and James M. Garrett, *The Tenuous Balance: Conventional Forces in Central Europe* (London: Westview Press, 1989).

38. A good survey of these issues can be found in Stephen J. Flanagan's book, *NATO's Conventional Defences: Options for the Central Region* (London: Macmillan in association with the International Institute of Strategic Studies, 1988). See also Ian Bellany and Tim Huxley, *New Conventional Weapons and Western Defence* (London: Frank Cass and Co., 1987).

39. Gerard Holden, *op. cit.*, p. 94.

40. Christopher Coker, 'The Myth of the Peace Dividend', in *The World Today*, vol. 46, no. 7 (July 1990), pp. 136–38.

41. These ideas were floated by General Hans-Henning von Sandrart, Commander-in-Chief Allied Forces Central Europe, at a talk at the Royal United Services Institute, London. See 'NATO Ponders how to Re-order the Ranks', in the *Financial Times*, 21 June 1990, and 'Still Central, not so Much a Front', in *The Economist*, 10 November 1990, p. 61.

42. See the collection of papers by Michael Randle and Paul Rogers (eds), *Alternatives in European Security* (Aldershot: Dartmouth, 1990).

43. Willem van Eekelen, 'The future of NATO and Warsaw Pact Strategy: Paper 1', in *The Strategic Implications of Change in the Soviet Union, Part 1*, Adelphi Paper 247 (London: Brassey's for the IISS, 1990), pp. 41–59.

44. Christian Krause, '"Strukturelle Nichtangriffsfaehigkeit" – A Yardstick for Conventional Stability', in *Current Research on Peace and Violence*, vol. 10, no. 3 (1988), pp. 121–29 (p. 124). For an excellent discussion of these and other related issues, see Ian M. Cuthbertson and David Robertson, *Enhancing European Security: Living in a Less Nuclear World* (London: Macmillan, in association with the IEWSS, 1990), pp. 210–11.

45. J. Dean, 'Alternative Defence: Answer to NATO's Central Front Problems?', *International Affairs*, vol. 64, no. 1 (Winter 1987–88), pp. 61–82 (p. 81).

46. For a useful guide to the issues raised by nuclear deterrence, see Philip Bobbit, *Democracy and Deterrence: The History and Future of Nuclear Strategy* (London: Macmillan, 1988); Barry Buzan (ed.), *The International Politics of Deterrence* (London: Frances Pinter, in cooperation with the UN Department for Disarmament Affairs, 1987); Philip K. Lawrence, *Preparations for Armageddon: A Critique of Western Strategy* (Brighton: Wheatsheaf, 1988); and Michael MccGwire, 'Deterrence: the Problem – not the Solution', *International Affairs*, vol. 62, no. 1 (Winter 1985–86), pp. 56–70.

47. See for example, Dan Smith (ed.), *European Security in the 1990s* (London: Pluto for the Transnational Institute, 1989).

48. This has been recognised even by some of those within the 'peace studies' camp; see for example, Vilho Harle and Pekka Sivonen (eds), *Europe in Transition: Politics and Nuclear Security* (London: Pinter for the Tampere Peace Research Institute, Finland, 1989), pp. 64, 20 and 74.

49. See Gerard Segal, Edwina Moreton, Lawrence Freedman and John Baylis, *Nuclear War and Nuclear Peace*, second edition (London: Macmillan, 1988), p. 163.

50. *Battlefield Europe: Conventional War and the Human Environment*, edited by A. Westing and B.A. Molski (London: Sage, 1989).

51. Lawrence Martin, *Minimum Deterrence*, Faraday Discussion Paper no. 8 (London: Council for Arms Control, 1987).

52. 'Deterrence after the INF Treaty', in the UK Government's *Statement on the Defence Estimates, 1989*, vol. 1, Cm 675-1 (London: HMSO, 1989), p. 11.

53. I am particularly indebted to John Baylis of the University College of Wales, Aberystwyth, for his helpful comments on an earlier draft of this chapter.

54. Field Marshall Lord Carver, 'The Nuclear Weapons Muddle', in *Tank: The Royal Tank Regiment Journal* (May 1988), pp. 4–8. See also Barry Nalebuff, 'Minimal Nuclear Deterrence', in *The Journal of Conflict Resolution*, vol. 32, no. 3 (September 1988), pp. 411–25.

55. Commission on Integrated Long-term Strategy, *Discriminate Deterrence*, Fred Ikle et al. (Washington, D.C.: US Government Printing Office, January 1988): 'However, there should be less ambiguity about the nature of the deterrent. The Alliance should threaten to use nuclear weapons *not as a link* to wider and more devastating war – although the risk of further escalation would still be there – but mainly as an instrument for denying success to the invading Soviet forces. The *nuclear weapons would be used discriminately* in, for example, attacks on Soviet command centres or troop concentrations. The Alliance's nuclear posture, like its posture for conventional war, will

gain in deterrent power from new technologies emphasizing precision and control' (p. 30). The charge that this amounted to a barely disguised call to limit nuclear war to Europe was denied by four prominent members of the Commission. In an article in the *International Herald Tribune* on 24 February 1988, Messrs. Brzezinski, Kissinger, Ilke and Wohlstetter stated that the report 'calls for the discriminate, effective use of intercontinental as well as theater-based forces against military targets in the Soviet Union as well as Eastern Europe, in response to attacks on military targets in the United States as well as attacks on Europe'.

56. See Malcolm McCall and Oliver Ramsbotham (eds), *Just Deterrence: Morality and Deterrence in the Twenty-First Century* (London: Brassey's, 1990), and Uwe Nerlich and Trutz Rendtorff (eds), *Nukleare Abschreckung. Politische und Ethische Interpretationen einer neuen Realitaet* (Baden-Baden: Nomos Verlag, 1989).
57. As Karsten Voigt has argued, 'Preventing war by deterrence is an ambivalent and paradoxical concept. It involves too many risks to suffice for a lasting preservation of peace. In particular, democratic societies cannot, in the long run consider legitimate the possibility of mankind's elimination as a precondition for the maintenance of peace. Citizens justifiably expect that the danger of deterrence failing be matched by political efforts to maintain peace. The strategy of deterrence is acceptable only as a transitional approach to less risky strategies for preserving peace.' See his contribution in Andrew J. Pierre's edited volume, *Nuclear Weapons in Europe* (New York: Council on Foreign Relations, 1984), pp. 117–18.
58. See William D. Bajusz and Lisa D. Shaw, 'The Forthcoming "SNF Negotiations"', in *Survival*, vol. XXXII, no. 4 (July–August 1990), pp. 333–48.
59. As one British official at the CFE negotiations put it, 'Not only are the East European officials unsure about whether they wish to be aligned with the Soviets, many are frankly uninterested in what they see as Cold War negotiations irrelevant to what is happening in the East'; quoted in the *Sunday Telegraph*, 28 January 1990, p. 11. See also Lawrence Freedman, 'The Politics of Conventional Arms Control', in *Survival*, vol. 31, no. 5 (September–October 1989), pp. 387–96, and David White, 'The Eclipse of the Arms Control Talks', *Financial Times*, 25 May 1990.
60. Hugh Beach, 'The Case for Arms Control Negotiations', in *The Council for Arms Control Bulletin*, no. 46 (October 1989), pp. 1–2.
61. Jonathan Dean, 'The CFE Negotiations, Present and Future', in *Survival*, vol. XXXII, no. 4 (July–August 1990), pp. 313–24 (p. 324).
62. For a useful discussion of Western Mediterranean cooperation, see Ian Gambles, *Prospects for West European Security Cooperation*, Adelphi Paper 244 (London: Brassey's for the IISS, 1989), pp. 53–56.
63. See Joe Nye, 'The Contribution of Strategic Studies: Future Challenges', in *The Changing Strategic Landscape, Part 1*, Adelphi Paper 235 (London: Brassey's for the IISS, 1989), pp. 20–34 (p. 25), and Harle and Sivonen, *op. cit.*, pp. 16 and 24.
64. Secretary Baker, 'Prerequisites and Principles for Arms Control', *United States Department of State Bureau of Public Affairs*, Washington, D.C., Current Policy No. 1215.

PART III

Four Scenarios for the Year 2010

Modelling Alternative Security Futures

Tesman: 'But, good heavens, we know nothing of the future.'
Lovborg: 'No, but there is a thing or two to be said about it all the same.'
Ibsen, *Hedda Gabler*[1]

In the first part of this book, we considered the nature of the post-war European security system – a system which proved remarkably stable and adaptable throughout its four decades of evolutionary development. In Part II, we looked at the key elements of change in contemporary Europe, from Soviet *perestroika* to German unification. Many of these elements are closely interconnected: Gorbachev's reform programme, for example, made possible Eastern Europe's 'Glorious Revolutions' of 1989. This in turn made possible both German unification and substantial conventional arms reductions in central Europe. Conversely, the growing integration and prosperity of Western Europe contributed to both the perceived need for radical reform in the Soviet Union, and the collapse of communism in Eastern Europe. Thus recent developments in Europe have only served to highlight the degree of interdependence and interconnectedness which has emerged in the continent, as changes in certain parts of Europe have stimulated related changes in others.

In this third part, however, our concern is not with the past, nor even with the present, but with the future. The security structures of the old bipolar, cold war Europe are increasingly anachronistic in an era of deepening interdependencies and growing East–West cooperation. They have been shaken to their roots by the strategic earthquake of late 1989, and are now in a process of fundamental transformation. As we have seen (Chapter 3), a new security agenda is emerging in post-cold war Europe, and this will stimulate the development of a very different configuration of security relationships and institutional structures. Many existing organisations will find their roles and functions changing, others will disappear, whilst some new bodies may be created. The result will be the development of a very different security system than that which has regulated the security concerns of the Europeans and their former superpower patrons in the post-war world.

Europe, therefore, stands at the crossroads of far-reaching change.

Developments in the next few years will greatly affect the nature of the new security system that emerges in a Europe beyond the cold war. There are many competing visions of Europe's future 'architecture', and many possible lines of institutional and political development. This raises a whole series of fascinating questions which are crucial to the future evolution of the continent. To begin with, what impact will the disintegration of the former 'socialist community' have on the process of West European integration? How will German unification affect the *Westintegration* of the FRG? What are the implications for the process of European integration of the nationalist fragmentation and deepening economic crisis of the Soviet Union? What are the implications of the rising tide of nationalism in the East, and how will it affect the border and minorities problems in the Balkans?

In terms of the structures of the European security system, a further series of questions suggest themselves: will NATO become an increasingly anachronistic alliance, or will it be able to reform itself and develop. in such a way that it becomes the bulwark of a new security system? Should the European Community seek to develop its own foreign and defence policy, and what impact would this have on the process of East–West rapprochement? What role will the CSCE play in a Europe no longer divided into antagonistic blocs, and can it provide the institutional basis for a pan-European system of collective security? Finally, with the passing of the East–West conflict, will Europe revert to its pre-war patterns of multipolar instability and nationalist rivalries? If so, can the security dilemmas that this balance of power system tends to generate be mitigated or resolved?

The purpose of this third part is thus to consider such questions as these in the light of the changing security structures of Europe. To this end, this part contains four scenarios of the European security system in two decades' time. These scenarios – which should be seen as 'ideal-types' – postulate a number of feasible alternative futures. Their purpose is to explore some of the possible outcomes of change and upheaval in European security today. In this sense, they should be seen as 'exploratory' rather than 'anticipatory' scenarios, in that they attempt to project current trends into the future (altering some of the key assumptions in order to produce different outcomes), rather than simply presenting a number of hoped-for futures.[2] By extrapolating current trends and thereby producing a number of different scenarios, I hope to illustrate some of the longer-term implications of current policy debates. In this way, it should be possible to identify and analyse some of the central issues affecting the future development of European security 'architecture'.

Modelling alternative futures is fraught with methodological problems. Nevertheless, it is an analytical technique which is well established in the social sciences (including international relations), and in the business world, especially in corporate strategic planning.[3] The last great spate of such studies of alternative security futures was in the late 1960s, at a time when the cold war seemed to be ending and East–West relations appeared to be in a state of considerable fluidity.[4] Given the breadth and scope of the changes currently under way in Europe, I believe that applying such model-building techniques to the contemporary European security system is a useful and illuminating exercise.

The purpose of these four scenarios is thus to elicit the long-term implications of the underlying structural dynamics in what is a complex system of interrelationships in Europe. Its aim is not to try and predict the future, nor is it to construct a series of snap-shot images or end-point models of Europe in 2010. I should add, of course, that this sort of modelling cannot accommodate the compromises, ambiguities, grey areas and blurred perspectives which are the everyday reality of international politics. Scenario-building 'cannot successfully take account of the element of chance in human affairs, the incidence of war, economic or social catastrophe, or the emergence of powerful idiosyncratic leaders .... Moreover, it is impossible to predict the clash of circumstance and personality which may modify the evolution of an international structure ....'[5] For example, no study written in the late 1970s could have predicted the full impact of a man like Gorbachev on the international scene, or the extraordinary events of 1989–90, which have unexpectedly transformed the whole political and strategic landscape in central and eastern Europe.

Nonetheless, despite the methodological problems inherent in this sort of model-building, these scenarios are offered as a contribution to the debate on the future of the European security system. By exploring the potential strengths and weaknesses of different security systems, I hope that these four scenarios of Europe in 2010 can stimulate an informed discussion of the policy choices facing the Europeans and the North Americans at this time of remarkable fluidity and uncertainty.

Notes

1. Quoted in Anton Deporte, *Europe Between the Superpowers* (New Haven, CT: Yale University Press, 1979), p. vii.
2. This methodological distinction is made by Peter Hall in *Europe 2000* (London: Duckworth, 1977), p. 6.
3. One example of this is the joint project of US–Soviet relations undertaken by the Center for Foreign Policy Development at Brown University and the Public Agenda Foundation; *The Public, The Soviets and Nuclear Arms: Four Futures – Alternatives for Public Debate and Policy Development.* (New York: Brown University C.F.P.D., 1987). The Center for Foreign Policy Development is currently engaged in a similar study of alternative security futures in Europe, entitled 'Mutual Security in Europe'.
4. See, for example, Alastair Buchan (ed.), *Europe's Futures, Europe's Choices: Models of Western Europe in the 1970s* (London: Chatto and Windus for

the Institute for Strategic Studies, 1969) and Pierre Hassner, *Change and Stability in Europe*, Adelphi Papers 45 and 49 (London: the Institute for Strategic Studies, 1968). See also Herman Kahn and Antony J. Wiener, *The Year 2000* (London: Collier-Macmillan for the Hudson Institute, 1967); Lincoln P. Bloomfield, *Western Europe to the Mid-Seventies: Five Scenarios* (Cambridge, Mass.: Center for International Studies MIT, 1968); Karl Kaiser and Willhelm Kewening, 'Alternativen für Europa: Modelle möglicher Entwicklungen in den 70er Jahren', *Europa Archiv*, Folge 23, 1968, pp. 851–64; and Warner Schilling et al., *American Arms and a Changing Europe: Dilemmas of Deterrence and Disarmament* (New York: Colombia University Press, 1985).
5. Buchan, *Europe's Futures, Europe's Choices*, p. 16.

9

Scenario A:
NATO and an 'Atlanticist' Europe

This first scenario envisages a NATO that has successfully adapted to the demands of the post-cold war world, and which has developed into one of the central institutions of the new Europe. The Atlantic Alliance, this scenario assumes, has remained a firm bulwark of the European security system, with NATO providing the key institutional expression of a strategic alliance between the 'old' and 'new' worlds. The transatlantic Alliance, however, has become a more equal partnership, resting on two 'pillars' – the USA and a more coherent and politically integrated Western Europe – as President Kennedy envisaged in his 1962 Philadelphia speech.[1] NATO has thus become a more 'European' alliance, reflecting the change in the economic power and political coherence of Western Europe since the early cold war years.

At the same time, this scenario assumes that NATO has become an important forum for security discussions and consultations in Europe as a whole. The Alliance will not only be the main forum for security discussions amongst the 16, it would also provide an important venue for East–West security debates. To this end, NATO will have developed an extensive network of diplomatic and political contacts with the Soviet Union and the countries of Eastern Europe. In this way, whilst providing a resilient framework for collective defence and deterrence for its Western members, NATO will seek to develop a more cooperative relationship with its former enemies in the Warsaw Treaty Organisation.

This scenario thus envisages a modification – albeit a significant one – of the existing security system, rather than its radical restructuring or the development of a fundamentally different security structure. It assumes that the Warsaw Pact will wither and die, but does not assume any symmetry in developments in the East and the West. It thus posits the gradual blurring of the eastern end of what has essentially been a bipolar system (with the Warsaw Pact fading away like the 'Cheshire cat' of Alice in Wonderland fame), leaving NATO as a strong and durable element within an increasingly pluralistic European security system. This model of European security therefore combines an 'Atlanticist' approach to West European security with both the 'Europeanisation' of NATO and the development of a more cooperative relationship between it and its former Warsaw Pact rivals.

I

This vision of Europe has its roots in the 1967 Harmel Report, which assigned to the Alliance not only the task of deterrence and defence, but also the management of detente and the cooperative aspects of the East–West relationship. It is a distinctly Anglo-American vision, but one which could nonetheless find support amongst centre-right political forces in other West European countries (such as the Christian Democrats in the FRG). Since late 1989, the Bush Administration has been pressing its European allies to agree that new European security arrangements should remain centred on NATO, with a changed, and possibly expanded role for the Alliance. This would preserve a significant degree of US influence on European developments, and may help cement transatlantic cooperation in other areas (such as trade). Margaret Thatcher has also called for NATO to adapt and develop to a world in which 'politically, NATO no longer has a front line'. Arguing that the need for an effective transatlantic alliance based on collective defence, a continued US military presence in Europe and a credible nuclear deterrence has made NATO as necessary as ever, she has also called for the Alliance to 'give more thought to possible threats to our security from other directions'.[2] With the Gulf crisis of August 1990, Margaret Thatcher has renewed her call for NATO to develop an 'out-of-area' capability, to help it remain relevant to the changing security agenda in Europe[3] – a call subsequently echoed by NATO's Secretary-General, Manfred Wörner, and its SACEUR, General Galvin.[4]

This concept of a NATO-based 'Atlanticist' Europe assumes that NATO itself is able to change and adapt to the new conditions in Europe. This would include the strengthening of NATO's 'political' role – something which has recently been given wide endorsement, but very little clarification. The North Atlantic Council meeting of NATO Foreign Ministers in Brussels on 15 December 1989, for example, resolved to strengthen the Alliance's political role and to help design a 'new architecture for Europe, whole and free'. Similarly Manfred Wörner has argued that,

> Ever since I took over it has always been my intention to strengthen the political role of NATO – not only the perception of this political role but also the substance. It means NATO has to serve more as a platform where you coordinate, where you harmonise the policy of the European member states with the United States and Canada, which gives us an influence on the Americans and the Americans an influence on us. There is no other platform and no better one.[5]

Whilst developing its political role, this model of an 'Atlanticist' Europe assumes that NATO will revise its military strategy and force structure. As we have seen in Chapter 6, the direction of this revision has already been suggested in the London Declaration of July 1990. The Alliance will field fewer active forces, and place considerable reliance on a reinforcement strategy. A multinational 'Rapid Deployment Force' will be created, capable of being deployed to cope with challenges to the security of the Alliance, wherever they occur. It will also reduce its reliance on nuclear weapons (which have already been defined as 'weapons of the last resort'), and will no longer deploy ground-launched theatre nuclear forces in Germany. At the same time, NATO will restructure its combat troops in multinational forces, integrated at the corps and perhaps divisional level. This scenario also envisages that at some stage in the future, some elements of NATO's command structures may be eliminated (perhaps, for example, NORTHAG and CENTAG), leaving SACEUR and a number of multinational corps.[6]

In this model of European security, the reform of the Alliance's military strategy and deployment patterns will be accompanied by the gradual 'Europeanisation' of NATO. This would include the development of a more cohesive West European security entity within NATO (perhaps based on the Eurogroup, or by associating the WEU more closely with NATO); giving the Europeans more senior command positions in the Alliance; and reducing America's direct military engagement in Europe. We have already considered some of the structural difficulties involved in developing a 'European pillar' within NATO (Chapter 6). Developing this new transatlantic balance within NATO will require careful political management by all parties involved. However, this scenario assumes that these political differences have been successfully overcome, and NATO has been successfully 'Europeanised' without self-destructing under the strain.

Along with the 'Europeanisation' of the Alliance, closer French and Spanish involvement in NATO's military structures is vital to the viability of this model of European security. The emergence of the Atlantic Alliance as the core of a post-cold war security system in Europe is only really possible if it has the backing of a country as strong and important as France. This might be possible if the American role in NATO were diminished; if the Alliance became a more 'European' body; and if France were offered some leading command positions within NATO (perhaps even a French SACEUR).

In this 'Atlanticist' Europe, expanding NATO's political role, restructuring its military profile and strengthening its 'European pillar' is to be accompanied by the development of new, more cooperative relations with the former communist countries to its East. Whilst preserving its deterrent capability in case of a recidivist backlash in the Soviet Union,

NATO will establish diplomatic and political relations with Warsaw Pact (and former Warsaw Pact) countries. In this way it will begin to function as a forum for broader pan-European security discussions (along with the CSCE). This might prove acceptable to a number of East European countries. Hungary, for example, has made it clear that it wishes to participate in as many Western institutions as possible, including NATO and the WEU, in order to effect its 'return to Europe'. Indeed, the former Hungarian Foreign Minister, Gyula Horn, has suggested that Hungary might seek a closer relationship with the political organs of NATO.[7] In the long term, it is even possible that at least some of the East European countries might request security guarantees from the Alliance, or even some form of 'associate' membership. As we have already seen, this would present NATO with a whole series of unwelcome dilemmas.

This scenario also envisages that a reformed NATO, functioning as the core of a new European security system, will revise its interpretation of the North Atlantic Treaty in order to permit Alliance forces to operate out of the 'NATO area'. Only in this way could NATO remain relevant to the changing security agenda in Europe. Indeed, a transformed NATO with an 'out-of-area' capability could begin to provide a focus for a new trilateral security partnership between the US, the West Europeans and the Japanese. The Japanese have expressed an interest in establishing closer security cooperation with NATO, and in June 1990, Japan officially participated for the first time in a NATO seminar in Knokke, Belgium. At this three-day meeting, the possibilities for closer trilateral security cooperation were explored, with a view to working towards a more stable global order in the wake of the decline in East–West tensions. Although there was no discussion of Japanese membership of NATO or direct military cooperation, the US Under Secretary of Defence, Paul D. Wolfowitz, urged the allies to consider the possibility of joint armed interventions, in conjunction with Japan, to respond to future crises outside of Europe.[8]

The biggest obstacle to this vision of a NATO-centred European security system is the attitude of France and a number of other Alliance countries like Spain, Greece and Italy. It is significant that France boycotted the Knokke meeting, on the grounds that NATO was violating its charter by seeking to expand its area of operations into Asia. President Mitterrand and other French officials have attempted to down-play the future significance of NATO whilst promoting that of the EC. One French official, for example, has argued that, 'As security depends increasingly on politics and economics, the EC is naturally better placed than NATO to cope with the new challenges, notably in Eastern Europe.' Another has specifically objected to American interest in expanding NATO's remit to cover crises in the Third World; 'We don't want NATO to become a directorate for global security affairs, and we fear that US attempts to invent impossible missions for NATO will only fuel Soviet fears and pacifism in Europe.'⁹ However, the ending of the cold war has thrown French foreign and security policy into a quandary, and it is possible that – given the problems inherent in giving the EC a defence dimension and the ambiguities surrounding the future development of the WEU – France might be willing to engage more actively in a 'Europeanised' NATO.

This scenario thus envisages the development of a NATO-based 'Atlanticist' system of European security. NATO would be at the core of this new post-cold war security arrangement, providing a guarantee for West European security, an institutional focus for the transatlantic partnership (perhaps buttressed by a 'North Atlantic Free Trade Association' involving the USA and the EC), and a forum for East–West security dialogue. The European Community – linked by Association Agreements to the countries to its East – would be a 'civilian' body, providing the engine of Europe's economic development and prosperity. Finally, the CSCE would provide a broader pan-European forum for continental-wide consultation and dialogue on political, economic and security issues – but would not attempt to provide a framework for a pan-European system of collective security.

II

Having outlined the principle features of an 'Atlanticist' security order, let us now consider the arguments in favour of this model of European security. They are as follows:

1. To begin with, a NATO-based European security system would be constructed around an already functioning alliance structure. NATO is a proven alliance of 16 democratic nations, which provides an effective system of collective defence. The Alliance would continue to provide an 'insurance policy' for its members in the event of a major European crisis or a deterioration of Soviet relations with the Western world. Meanwhile, it is argued, the rest of Europe would benefit from this arrangement, because NATO would provide a factor of stability in an otherwise turbulent strategic environment. Furthermore, given that alliances of democratic countries have an in-built 'structural incapacity for attack', NATO would not present a threat to any other peaceful state in Europe.

2. An 'Atlanticist' system of European security would cement a US military commitment to Europe, and ensure a continued strong role for the USA in European affairs. This is seen as essential by some because it preserves a strategic balance with the USSR in Europe, and thus provides a further factor of stability on the continent. In December 1990, the British Foreign Secretary, Douglas Hurd, argued that 'European security without

the United States simply does not make sense, and urged Europeans to 'say loud and clear that we welcome US forces in Europe'. On the other hand, his colleague Alan Clarke, the Minister for Defence Procurement, in response to a suggestion that NATO is vital to keep US forces in Europe, has said, 'Why should we want to keep the United States in Europe?'.[10] Some commentators also suggest that the American presence in Western Europe helps contain the historical and political rivalries amongst its European allies – a function which, some argue, will remain essential given the tensions likely to emerge in Europe with a united and economically powerful Germany. At the same time, a solid transatlantic strategic relationship may assist the development of broader economic, political and trade relations. Finally, a close strategic relationship with the USA is essential for Europe because the US is the only country with the resources and political will able and willing to defend Western interests around the globe or – as the Gulf crisis shows – to take the initiative in enforcing UN Security Council decisions. Only by cooperating with the Americans, it is suggested, can the West Europeans hope to be able to have an effective influence on the course of international events.

3. An 'Atlanticist' Europe would provide a security framework through which German power could be integrated into broader European and transatlantic structures. This gives implicit security guarantees to Germany's neighbours, without the singularisation of Germany implied by some other proposals. It was clear from the Warsaw Pact Summit in March 1990, for example, that Moscow's call for a united Germany to be neutral was not welcomed by countries like Poland, Czechoslovakia and Hungary, and that these countries looked much more favourably than the Soviets did at this time on German membership of NATO.

4. A reformed and militarily restructured NATO could preserve the elements of collective defence planning and integrated military command structures it has developed over the years, thereby avoiding the 'renationalisation' of defence policies in Western Europe. This would facilitate the coordination of defence cuts and military restructuring amongst the 16, thus preserving a balanced military structure at lower levels (with perhaps a higher degree of functional specialisation within the Alliance). Utilising NATO's existing military command structures could also provide a mechanism for coordinating joint Western 'out-of-area' operations, if NATO countries so wished.

5. Finally, by providing an element of stability in a turbulent and fluid strategic landscape in Europe, NATO could serve as the bulwark for a new security system in the continent. NATO would guarantee the security of its members, and would act as the focus for the transatlantic partnership and as a forum for East–West security dialogue. Meanwhile, the EC could act as the engine of Europe's economic development, whilst the CSCE could provide a forum for pan-European discussion of political,

economic and strategic issues facing its 34 members (35 if Albania joins). In this way, therefore, NATO could provide the scaffolding during the transition to a more cooperative security system, based on political trust and economic interdependence.

III

Having considered the strengths of a NATO-based security system, what are its main disadvantages? Critics of this concept of European security argue as follows:

1. Firstly, it is alleged, NATO is a child of the cold war, designed to 'keep the the Russians out of Europe, the Americans in, and the Germans down'. Such a cold war alliance, based on notions of 'containment' and nuclear deterrence, is not a suitable organisation to provide the core of a new and more cooperative security system in Europe. NATO has not in the past been very successful in functioning as a means of managing the cooperative aspects of the East–West relationship, despite the creation of new committees such as those covering the 'Challenges of Modern Society' or 'Science and Technology'. In the 1970s and 1980s, for example, West European states tended to coordinate their detente policies and the cooperative aspects of the East–West relationship through the EPC (European Political Cooperation), whereas decisions on defence and deterrence were left to NATO.[11]

2. Some would argue that it is potentially counterproductive to react to the changing scene in the East 'by insisting upon "Steady as we go" as the basis for our own defence postures'.[12] The failure to think of any bold and creative new approaches to the problems of European security – by, for example, considering a new security system based on the CSCE, or changes in NATO's doctrine of 'flexible response' (ie, the adoption of 'no first use') – is undermining Gorbachev's efforts to reform and democratise the Soviet Union. Unless the West takes measures to reassure the Soviet leadership and the Soviet military about the security of their heartland, some have argued, then Gorbachev is vulnerable to charges that he is leading the country to disaster. Hanging on to cold war structures like NATO may thus not be in our own long-term interests.[13]

3. NATO does not provide a suitable framework for addressing 'out-of-area' security problems. Article 5 of the North Atlantic Treaty (which founded NATO in 1949) commits its signatories to come to each other's defence if their territories or forces are attacked within the Treaty area (defined by Article 6). But it does not provide this cover for so-called 'out-of-area' challenges (although there is nothing to stop member countries from discussing these issues, or even acting together if

they so choose). As we have seen in Chapter 3 – and as the Gulf crisis of August 1990 dramatically highlights – many security challenges to the Europeans are likely to originate outside of the NATO area in the future. Although there have been some calls for extending NATO's remit to cover such issues, such proposals are likely to be vigorously opposed by the French and Germans (for different reasons) amongst others, and would face stiff opposition in the US Congress. Extending NATO's responsibility so that it acts as a self-appointed global policeman is unlikely to be acceptable to the rest of the world, and would therefore not be conducive to the development of a new international order based on the UN.[14]

4. Basing a new security system around a reformed NATO would preserve US hegemony over West European affairs. US leadership within NATO 'both reflects and reinforces a low level of political cohesion in Western Europe', and 'prevents the development of higher levels of West European cohesion'.[15] For those committed to the vision of a more independent and politically cohesive Western Europe, this is a disturbing state of affairs. Western Europe, it is argued, no longer requires its 'American pacifier', given the extensive networks of integration and cooperation that have developed in the region over the last four decades. Moreover, American interests – from strategic issues to trade questions – frequently diverge from those of the West Europeans. Thus although there is considerable scope for transatlantic cooperation, some now argue that developing a security system which preserves a central role for a US-led Alliance no longer corresponds to the objective need for greater West European self-determination and autonomy.

5. Finally, this scenario of a NATO-based 'Atlanticist' Europe does not really provide a viable solution to the specific security problems of the East Europeans. Although it provides the West Europeans with an insurance policy against the prospect of a renewed security threat from the Soviet Union, it does not address the security needs of those countries situated between NATO and the USSR. These countries face the potential threat of national and ethnic conflicts, and perceive themselves to be caught between the Charybdis of a resurgent Germany and the Scylla of a disintegrating Soviet Union. If NATO were to offer security guarantees to these countries, or even admit them to membership of the Alliance, this might antagonise Moscow, and present SACEUR and NATO's military command with an impossible military mission. It is therefore extremely unlikely that NATO would offer security guar-antees to the East Europeans. But this means that a NATO-based security system fails to address one of the central tasks facing the new Europe: namely, how to manage the security problems of Eastern Europe in the wake of the effective disintegration of the 'socialist community'.

IV

A NATO-based 'Atlanticist' Europe represents a largely Anglo-American and politically conservative view of European security. Its biggest obstacle is the opposition of the French and some other West European states (such as Spain, Italy and Greece). In assessing the viability and desirability of this model of Europe, there are a number of central questions to consider. First, whether NATO can prove sufficiently adaptable to remain relevant to the new security situation in Europe, or whether it is a cold war 'dinosaur' which will die out with the thaw in East–West relations. Second, the role of the USA in Europe: what sort of balance should be struck between the desire for transatlantic partnership on the one hand, and West European political cohesion and autonomy on the other? Third, should NATO develop an 'out-of-area' capability? The major weakness of this scenario is that it fails to address the specific security needs of the East Europeans – and it is Eastern Europe and the Balkans which constitute the most unstable elements of the post-cold war security system on the continent.

Notes

1. In his 1962 Independence Day speech in Philadelphia, President Kennedy declared that the US favoured the development of a united Europe which could share with the USA the burdens of global economic development and the defence of the West. He called for Western Europe to assume the role of 'a partner with whom we could deal on a basis of full equality in all the great and burdensome tasks of building and defending a community of free nations'. Quoted in Ian Gambles' Adelphi Paper, *Prospects for West European Security Cooperation* (London: Brassey's for the IISS, 1989), p. 3.
2. Margaret Thatcher speech to the meeting of NATO Foreign Ministers in Turnberry, Scotland, Thursday, 7 June 1990.
3. At a meeting of centre-right European political leaders in Helsinki, Mrs Thatcher said, 'I recall that I was criticised by some at the time for being so intemperate as to suggest that NATO should get involved in out-of-area problems. But events since then have driven home the lesson; Europe's security is vitally affected by events outside the NATO area.' Quoted in the *Financial Times*, 30 August 1990, p. 4.
4. See the *Financial Times*, 30 November 1990.
5. Manfred Woerner, interviewed by Isabel Hilton in *The Independent*, 4 December 1989.
6. See the *Financial Times*, 9 April 1990, p. 3.
7. In a lecture held at the Hungarian Political Science Association on 20 February 1990, the former Hungarian Foreign Minister, Gyula Horn, mapped out a long-term strategy for Hungary's integration into Europe. The first step would be to join the Council of Europe, the next would be entering the EC, and at a later stage it might be possible to cooperate with the political organs

of NATO. Quoted by Pal Dunay in his paper presented at a conference on 'European Security in the 1990s', organised jointly by the Royal Institute of International Affairs and the Peace Research Institute, Frankfurt, and held at Wilton Park, Sussex, 8–10 April 1990.

8. Joseph Fitchett, 'At NATO Meeting, Japan Seeks Wider Security Link', *International Herald Tribune*, 20 June 1990, p. 1.

9. Joseph Fitchett, 'Defining NATO's Role in a New Europe', *International Herald Tribune*, 6 April 1990, p. 1.

10. Quoted in *The Independent*, 13 December 1990, p. 18.

11. See Peter Schmidt, 'Die Westeuropaeische Union und ihr Verhaeltnis zur NATO', in Lothar Brock and Matthius Jopp (eds), *Sicherheitpolitische Zusammenarbeit und Kooperation der Ruestungswirtschaft in Westeuropa* (Baden-Baden: Nomos, 1986), pp. 95–104.

12. Ken Booth, 'Steps towards Stable Peace in Europe: a Theory and Practice of Coexistence', in *International Affairs*, vol. 66, no. 1 (1990), pp. 17–45 (p. 38).

13. Admiral Sir James Eberle, 'Bold Steps towards a Secure Future', *The Guardian*, 8 March 1990.

14. Edward Heath has argued that attempts to change NATO into a worldwide peacekeeping force are misguided: 'That could only lead to the creation of a new imperialism to replace that banished after the Second World War. It would be costly in money and lives, and politically unacceptable to those countries outside the north Atlantic alliance.' See his article in the *Sunday Correspondent*, 7 October 1990.

15. Barry Buzan, 'The Future of Western European Security', in Ole Waever et al. (eds), *European Polyphony: Perspectives Beyond East–West Confrontation* (London: Macmillan, 1989), p. 36.

10

Scenario B:
A West European Defence Community

This scenario posits a much more radical change in the character of the European security system than scenario A. It is based on two key assumptions. First, a decline in the significance of NATO as a viable military-political alliance. And second, the emergence of a 'West European Defence Community', based on a much more politically cohesive European Community. In this model of Europe, a West European Defence Community has been established, linked by a treaty of mutual security cooperation with the USA. The product of a fusion of the EPC with the WEU, this new security entity would signify the belated creation of the failed 'European Defence Community' (EDC) of the early 1950s. In this scenario, the West European Defence Community has become the central guarantor of West European security, whilst providing the lodestone of a broader European security system – as a bulwark of stability in a Europe of 'concentric circles'.

I

As we have already seen (Chapter 6), the dynamics for West European security cooperation are now weaker than in the mid-1980s, and the prospects for the emergence of a West European Defence Community appear slim. Nonetheless, the impetus for a more cohesive West European security entity could appear in the event of a future security challenge emerging in a situation where NATO had been significantly weakened, whilst the CSCE remains an ineffective body for implementing collective security. As Pierre Hassner has argued, the time 'for a reassertion of a West European defence identity (which is unlikely to constitute a priority for any country in the present atmosphere)' may come 'after bipolarity and the Cold War, and after the euphoria and the disappointment of all-European cooperation';

> Put differently, after the thesis constituted by NATO and the antithesis of CSCE, some kind of European Defence Community may come to represent a synthesis. All the more so since this might be conceived as a West European pillar either of NATO or of CSCE, depending on America's wish to maintain its presence in Europe and Germany's wish to maintain special links in the West.[1]

An autonomous West European security entity could emerge either within the ambit of the European Community, or from a reinvigorated WEU. A possible scenario for the emergence of a West European Defence Community is via the fusion of the EPC with the WEU, and their incorporation into the Community's institutional ensemble – as proposed by the Italian Foreign Minister, Gianni De Michelis, in September 1990.[2] Indeed, the Secretary-General of the WEU, Willem F. van Eekelen, and his predecessor, Alfred Cahen, have both suggested that the WEU should be seen as a 'holding-body' pending the assumption of defence responsibilities by the EC.[3]

Proposals for West European defence cooperation have multiplied in recent years, as the European Community has entered a period of dynamic development and deepening integration. The former NATO Secretary-General, Lord Carrington, has called for the EC to take over responsibility for West European defence from the Alliance, arguing that it was ridiculous to exclude defence matters from a Community which is trying to coordinate its foreign policy, construct an internal market and abolish frontiers between the 12. An EC responsible for its own defence would still need an alliance with the USA, he has argued, and this could include the stationing of US forces in Europe. But with the ending of the cold war in Europe, 'it may be the threat comes from somewhere quite different'. In this situation, Lord Carrington has suggested, the Europeans might need a capacity for independent military action.[4]

In a similar vein, Sir Leon Brittan, vice president of the European Commission, has called for the establishment of a 'European Security Community' within the EC, as a 'European defence pillar' for NATO. Arguing that 'now is the time to develop a security dimension to the European Community', he called for the creation of a European Security Community alongside Euratom, the Coal and Steel Community and the European Community. Although it should be 'assimilated as closely as possible into the existing Community institutions', it would have to have 'slightly different' decision-making arrangements 'because of the problem of Irish neutrality on the one hand, and Norwegian, Icelandic and Turkish membership of NATO on the other'. The new body should subsume within it the existing structures for defence and security cooperation, such as the NATO Eurogroup, the Independent European Programme Group and the WEU. It could then become 'the forum in which Europe developed a common defence strategy, and a coherent arms procurement policy'. It could also organise joint training and joint manoeuvres. In the long term, such a body could even 'manage' a European nuclear deterrent, as an equal partner with the 'American pillar' of NATO, and could encourage greater military integration, 'both in terms of joint forces and specialisation of roles'.[5]

This scenario envisages a West European Defence Community based on two key elements: a European nuclear deterrence and integrated conventional forces. A European nuclear deterrence would be required because of the prohibitive costs of a purely conventional deterrence, and because a mix of nuclear and conventional forces provides a better way of deterring all forms of war, conventional as well as nuclear.[6] Such a European nuclear deterrent would be based on Anglo-French nuclear cooperation, and would involve the creation of a European version of NATO's 'Nuclear Planning Group'. Integration of West European conventional forces would begin at the corps or divisional level, and could draw upon the past experience of Franco-German military cooperation. Indeed, as Helmut Schmidt has suggested, a 30-division Franco-German army could act as the 'European nucleus for Europe's defence', with a French commander-in-chief and French extended nuclear deterrence.[7] Similarly, Edward Heath has proposed the creation of a European army, 'with British, French and German troops serving shoulder to shoulder in times of tension, like the present Gulf crisis'.[8]

A West European Defence Community would thus have two key axes of military-political cooperation: Paris–London (given their possession of nuclear weapons, their membership of the UN Security Council, and their 'out-of-area' commitments[9]); and Paris–Bonn (a relationship which has long been regarded as the political motor of West European cooperation). It is no coincidence that Paris emerges as the pivot of this model of Europe. This vision of a West European security entity at the heart of a refashioned European security system has long enjoyed substantial support in many circles in French political life. Such a model of Europe would correspond to many of the traditional political and strategic interests of France. It is no surprise, therefore, that the current Mitterrand Administration has trumpeted the notion of giving a defence and foreign policy competence to the Community, at the expense of NATO. Although this would require a dilution of France's traditional Gaullist independence, it could nonetheless strengthen French influence over European affairs – a long-standing goal of French foreign policy.

A West European Defence Community, based on the European Community, would not only appeal to many in France, it would also be welcome to many in countries like Spain and Italy. Even in Germany, which has traditionally been firmly committed to post-war Atlanticism, there is considerable support for the notion of a European security system based on 'concentric circles'.[10] In this scenario, a strong and politically coherent Western Europe would provide the anchor and foundation of a Europe of concentric circles. At its core would be a federated European political entity (composed of an inner-grouping of EC countries committed to political and economic union); a second circle would be formed of EC countries not willing to pool their sovereignty to such an extent; a third circle would encompass EFTA countries and former communist states linked to the Community in a broader 'European economic space'; and the outer circle would embrace all 34 CSCE countries, including the USA and the USSR. At the core of this Europe, therefore, would be the West European Defence Community, as an organic part of a federated EC grouping.

This scenario assumes that the West Europeans would not have completely severed their security ties to the North Americans, but would have negotiated a new mutual security treaty with the USA. These strategic links would be much looser than in the previous scenario of a transatlantic 'partnership'. There would, for example, be no American forces in the West European Defence Community's integrated military command structures, and only token – if any – US combat forces deployed in Europe. The concept of linking any new West European security entity by treaty to the US is widespread amongst those who favour this model of a more militarily self-reliant and autonomous Western Europe. Stanley Hoffmann, for example, arguing that the present alliance system should be replaced, has called for

> a West European security organisation allied to the US. It could perhaps be based on the currently sleepy West European Union, but it certainly should be incorporated in the institutional system of the European Community. ...this transformation would require no revision of the North Atlantic Treaty of 1949, which is remarkably flexible. Only symbolic or very small numbers of American and Soviet troops would remain on the continent.[11]

Similarly, Professor Werner Link has proposed that a restructured WEU should be allied to the USA in a reformed Atlantic Alliance. This, he suggests, would provide an ideal military framework for a unified Germany, signifying the belated creation of the ill-fated EDC of the 1950s. At the same time, such a revamped WEU would provide an element of military stability within a pan-European security order.[12] This might prove attractive to some of the East Europeans: Geza Jeszenszky, for example, the Hungarian Foreign Minister, has told a meeting of WEU parliamentarians in Paris that Hungary wanted to leave the Warsaw Pact, and that it would apply for 'special guest status' with the WEU Assembly.[13]

The political prerequisites for the emergence of a European security system centred on a West European Defence Community include the development of a much higher degree of political and institutional cohesion in the European Community. A political structure approaching some form of federalism (based on the principle of 'subsidiarity') would be required, although this would certainly be more pluralistic than the sort of federalism found, for example, in the USA. Furthermore, it would require a common West European assessment of the security 'risks' and 'challenges' emanating from the Soviet Union, Eastern Europe or regions of geostrategic significance to the Europeans (such as the North African littoral, the Middle East or the Gulf). Militarily, it would require agreement on (i) a European *Gesamtkonzept* which defined a mutually acceptable mix of nuclear and conventional weapons, and (ii) an expansion of industrial and technological cooperation involving both military research and development, and more joint arms production agreements.

II

Proponents of an autonomous and integrated West European defence entity argue that this model of European security offers the most realistic solution to the security dilemmas of Europe after the cold war. They claim that:

1. The emergence of a West European Defence Community would give Western Europe a much higher profile in world affairs, and would 'crown' the process of West European integration.[14] 'Western Europe', Luc Reychler has argued, 'can no longer function as an economic superpower, a political schizophrenic, and a military vassal.'[15] If Western Europe were to develop a defence and foreign policy competence (including a capacity for collective power projection in areas such as the Gulf), it would be able to assert its interests in an increasingly polycentric and turbulent world. The EC would therefore have a military potential to match its existing economic and political power.

2. West European security interests, it is often argued, can no longer be seen as identical with – or even necessarily compatible with – US security interests, in the way they could in the early cold war years. This became increasingly evident in the 1980s. Such transatlantic strategic differences are likely to become even more pronounced in an increasingly polycentric world no longer divided into two antagonistic blocs. It is therefore essential, it is suggested, that Western Europe develops its own independent military capacity for defence and international power projection. This would provide a safeguard against a precipitate withdrawal of US military forces from Europe – in the event, for example, of a serious conflict over 'burden-sharing', or a deepening mood of 'isolationism' in American foreign policy circles. It would also help mitigate some of the problems arising from 'extended nuclear deterrence' and its associated 'coupling/decoupling' conundrum.

3. A West European Defence Community would provide a means of anchoring a united Germany firmly in the West. Germany would be militarily integrated into a West European Defence Community, and politically and economically integrated into a more integrated European Community. This would provide assurance to the French and other West

Europeans, and would be welcomed by Germany's eastern neighbours.

4. A West European Defence Community, organically linked to the EC, could provide a strong element of stability for Europe as a whole, as the core of a system of 'concentric circles'. Proponents of this model of Europe would argue that in attempting to develop a new security system, it is a mistake to begin by attempting to construct a pan-European system of collective security. It is much more realistic to start by building on the existing 'security community' in Western Europe, and developing it as the stable foundation or bulwark of a broader, pan-European security order.[16]

5. Finally, a West European security entity could emerge as a force for peace in the world. The Europeans, it is suggested, have tended to be much less prone to military interventions in regional conflicts than have the Americans, and tend to place a greater emphasis on diplomatic and political solution to such disputes.[17] There may in the future be a need for European peacekeeping forces in areas of international tension, and these forces could most effectively be supplied by a West European Defence Community. Such a defensive organisation could thus be a force for stability and peace in Europe and the broader international system. Indeed, Barry Buzan has argued that what he dubs a 'West European Treaty Organization' (WETO), 'in which a robust, but non-provocative, defence policy is used to loosen the pressure of the superpower nutcracker, could enhance security not only for Europe but for both superpowers as well'.[18]

III

Despite its apparent strengths, this *Kleineuropa* concept of European security has many critics. They argue that the creation of a West European Defence Community would not be conducive to the emergence of a durable peace order in Europe, and that it would be a risky project with undesirable consequences:

1. To begin with, it risks recreating the division of Europe. By deepening the process of West European integration and constructing a *de facto* West European superpower, it is argued, the opportunity for overcoming the division of Europe will be lost. Adding defence and foreign policy to the responsibilities of the EC would make it extremely difficult to open up the Community to new members from neutral or former Warsaw Pact countries. The result might therefore be to create a new set of political and strategic cleavages on the European mainland. Furthermore, the proposed system of 'concentric circles' – a concept which already implies elements of hierarchy and exclusion – would not necessarily mesh together in a harmonious and constructive manner.

Instead, they could lead to new forms of division, would which not be in the long-term interests of either the 'core' or 'periphery' countries.

2. Convinced Atlanticists argue that this model of European security would weaken the transatlantic partnership, thereby undermining the strategic alliance which has been the bed-rock of West European security and prosperity for over forty years. The post-war Atlantic community, people like Helmut Kohl and Margaret Thatcher insist, has safeguarded the prosperity and security of the West Europeans. Severing the existing security ties between the 'old' and 'new' worlds could leave transatlantic relations prone to recurrent tensions and rivalries which, without the institutional bond of NATO, might result in a drastic realignment of global politics. Given US fears of a post-1992 'fortress Europe', American disenchantment with Europe could accelerate a reorientation of its strategic commitments to the Pacific, or precipitate a period of US isolationism. Even if a West European Defence Community were to sign a new mutual security treaty with Washington, and the Americans were to establish new institutional links with the EC, these might not be strong enough to survive serious trade disputes or differences over strategic global issues.

3. Not only could a West European Defence Community weaken the transatlantic partnership, it is argued, it might also antagonise conservative forces in the Soviet Union and undermine the reform process there. The emergence of a powerful new economic, political and military 'superpower' on its Western borders – which included a united Germany – could reinforce conservative, nationalist and atavistic forces in the Soviet Union. Soviet concern about the possible emergence of a 'West European superpower' was particularly evident in the early 1980s. Since then, however, a number of influential Soviet security analysts have challenged the conventional Soviet view that closer West European security cooperation would necessarily represent a threat to Moscow's interests. Nevertheless, there is a very real danger that the emergence of an autonomous West European power centre could be perceived as threatening by many conservative and nationalist groups in the Soviet Union.[19]

4. The emergence of a 'West European superpower' is not only worrying to some in the Soviet Union, but is also becoming one of the major bugbears of the West European peace movement and the radical left. They fear that this could lead to the development of a West European nuclear-armed superpower which might then play an aggressive and neo-imperialist world role. West European nuclear and conventional military cooperation, it has been alleged, 'could be the route to its becoming the fifth world power (along with the USA, USSR, China and Japan) of the early twenty-first century, dominating and looting weaker and poorer countries'.[20] According to this school of thought, there

is a very real potential danger of a 'nascent neo-imperialism in Western Europe'. The creation of a new military bloc in Western Europe, it is argued, in which British and French nuclear forces replace those of the Americans, would place both Europe and the Third World at risk:

> For Europe, it could lead to a new round of confrontation and higher military spending. For the Third World, it would pose a new threat to independence. Third World countries often want greater Western European involvement to moderate the USA's interventionism; but if Western Europe starts operating as a new bloc, the result could be a military temptation to exert greater power over less-developed countries.[21]

Radical critics of military cooperation and supranational integration in Western Europe, therefore, suggest that despite the liberal and humanist traditions in Europe, the creation of a new power bloc might rekindle the imperialist aspirations of the past.[22] They also argue that it would recreate the division of Europe in a new guise, and fuel a new arms race on the continent.

5. Some argue that a West European Defence Community does not provide a solution to the security problems of the East Europeans. It would not address the problems of rising nationalism, political instability and economic restructuring which plague the former communist countries in the East. Giving security guarantees or membership to one or more of the East European countries would cause more problems than it would solve, and would provoke serious concern in Moscow. This scenario therefore fails to address the security concerns and requirements of the newly democratising countries of Eastern Europe.

6. Finally, it has been argued that seeking to give the EC a defence dimension involves a mistaken application of the nineteenth-century process of nation-state building to a community of twelve nations, which is a very different animal. The creation of a West European Defence Community, its critics suggest, would not correspond to the national and political diversity of the region. As we have seen in Chapter 6, the national differences and political diversity of the West Europeans makes the task of deepening West European security cooperation enormously difficult. It would therefore prove a largely ineffective and ultimately fragile creation.

IV

A West European Defence Community, at the heart of a Europe of 'concentric circles', is seen by some in Western Europe as the only real alternative to an 'Atlanticist' Europe based on NATO. It is a vision of European security which is very popular amongst advocates of West European supranational integration, and in key sections of the French,

Italian and Spanish political elites. It also enjoys some political support in German political circles, but much less in the Anglo-Saxon world.

It is a more radical model of European security than scenario A, but perhaps at the same time more risky. More risky because it proposes the creation of a security system based on a degree of political and military cohesion in Western Europe which is without historical precedent in the region. On the other hand, however, it is a model of European security which seems to correspond to the growing political cohesion and economic integration of the West European countries. It might, therefore, be the only solid foundation for a new system of European security beyond the cold war (of which NATO was a product).

The main issues which this model of security raises are similar to those in scenario A, namely (i) the question of the desirability and feasibility of greater West European security autonomy vis-a-vis the Americans, and (ii) the effect of closer West European defence cooperation on the Soviet Union. Another important issue of controversy is whether or not a West European Defence Community would represent a nuclear-armed, neo-imperialist superpower, or a force for peace and stability in the world? There is no clear answer to this latter question. As Barry Buzan has argued, such a body 'could represent anything from an emergent Western European superpower to some kind of semi-neutral zone of disengagement between the superpowers concerned principally with defending itself in ways that would maximise its value as a buffer between them'.[23]

Finally, the main limitations of this concept of European security are that (i) it does not directly address the specific security problems of the East Europeans, and (ii) it risks establishing a new set of political and strategic cleavages in Europe, which would replace those created by the old 'iron curtain'.

Notes

1. Pierre Hassner, 'Europe beyond Partition and Unity: Disintegration or Reconstitution?', *International Affairs*, vol. 66, no. 3 (July 1990), pp. 461–75 (p. 468).
2. 'Italy Says EC Should Consider Forming its Own "Army for Defence"', *The Independent*, 19 September 1990, p. 11.
3. See, for example, Alfred Cahen, 'The WEU and the European Dimension of Common Security', in *RUSI and Brassey's Defence Yearbook* (Oxford: Brassey's for the Royal United Services Institute for Defence Studies, 1989), pp. 25–37, and Alfred Cahen, 'The Emergence and Role of the Western European Union', in Michael Clarke and Rod Hague (eds), *European Defence Co-operation: America, Britain and NATO* (London: Manchester Univerity Press, 1990), pp. 55–72.
4. Colin Brown, 'Carrington Proposes Defence Role for EC', *The Independent*, 12 April 1990, p. 10.

5. 'Brittan Proposes Defence Role for EC within NATO', *Financial Times*, 18 May 1990, p. 2.

6. See Dominique David, 'A French View of European Security', in *European Polyphony: Perspectives Beyond East–West Confrontation*, ed. by Ole Waever et al. (London: Oxford, 1989), pp. 99–109.

7. See Ian Gambles, *Prospects for West European Security Cooperation*, Adelphi Paper 244 (London: Brassey's for the IISS, 1989), p. 13.

8. Edward Heath, 'Now We Need a New Army for Europe', *Sunday Correspondent*, 7 October 1990.

9. See Yves Boyer, Pierre Lellouche and John Roper, *Franco-British Defence Cooperation. A new entente cordiale?* (London: Routledge for the RIIA and IFRI, 1989), and Francoise de la Serre, Jacques Leruez and Helen Wallace, *French and British Foreign Policies in Transition. The Challenge of Adjustment* (Oxford: Berg for the RIIA and CERI, 1990).

10. See for example Michael Mertes and Norbert Prill, 'Eine Vision für Europa', *Frankfurter Allgemeine Zeitung*, 19 July 1989, p. 8.

11. Stanley Hoffmann, 'A Plan for the New Europe', *New York Review of Books*, 18 January 1990, pp. 18–21 (p. 21).

12. Werner Link, 'Ein neuer Rahmen fuer die deutsche Macht', in *Rheinischer Merkur*, 16 February 1990.

13. See *Report on Eastern Europe*, 15 June 1990, p. 36.

14. Jean-Pierre Chevenement, the French Minister of Defence, has declared that 'without doubt, a European system of defence will *crown* the process of European construction, which will pass an important milestone in 1992 with the establishment of a single market, and which will have to be developed through closer political relationships'. Quoted in Ian Gambles, *Prospects for West European Security Cooperation*, p. 12.

15. Robert Rudney and Luc Reychler (eds), *European Security Beyond the Year 2000* (New York: Praeger, 1988), p. 2.

16. Valery Giscard D'Estaing, 'The Two Europes, East and West', *International Affairs*, vol. 65, no. 4 (Autumn 1989), pp. 653–58.

17. Trevor Taylor, *European Defence Cooperation*, Chatham House Paper no. 24 (London: Routledge & Kegan Paul for the RIIA, 1984), p. 70.

18. Barry Buzan, 'The Future of Western European Security', in *European Polyphony*, p. 38.

19. According to the Soviet analyst A.I. Utkin, 'Europeanism as an ideology focuses on greater independence from the hegemonic power of the capitalist world – the United States – which results in the definite anti-American trend of Europeanism', and it constitutes 'an ideology of isolating Western Europe, of forming the West European alliance as an autonomous center in the world arena'. Quoting these remarks, Robin F. Laird has argued that, '...the Soviets hope to contribute to the decline of Atlanticism without encouraging the further development of European cooperation in the economic, political and military security areas', and that the emergence of such a West European superpower would be of major concern to the USSR. Robin F. Laird, 'The Soviet Union and the Western Alliance', in *The USSR and the Western Alliance*, edited by R.F. Laird and Susan L. Clark (London: Unwin Hyman, 1990), p. 251.

20. Dan Smith, 'The Changing Strategic Context', in *European Security in the 1990s*, edited by Dan Smith (London: Pluto, 1989), pp. 1–24 (p. 23).

21. Mariano Aguirre, 'Looking Southwards', in Dan Smith (ed.), *op. cit.*, pp. 123–150 (p. 149).

22. Other proponents of this view include Michael Randle in *Alternatives in European Security*, edited by M. Randle and Paul Rogers (Aldershot: Darmouth, 1990), p. 93, and Richard Falk, 'The Superpowers and a Sustainable Detente for Europe', in *The New Detente: Rethinking East–West Relations*, edited by Mary Kaldor, Gerard Holden and Richard Falk (London: Verso, 1989), pp. 133–153 (p. 150).

23. B. Buzan, in *European Polyphony*, p. 38.

11

Scenario C:
The CSCE and a Pan-European
Collective Security System

This scenario envisages the emergence of a pan-European system of collective security, based on an institutionalised CSCE. There is now a broad constituency across Europe for giving an institutionalised CSCE a more important role in European affairs. What is distinctive about this model of European security, however, is that it conceives of the CSCE developing into the central security structure in the continent – providing an institutional basis for a pan-European collective security system, and gradually absorbing the functions and responsibilities of existing alliances and security arrangements.

In this model of Europe, the CSCE has developed as an institutionalised framework for pan-European cooperation and collective security. It consists of an institutional ensemble comprising a CSCE Parliamentary Assembly; regular meetings of heads of state and government, and of foreign and other ministers; a number of specialist agencies covering the major concerns of the November 1990 'Paris Charter for a New Europe'; and, at its core, a European Security Council, which would provide a mechanism for conflict resolution and crisis management. This European Security Council would act as a mandatory arbitration and conciliation centre in cases of inter-state conflict, and would have at its disposal European peacekeeping and possibly interventionary forces. This CSCE-based structure would therefore provide the framework for managing and containing the security problems of a Europe 'whole and free'.

I

This is a vision of European security which has a strong constituency in central and eastern Europe, given their unhappy experience of the division of the continent and the old 'bloc' system. It expresses an aspiration for a Europe in which security is indivisible, and in which national independence and democracy are guaranteed for all the peoples of the continent. It differs from De Gaulle's notion of *l'Europe de l'Atlantic à l'Oural*, however, because nationalism and the nation-state will no longer provide the motor-forces of this new security system. Instead, European security would be regulated by a strengthened and institutionalised CSCE.

The creation of a system of pan-European collective security is now championed primarily by the newly democratising countries of East Central Europe. It has been, however, a long-standing goal of Soviet foreign policy. Indeed, the preamble to the Warsaw Treaty of 14 May 1955 declared its aim to be the establishment of a 'system of collective security in Europe, with the participation of all the Europeans states, irrespective of their social and political systems, which would make it possible to combine their efforts in the interests of securing peace in Europe'.[1] The Soviets also proposed an 'All-European Agreement on Collective Security in Europe' in October 1955 at the Geneva Conference of the four great powers' foreign affairs ministers. Given Soviet behaviour in Eastern Europe, however, this was not a realistic possibility for most of the post-war period. It was only with the Soviet 'new political thinking' – and the democratic revolutions of 1989 – that it has become a more feasible objective.

The most coherent and ambitious proposals for a system of collective security based on the CSCE have come from the new democratic Czechoslovak government. In April 1990, President Vaclav Havel, and his foreign minister, Jiri Dienstbier, outlined a three-stage proposal aimed at moving from the 'bloc' system to one of collective security.[2] The first stage (to be completed by the end of 1991) would involve the creation of a 'European Security Commission' at the level of foreign ministers, based on the CSCE processes, which would seek to foster a more cooperative relationship between NATO and a democratised Warsaw Pact. The Commission would consist of a small Executive Secretariat and a 'Military Section' subordinated to an Advisory Committee of the foreign ministers. In the second stage (which is expected to take about five years), an Organisation of European States – based on the Helsinki Final Act 'Decalogue' – would be established to coordinate relations, foster cooperation and ensure common defence amongst the European member countries in the event of any one of them being attacked. In the final stage (to be reached by about 2000) a European Confederation (as proposed by President Mitterrand) would be created, which would integrate all European countries into a single commonwealth of nations.[3]

These Czechoslovak proposals were subsequently coordinated with the Polish and East German governments, who formally presented a version of them to the CSCE in June 1990.[4] They called for: biannual summit meetings to discuss political developments and draw up an agenda for follow-up conferences and expert meetings; the establishment of a Council of Security and Cooperation involving foreign ministers (and others as appropriate) meeting twice-yearly to discuss common issues in greater detail; monthly meetings of the 34 CSCE Ambassadors; and the creation of a small secretariat (to be based in Prague). The Council on Security and Cooperation was to be responsible for the work of two specialist agencies or centres: one dealing with confidence-building measures, arms controls and verification (and based in Berlin); the other to act as a centre for conflict-prevention and non-mandatory conciliation in Europe. In time, it was suggested, the CSCE could develop a mechanism for the peaceful settlement of all conflicts between its members. Ultimately, it would grow into a European Confederation, in which national military forces would be supplemented and later replaced by a CSCE peace-keeping corps.[5]

In the West, calls for an institutionalisation of the CSCE also multiplied in the course of 1990. But Mrs Thatcher, for example, argued that it should 'develop as a forum, not for defence, but for wider East–West political consultation and as a framework for drawing East European countries into the mainstream of Europe'.[6] More ambitiously, the Danish Foreign Minister, Uffe Ellemann-Jensen, called for the establishment of a 'European Security Council' within the CSCE framework, as a supplement to a reformed NATO and WTO. Such a body, he suggested, could help tackle the ethnic and national conflicts surfacing in Europe, and 'it is possible that such a council should even have a peace-keeping force at its disposal'.[7] A still more visionary approach was articulated by President Mitterrand, who called for the creation of a secretariat to begin work on a 'European Confederation', embracing East and West: 'There must be a pact between countries that have democratic institutions. Why not a flexible structure, more flexible than the EC, where one could discuss economic and cultural questions, start talks on security and where everyone would be equal? ... We should work around a permanent flexible secretariat that would represent all European nations, prepare joint briefs, inform all parties on the progress needed and on the problems.'[8]

Furthermore, in July 1990 NATO as an organisation committed itself to an institutionalisation of the CSCE in order to make it 'more prominent in Europe's future' and to establish it as 'a forum for wider political dialogue in a more united Europe'. To this end, the 'London Declaration' of 6 July 1990 made the following proposals: regular meetings of Heads of State and Government or ministers at least once a year; CSCE review conferences once every two years; a small secretariat; a CSCE mechanism to monitor elections based on the Copenhagen Document;[9] a Centre for the Prevention of Conflict to serve as a means of greater military transparency and the reconciliation of disputes amongst CSCE member states; and an 'Assembly of Europe', based on the existing parliamentary assembly of the Council of Europe, but including representatives of all CSCE member states.[10]

By the time of the November 1990 CSCE summit in Paris, therefore, a broad consensus had formed around the notion of institutionalising the CSCE, and giving it a more prominent role in European affairs. The Paris summit of 19–21 November saw the signing of the CFE treaty by 22 of the 34 CSCE countries, and a declaration by NATO and Warsaw Pact members that 'they were no longer adversaries, and would extend to each other the hand of friendship'.[11] The CSCE was also given a more permanent institutional structure, consisting of: a permanent secretariat of about 10–15 officials, to prepare and serve regular follow-up meetings (to be based in Prague); regular summits of heads of state and government (at least once every two years), and annual meetings of foreign ministers; a Conflict Prevention Centre (to be based in Vienna), which would supervise the exchange of military information, monitor 'unusual military activity' and convene meetings of its 34 members to discuss such 'unusual' developments when necessary; an Office of Free Elections (based in Warsaw), which would monitor national and local elections, and supply expert advice and observers when requested; and an Assembly of Europe, composed of delegates from national parliaments, which would use the facilities of the Council of Europe's Assembly in Strasbourg. Finally, the 34 participating countries agreed a 'Paris Charter for a New Europe', which included a series of commitments to peace, common security, democracy, human rights and market economies.

The Paris summit was hailed by many as the start of a new era of peace, human rights and democracy in Europe. Whilst welcoming these developments, however, most Western statesmen continued to insist that the CSCE could not replace NATO and other security bodies such as the WEU. They also underlined their doubts about the feasibility of proposals for a pan-European collective security arrangement based on the CSCE. Secretary of State James Baker, for example, insisted that 'suggestions for new institutions should complement rather than duplicate roles assigned to exisiting institutions and fora'.[12] The exception here has been Hans-Dietrich Genscher, the West German Foreign Minister. He alone amongst leading NATO ministers has envisaged the creation of 'new European security structures' based on the CSCE which could eventually absorb both NATO and the Warsaw Pact.[13] This idea is increasingly popular amongst opposition West German Social Democrats, and given early signs of diminishing popular support for the traditional Atlanticist orientation of German foreign policy in the wake of unification,[14] it is possible that the notion of a CSCE-based system of European collective security could find growing political support in Germany.

Outside official circles, there have been a number of ambitious proposals for pan-European cooperation and collective security. In a Fabian Society pamphlet published in September 1990, Mike Gapes proposed the creation of a 'European Security Organisation' (ESO), involving in the first instance the existing members of both NATO and the Warsaw Pact, but open to all CSCE states. The ESO would organise 'regular exchanges of civilian and military personnel, joint exercises, establishment of a joint verification agency, and shared use of military and observation satellites. In time a joint military structure and a Chief of Staff, equivalent to the NATO Supreme Allied Commander Europe (SACEUR) could be established.' He also proposed the establishment of 'joint peace keeping forces which could operate within Europe at the request of national governments'; the development of 'joint multi-national brigades' (for example between the Poles and Germans or Italians and Hungarians); and tours of duty by Soviet troops in Western Europe, and by British and American forces (for example) in Eastern and Central Europe.[15]

Another proposal for a European system of collective security (by Jane Sharp and Gerhard Wachter) advocates the creation of Central European Security Commission comprising all CSCE countries (plus Albania), based in Berlin. This would be supplemented by four regional security commissions, covering central Europe, northern Europe, the western Mediterranean and the eastern Mediterranean (with their headquarters based respectively in Stockholm, Vienna, Rome and Budapest). The two superpowers would be represented on the Central European Security Commission, and on each of the four regional commissions.[16]

More recently, Hans-Joachim Schmidt of the Peace Research Institute Frankfurt has suggested the creation of a 'Military Council for Europe' within the CSCE framework, to which all the active forces of a unified Germany and all stationed forces in Germany would be assigned. In the future, other European countries could assign part of their active forces to the Military Council, which would operate according to a mandate drawn up by a CSCE summit meeting. This Military Council would provide a mechanism for controlling German military forces; help reduce the danger of increased nationalism in the East; coordinate the defensive restructuring of European armed forces; and facilitate the development of 'a new cooperative security structure to absorb the breakup of the alliances'.[17]

There are a number of prerequisites for a Europe-wide collective security system, as envisaged in this third scenario. First, the continuation of the reform processes in the Soviet Union and elsewhere in Eastern Europe. If authoritarian nationalist or recidivist political forces were to come to power in Moscow, for example, it would be very hard to imagine the development of a pan-European collective security system. Second, a high degree of consensus and cooperation between the major powers in the CSCE – such as the two superpowers, Germany, France, Britain and Italy. This would facilitate the development of a collective security regime in Europe, in contrast to the 1930s, when the League of Nations was faced with a number of major 'rogue' or revisionist powers (including Nazi Germany, fascist Italy, and Soviet Russia). Third, a continuing build-down and defensive restructuring of military forces in Europe.[18] Fourth, the formation of a broad consensus on normative values such as human rights (both collective and individual), parliamentary democracy and political freedom. Fifth, the evolution of a pan-European 'economic space', based on market principles, with the EC at its core. This would facilitate the development of more intensive forms of economic interdependence, which in turn would give a more solid basis to pan-European political cooperation. And finally, it requires agreement on the definition of the common security interests of all 34 CSCE nations, and their coordination in joint institutions within the CSCE process. A system of collective security is incompatible with exclusive alliances directed against other states: instead, it requires a commitment by every state to the defence of every other state, on the basis of reciprocity and solidarity. This entails reciprocal guarantees of common, concerted action, either by 'closing the circle' against the most menacing member of a group, or against an external threat. Such a system should not be directed against any particular enemy or threat defined in advance, but against any aggression from whatever source. Any state that committed aggression would be regarded as the enemy of all, and would be punished accordingly, by whatever sanctions the collective agreed.[19]

In this scenario, therefore, the pan-European interests of a continent 'whole and free' would be regulated by a network of pan-European bodies. An institutionalised CSCE would provide the overall framework for cooperation and collective security, through its specialised agencies, its regular follow-on meetings and expert conferences, and its conciliation and arbitration mechanism. But it would also cooperate with other pan-European bodies, such as the UN Economic Commission for Europe, and the Council of Europe (with its European Court of Human Rights in Strasbourg). This arrangement would be compatible with a range of regional and sub-regional forms of cooperation and integration, such as the EC, the Pentagonale and the Nordic Council. The existing alliance structures – NATO, the WEU and the Warsaw Pact – would, however, ultimately be absorbed into the CSCE itself, which would take on responsibility for the security and independence of all its member states.

II

A CSCE-based collective security regime in Europe is seen by its proponents in Central and Eastern Europe as a long-term solution to many of the security problems of the continent. They believe that it can fulfil this role for the following reasons:

1. Such a pan-European system, founded on an institutionalised CSCE, would include both the USA and the USSR. Although Vaclav Havel has argued that a system of collective security would ultimately make possible the withdrawal of American troops from Europe, the USA would still be an important element of a European collective security system, given its participation in the CSCE. Similarly, the USSR would be included in this security order, despite having withdrawn its stationed forces from Eastern Europe. The inclusion of the Soviet Union in this system of collective security is seen by many as essential because it would help avoid the danger of the USSR perceiving itself excluded from the process of European construction (such a perception of exclusion might leave the Soviet Union feeling increasingly isolated and embittered).

2. The CSCE is regarded by some as the ideal framework for a new security order in Europe given the high standing and political legitimacy it won for itself in the course of the 1970s and 1980s.[20] This high regard for the possibilities of the CSCE is especially strong in Eastern Europe, where it is credited with both having kept the issue of human rights at the forefront of the European agenda over the last decade, and having expanded the East European states' room for manoeuvre vis-a-vis the Soviet Union.

3. An institutionalised CSCE – including a European Security Council which could act as a centre for conflict prevention and international arbitration, backed up by multinational peacekeeping forces – is seen as the one institution which can really address the security concerns of the East European and Balkan countries. No other institution, it is suggested, possesses the potential of the CSCE to act as a mechanism for managing, containing and possibly resolving the intra-European conflicts which are bound to occur in the post-cold war setting.[21]

4. The CSCE, it is argued, provides an important pan-European framework for integrating a united Germany into broader European structures without destabilising the equilibrium of the continent.[22] The commitment of a united Germany to a system of collective security within the ambit of the CSCE is seen as a vital condition of this model of Europe. A united Germany, committed to the CSCE, could then act as a lynch-pin of East–West cooperation. In this way, it may be possible to build a new *europäische Friedensordnung* (a 'European peace order') **around** Germany, not **against** or **under** her.[23]

5. Finally, this collective security structure could provide the institutional framework for developing a durable and just peace in Europe. A peace founded on the spread of democracy and the acceptance of collectively agreed principles of human rights, and facilitated by growing economic interdependence, based on market relations. Europe today is no longer divided into two hostile and antagonistic blocs, and for the first time in its long and troubled history, the prospect of building a Europe

'whole and free' now seems a realistic proposition. For many visionaries in Europe, an institutionalised CSCE presents the ideal framework within which pan-European cooperation and understanding can flourish.

III

This vision of Europe has obvious attractions. Its optimistic assumptions seem to reflect the *Zeitgeist* of an age in which the Berlin Wall has collapsed, and in which authoritarian governments have been swept aside by 'people's power'. Given the commendable motives behind this concept of a post-cold war Europe, criticisms of this notion of European security tend to focus on its feasibility, rather than its desirability. Sceptics make a number of points concerning the futility of seeking to develop a collective security system based on an institutionalised CSCE:

1. To begin with, critics of what *The Economist* has disparagingly dubbed 'the dream of Europax' point out that, as a framework for regulating the security affairs of Europe, the CSCE is completely untried and untested. The CSCE has only recently acquired a more permanent institutional structure, and no-one yet knows quite how its agencies and ministerial meetings will work in practice. The CSCE has indeed won substantial support and acceptance for itself over the last decade and a half of its existence, but only as a forum for consultation and dialogue based on consensus and the unanimity principle. In attempting to change its fundamental character as a pan-European 'talking-shop', a more assertive CSCE could lose the legitimacy and acceptability it has won for itself over the years.

2. Apart from this reservation, the main criticisms of this model of European security are the same as traditional criticisms of any collective security arrangement – namely, how to make it work? How to ensure common and concerted action against an aggressor or aggressors, without thereby provoking generalised conflict? 'Collective security' assumes that all participating states agree to enforce general standards of acceptable behaviour. However, this is bound to cause controversy. What exactly is 'acceptable behaviour'? Furthermore, many disputes are highly complex and involved, with the rights and wrongs of the issue clouded by historical complexities and uncertain causality. These more general criticisms of collective security lead on to two more specific criticisms of the CSCE process.

3. The CSCE's decision-making mechanism is based on the unanimity principle. If this consensual principle is retained, it is hard to see how the CSCE could avoid paralysis at times of crisis, given the divergent interests of the 34.[24] If some form of 'qualified majority voting' (as Egon Bahr for one has suggested[25]) were to be adopted, the range of

permutations which could result is mind-boggling. Would the Soviet Union allow itself to be outvoted – any more than Britain, France or Germany, for that matter? Should Malta or the Vatican have the same weight in the decision-making processes as Germany or the USA? Should some (or all) states be given the right of veto, as on the UN Security Council? It is certainly most unlikely that the US Senate would agree to a collective security arrangement which committed American troops to combat by majority vote not subject to a US veto.[26] It is therefore difficult to imagine developing any effective decision-making process for the CSCE which could win the support of all 34 participating countries.

4. The CSCE has no enforcement mechanism.[27] To be effective, a system of collective security requires a means of being able to impose its decisions on recalcitrant states. This could be anything from diplomatic ostracism, through economic sanctions, up to and including military peacekeeping or intervention forces. The biggest problem is how to enforce collective security against a major 'rogue' country, as Henry Kissinger has pointed out.[28]

5. A further criticism of this concept of European collective security is that neither the historical precedents nor the contemporary models are very encouraging. The League of Nations was handicapped from the start by US isolationism, and collapsed in the face of German, Japanese and Italian aggression. The Concert of Europe has been put forward by some as a model, but as Robert Jervis has pointed out, it only functioned effectively for a relatively brief period of its existence (1815–23).[29] More contemporaneously, neither the Organisation of African Unity nor the Organisation of American States have shown themselves to be adequate to the task of ensuring collective security for their members.[30]

6. Finally, the foundations of a CSCE-based collective security structure are not of uniform strength.[31] They are strongest in Western Europe, less firm in East Central Europe, and weak in the Balkans and the Soviet Union. It is therefore risky to attempt to construct a uniform and symmetrical structure embracing all of Europe from the Atlantic to the Urals. Europe is likely to remain politically diverse and strategically fragmented for many decades to come, and therefore, it is argued, it is hard to envisage a single security structure which can address the security needs of countries as diverse as Turkey and Iceland, or Poland and Ireland.

IV

A CSCE-based European collective security system is the favoured goal of the governments of East Central Europe and the Soviet Union. It also enjoys increasing popularity in Germany and other parts of central Europe – especially on the left and centre-left of the political spectrum.

It is a much more visionary and radical model of European security than either an Atlanticist Europe or a West European Defence Community, and would require a far-reaching transformation of the behaviour and expectations of European states, their governments and their peoples. Its advantages are that it embraces all 34 participating states on an equal basis (even Albania has now expressed an interest in joining); it includes both superpowers; and it provides a possible means of actually addressing the security needs of the East Europeans – which the other two models of European security we considered fail to do.

The main problems with such a system of European collective security, however, stem from the difficulty of enforcing the decisions of the collective against recalcitrant states. Proposals for such a system of collective security need to address two key questions: an adequate decision-making process for the CSCE; and secondly, an effective enforcement mechanism. Until these issues are addressed, the CSCE is likely to remain a forum for consultation and dialogue, rather than an effective framework for collective security.

Notes

1. Gerard Holden, *The Warsaw Pact: Soviet Security and Bloc Politics* (London: Blackwell, 1989), p. 158.
2. See the *Guardian*, 7 April 1990.
3. The proposals of Jiri Dienstbier and Vaclav Havel have been described and expanded upon by Jiri Stepanovsky. See his two papers: (a) 'Future of the Warsaw Pact and the European Security', presented at the FOA Symposium on the future of NATO and the WTO in Stockholm, 11–13 June 1990; and (b) 'The Havel Plan: What Security Arrangements for Central Europe', presented at the CeSPI-Friedrich Ebert Stiftung international workshop on 'The New European Security Order', Rome, 19–20 July 1990.
4. Jan B. de Weydenthal, 'Changing Views on Security in Eastern Europe', in *Report on Eastern Europe*, 20 July 1990, pp. 45–47.
5. Speech by Markus Meckel, Minister of Foreign Affairs of the German Democratic Republic, delivered at the Royal Institute of International Affairs, London, 19 June 1990.
6. At the meeting of Mrs Thatcher and President Bush in Bermuda in April 1990; quoted in *The Independent*, 14 April 1990.
7. Quoted in the *Financial Times*, 14 May 1990, p. 2.
8. Quoted in the *Financial Times*, 11 May 1990, p. 2.
9. A CSCE meeting on human rights was held in Copenhagen from 5–28 June 1990. It agreed to a 19–page document on political democracy, human rights, the rule of law and the rights of national minorities. This meeting was also significant because, for the first time ever, Albania attended as an observer (having shortly before declared its desire to join the CSCE process). See the *Financial Times*, 29 June 1990.
10. The London Declaration on a Transformed North Atlantic Alliance, issued by Heads of State and Government participating in the meeting of the North Atlantic Council in London on 5–6 July 1990, paragraphs 21–22.

11. Quoted in *The Independent*, 20 November 1990.
12. Secretary of State James Baker, Address at the CSCE Conference on the Human Dimension at Copenhagen, 6 June 1990 (United States Information Service, US Embassy London, Official Text, 7 June 1990).
13. See for example his address to a special meeting of the WEU Assembly on 23 March 1990, documented in the Bulletin of the Press and Information Office of the FRG Government, 27 March 1990, p. 312.
14. In a major poll of German public opinion by Infratest, 59 per cent declared that they wanted to see 'particularly close relations' with the USSR, against only 44 per cent desiring the same thing with the USA. See the *Süddeutsche Zeitung*, 4 January 1991.
15. Mike Gapes, *After the Cold War: Building on the Alliances*, Fabian Tract 540 (London: Fabian Society, 1990), pp. 20–21.
16. Jane Sharp, 'Alternative European Futures', in a lecture given at the International Institute for Strategic Studies, 18 July 1988.
17. Hans-Joachim Schmidt, 'A Germany Neither Neutral nor Allied', in *Defense and Disarmament Alternatives*, vol. 3, no. 4 (April 1990), pp. 1–2.
18. As Jürgen Nötzold and Reinhardt Rummel have suggested, steps towards 'collective all-European security instruments could be a European Security Council, a contingent of multinational peacekeeping troops for Europe, and an all-European arbitration organ for the settlement of conflicts. The time is not yet ripe to consider and realise these proposals. First of all, processes of disarmament and reform must create better preconditions.' See their article, 'On the Way to a New European Order', in *Aussenpolitik*, vol. 41, no. 3 (1990), pp. 212–24 (p. 220).
19. Pierre Hassner, *Change and Security in Europe*, Part II, Adelphi Paper 49 (London: The Institute for Strategic Studies, 1968), pp. 2–3.
20. Karl Birnbaum and Ingo Peters, 'The CSCE: a Reassessment of its Role in the 1980s', in *Review of International Studies*, vol. 16, no. 4 (October 1990), pp. 305–19.
21. Bruce Kent, 'Vision of a New Europe', *New European*, vol. 3, nos. 2/3 (Summer/Autumn 1990), pp. 13–16.
22. Nicholas Henderson, 'One Germany Will Still Leave Two Europes', in *The Independent*, 18 April 1990.
23. This formulation is used by Pierre Hassner, *Change and Security in Europe*, p. 31.
24. 'The Dream of Europax', *The Economist*, 7 April 1990, pp. 14–15.
25. Egon Bahr, for example, suggested in June 1990 that the CSCE should be able to send an armed force into action to settle a European dispute by a 'qualified majority vote'; see 'CSCE, OAU, OAS, etc.', *The Economist*, 1 September 1990, p. 21.
26. Hans Binnendijk, 'How Bush Can Help Build a New Europe', *The Times*, 3 April 1990.
27. Timothy Garton Ash, 'The New Continental Drift', *The Independent*, Thursday 1 March 1990, p. 27.
28. 'A system of general collective security has historically proved useless against the biggest threat to peace – a major rogue country', Henry Kissinger, *The Washington Post*, 15 April 1990.
29. Robert Jervis, 'Security Regimes', in *International Organization*, vol. 36, no. 2 (Spring 1982), pp. 357–78 (pp. 362–68).

30. 'Organisation of European Unity', *The Economist*, 14 July 1990, p. 13.
31. Lawrence Freedman, 'Architecture with Eurovision', *The Independent*, Thursday 8 March 1990.

12

Scenario D:
L'Europe des Etats

The preceding three scenarios all have one feature in common. They all assume that the post-cold war security system in Europe will be built around pivotal institutional structures – either a reformed NATO, a West European Defence Community centred on the EC, or an institutionalised CSCE. They all therefore tend to envisage a European system which incorporates the features of an 'architectural' structure – solidity, stability, firmness, order. This final scenario, however, posits a Europe without cohesive blocs, military alliances or multilateral security structures. A Europe, in other words, in which the 'European idea' does not assume institutional form, and in which there is limited faith in the value of supranational forms of integration.

In this *Europe des Etats*, the Warsaw Pact has collapsed; NATO has gone the way of SEATO, CENTO and the WEU of the 1960s and 1970s; America no longer remains committed to the collective defence of West Europe through NATO, although it retains important bilateral security arrangements with countries such as, for example, Britain, Germany, Turkey and Italy; the European Community has completed its internal market and expanded to include new members, but has made no substantial progress towards political union or a single currency; West European security cooperation remains constrained by national differences; and a partially institutionalised CSCE, still based on the unanimity principle, has failed to develop as an effective forum for collective security. The result of these developments is a bloc-free, more fragmented Europe, in which the continued strength and vitality of the nation-state in Western Europe is complemented by the rise of nationalism in the East.

At the heart of this scenario is a neutral Germany, no longer integrated in NATO, and free to act as a 'wanderer between East and West'. In this fragmented and polycentric Europe of autonomous nation-states, security would no longer be guaranteed by multinational alliance structures or collective security arrangements, but by a looser and more fluid pattern of bi- and multilateral security agreements and non-aggression pacts. At the core of these new security arrangements would be a series of 'Eastern Locarno Treaties', between Germany and its neighbours to the east. At the same time, new bilateral relationships would have developed around

Germany and with Germany, as states seek to establish a new equilibrium on the continent. This would mean a reversion to the logic of traditional polycentric 'checkerboard' politics, with shifting patterns of alliances, multipolar instability and rival nationalisms. Europe would thus once again return to the pre-1945 pattern of balance of power politics, but in the context of a continent transformed by economic interdependence and nuclear deterrence.

I

This scenario of Europe in 2010 is very much inspired by De Gaulle's notion of *l'Europe de l'Atlantique à l'Oural* – a Europe transcending the bloc system derived (as the French would have it) from the 1945 Yalta conference, and in which the bipolar hegemony of the two superpowers is replaced by a new political and security arrangement based on European nation-states. Cooperation in this *Europe des Etats* would be based on inter-governmental agreement, rather than supranational integration. This arrangement, De Gaulle felt, would shift power to middle-ranking countries like France, especially given its possession of nuclear weapons.[1] Such notions have now been revived by France's Gaullist Party, the RPR (*Rassemblement pour la République*), which in December 1990 came out against what were perceived to be the federalist schemes of President Mitterrand and Jacques Delors.[2]

A Europe without the blocs has also been the long-standing goal of many in the peace movement.[3] They believed that, freed from the hegemony of the superpowers, and without the constraints of the blocs, a new, peaceful equilibrium between the European states could be achieved. A denuclearised Europe could then base its military security on some form of 'defensive defence', whilst making extensive use of political cooperation to diffuse potential conflicts and build mutual trust.

This fourth scenario envisages a situation in which the security 'system' in Europe has fragmented, and become increasingly polycentric, pluralistic and diverse – largely as a result of the fading of the old East–West divide, and the emergence of a more diffuse and fragmented security agenda. It assumes NATO has lost its cohesiveness, perhaps as a result of Germany leaving the integrated military command and asking all allied troops to leave its territory. In this *Europe des Etats*, the EC remains an important forum of economic integration and intergovernmental cooperation, but the grander schemes for political and economic union have long since been abandoned. In this context, the emphasis would be on expanding the Community to include new members, rather than on 'deepening' its supranational political integration. Similarly, although the CSCE would have a permanent institutional structure with regular ministerial meetings and a number of specialist agencies, it would remain a centre for consultation and dialogue, rather than collective security.

With the fragmentation of the European security system, regional and sub-regional forms of cooperation and conflict will reassert themselves. Western Europe will remain the 'core' area of the continent, in terms of the high degree of economic interdependence within the region, and the intensity of its informal social and cultural exchanges. However, the countries bordering the Western Mediterranean – Spain, Italy, France and Portugal (given its proximity to the region) will deepen their bi- and multilateral forms of security and defence cooperation, in the light of their common security problems arising from economic and demographic trends on the North Atlantic littoral; the unpredictable behaviour of radical states like Libya; and the spread of Islamic fundamentalism.

In central Europe, a German-dominated *Mitteleuropa* will inevitably emerge, given Germany's economic hegemony and cultural influence. In response to this, regional forms of cooperation in the Baltic area and between the countries of the old Habsburg empire will be strengthened, as neighbouring countries seek to develop alternative centres of gravity and influence to that of Germany. Such regional groupings could include a modern-day version of the 'Hanseatic League' around the Baltic Sea, and the Italian-led 'Pentagonale' grouping in south-central Europe. In the East, this scenario envisages the development of a much looser confederation in the Soviet Union, with individual republics deepening their bilateral relations with regional neighbours – ie, the Baltic Republics with their Nordic neighbours, the Ukraine with Poland, and Azerbaijan with Turkey. The most problematical area would be the Balkans, given the ethnic, national, religious and political rivalries in the region. Here traditional conflicts could reassert themselves – for example, the Macedonian problem – despite the attempts to establish high-level political consultations amongst the six Balkan countries. New friendships could also develop in the face of common enemies – for example, between Greece and Bulgaria, given their common mistrust of Turkey.

In this situation, the development of regional and sub-regional forms of cooperation would be accompanied by the establishment of a tangle of shifting bipolar alliances, reminiscent of the turn of the century. The aim of much of the diplomacy in this *Europe des Etats* would be to establish a 'balance and concert between Gauls, Germans and Slavs'.[4] France, for example, will be concerned to reconstruct old alliances to 'contain' Germany. This will mean the cultivation of France's traditional links with East European countries like Poland and Romania; the establishment of a new 'entente cordiale' with Western Europe's other nuclear power, Great Britain; and closer diplomatic and political ties with the Soviet Union. At the same time, Germany itself will be subject to growing pressures to balance its substantial economic and political links with

Western Europe (above all, with France), whilst extending its influence in *Mitteleuropa*, the Baltic and the Soviet Union. The Soviet–German relationship will be of particular importance in this *Europe des Etats*. After unification, Germany is the only Western country with an 'organic' economic relationship with the Soviet Union (given the legacy of former Soviet–GDR industrial and technological cooperation). Many Soviets and Germans argue that a close bilateral relationship between their countries is the 'natural' state of affairs, given their common geostrategic interests. This will raise the spectre of a new 'Rapallo' between Germany and the USSR – a perennial concern of both the French and East European countries like Poland and Czechoslovakia. Italy will want to strengthen its regional influence in south-central Europe and the Balkans, through such bodies as the Pentagonale. Meanwhile Britain may remain somewhat aloof from continental affairs, whilst cultivating its 'special relationship' with the USA and the Commonwealth. Enoch Powell has even suggested that Britain will have a particularly strong geopolitical community of interests with the Soviet Union, given that they are both peripheral European countries with an interest in maintaining a balance in the central European heartlands.

Security arrangements in this model of Europe would be based on national military capabilities and a multipolar system of defence agreements and non-aggression pacts, rather than on collective defence alliances like NATO, the WTO or the WEU. This would tend to produce a complex pattern of overlapping and criss-crossing security relationships throughout Europe.[5] At the core of this multifaceted and loosely knit structure would be a series of Eastern 'Locarno Treaties' between Germany and its eastern neighbours, similar to those of the inter-war period. These arrangements could be supplemented by the creation of a number of nuclear and chemical weapons free zones, and by zones of disengagement – perhaps involving the Baltic area, central Europe and the Balkans. Along with the Locarno Treaties, a further historical parallel would be Bismarck's diplomatic creation of a system of defensive multipolar alliances. In modern-day terms, this could mean, for example, that France, Germany and the USA would guarantee German security against the Soviet Union, whilst at the same time, these three nations would guarantee Soviet security against an attack by Germany.[6]

In this situation, countries like France, Britain and the USSR might place greater reliance on nuclear deterrence, hoping that a multipolar nuclear stand-off might contribute to the overall security of the continent. The existence of nuclear weapons would certainly contribute to the prevention of major large-scale wars in the region, but has three main failings. First, it would not prevent limited wars, national and ethnic unrest or economically generated conflicts. Second, it would not protect the USSR from the economic colonialisation of its peripheries, or from ethnic separatism (both of which are significant Soviet security concerns). Third, one major power, Germany, does not belong to the nuclear club. In this situation, the prospect of a future generation in Germany wanting to acquire nuclear weapons – with all the unease that this might cause in Europe – could not be discounted (although it remains an unlikely development).[7]

As we have seen, in this Europe of independent nation-states, a united Germany will play a pivotal role. As the divisions of the post-war period gradually heal, Germany's geographical location in the heart of the continent is already giving it a crucial role in the new Europe. As the strongest economic and financial power in an *Europe des Etats*, Germany would wield enormous influence. This would make it the object of considerable suspicion and concern. Germany would find itself having to balance its relations with the West with those to its East – doomed, perhaps, to play the role of 'wanderer' between East and West. In this unsettling situation, Europe could find itself having to face an old historical dilemma – how to accommodate a country with the energy and ambition of Germany at the heart of a loosely knit and polycentric Europe?

II

A European security system based on the old Gaullist idea of a bloc-free *Europe des Etats* is popular amongst those in Europe who believe in the continued viability and efficacy of the nation-state. The advantages claimed for this bloc-free and fragmented security system are as follows:

1. To begin with, it is argued that such a Europe would correspond to the historical diversity and pluralism of the European peoples. A Europe of individual nation-states, cooperating together without the constraints of supranational institutions, could provide the best guarantee of the national sovereignty, political independence and cultural diversity of the continent's varied peoples. This position has been frequently expounded by Margaret Thatcher,[8] and by the nationalist right's more articulate and intellectual elder spokesmen, such as Enoch Powell. Mr Powell has suggested that 'the Europe of the blocs is being replaced by the Europe of independent sovereign states', and that the old vision of a West European political unit needs to be replaced by that of 'a new and realistic policy of co-operation between independent sovereign states'. He argues that for the first time since the rise of Prussian imperialism in the last third of the nineteenth century, a 'Europe of the nations' is becoming possible. The EC therefore has to develop 'in a manner which matches the other movements that are going on in Europe, the re-emergence of independent sovereign states in East and Central Europe

and the consequent realignment of the two Germanies with one another and with the rest of the European nations'.[9]

Similarly, right-wing pressure groups like the Bruges Group and the Adam Smith Institute argue that the economic prosperity of the continent does not depend on the creation of political union within the EC. They believe that Europe's material welfare can best be provided within a free market without _dirigiste_ and interventionist political structures. They therefore tend to advocate the extension of the EC to include new members from EFTA and Eastern Europe, in order to dilute the drive for deeper political integration.[10]

2. It is also argued that this scenario would best correspond to the more diffuse and varied security agenda in Europe after the cold war. Regional problems such as political instability in the Balkans, population trends in North Africa or ethnic conflict in Eastern Europe, for example, will affect countries like Ireland, Austria or Norway very differently. It is thus mistaken to expect a pan-European response, or even a common response by the EC, NATO or the WEU. Regional or sub-regional groupings are therefore much more appropriate, and when necessary, these could be supplemented by temporary forms of intergovernmental cooperation between European states.

3. At the same time, a Europe free of superpower hegemony and the constraints of the bloc system would be free to develop extensive forms of regional or sub-regional development. European governments could abandon any pretence towards constructing either a pan-European collective security order or supranational organisations, and could instead concentrate on developing specific forms of intergovernmental cooperation with their immediate neighbours and traditional friends. In fact, this _Europe des Etats_ could well be a Europe of several competing blocs, rather than a Europe of individual nation-states. New forms of economic, political, security, environmental and cultural cooperation might develop in central Europe (based on the old Habsburg Empire); in the Balkans; in southern Europe (between those countries which border on the Mediterranean, such as Spain, Italy and France); and in the Baltic (including Poland and the three Baltic Republics). At the same time, individual European countries would be free to cultivate their own specific relations with the external world. Spain, for example, could invest more energy in developing its relations with Latin and Central America; France, its traditional ties with North Africa; and Britain its links with the Commonwealth and its 'special relationship' with the USA.

4. It is argued that this _Europe des Etats_ avoids the danger of a more deeply integrated EC being dominated by Germany, the power it is meant to contain.[11] The attempt to 'rein in' a unified Germany by developing supranational forms of political and economic decision-making within the Community might mean, it is alleged, that the other eleven EC

members find themselves being dragged long in the wake of a powerful German economy. In France, this argument has been forcefully made by the Gaullist RPR. In Britain, both Margaret Thatcher and Nicholas Ridley have argued that it is far more likely that a united Germany would be dominant in a federated Europe – by virtue of its 80m population – than in the Europe of sovereign nation-states they would prefer to see.

5. Finally, it is argued that an *Europe des Etats* would not necessarily mean a return to the instabilities of the old pre-war 'balance of power' system, for four reasons: first, because there is a much higher degree of interdependence in Europe today than in 1939 or 1914 – economic interdependence, as well as cultural, political and social; second, because of the existence of bodies like the EC (even if it doesn't develop into a fully fledged economic and political union), which institutionalises economic interdependence between West European countries; third, because of the transformation in political culture in Europe today – Europeans, particularly in western and central Europe, are more prosperous, democratic and tolerant, and less aggressive, chauvinistic and nationalistic than they tended to be in the first half of the century; and finally, because Europe is now living in a post-Clausewitzian world, thanks to the existence of nuclear weapons. As long as nuclear deterrence continues to underpin the stability and security of Europe, it is claimed, the worst excesses of balance of power politics can be avoided.

III

Despite the arguments in favour of a loosely bound, polycentric *Europe des Etats*, critics of this model of European security tend to outnumber its advocates. They make a number of trenchant criticisms of it in terms of its potential for preserving the security and stability of the continent:

1. The military disengagement of the USA from Europe and the demise of NATO, it is argued, would leave the Soviet Union as by far the largest conventional and nuclear power on the Eurasian continent. Even if the USSR were to break up, Russia itself would still have a massive military potential, which it might seek to use for political purposes. The smaller East European countries would be left dangerously exposed to the Soviet Union (or even to Russia on its own), and many in Western Europe would have considerable grounds for concern – especially on the flanks, given the proximity of countries like Sweden or Turkey to the Soviet Union. An *Europe des Etats*, therefore, would not provide a reassuring security system in Europe in the event of the collapse of the reform process in the USSR, given that country's massive military might.

2. An economically and politically powerful united Germany, which was no longer firmly bound into NATO, and which was not contained by a tightly integrated European Community, would – it is argued – be

of concern to Germany's neighbours, friends and former enemies alike. The Deutschmark would be the dominant currency in Western Europe, and German capital would exert a hegemonic role throughout Eastern Europe and much of the Balkans. A strong and united German state might be susceptible to bouts of assertiveness and nationalist pride, and may find it hard at times to reconcile its interests in the West with its interests in the lands to its East. Franco-German tensions could well increase, and East European fears of 'German revanchism' – particularly in Poland and Czechoslovakia – would almost certainly be rekindled. Without broader European structures to integrate and channel the energy of a dynamic new Germany, it would be difficult to maintain a stable balance in Europe in the face of a renascence of German power and influence. This could then revive the old German 'nightmare of coalitions' which was the ultimate downfall of the diplomatic arrangement created by Bismarck's system of defensive multipolar alliances.

3. A Europe of independent nation-states could lead to the 'Balkanisation' of European politics, and to the multipolar instabilities of the old pre-war 'balance of power' system, which ultimately resulted in the disasters of 1870, 1914 and 1939. Europe is strewn with ancient antagonisms, past feuds and unresolved *irredenta*. In an *Europe des Etats* – without firm supranational structures that can help institutionalise cooperation – nationalist rivalry, envy and mistrust could well increase. To rely on loose forms of limited intergovernmental cooperation might not be sufficient to generate a durable commitment to long-term cooperation. Without formal structures for collective decision-making and common action, national rivalries could re-emerge in Western Europe. For example, the small and medium powers in Western Europe – Italy, and the Scandinavian, Iberian and Benelux countries – may grow to distrust the larger powers – France, Germany and the UK – whilst these three powers could begin to distrust each other or any combination of the other two. Above all, Germany would be the object of mistrust, jealousy and suspicion. In this situation, the reconciliation of the post-war period could be badly eroded.

In other parts of the continent, there are barely suppressed national and ethnic conflicts – for example, between Germany and Poland, Greece and Turkey, Yugoslavia and Bulgaria, Hungary and Romania, and Romania and the Soviet Union – and in a fragmented and polycentric Europe, these could lead to the resurgence of inter-state and inter-communal disputes. Furthermore, it should not be forgotten that many of these countries are in the Balkans or south-eastern Europe, an area which has proven to be the tinder-box of more explosive Europe-wide conflicts in the past. It is therefore perhaps no surprise that one Turkish official has argued that, 'To go back to Metternich and the Balance of Power would be very damaging and risky for the continent's future.' Calling for a multilateral collective security system in post-communist Europe, he insisted that, 'We don't want to see countries trying to balance each other out in a system of bilateral arrangements.'[12]

4. The emergence of a bloc-free and polycentric Europe in place of the old alliance systems would enormously complicate the process of arms control negotiation and verification. The CFE and CDE negotiations in Vienna have been facilitated by a process of intra-alliance consultation and consensus-building. Without this, it would be much more difficult to negotiate further arms control and confidence-building measures on a broader European basis. Whilst it might be possible to negotiate some limited regional or bilateral arms control agreements or CSBMs, wider multilateral agreements would be much more difficult to negotiate, implement and verify.

5. A Europe which remained politically fragmented would, it is argued, be a diplomatically weak one. In an increasingly multipolar global world, it would at best be an 'economic giant but a political dwarf' – what *The Economist* has dubbed a 'headless superpower'.[13] A Europe of sovereign and independent nation-states – only loosely bound together by free trade and intergovernmental cooperation – would, many argue, be one which failed to live up to its promise and potential. It would lack the political cohesion to speak with one voice in international forums, and would tend to be inward-looking and parochial – too preoccupied with its own internal problems to concern itself with broader, global developments. Such a weak and fragmented Europe would be susceptible to outside interference and manipulation by stronger powers, or even by 'rogue' countries such as Iraq or Libya. It would also be vulnerable in the event of a break-down in cooperation with the Soviet Union, and the emergence of a stronger and more aggressive USSR.[14] Critics of an *Europe des Etats*, therefore, suggest that it would leave Europe weak and fragmented, and exposed to both external security challenges and to the unpredictable risks of resurgent nationalism from within.

6. Finally, as with the model of a European collective security system, the historical precedents for this scenario are not reassuring. Balance of power arrangements have proved notoriously unstable and risky. Neither the Locarno Treaties of the inter-war years nor Bismarck's system of defensive multipolar alliances prevented the outbreak of continent-wide conflict. In military and strategic terms, it might not be possible to limit alliance commitments to defensive action. In checkerboard multipolar alliance patterns, it may be necessary to honour defence commitments with offensive military actions, in order to attack an aggressor in the rear, or liberate occupied territory. Developing this capability, however, could exacerbate the security fears of other states, thereby undermining the pacific intentions of purportedly defensive strategies.[15] Even if nuclear deterrence helps mitigate some of these specific military concerns, the politics that these kind of balance of power arrangements tend to breed

could prove equally as destabilising, given the danger of resurgent nationalism, economic rivalry and long-suppressed historical animosities.

IV

In this scenario, therefore, little faith is invested in supranational forms of integration (such as the EC), multinational peacetime alliances (such as NATO and the Warsaw Pact) or pan-European collective security regimes. Instead, a new European security system would be founded on the continued centrality and vitality of the nation-state, in a Europe free from superpower hegemony and bipolar bloc structures. In many respects, this would correspond to De Gaulle's notion of *l'Europe de l'Atlantique à l'Oural*. Europe would thus be polycentric, fragmented and pluralistic, with political and strategic relationships characterised by a tangle of shifting bipolar alliances and regional groupings.

The debate on the viability and desirability of this model of an *Europe des Etats* revolves around three main areas of contention. To begin with, this scenario raises the familiar question of the balance to be struck between national sovereignty and supranational integration, in an age of complex interdependence and the growing permeability of national borders. Second, it raises the question of how best to contain and channel the energies of a united Germany in the new, post-cold war Europe. Can German economic might and political influence best be countered in a Europe of autonomous nation-states, or by constructing supranational institutions of pooled sovereignty? Finally, would an *Europe des Etats* mean a return to pre-war balance of power politics, with all its old national rivalries and multipolar instability? Or would this be prevented by nuclear deterrence, economic interdependence, institutions like the EC or the Council of Europe, and the changed political culture of contemporary Europe?

This model of European security has fewer advocates than any of the three previous scenarios. Nevertheless, it could emerge less by conscious plan than by default, in the event of the demise of NATO, and the failure to construct either a West European Defence Community or a pan-European collective security system. In this situation, many long-dormant patterns of both cooperation and conflict in Europe could re-emerge, albeit in a continent deeply marked by economic interdependence, nuclear deterrence and the spread of democracy.

Notes

1. See Jolyon Howorth, 'Atlanticism, Gaullism and the Community of Europe: The Debate Between Security and History in the Post War World', *Foreign Policy*, no. 65 (Winter 1986–87).

2. See 'Gaullist Demonology Resurrected', in the *Financial Times*, 10 December 1990, p. 30.
3. Mary Kaldor, 'Beyond the Blocs: Defending Europe the Political Way', in *World Policy*, vol. 1, no. 1 (Fall 1983), pp. 1–21, and E.P. Thompson, 'Beyond the Blocs', in *END Journal*, no. 12 (October–November 1984), pp. 12–15.
4. Pierre Hassner, *Change and Stability in Europe*, Part I, Adelphi Paper 49 (London: Institute of Strategic Studies, 1968), p. 8.
5. For a discussion of the logic of alliance patterns in a multipolar system, see Thomas J. Christensen and Jack Snyder, 'Chain Gangs and Passed Bucks: Predicting Alliance Patterns in Multipolarity', in *International Organization*, vol. 44, no. 2 (Spring 1990), pp. 137–68.
6. See Jack Snyder, 'Averting Anarchy in the New Europe', *International Security*, vol. 14, no. 4 (Spring 1990), pp. 5–41 (p. 14).
7. Indeed, John Mearsheimer has argued that the acquisition of a nuclear capability by the Germans should be encouraged as a factor of stability in an otherwise turbulent Europe. See his provocative article, 'Back to the Future: Instability in Europe after the Cold War', in *International Security*, vol. 15, no. 1 (Summer 1990), pp. 5–56.
8. Her last major statement of her 'little-Englander' views on Europe whilst Prime Minister was her *Financial Times* article, 'My Vision of Europe Open and Free', published on 19 November 1990.
9. Enoch Powell, 'Towards a Europe of Sovereign Nations', in *The Independent*, 6 September 1989.
10. See the report published by the Adam Smith Institute on 16 February, 1990, which was reported in *The Independent* on 17 February 1990, p. 6. The Bruges Group have published a number of occasional papers on this and related themes, including, *'Good Europeans?'*, by Alen Sked (November 1989); *Is National Sovereignty a Big Bad Wolf?*, by Stephen Haseler et al. (February 1990); and *A Europe for the Europeans* by François Goguel et al. (April 1990).
11. See Frédéric Bozo and Jérôme Paolini, 'Trois Allemagnes, deux Europes et la France', *Politique Etrangère*, no. 1 (1990), pp. 119–38.
12. Quoted in the *Financial Times*, special supplement on Turkey, 24 May 1990, p. iv.
13. *The Economist*, 16 December 1989, p. 17.
14. Jürgen Nötzold and Reinhardt Rummel have argued that the least favourable variant of future developments in European security would be a combination of (a) stagnation in West European integration, and (b) the simultaneous collapse of the Soviet reform process. See their article 'On the Way to a New European Order' in *Aussenpolitik*, vol. 41, no. 3 (1990), pp. 212–24 (p. 224).
15. See Christensen and Snyder's article, 'Chain Gangs and Passed Bucks: Predicting Alliance Patterns in Multipolarity'.

13
Conclusion

1989 and 1990 have been years of astounding change in Europe. The comfortable assumptions of nearly four decades have been abruptly overturned, as the seemingly immutable structures of post-war Europe have broken asunder. This period of accelerated historical change has witnessed the sorts of revolutionary transformations which have only previously occurred as the by-product of war or bloody insurrection. After four decades of East–West confrontation, a series of historical milestones marking the end of the post-war era have finally been passed. One such milestone was the signing of the historic 'two plus four' agreement in September 1990, which cleared the way for German unification. The signing of the treaty was the occasion for some stirring rhetoric: the British Foreign Secretary, Douglas Hurd, declared that 'This is the end of one road but also a milestone on a new road to a new and harmonious world order.' For the Soviet side, Eduard Shevardnadze argued that 'We are going through an emotional and historic event. We have drawn the line under World War Two, and we have started counting the time of the new age.' In a similar vein, Secretary of State James Baker declared that, 'We consign to history forever one of the most corrosive conflicts of this century.'[1]

German unification has been but one – if not perhaps the most momentous and unexpected – of the historic events which have transformed the continent in recent years. Of similar importance are the reform programme of Mikhail Gorbachev, the collapse of communism in Eastern Europe, and the deepening of the integration process in the European Community. Indeed, many of the changes in Europe as a whole can be attributed to the interaction of Soviet *perestroika* in the East with the process of deepening integration in Western Europe. Together, they have produced a dynamic new phase in European history. The post-war period – characterised by four decades of East–West conflict – is now over. With the fall of the 'iron curtain', a new chapter in the long and frequently turbulent history of the 'old continent' has begun.

The transformation of the political and strategic situation in Europe has rendered obsolete existing security relationships in the continent. The post-war security system – so stable yet so unacceptable – was characterised by the dominance of the two superpowers within their respective alliance structures; a divided Germany; nuclear deterrence; and a small but distinct group of neutral and non-aligned countries. For both East and West, the overwhelming security concern was preventing a full-scale military conflict in Europe. This resulted in the biggest concentration of conventional and nuclear forces in one region the world has ever seen.

The danger of a major continental conflagration is now a very remote prospect. There are few realistic scenarios in which a large-scale military conflict involving leading European powers is conceivable.[2] Thus there are considerable grounds for optimism about the future prospects for peace and stability in Europe. The continent is no longer split into two hostile and antagonistic political-military blocs; political relations between the superpowers are increasingly characterised by cooperation and constructive dialogue; and there is little reason to fear a return to either the systemic divisions of the cold war, or the Great Power rivalries of the pre-war years. Moreover, the foundations for a new Europe are being built as pluralist democracies and market economies are constructed – albeit painfully at times – in the East. At the same time, the CFE Treaty – which builds on the achievements of the 1986 CSBM Agreements and the 1987 INF Treaty – is an important contribution to the process of reducing the level of military confrontation in Europe. Finally, the CSCE Summit in November 1990 has demonstrated the font of goodwill which now pervades the diplomatic scene in Europe, and the widespread desire to fashion a continent which will finally be 'whole and free'.

Nevertheless, this does not mean that Europe will soon become an oasis of peace and stability in an otherwise turbulent world. To begin with – as the Gulf crisis has so vividly illustrated – the security of Europe is vulnerable to challenges arising on the peripheries of the continent, or through the interaction of Europe with other regions of the world. Of these so-called 'out-of-area' risks and challenges, the most significant are: threats to both maritime routes and supplies of raw materials, strategic resources and markets; the spread of ballistic missile technology, coupled with the proliferation of nuclear and chemical weapon capabilities; Third World poverty, with its attendant social, economic and political problems (including large-scale population movements and economically motivated immigration); and international terrorism.

Furthermore, Europe itself is not without its own indigenous sources of conflict. If the bipolar bloc system had one saving grace, it was that it contained many of the deep-seated national, ethnic, religious and political tensions which have plagued the continent for centuries. With the demise of the cold war, many of these historical animosities and pent-up frustrations have been released. Of particular concern is the rising tide of nationalism in much of Eastern Europe and the Balkans, coupled with a severe economic crisis and fragile political institutions. This problem is especially acute for the Soviet Union and Yugoslavia – both multinational states faced with the collapse of their post-war communist systems of government. On top of these problems are two further major intra-European security concerns. Firstly, the residual military strength of the Soviet Union, which retains substantial conventional and nuclear forces. And secondly, the worries that many have about the consequences of German unification for the stability and equilibrium of the continent.

Thus although the old divisions between a 'capitalist West' and a 'communist East' no longer blight the politics of Europe, there is still a need for a new system of European security which can preserve peace and stability throughout the continent. Any future European security system must be able to manage – and, if possible, resolve – a much more diffuse and multifaceted series of security 'challenges', in the context of an increasingly polycentric and heterogeneous continent. This is likely to prove a much more difficult task than managing what was essentially a bipolar system of European security. This in turn will place much higher demands on the diplomatic skills and statesmanlike qualities of political elites in both East and West.[3] Many of the future security concerns of the Europeans will be economic and political in nature – reflecting the declining saliency of military force as a currency of power in a continent increasingly marked by complex interdependence and common security. Nevertheless, the possibility of limited outbreaks of armed conflict – however slight – cannot be entirely ruled out, especially given the nationalist turbulence and economic problems which are rife in much of Eastern Europe, the Balkans and the Soviet Union.

Security 'Architecture' in Europe

The widespread belief that a new system of security for Europe is urgently required has given rise to an intense debate on what is frequently described as the future security 'architecture' of the continent.[4] The proclivity towards the use of 'architectural' metaphors in the discussion on security issues has a long pedigree – from talk of a 'European pillar' and East–West 'bridges', to the 'common European house' and a 'fortress Europe'. Nonetheless, the use of architectural images is in some ways misleading and inappropriate. It implies the existence of an architect with a conscious plan; it suggests fixed, permanent structures, designed to serve clearly defined sets of purposes; and, as Lawrence Freedman has argued, 'It reflects the tendency to elevate stability as the dominant value in discussions of security.'[5] Thus although it is often difficult to escape using architectural metaphors when discussing European security, it should be noted that the use of more organic images – perhaps drawn from the disciplines of biology, evolutionary science or geology – might be more appropriate. Indeed, T.C.Shelling's words of over twenty years ago are even more apposite today: 'The time for the Grand Schemes is over. We are moving out of our architectural period in Europe into the age of manoeuvre.'[6]

The new structures of European security in the post-cold war world will therefore not be the result of any 'Grand Scheme' or prize competition between European security 'architects'. Many such schemes and architectural plans are now on offer in Europe – for example, Mikhail Gorbachev's 'Common European house'; President Bush's vision of a Europe 'whole and free'; President Mitterrand's 'European Confederation'; the notion of a 'European village' espoused by both Giscard D'Estaing[7] and the Norwegian Minister of Defence, Johan Jorgen Holst;[8] and Margaret Thatcher's vision of a Europe 'free' and 'open'.[9] But it is not the purpose of this concluding chapter, either to try and predict the future direction of institutional development in Europe, or to advocate a particular security model for the continent. Rather, it is fourfold: to outline some of the structural requirements of a new European security system; to specify the major trends and issues in European security; to consider the impact of the Gulf crisis on the future evolution of the European security system; and to suggest a series of principles which should underlie the construction of a new European order.

Towards a New European Order

What are the structural requirements of a new European security system? As with all political constructs, the central requirement is to find an adequate balance between firmness and flexibility. A new system of European security must be firm enough to contain future stresses and strains, arising from political instability in the East, national and ethnic tensions, economic problems, population movements and 'out-of-area' challenges. On the other hand, it must be flexible enough to respond to a wide range of security challenges arising from an increasingly complex and shifting security agenda. At the same time, it must be able to adapt to new conditions and changing circumstances.

The goal of this new European order should be to foster a continent at peace with itself and its neighbours, in which basic human rights are respected and the fruits of economic prosperity equitably distributed. A Europe, in other words, 'whole and free', in which disputes between and within European states are settled peacefully, within the framework of a legimate European peace order.

What this requires above all is the creation of a constructive synergy between the process of West European integration on the one hand, and that of overcoming the legacy of the East–West divide on the other. The central problem facing post-cold war Europe is how to forge an organic bond between the two halves of a continent severed by the 'iron curtain'. In the long term, Europe will not enjoy stability and a durable peace if the fall of the Berlin Wall is followed by the erection of a new 'silver curtain' to its east (perhaps along the Bug River – which marks the Polish–Soviet border) or south-east (either along the historical borders of the old Habsburg Empire, or running through the Balkans and dividing Christians from Muslims, or even Roman Catholics from Orthodox Christians). Given the severity of the mounting economic and political problems in Europe's East, there is a very real risk that a new division of Europe could emerge in the wake of the cold war. This time, however, the cause of the division would not be ideological or military, but economic and social – with all the attendant political, strategic and cultural problems that that would entail.[10]

The Future of the European Security System: Trends and Issues

In the course of this book, we have considered at some length the key factors determining the future of European security. It is now time to summarise our findings, and to outline some preliminary conclusions concerning future trends and issues in the European security system. These conclusions are as follows:

1. In any future structure of European security, three bodies will play a crucial role – the European Community, NATO and the CSCE. These three organisations will provide the structural core of the new European security system, with other bodies – such as the Council of Europe, EFTA, the WEU, the Pentagonale, the CMEA and the Warsaw Pact – playing a supporting or supplementary role. Some of these secondary bodies will perhaps fade away or be subsumed within other institutional structures: the prime candidates for this are the CMEA, the WTO and EFTA. Others – such as the Council of Europe[11] or the WEU – are likely to grow in importance. The character and structural dynamics of the new European order, however, will depend crucially on the division of functions between the EC, NATO and the CSCE. All three bodies will undoubtedly change, perhaps beyond recognition, but it is the relationship between them that will determine the overall shape of the new Europe.

2. The new European order will not emerge as the result of a conscious architectural plan, nor from any grand scheme in geostrategic engineering – however far-sighted and inspired Europe's self-styled security architects (such as Gorbachev, Mitterrand, Genscher or Delors) may be. Rather, the future morphology of the new Europe will be the result of series of *ad hoc* and largely pragmatic responses to specific crises, problems and challenges. The new European order, in other words, will tend to evolve

organically on a piecemeal and incremental basis, through a process of 'trial and error'. There is now a sort of 'free market' in institutions, in which existing organisations are competing to prove how well suited they are to dealing with specific problems. The clearest examples of this are the rivalry between the CSCE and the Council for Europe, and the efforts by the WEU to demonstrate its relevance to European security interests.[12] Furthermore, the scope for constructing new institutions in Europe is likely to be fairly limited, given that existing organisations are already jostling for space in a crowded institutional landscape. 'Occam's Razor'[13] is therefore likely to apply, except for some new bodies within the CSCE framework and some new economic structures for managing East–West economic relations.[14]

This suggests that the basic contours and distinguishing institutional features of the new European security system will be determined by how well existing institutions – above all the EC, NATO and the CSCE – respond to specific crises and security challenges. It will also depend on what sort of security risks and challenges appear on the policy agenda, and in what order. For example, if the security agenda is dominated by economic and social issues, then the relative importance of the EC will continue to grow; if national and ethnic tensions intensify, and the political entente between the major actors in Europe (ie, the USSR, Germany, the USA, France and the UK) continues, then the security responsibilities of the CSCE may be expanded; if, however, there is a recidivist backlash in the Soviet Union, then the relative importance of NATO (or perhaps the WEU) will be strengthened.

3. The major test of the new security system in Europe is not the Gulf crisis, but rather its response to the power vacuum which is developing in the old communist world, especially in the Balkans. The sudden implosion of communist power has unleashed a wave of nationalism and ethnic conflict, which – along with the savage fall in living conditions – threatens to overwhelm Eastern Europe's fragile democracies. Many now fear the 'Balkanisation' – still worse, the 'Lebanonisation' – of much of Eastern Europe and the Soviet Union.[15]

At the same time, the disintegration of the Warsaw Pact has left the East Europeans in a security limbo. Many now pin their hopes on a 'return to Europe', meaning a reorientation away from the Soviet Union towards the West. As a new European security system emerges, therefore, a series of major international re-alignments are likely to occur in Eastern Europe, affecting the totality of their political, economic and security relationships. One problem is that Western Europe's security organisations, NATO and the WEU, are of limited value in tackling the security problems of Eastern Europe and the Balkans. Any new security structures in Europe must therefore be able to address the specific security requirements of the East Europeans, and provide a resilient enough framework for containing the conflicts which threaten the peace and stability of the continent's East.

4. The most pressing question facing Europe in the 1990s is the future of the Soviet Union, and the place of that unhappy and troubled country in the political, economic and strategic structures of Europe. The USSR is now in an advanced state of decay: Mikhail Gorbachev's valiant attempt to reverse the steady decline of the Brezhnev years has precipitated a major political and economic crisis. In a situation of economic dislocation, nationalist unrest and political fragmentation, the very survival of the Soviet state is now in question. The domestic travails of the USSR will leave it weakened and potentially unstable, but the very size of the country – or even of its Slavic heartlands on their own – will mean that it will continue to cast a very long geopolitical shadow over Europe. Russia itself would still be a major European power, with a considerable conventional and nuclear military capability.

The fate of the Soviet Union is therefore the biggest unknown factor in the European security equation. The prospect facing the Soviet peoples is of a sustained period of domestic instability, perhaps lasting a generation or more. The Soviets themselves are uncertain about their real interests in Europe – as the debate between the latter-day 'Slavophiles' and 'Westernisers' illustrates all too clearly.[16] However, to exclude the Soviet Union from the process of European integration might engender a debilitating 'Versailles syndrome' in the USSR, leaving it embittered and vengeful. Widespread instability and disorder in a disintegrating Soviet Union would also not be in the interests of Europeans in either West or East. The problem facing the West is how to integrate the Soviet Union (or more precisely its constituent elements[17]) in the new Europe in ways that reinforce the Soviet domestic reform process, without at the same time compromising the security of other European states, or weakening the process of pan-European integration.

Europe and the Gulf Crisis

Saddam Hussein's invasion and annexation of Kuwait in August 1990 has provided the first major test of the post-cold war international system.[18] In doing so, it has illustrated the changing structure of international relations in the last decade of the twentieth century. At the time of writing the Gulf crisis has only had a limited and indirect impact on the nature of the emerging 'post-Yalta' security system in Europe itself. Nevertheless, the crisis illustrated both the strengths and weaknesses of existing European institutions, and the political character of the leading protagonists in the European security area. In the medium term, the Gulf crisis may accelerate certain trends in Europe (such as the development of a common foreign and security policy by the European Community), whilst slowing down others.

How have Europe's main security institutions responded to the Gulf crisis?

1. NATO

The provisions of the 1949 Washington Treaty – most importantly, the commitment to a concerted military response to aggression – do not apply to crises out of the North Atlantic area. Thus, although the Gulf crisis has been discussed within NATO, the Western military response has not been coordinated through the Alliance. Its only substantive role has been in guaranteeing the security of Turkey.[19]

The direct involvement of NATO in the Gulf war would perhaps ease the problems of multinational command and control, but it would generate enormous political problems. It would transform a regional crisis into a North–South conflict (between the Christian or secular West, and a Muslim Arab country); it would make it much more difficult to secure Soviet support and wider international collaboration; and it would precipitate a major debate within NATO countries on the Alliance's very legitimacy. As Karsten Voigt has argued, 'In the Gulf crisis, NATO is not the answer, because it is alien to the region. We must use the United Nations and other multilateral structures.'[20]

2. The European Community

As a 'civilian' body, with responsibility only for the 'economic and social' aspects of security, the EC has played no direct role in the American-led military build-up in the Gulf. Nevertheless, it has played a significant diplomatic, political and economic role. The EC was swift to respond to the Iraqi invasion, imposing economic sanctions on Iraq even before the UN Security Council resolution. It has also attempted to develop a coordinated EC response to the hostages (thereby implicitly introducing a principle of European citizenship), and to the closure of foreign embassies in Kuwait. Moreover, the Community has been forthcoming with financial aid for the front-line states in the Middle East, although it has ruled out direct economic assistance to the US military effort.

One problem for the EC has been the refusal of both Britain and France to coordinate their UN Security Council policies with their EC partners through the EPC. Both countries have stressed that their policies at the UN Security Council are national issues, and not the concern of the EC.

In the immediate future, the Gulf crisis is likely to bolster the arguments of those who believe that the EC must develop a common foreign and defence policy.[21] This view is particularly strong in France. Dominique Moisi (of IFRI), for example, has argued that 'If the gulf proved something, it is the need for a European security umbrella. ... Defence is vital for Europe's political self-definition. We must reinforce the EC by giving it this role, for it will not be strong without a clear security dimension.'[22]

3. *The WEU*

The Gulf crisis has once again given the WEU the chance to prove its value to the West Europeans as a convenient forum for coordinating their response to *ad hoc* 'out-of-area' crises. At a meeting in Paris on 21 August 1990, the WEU agreed to coordinate West European naval forces in the Gulf. This had the welcome effect of encouraging other West European countries – namely Italy, Spain and Belgium – to contribute naval forces to the Gulf, which they were only willing to do in the context of a multilateral West European effort. The WEU action proves an important political symbol of West European security cooperation.[23] Nevertheless, the WEU's military role is still rather limited: the WEU has no integrated military command, and can at best provide only a loose degree of West European military coordination.[24]

If the Gulf crisis has cast a spotlight on the strengths and weaknesses of Europe's security institutions, it has also demonstrated the political character of some of the key actors in Europe:

1. *The USA*

The Gulf crisis has shown that the USA is the only real superpower left in the world today. Unlike the USSR, it has the economic wherewithal (despite its budget and trade deficits) to back up its military strength. And unlike the emergent economic superpowers of Japan and the EC, it has global interests and concerns. This means that it is the only country with the political will and the military capacity to take the lead in international crises.

America's lead in organising the multinational military effort in the Gulf underlines the importance of good transatlantic relations for the stability of Europe itself. Whether or not US power has suffered from 'relative decline' and 'imperial over-stretch', America remains a powerful international actor, and a continued US political and military engagement in European affairs could act as a significant force for continental stability.

On the other hand, the Gulf crisis also shows that US power has indeed declined – at least in relative terms – over recent decades. Washington has been forced to request financial contributions from its prosperous Western allies, in order to help pay for the costs of the economic sanctions and military action. This means that the long-running 'burden-sharing' debate is likely to receive a new and possibly vicious twist.[25] At the same time, the Gulf crisis indicates that whilst the Americans are keen on 'burden-sharing', they are not so keen on involving their allies in decision-making. There is still a tendency for the USA to prefer unilateral action to multilateral consultation and coordination. Yet America's allies are likely to insist on the principle that 'he who pays the piper, calls the tune' – or at least, has a major say in what sort of music is played. This does not mean that close transatlantic relations are not in the interests of both the USA and the West Europeans – quite the contrary. But it does underline the fact that a 'new Atlanticism' must be based on real partnership and institutionalised consultation – and not on an American presumption that they are 'bound to lead'.[26]

2. The USSR

One of the most important lessons of the Gulf crisis is that the Soviet Union can no longer be seen simply as a rival and a competitor with the West. Rather, it is increasingly a collaborator and a partner of both Western Europe and the USA. Soviet behaviour in the UN Security Council; the shuttle diplomacy of Gorbachev's special envoy, Yevgeny Primakov; its close cooperation and consultation with the USA; and its regional diplomatic initiatives, have all revealed Moscow to be a constructive and responsible member of the international community.[27] The Soviet Union retains its distinctive concerns in the region, and has clearly been less happy to see the military option employed, but this is a position it has shared with France – a leading Western power. It is also significant for the management of future regional crises that the USSR has been particularly keen to see the multinational effort against Saddam Hussein coordinated through the United Nations, and has persistently advocated reviving the moribund UN Military Staff Committee.

3. The United Kingdom

From the very earliest hours of the Gulf crisis at the start of August 1990, President Bush and Prime Minister Thatcher cooperated closely together in coordinating a common international response to the Iraqi invasion. The rapid dispatch of British naval, air and later ground forces to the Gulf, and the important role the British Government has had in convincing the Europeans and others of the need for a firm response to Iraqi aggression, has resuscitated a 'special relationship' which otherwise seemed to wilt in the post-cold war thaw. The British Government seems to have utilised the Gulf crisis to reaffirm the closeness of Anglo-American relations, much to the chagrin of the French and the irritation of the Germans. Nevertheless, the overwhelming weight of Britain's economic and political interests increasingly lie in Europe, and however close Anglo-American military cooperation in 'out-of-area' conflicts in the Gulf may be, such a 'special relationship' cannot obviate the need for

Britain to play a more constructive and committed role in the process of European integration.

4. France

If the Gulf crisis has demonstrated that the traditional reflexes of British foreign policy (ie, close alignment with American foreign policy) are still very much alive, it has also exposed the idiosyncracies of post-war French foreign policy. Although France sent military forces to the Gulf, Paris made strenuous efforts to distance itself from Anglo-American initiatives. French military cooperation with the other multinational forces in the Gulf is minimal, and, like Britain, France has pursued a distinctly nationalistic position at the UN. In fact, the position of the French has frequently been closer to that of the Soviet Union than it has been to its NATO allies, America and Britain.

5. Germany

As the Gulf crisis unfolded in the autumn of 1990, German eyes were focused on a much more pressing domestic concern – completing the long-standing dream of national unification. The Bonn Government has supported economic and diplomatic sanctions against Saddam's regime, but its 1949 Constitution prevents it from deploying Bundeswehr troops out of the NATO area. Instead, Germany has been a generous supplier of substantial financial and material support to the multinational effort in the Gulf.[28] At the same time, Hans-Dietrich Genscher has been active in seeking to fashion a common EC diplomatic response to the crisis.

One result of the Gulf crisis for Germany, however, has been to provoke a lively debate on the possibility of revising or reinterpreting the *Grundgesetz* in order to allow German military forces to be deployed abroad in support of UN peacekeeping operations. Both Hans-Dietrich Genscher and Gerhard Stoltenberg, for example, have made clear their determination to see such a change in the Basic Law, whilst Chancellor Kohl has declared that the constitutional ban on involvement in UN peacekeeping operations was 'in no way tolerable for the future'.[29] Nevertheless, such a change in the status of the Bundeswehr is bound to provoke serious domestic controversy within Germany.

Ten Principles for a New European Security System

The Gulf crisis has focused attention on Europe's vulnerability to external security challenges, and has stimulated the debate on Europe's security needs in a world 'beyond containment'. As we have already seen, however, the new European security system is not likely to emerge as the result of any grand scheme or 'architectural plan', but as part of an organic process of incremental change, in response to specific crises and security challenges. I will therefore avoid concluding this study of European security by attempting to predict future trends, or outlining yet another vision of Europe in 2010. Rather, I will suggest a set of principles which I believe should underpin the construction of a new security system. These ten principles would, I believe, facilitate the gradual development of a durable and just peace order in Europe. To use (despite my earlier caveats!) the architectural metaphors which are so prevalent in the debate on security issues, these ten points could be seen as the strategic equivalent of HRH The Prince of Wales' ten points on contemporary architecture in his book, *A Vision of Britain*. My ten points are not meant to provide an architectural blue-print for European security, but to suggest a series of guidelines on security issues which could help Europe's policy-makers reach decisions which contribute to the process of forging a continent 'whole and free'.

These ten points are as follows:

1. Common Security

One of the positive consequences of the 'Second Cold War' in the early 1980s was the growing recognition that – especially in the nuclear age – security can only ever be mutual. Although the concept of 'mutual' or 'common' security was one that was originally developed in the context of a deep-seated systemic conflict between East and West, its central message is still relevant to the new post-cold war Europe.

'Common security' is based on a number of important insights into the nature of European security in the late twentieth century. First, that the attempt to achieve one-sided security against an opponent by a nation-state or an alliance is likely to prove self-defeating, in that it is bound to stimulate countervailing measures by other states – thus provoking a costly arms race.[30] Security in Europe should therefore not be seen in zero-sum terms. Second, that there can be no military-technical solution to the security problems of the continent. This means that security can no longer be reduced to a simple military equation: it cannot be guaranteed by any 'mix' of conventional and nuclear weapons, or by any particular balance or structure of military forces. Security ultimately rests on political guarantees. Third, this in turn suggests that we need an expanded concept of security, capable of including the whole range of factors – military, economic, political, social and cultural – which affect the security of Europe. To focus exclusively on the military dimension of security is to overlook the broader spectrum of vulnerabilities and threats with which the Europeans are now confronted. Thus we need to develop a concept of security which, whilst not ignoring the significance of military factors, is comprehensive enough to include the other vital determinants of contemporary European security.

The acceptance of the validity of the notion of mutual or common security places a high premium on developing structures for international consultation and negotiation (which could best be established within the CSCE framework[31]), in order to identify common security interests and concerns, and to direct competition along non-military paths.

2. The Need to Institutionalise Interdependence

Interdependence is an increasingly important feature of the global system, and is particularly pronounced in Europe. Complex interdependence is a phenomenon which has transformed the nature of international relations in the late twentieth century. It provides an economic and political basis for closer international cooperation, by forging structural bonds between different countries and nations. However, it does not automatically produce peaceful relations and mutual cooperation between former rivals in the international system. Indeed, it can produce conflict, as states seek to struggle to escape the vulnerability that interdependence creates.

If complex interdependence is to facilitate a process of closer inter-state cooperation and 'peaceful competition' (in the literal sense of this term), then it has to be institutionalised. This involves the development of institutional frameworks for bi- and multilateral forms of diplomacy, which can draw up mutually acceptable rules, regulations and codes of behaviour. As the experience of the European Community suggests, in this way it might be possible to help pattern the expectations and behaviour of the participants, thereby encouraging the emergence of habits and constituencies that will support a cooperative international regime.[32]

One goal of a new European security system, therefore, should be to enmesh European countries in an institutionalised network of deepening interdependencies. By institutionalising interdependence, it may be possible to create a new cooperative security regime in Europe. This in turn will contribute to the progressive demilitarisation of inter-state relations in Europe, producing what Francis Fukuyama finds so boring about the end of the cold war: namely, the growing 'Common marketizing of international relations'.[33]

3. Rejection of a Single, Unitary Structure of European Security

There have been some ambitious proposals for a new system of European security which envisage the creation of a single, all-encompassing structure. This unitary structure, it is suggested, could absorb the functions of other institutions and alliances, thereby assuming responsibility for all security concerns within Europe. The CSCE is frequently regarded as the institutional basis for such a unitary system of European security, as the proposals of President Havel and some of his East European colleagues make clear. The idea is also popular within left-wing and pacifist circles in Germany and elsewhere in Western Europe.[34] Even a mainstream conservative like Michael Howard has argued that,

> A single security system embracing the whole of Europe, involving the dissolution or the amalgamation of the existing pacts, is certainly a reasonable long-term goal. This is the objective at which we should aim in the CSCE negotiations at Helsinki. But political circumstances dictate that we must take our time getting there.[35]

A 'single security system embracing the whole of Europe' is certainly not a viable proposition in the short or medium term. But it is also questionable whether it is a 'reasonable long-term goal'. The very heterogeneity of Europe; its blurred edges; its varied historical experiences and political cultures; and its increasingly diverse security agenda – all suggest that a unitary, all-embracing security system would not correspond to the pluralism of Europe's existing structures and future security requirements.

This does not mean that the role of the CSCE in the new Europe should be regarded as marginal or even irrelevant – quite the contrary. After the November 1990 Paris Summit, there is good reason for believing that the CSCE can play an important role in providing a framework for pan-European consultation, dialogue and cooperation. The Paris Summit resulted in a number of proposals for giving the CSCE a more permanent institutional structure: these proposals included the establishment of a permanent CSCE Secretariat and an Assembly for Europe; regular meetings of Heads of State and Government; and the creation of a Conflict Prevention Centre in Vienna and an Office for Free Elections in Warsaw. These developments all indicate that the CSCE could well emerge as a key pan-European forum for multilateral cooperation and consultation. One of its main advantages is that it includes all the main European states (with the exception of Albania, which is now seeking to join), along with the USSR, the USA and Canada. It is not inconceivable that the CSCE could in the long term develop an effective institutionalised mechanism for a voluntary conciliation procedure.[36] But the problems inherent in modifying the CSCE's unanimity principle, and its lack of an effective enforcement mechanism, mean that it is not a suitable body for providing a unitary and all-embracing system of collective security in Europe.

This leads on to the next three points.

4. European Security Should be Based on a System of Interlocking and Overlapping Structures, with No Institutional Hierarchy.

Rather than seeking to construct a unitary system of European security, a more pluralist and multi-layered system should be developed. It should consist of a series of interlocking and overlapping structures, involving a network of alliance systems, mutual security guarantees, multi- and bilateral defence arrangements, and criss-crossing security regimes. In such an institutional ensemble, functions and responsibilities would be distributed between different bodies and through different levels. In other words, pluralism and a diffusion of power throughout all levels of the security system would provide the broadest and most stable basis for a durable peace order in Europe.

A pluralist European security system with a multi-layered structure would inhibit the excessive concentration of power either in one set of institutions or in one group of states, which has so often been a source of instability in the past. As Barry Buzan has argued,

> Just as security cannot be created by individual actors, neither can it be created by concentrating all power and responsibility at the upper levels. When such concentration happens, as we have seen in the case of individuals and the state, the collective institution becomes a major source of threat to those smaller actors it was supposed to protect. For the same reason, states fear submergence of their powers and authorities in larger regional or global entities .... The more actors at every level retain some control over their security, the more stable the system will be, for a collapse at any point will not entail a collapse of the whole security system.[37]

In such a multi-layered structure, the CSCE could provide a framework for pan-European security dialogue, and might also provide a mechanism for addressing some of the national and ethnic conflicts in Eastern Europe and the Balkans. NATO could remain the bed-rock of West European collective defence, whilst the WEU could provide a forum for independent West European security cooperation (especially 'out-of-area'). Meanwhile, the EC could deal with the 'economic and social' aspects of security. These structures could be complemented by regional forms of cooperation, from the Pentagonale to the proposed 'Conference on Security and Cooperation in the Mediterranean'.

At the same time, a series of bilateral treaties recognising existing borders and renouncing the use of force in intra-European disputes (perhaps with, as in the case of the Soviet–German 'Grand Treaty' of November 1990, a specific non-aggression clause) could provide another element in this multi-structured security system. Although such a complex and diversified security system would inevitably be prone to a degree of structural incoherence and institutional confusion, these disadvantages would be outweighed by its advantages – in terms of the stability and predictability it would provide through its pluralist diffusion of power.[38] A system of intersecting circles and overlapping structures would also correspond more to the specific traditions and dynamics of European development than would a unitary system with a clear institutional hierarchy.

5. Functional Diversity within the European Security System

As we have already seen, with the passing of the bipolar East–West conflict, a much more diversified security agenda is emerging in Europe. The growing multiplicity of security risks and challenges requires a more differentiated spectrum of responses to different problems – whether economic, political, diplomatic or military. The existence of a variety of different institutions and forums – each capable of dealing with different sorts of security problems – could provide an effective and flexible way of managing this more diffuse security agenda.

For example, the problems of illegal immigration and economically motivated refugees are best dealt with through the EC or the Schengen group, rather than by NATO or the WEU. On the other hand, strategic issues can be addressed through the military alliances, or perhaps through the CSCE. A high degree of functional diversity within the European security system should therefore not necessarily be seen as a structural weakness: it could well serve as a source of considerable flexibility and effectiveness.

6. Regional Differentiation in Europe

For over forty years, the primary security concern within Europe was the East–West conflict, the focus of which was Germany and the central front. The priority both sides attached to the systemic rivalry between 'socialism' and 'capitalism' in Europe had the effect of suppressing some of the more traditional patterns of confrontation and cooperation in Europe. Nevertheless, some of these old conflicts still flickered on – the best examples being the Greco-Turkish conflict in the Eastern Mediterranean, and the Hungarian–Romanian dispute over Transylvania. Similarly, older patterns of regional cooperation persisted throughout the cold war, and began to reassert themselves from the 1970s onwards: examples of this being relations between Austria and Hungary, Italy and Yugoslavia, and between the two German states.   The end of the cold war in Europe has led to a resurgence in the more traditional patterns of cooperation and conflict in Europe. One of the key features of the new security system in Europe is thus likely to be a much higher degree of regional and sub-regional interaction. A patch-work of different regional security regimes is already beginning to emerge in Europe. The main examples of this are:

The Pentagonale: this grouping of five south-central European countries brings together Italy, Austria, Hungary, Yugoslavia and Czechoslovakia (in other words, the countries of the former Habsburg Empire). It has no direct security function, but seeks to encourage both diplomatic coordination (in both the UN and the CSCE), and regional economic projects. One of its unspoken functions is to provide a counter-weight to German influence in northern and eastern Europe. More importantly, it provides a link between Italy (an EC member) and four countries aspiring to Community membership.

Scandinavia and the Baltic: The Nordic countries have throughout the post-war period constituted a specific grouping within Europe. The region has enjoyed a unique 'Nordic balance' between NATO countries such as Iceland, Norway and Denmark; Sweden (with its policy of 'active neutrality'); and Finland (with its more intimate relations with the USSR). As a new chapter of European history begins, the Baltic is likely to become the focus of a network of close regional cooperation. This will provide a means of involving the three Baltic Republics in a broader regional grouping – a sort of 'Hanseatic League', linking the old trading centres of northern Germany with Poland, the Baltic Republics, Kaliningrad and the Scandinavian countries. The Nordic region also has its own specific security concerns, given (i) its proximity to the Soviet Kola peninsular (with its large concentration of military bases); (ii) the huge Soviet fleet in Murmansk; and (iii) the Soviet-Norwegian demarcation dispute in the Barents Sea.[39]

The Balkans: The Balkans – once described as 'the powder keg of Europe' – has long been an area riven by ancient and irreconcilable antagonisms. Fuelled by mounting economic problems, national, ethnic, religious and political tensions have risen in recent years. Nevertheless, there has been an attempt by the six Balkan countries (Greece, Turkey, Yugoslavia, Albania, Bulgaria and Romania) to try and play down their various differences and to work to promote yet another example of regional cooperation in a rapidly changing Europe. To this end, a series of meetings of foreign ministers, deputy ministers and experts has been held, starting in February 1988 with a meeting of the six foreign ministers in Belgrade. Since then, a succession of gatherings has been held in various Balkan capitals, to discuss a broad range of common concerns, from tourism and trade, to drugs, terrorism and ecological issues. The substantive results to date have been modest. Yet the fact that such contacts have multiplied in recent years is in itself a positive sign. It reflects a broad Balkan commitment to overlook their differences and to work together on the basis of the lowest common denominator.[40]

The Mediterranean: the countries of southern Europe have increasingly been concerned with the security problems emanating from NATO's 'southern flank' – the North African littoral, the Eastern Mediterranean and the Middle East. The security agenda in the Mediterranean area is very diverse: from the Arab–Israeli conflict in the Middle East, through the rising tide of Islamic fundamentalism, to what is becoming a major security problem – the influx of economic migrants from the North African coast into Europe's exposed southern underbelly. Military cooperation between Spain, France and Italy has been gaining momentum over the last ten years. A more ambitious proposal, championed primarily by the Italians and Spanish, is the convocation of a 'Conference on Security and Cooperation in the Mediterranean' (a 'CSCM') modelled on the 34-nation CSCE.[41] Such a conference, its advocates suggest, could address the whole range of security problems in the Mediterranean area, from the economic and social problems of the Maghreb, to the Palestinian *intifada* in the West Bank and Gaza strip.

The Black Sea: The apparent reluctance of the EC countries to countenance Turkish membership of the Community has led Turkey to seek a regional alternative to EC membership. This has led to a discussion on the possibility of developing economic cooperation across and around the Black Sea. Underpining this would be bilateral trade with the Soviet Republics of Georgia, the Ukraine, Moldavia and Azerbaijan, and Balkan countries like Bulgaria and Romania. Although President Ozal's vision of a Black Sea grouping in which Turkey would play a dominant role has raised the unwelcome spectre of the Ottoman Empire in some quarters, there is nonetheless growing interest in regional cooperation in economic, environmental and infrastructural projects.[42]

7. No Primacy for Military Structures within the European Security System

In the cold war period, it was the two military alliances – NATO and the Warsaw Pact – which constituted the vital core of the European security system. In the West, an organisation like the EC was able to flourish because it enjoyed the strategic protection afforded by the Atlantic Alliance. Similarly, the institutional heart of the 'socialist community' was the Warsaw Pact, not COMECON. However, with the demise of the cold war, the relative importance of military alliances like NATO (let alone the WTO) is likely to decline in relation to primarily 'civilian' bodies such as the EC. Military structures like NATO and the WEU will still have a significant role to play within the overall system of European security, but they will no longer be as central as they were in the past.

Military structures should thus no longer be seen as the institutional core of European security, but as one element – albeit a significant one – within a broad system of political, economic and cultural relationships. This reflects the declining utility of military force in a Europe of deepening interdependencies. It also reflects the recognition that security is much more than a problem of weapons: focusing on achieving peace in Europe either through radical disarmament measures or by building up strong military forces is equally misguided.[43]

8. Restructuring Military Forces: 'Mutual Defensive Dominance'

Although military structures will no longer provide the primary element of a new security system in Europe, military forces themselves remain an integral factor in the overall security equation. The concentration of conventional forces on the central front has been dramatically reduced as a result of both unilateral cut-backs and the CFE Treaty of November 1990. But if a stable military balance is to be ensured on the continent, it is important that the remaining armed forces be restructured in a defensive manner. The goal should be to establish a situation of mutual defensive dominance, in which all major military powers or alliances in Europe are structurally incapable of conducting large-scale offensive operations on a strategic scale. A comprehensive arms control and verification regime, designed with the concept of 'non-offensive defence' in mind, and with an institutionalised framework of confidence and security building measures to ensure military transparency, would provide a sound military basis for a durable peace order.

As we have seen in Chapter 8, there are some major difficulties in defining exactly what constitutes a 'defensive' configuration of military forces, and which weapon systems can accurately be described as either 'defensive' or 'offensive'. This means that there can be no easy, sweeping solutions to the problem of military restructuring. Progress in this difficult area will therefore only be achieved through a piecemeal, incremental, and pragmatic approach. Once again, this underlines that there can be no military-technical solution to the problems of European security. In the end, security can only be achieved through political means, by extending the sort of security community that now exists in Western Europe across the rest of the continent.

9. Nuclear Deterrence in Europe

We have already considered the weight of arguments in favour of the continuation of a minimum nuclear deterrence in Europe (see Chapter 8, pp. 176–78). Suffice it to say here that the awesome destructive capabilities of modern nuclear weapons renders large-scale war in Europe as a conscious instrument of policy (in the Clausewitzian sense) completely unthinkable. A minimum nuclear deterrence, designed for war-prevention rather than war-fighting, could thus provide a powerful element of stability at a time of considerable strategic flux and uncertainty. Nevertheless, the role of nuclear weapons will remain limited: as 'weapons of last resort', they will provide an ultimate insurance policy against continental-wide war. They do not, however, provide an answer to many of the security problems facing Europe after the cold war. In particular, they do not provide an answer to the security problems arising from the rising tide of nationalism in the post-communist world, or the worsening economic and social problems to the continent's East and South. Specious arguments in favour of a 'process of limited nuclear proliferation in Europe' (as a technical panacea to Europe's security problems),[44] therefore, are not helpful: they are based on a lack of familiarity with contemporary

European politics; a failure to comprehend the impact of interdependence on late twentieth-century Europe; and an unfortunate tendency of some strategic analysts to seek military-technical solutions to complex security problems.

10. European Integration

In the long term, the best way to achieve a stable peace order in Europe is by deepening and broadening the process of European integration. In Western Europe, integration – led primarily by the European Community – has facilitated the development of a 'security community', in which military factors no longer play a significant role in state-to-state relations in the region. The EC also provides the historic answer to the long-standing 'German problem', which has plagued the continent for over a century (as we saw in Chapter 6, p. 117 and Chapter 7, p. 149). European security will therefore be enhanced if individual countries can be integrated into a system of interlocking and overlapping institutions, in which national sovereignty can increasingly be pooled in the interests of all.

It is particularly important that as the Europeans seek to develop a new security structure, they avoid the reconstitution of unrestricted national sovereignty in military matters. The 'renationalisation' of defence policy would be a set-back to the process of constructing a European peace order. This is already a pressing problem in Eastern Europe, given the break-up of the Warsaw Pact, and the looming shadow of nationalism. The development of new regional or pan-European security structures is therefore an urgent necessity if the 'renationalisation' of defence policy in Eastern Europe is not to aggravate the military and political tensions in the region.

The risk of a renationalisation of defence policy is one that also hangs over Western Europe. The danger is that NATO may disintegrate without a robust West European collective defence organisation taking its place. One of the more unfortunate consequences of this would be the 'renationalisation' of German defence policy, which could be a cause of considerable concern in many parts of the continent. As has already been argued (in Chapters 6 and 8), integrating military forces into a democratic alliance for collective defence produces what could be termed a 'structural incapacity for unprovoked aggression'. It is thus important that as NATO changes and adapts to the new political environment, it does not discard its integrated military command structures. Moreover, there are very good grounds – militarily as well as politically – for developing integrated multinational forces in NATO, with reciprocal stationing rights where appropriate. By preserving the existing elements of integration in Europe, therefore, and extending them where possible, the chances of avoiding a return to the debilitating balance of power politics of the pre-war period (which some now fear[45]) may be enhanced.

Concluding Remarks

After the watershed years of 1989–90, a new era in European history has now begun. In the course of this book we have considered the various elements which together will determine the nature of European security beyond the cold war. There are substantial grounds for optimism about the future. For the first time in its long and turbulent history, the prospect of a continent democratic and at peace with itself seems to be a realistic possibility. This, however, is no reason for euphoria or complacency. There are a myriad of security issues – economic, political and military – which need to be tackled before Europe enjoys a durable peace order. Above all, Europeans will have to recognise that they will have to live with some painful uncertainties for several years to come: uncertainties about the compatibility between West European integration and the task of overcoming the legacy of the East–West divide; about the role of a united Germany in the new Europe; about the future of the Soviet and Yugoslav states; and about the relationship of Europe with its major partners, both across the Atlantic and across Eurasia.

The most positive outcome of today's period of uncertainty would be one which led to the following sorts of developments: growing pan-European cooperation, within the CSCE framework; the deepening and widening of the European Community; a united German state acting as a bridge between East and West; a continuation of the Soviet reform programme; a successful 'return to Europe' by the east central Europeans; and the development of a more balanced 'new Atlanticism' between Western Europe and the USA. Clearly, this is a very optimistic scenario! The least favourable outcome would be the stagnation of West European integration; the disintegration of the Atlantic Alliance and a transatlantic trade war; the collapse of Soviet *perestroika*; the emergence of 'authoritarian nationalism' in Eastern Europe and the Balkans; and a restless Germany in the heart of a Europe of competing nationalisms.

Given the widespread uncertainties of today's Europe, the most prudent course of action would be to concentrate on improving existing security arrangements, rather than devising desirable but abstract models of future European security structures. As Ken Booth has argued, 'if we look after the processes in international politics, the structures will look after themselves'. This he calls the 'process utopian' approach, which, following Joseph Nye, he distinguishes from the 'end-point utopians' approach.[46] Antonio Gramsci's old adage also seems appropriate for those considering the problems of European security: 'Optimism of the will, pessimism of the intellect'.

One final point is that Europe is unlikely to be the scene of high international drama in the way it was in the *annus mirabilis* of 1989.

Nevertheless, developments in Europe – especially in the EC and the USSR – will have a profound effect on the global economic and political system in the 1990s and beyond. There is currently much talk of the twenty-first century being the 'Pacific century', in the same way as the nineteenth century was a British century, and the twentieth century an American century. But as Samuel Huntington has suggested, the challenge to America's global pre-eminence is more likely to come from a united European Community than it is from the Pacific.

> The European Community, if it were to become politically cohesive, would have the population, resources, economic wealth, technology and actual and potential military strength to be the pre-eminent power of the twenty-first century. Japan, the United States and the Soviet Union have specialized respectively in investment, consumption and arms. Europe balances all three ....
>
> It is quite possible to conceive of a European ideological appeal comparable to the American one. Throughout the world, people line up at the doors of American consulates seeking immigration visas. In Brussels, countries line up at the door of the Community seeking admission. A federation of democratic, wealthy, socially diverse, mixed-economy societies would be a powerful force on the world scene. If the next century is not the American century it is most likely to be the European century. The baton of world leadership that passed westwards across the Atlantic in the early twentieth century could move back eastward a hundred years later.[47]

Notes

1. *The Japan Times*, 14 September 1990, p. 1.
2. Even Richard Perle, the 'Prince of Darkness' in the Reagan Administration, has recognised that 'It is simply no longer possible to imagine a cohesive Warsaw Pact, led by Soviet troops, forcing its way through the centre of Europe in a massive invasion ... of territory under the control of the North Atlantic Treaty Organisation ... the canonical threat against which a defensive NATO alliance has long been poised is no longer credible' (February 1990).
3. Peter Calvocoressi makes this point in his stimulating article, 'World Power 1920–1990', in *International Affairs*, vol. 66, no. 4 (1990), pp. 663–74. He argues that 'Bipolarity produced stability, ... and substituted data for statecraft. It is only a bit extravagant', he goes on to suggest, 'to ascribe the chilling mediocrity of statesmanship over the past 45 years to the fact that it has been relatively little needed. But it now is; for with the abatement of the Cold War and the dissolution of bipolarity the flux in international politics is back' (p. 674).
4. In April 1990, for example, the French and West German Governments agreed to set up a joint study on 'The future architecture of Europe's security; the role and possible developments of the structures of the Atlantic Alliance; methods of bilateral cooperation in a changing European context'. Reported in the *Financial Times*, 27 April 1990.
5. L. Freedman, 'Architecture with Eurovision', *The Independent*, 8 March 1990.

6. Quoted in Alastair Buchan (ed.), *Europe's Futures, Europe's Choices: Models of Western Europe in the 1970s* (London: Chatto and Windus for the Institute of Strategic Studies, 1969), p. 158.

7. Valery Giscard D'Estaing, 'The Two Europes, East and West', *International Affairs*, vol. 65, no. 4 (Autumn 1989), pp. 653–58. He speaks of a 'European village' consisting of 'five groups of "houses" destined for different futures': the EC, EFTA, Eastern Europe, the 'isolated' countries (Yugoslavia, Albania and Malta) and the European part of the Soviet Union (p. 654).

8. Johan Jorgen Holst, 'Uncertainty and Opportunity in an Era of East–West Change', *The Strategic Implications of Change in the Soviet Union*, Adelphi Paper 247 (London: Brassey's for the IISS, 1989), pp. 3–15 (p. 8). He has advocated 'the model of an open village in Europe where the inhabitants choose their preferred dwellings, and where life depends on co-operation, tolerance, divisions of labour, mutual respect and restraint; a village where serfdom has been abolished and which maintains open gates to the outside world, rather than the forbidding walls of a fortress Europe. The open village in Europe will be sustained by invisible but recognized bonds of interdependence, and by indispensable safety nets' (p. 8).

9. Margaret Thatcher, 'My Vision of Europe Open and Free', *Financial Times*, 19 November 1990.

10. At the historic CSCE Summit in Paris in November 1990, the then Polish Prime Minister, Tadeusz Mazowiecki, warned of 'dark clouds' caused by the resurgence of old conflicts if the gap between haves and have-nots was not overcome. The Hungarian Prime Minister, Jozsef Antall, also called for more economic integration, otherwise 'a new wall could take shape'. In a similar vein, Chancellor Kohl of Germany insisted that 'Following the opening of national borders, there must now be no borders which perpetuate the prosperity divide. The ideological gulfs that have been overcome must not be torn open again by social gaps.' Quoted in *The Independent*, 21 November 1990, p. 10

11. For a brief analysis of the history and potential of the Council of Europe, see Cosmo Russel, 'The Council of Europe – Forty Years On', *New European*, vol. 3, no. 1 (Spring 1990), pp. 15–19.

12. See Edward Mortimer, 'Springtime for Euro-institutions', *Financial Times*, 12 June 1990.

13. William of Occam coined the adage, *Entia non sunt multiplicanda praeter necessitatem*, ie, 'Bodies should not be multiplied except when necessary.'

14. It is significant that the first major new organisation created to cope with the problems arising from the end of the cold war in Europe was the European Bank for Reconstruction and Development (sometimes known by its French acronym, BERD).

15. In his speech to the CSCE Paris Summit in November 1990, President Gorbachev outlined his vision of a 'united and democratic Europe' becoming an 'irreversible reality in the coming century'. However, he also warned against 'impermissible euphoria' because of the danger of 'Balkanisation, or even worse, Lebanonisation of entire regions'. Quoted in *The Independent*, 20 November 1990.

16. The current debate inside the Soviet Union on the desirability or otherwise of adopting the 'Western model' recalls the words of Alexander Blok in the

last century. He wrote that as Russia looks to the West, '... bleeding with black blood, she gazes with both hatred and love'.

17. 'The process of integration of the Soviet Union (and Russia proper) into the rest of Europe can take different routes. But all of them must go through a disintegration of what some call the Soviet Union – and others the Soviet Empire'. Alexander Kustaryov, 'Russia and Europe', in *New European*, vol. 3, nos. 2/3 (Summer/Autumn 1990), pp. 6–9 (p. 9).

18. The *Financial Times's* editorial comment of 3 August 1990 was indicative of the widespread sense of outrage in the Western world: 'Iraq's invasion and effective annexation of Kuwait is the most direct and flagrant challenge to international order since the Second World War.' President Bush was subsequently to argue that the Gulf crisis was 'a defining moment of the post-cold war era'.

19. This was made clear at a special meeting of the Atlantic Council on 10 August. Manfred Wörner, NATO's Secretary-General, declared that the Alliance would consider an Iraqi attack on Turkey to be 'an attack on all member nations under Articles 5 and 6 of our Treaty'. He also said that although there was no question of NATO coordinating the military action in the Gulf through its integrated command structures, it would prove a 'key forum for close consultation between the allies'. *Financial Times*, 11/12 August 1990, p. 2. Later (in early January 1991), NATO agreed to Turkey's request for the deployment of 42 aircraft from NATO's Allied Mobile Force (the AMF, composed of three squadrons of fighters from Germany, Belgium and Italy) as a deterrent against Iraq.

20. Quoted in an article entitled, 'Redefining European Security', in *Time*, 8 October 1990, p. 24.

21. See Michael Binyon, 'Will Saddam Bring about a More United Europe?', *The Times*, 22 August 1990.

22. *Time*, 8 October, 1990, p. 25.

23. Interview with Willem van Eekelen, the WEU Secretary-General, published in the *International Herald Tribune*, 20 August 1990, p. 2.

24. The WEU Communiqué of 21 August spoke of coordination covering 'overall operational concepts and specific guidelines for co-ordination between forces in the region, including areas of operation, sharing of tasks, logistical support and exchange of intelligence'. *The Times*, 22 August 1990, p. 3. However, on 23 November 1990, the WEU made public two reports which proposed the establishment of a Rapid Deployment Force, possibly consisting of as many as 100,000 troops and a naval counterpart, in order to be able to help deal with out-of-area regional crises such as that in the Gulf.

25. Col. Harry G. Summers, 'The Cost of that Line in the Sand', *Defence and Diplomacy*, vol. 8, nos. 11–12 (Nov–Dec 1990), pp. 8–11.

26. To quote the title of a recent book by Joseph Nye – *Bound to Lead: the Changing Nature of American Power* (New York: Basic Books, 1990).

27. Richard Weitz, 'The USSR and the Confrontation in the Gulf', *Radio Liberty Report on the USSR*, vol. 2, no. 33 (17 August 1990), pp. 1–7.

28. In mid-September, for example, the Bonn Government announced that it would be giving DM 3.3bn of 'immediate aid' to the multinational effort in the Gulf, just under half of which would go to US military effort, and the rest to Jordan, Turkey and Egypt. This was significantly more than

the US Government had requested and expected. See *The Independent*, 17 September 1990.
29. *Financial Times*, 10 September 1990, p. 2.
30. That the concept of 'common security' has now become the 'common sense' of Europe is evident from the Joint Declaration of Chancellor Kohl and President Gorbachev in the Joint Declaration of 13 June 1989; 'The Federal Republic of Germany and the Soviet Union declare that one's own security must not be obtained at the expense of the security of others. They therefore pursue the goal of eliminating the causes of tension and distrust through a constructive and forward-looking policy so that the feeling of being threatened that still exists today can be replaced gradually by a state of mutual trust.'
31. As Rita Süssmuth suggested in her address to the New York Institute of East–West Security Studies (IEWSS) on 'German Reunification and the Future Political Architecture of Europe', 20 March 1990.
32. Jack Snyder, 'Averting Anarchy in the New Europe', *International Security*, vol. 14, no. 4 (Spring 1990), pp. 5–41 (p. 30).
33. Francis Fukuyama, 'The End of History', in the *National Interest* (Summer 1989), pp. 3–18.
34. See for example Bruce Kent, 'Vision of a New Europe', *New European*, vol. 3, nos. 2/3 (Summer/Autumn 1990), pp. 13–16. He suggests that 'a common security system for Europe is essential, sooner rather than later. The CSCE process is a better starting point for such a system than the WTO or NATO.' He then goes on to refer to the proposal by Admiral Elmar Schmäling for a negotiated dissolution of the two alliances within the CSCE by 1997, and concludes by arguing that 'The most pressing tensions Europe faces lie within the USSR, Yugoslavia, Turkey, Cyprus, Bulgaria, Romania, France, Spain and Northern Ireland .... The only way to deal with these issues is through a pan-European arangement of CSCE "United Nations" peace-keeping type forces.'
35. Michael Howard, 'The Remaking of Europe', *Survival*, vol. XXXII, no. 2 (March/April 1990), pp. 99–106 (p. 103).
36. As proposed by the British Foreign Minister, Douglas Hurd, at the Paris Summit. His proposal is to be discussed at a follow-up meeting in Malta in early 1991.
37. Barry Buzan, *People, States and Fear. The National Security Problem in International Relations* (Brighton: Wheatsheaf, 1983), p. 253.
38. This point is well made by Karsten Voigt in his 'Draft General Report on Alliance Security' for the North Atlantic Assembly (May 1989); In a section entitled 'Strength and Security through Diversity', he argues that, 'This Rapporteur sees positive developments which point in the direction of pluralism in Europe and which have the capacity to overcome the antagonism between East and West. This is surely in the interests of all. To be sure, it will mean a Europe characterized by differing speeds, differing levels of integration, and differing boundaries of various territorial and functional unions: the Europe of the CSCE, including the United States and Canada; the Europe of the Council of Europe; the Europe of the EC; and the Europe of the CMEA .... Regional forms of co-operation, such as the Nordic Council, transcend the frontiers of NATO and the EC'. He concludes by suggesting that, 'The Various degrees of integration and the diversity of

institutions' functions and boundaries are not something negative. Indeed, they are uniquely and historically European' (paragraphs 137 and 138).

39. Hence the long-running Nordic interest in the idea of a 'Nordic Nuclear-Free Zone', and the more recent sympathy for Maritime Confidence-Building Measures (in the light of the Forward Maritime Stratey). These and other related issues are discussed in Richard Latter, *Northern Europe in Transition*, Wilton Park Paper 14 (London: HMSO, 1990); *NATO's Sixteen Nations*, vol. 33, no. 7 (December 1988), which is devoted to 'The Northern Perspective'; and Falk Bomsdorf, 'The Soviet Union's Nordic Initiative', *Aussenpolitik*, vol. 40, no. 1 (January 1989), pp. 55–65.

40. Patrick Moore, 'Balkan Cooperation Revisited', *Report on Eastern Europe*, 23 March 1990, pp. 31–34.

41. Francisco Fernandez-Ordonez, 'The Mediterranean – Devising a Security Structure', *NATO Review*, vol. 38, no. 5 (October 1990), pp. 7–11.

42. See Jim Bodgener, 'Black Sea initiatives', in the *Financial Times*, Survey on Turkish Finance and Industry, 21 November 1990, p. 2.

43. Barry Buzan, *People, States and Fear*, p. 253.

44. See for example the influential piece by John J. Mearsheimer entitled 'Back to the Future: Instability in Europe After the Cold War?', *International Security*, vol. 15, no. 1 (Summer 1990), pp. 5–56.

45. *Ibid.*

46. Ken Booth, 'Steps towards Stable Peace in Europe: a Theory and Practice of Coexistence', *International Affairs*, vol. 66, no. 1 (1990), pp. 17–45 (p. 32).

47. Samuel P. Huntington, 'The U.S. – Decline or Renewal?', in *Foreign Affairs*, vol. 67, no. 2 (Winter 1988/89), pp. 76–96 (pp. 93–94).

Suggestions for Further Reading

Books:

Ashton, S.R., *In Search of Detente: The Politics of East–West Relations Since 1945* (London: Macmillan, 1989).

Bluth, C., *New Thinking in Soviet Military Policy* (London: Pinter for the RIIA, 1990).

Bowker, M., and Williams, P., *Superpower Detente: A Reappraisal* (London: Sage for the RIIA, 1988).

Boyer, Y., Lellouche, P., and Roper, J., (eds), *Franco-British Defence Co-operation: A New Entente Cordiale?* (London: Routledge for the RIIA and IFRI).

Buzan, B., Kelstrup, M., Lemaitre, P., Tromer, E., and Wæver, O., *The European Security Order Recast: Scenarios for the Post-Cold War Era* (London: Pinter, 1990).

Cerutti, F., and Ragionieri, R. (eds), *Rethinking European Security* (New York: Crane Russak, 1990).

Clarke, M., and Hague, R. (eds) *European Defence Cooperation: America, Britain and NATO*, Fulbright Paper 7 (Manchester: Manchester University Press, 1990).

Cuthbertson, I., and Robertson, D., *Enhancing European Security: Living in a Less Nuclear World* (London: Macmillan, 1990).

Dawisha, K., *Eastern Europe, Gorbachev and Reform. The Great Challenge*, second edition (Cambridge: Cambridge University Press, 1990).

Eavis, P., et al., *Security After the Cold War: Redirecting Global Resources* (Bristol: Saferworld Foundation, 1990).

Gambles, I., *Prospects for West European Security Co-operation*, Adelphi Paper 244 (London: Brassey's for the IISS, 1989).

Gapes, M., *After the Cold War: Building on the Alliances*, Fabian Tract 540 (London: Fabian Society, 1990).

Golden, J., et al. (eds), *NATO at Forty: Change, Continuity, and Prospects* (London: Westview, 1989).

Halliday, F., *The Making of the Second Cold War*, second edition (London: Verso, 1988).

Harle, V., and Sivonen, P. (eds), *Europe in Transition: Politics and Nuclear Security* (London: Pinter, 1989).

Holden, G., *The Warsaw Pact: Soviet Security and Bloc Politics* (London: Basil Blackwell for the United Nations University, 1989).

Hopman, P., Terence, P., and Barnaby, F. (eds), *Rethinking the Nuclear Weapons Dilemma in Europe* (London: Macmillan, 1988).

Jopp, M., Rummel, R., Schmidt, P., and Wessels, W. (eds), *Integration and*

Security in Western Europe: Inside the European Pillar (London: Westview, 1991).

Kaiser, K., and Roper, J. (eds), *British–German Defence Co-operation* (London: Janes for the RIIA and the DGAP, 1988).

Kaldor, M., Holden, G., and Falk, R. (eds), *The New Detente: Rethinking East–West Relations* (London: Verso for the United Nations University, 1989).

Kennedy, P., *The Rise and Fall of the Great Powers: Economic Change and Military Conflict from 1500 to 2000* (London: Fontana, 1989).

Laird, R., and Clark, S. (eds), *The USSR and the Western Alliance* (London: Unwin Hyman, 1990).

Light, M., *Soviet Theory of International Relations* (Brighton: Harvester-Wheatsheaf, 1988).

McCall, M., and Ramsbotham, O. (eds), *Just Deterrence: Morality and Deterrence in the Twenty-First Century* (London: Brassey's, 1990).

MccGuire, M., *Perestroika and Soviet National Security* (Washington, D.C.: The Brookings Institution, 1987).

Malcolm, N., *Soviet Policy Perspectives on Western Europe* (London: Routledge for the RIIA, 1989).

Nevers, R. de, *The Soviet Union and Eastern Europe: The End of an Era*, Adelphi Paper 249 (London: Brassey's for the IISS, 1990).

Pugh, M., and Williams, P. (eds) *Superpower Politics: Change in the United States and the Soviet Union* (Manchester: Manchester University Press, 1990).

Pugh, M. (ed.), *European Security – Toward 2000* (Manchester: Manchester University Press, 1991).

Randle, M., and Rogers, P. (eds), *Alternatives in European Security* (Aldershot: Dartmouth, 1990).

Rollo, J. (ed.), *The New Eastern Europe: Western Responses* (London: Pinter for the RIIA, 1990).

Rudney, R., and Reychler, L. (eds), *European Security Beyond the Year 2000* (New York: Praeger, 1988).

Rummel, R. (ed.), *West European Security Policy: Asserting European Priorities* (London: Westview, 1990).

Sharp, J. (ed.), *Europe After an American Withdrawal: Economic and Military Issues* (Oxford: Oxford University Press for SIPRI, 1990).

Shenfield, S., *The Nuclear Predicament: Explorations in Soviet Ideology* (London: Routledge & Kegan Paul for the RIIA, 1987).

Smith, D. (ed.), *European Security in the 1990s* (London: Pluto, 1989).

Waever, O. et al. (eds) *European Polyphony: Perspectives Beyond East–West Confrontation* (London: Macmillan, 1989).

Wallace, H., *Widening and Deepening: The European Community and the New European Agenda*, Chatham House Discussion Paper No. 23 (London: RIIA, 1989).

Wallace, W., *The Transformation of Western Europe* (London: Pinter for the RIIA, 1990).

Articles:

Bialer, S., 'The Passing of the Soviet Order?', in *Survival*, vol. XXXII, no. 2

(March/April 1990), pp. 107–20.

Birnbaum, K., and Ingo, P., 'The CSCE: a Reassessment of its Role in the 1980s', in *Review of International Studies*, vol. 16, no. 4 (October 1990), pp. 305–19.

Booth, K., 'Steps towards Stable Peace in Europe: a Theory and Practice of Coexistence', in *International Affairs*, vol. 66, no. 1 (1990), pp. 17–45.

Brzezinski, Z., 'Post-Communist Nationalism', in *Foreign Affairs*, vol. 68, no. 5 (Winter 1989/90), pp. 1–25.

Corterier, P., 'Quo Vadis NATO?', in *Survival*, vol. XXXII, no. 2 (March/April 1990), pp. 141–56.

Halliday, F., 'The Ends of Cold War', in *New Left Review*, No. 180 (March–April 1990), pp. 5–24.

Hassner, P., 'Europe beyond Partition and Unity: Disintegration or Reconstitution?', *International Affairs*, vol. 66, no. 3 (July 1990), pp. 461–75.

Howard, M., 'The Remaking of Europe', in *Survival*, vol. XXXII, no. 2 (March/April 1990), pp. 99–106.

Kaldor, M., 'After the Cold War', in *New Left Review*, No. 180 (March–April 1990), pp. 25–40.

Kielinger, T., Dijlas, M., Davidson, I., Krol, M., Lengyel, L., and Dassu, M., 'The Future of Europe: A Debate', in *International Affairs*, vol. 66, no. 2 (April 1990), pp. 249–312.

Joffe, J., 'After Bipolarity: Eastern and Western Europe', in *The Strategic Implications of Change in Soviet Union, Part 1*, Adelphi Paper 247 (London: Brassey's for the IISS, 1990), pp. 66–80.

Malcolm, N., 'The "Common European Home" and Soviet European Policy', in *International Affairs*, vol. 65, no. 4 (Autumn 1989), pp. 659–76.

Mearsheimer, J., 'Back to the Future: Instability in Europe after the Cold War', in *International Security*, vol. 15, no. 1 (Summer 1990), pp. 5–56.

Nötzold, J., and Rummel, R., 'On the Way to a New European Order', in *Aussenpolitik*, vol. 41, no. 3 (1990), pp. 212–24.

Petersen, P., 'A New Security Regime for Europe?', in *Problems of Communism*, vol. XXXIX, no. 2 (March–April 1990), pp. 91–97.

Snyder, J., 'Averting Anarchy in the New Europe', in *International Security*, vol. 14, no. 4 (Spring 1990), pp. 5–41.

Wæver, O., 'Three Competing Europes: German, French, Russian', in *International Affairs*, vol. 66, no. 3 (July 1990), pp. 477–94.

Index